Shaping Contracts for Work

OXFORD LABOUR LAW

Series Editors: Professor Alan Bogg (University of Bristol Law School), Professor Anne Davies (University of Oxford, Faculty of Law), Professor Keith Ewing (School of Law, King's College London), and Mark Freedland (University of Oxford, Faculty of Law).

The *Oxford Labour Law* series (formerly known as the *Oxford Monographs on Labour Law* series) has come to represent a significant contribution to the literature of British, European, and international labour law. The series recognizes the arrival not only of a renewed interest in labour law generally, but also the need for fresh approaches to the study of labour law following a period of momentous change in the UK and Europe. The series is concerned with all aspects of collective labour law and individual employment law, including the growing role of human rights and discrimination in employment. It is concerned also with the influence of politics and economics in shaping labour law, as well as the importance of legal theory and international labour standards. Recent titles address developments in multiple jurisdictions.

Also Available in the Series

Human Rights Due Diligence and Labour Governance
INGRID LANDAU

*Catholic Social Teaching and Labour Law
An Ethical Perspective on Work*
MARK BELL

Structural Injustice and Workers' Rights
VIRGINIA MANTOUVALOU

*Reforming Age Discrimination Law
Beyond Individual Enforcement*
ALYSIA BLACKHAM

*Putting Human Rights to Work
Labour Law, the ECHR, and the Employment Relation*
PHILIPPA COLLINS

Strike Ballots, Democracy, and Law
BREEN CREIGHTON, CATRINA DENVIR, RICHARD JOHNSTONE, SHAE MCCRYSTAL, ALICE ORCHISTON

*Living Wage
Regulatory Solutions to Informal and Precarious Work in Global Supply Chains*
SHELLEY MARSHALL

A Purposive Approach to Labour Law
GUY DAVIDOV

Shaping Contracts for Work

The Normative Influence of Terms Implied by Law

GABRIELLE GOLDING

OXFORD
UNIVERSITY PRESS

Great Clarendon Street, Oxford, OX2 6DP,
United Kingdom

Oxford University Press is a department of the University of Oxford.
It furthers the University's objective of excellence in research, scholarship,
and education by publishing worldwide. Oxford is a registered trade mark of
Oxford University Press in the UK and in certain other countries

© Gabrielle Golding 2023

The moral rights of the author have been asserted

First Edition published in 2023

All rights reserved. No part of this publication may be reproduced, stored in
a retrieval system, or transmitted, in any form or by any means, without the
prior permission in writing of Oxford University Press, or as expressly permitted
by law, by licence or under terms agreed with the appropriate reprographics
rights organization. Enquiries concerning reproduction outside the scope of the
above should be sent to the Rights Department, Oxford University Press, at the
address above

You must not circulate this work in any other form
and you must impose this same condition on any acquirer

Public sector information reproduced under Open Government Licence v3.0
(http://www.nationalarchives.gov.uk/doc/open-government-licence/open-government-licence.htm)

Published in the United States of America by Oxford University Press
198 Madison Avenue, New York, NY 10016, United States of America

British Library Cataloguing in Publication Data

Data available

Library of Congress Control Number: 2023947288

ISBN 978–0–19–286782–7

DOI: 10.1093/oso/9780192867827.001.0001

Printed and bound by
CPI Group (UK) Ltd, Croydon, CR0 4YY

Links to third party websites are provided by Oxford in good faith and
for information only. Oxford disclaims any responsibility for the materials
contained in any third party website referenced in this work.

General Editors' Preface

Contracts of employment are one of the major building blocks of employment law. One of their distinctive features is the law's willingness to imply a wide range of terms, creating obligations for both employers and employees, to 'fill in the gaps' in what the parties themselves have specified by means of express terms. There is an increasing tendency to extend some of these terms beyond standard contracts of employment to other contracts for personal work.

In this welcome addition to the series, Dr Gabrielle Golding explores the historical evolution and development of terms implied by law into contracts of employment and contracts for personal work in England and Australia, drawing also on jurisprudence from other common law jurisdictions. Her deep analysis reveals the slender basis on which this crucial legal development rests. She argues that the courts do not have a clear understanding of employment contracts as a 'class', nor have they developed a consistent or convincing test for determining why it is 'necessary' to imply a particular term.

These weaknesses in the judicial approach have, in turn, led to difficulties in answering some important practical questions which Golding explores in the book. For example, without a proper understanding of employment contracts as a 'class', it is difficult to decide the extent to which terms usually implied into contracts of employment should also be implied into contracts for personal work. Without a good grasp of the 'necessity' test, it is difficult to produce a coherent answer to the vexed question whether terms standardly implied into contracts of employment can be excluded by express terms.

From this detailed analysis, richly illustrated with historical and comparative examples, Golding develops proposals for statutory reform and case-law development with a view to bringing much-needed clarity and coherence to this area of law. This book is sure to prompt debate among scholars, policy-makers, judges, and practitioners and will be a key reference point for discussions about implied terms for many years to come.

ALB, ACLD, KDE, MRF

Acknowledgements

There have been many who have helped shape this book. I feel tremendously grateful to everyone who has supported me in writing it in many invaluable respects. I hereby forgive all those who thought it would be funny to point out that a book on shaping contracts for work might, in turn, shape how I spend much of my time working over the last few years. (And it *was* funny, sort of, the first couple of times.)

This project would have gotten precisely nowhere without the supervisors of my doctoral thesis on which this book is foundationally based: Professors Andrew Stewart and Joanna Howe, whom I thank for their expert guidance, unwavering support, and for the many insights, which remain embedded here. The institutional support I have received from the University of Adelaide, especially as a recipient of the 2022 Barbara Kidman Women's Fellowship, has made this book's completion possible.

During 2018, I was extremely fortunate to work as Associate to the Honourable Justice Besanko of the Federal Court of Australia, who decided, at first instance, a case, which infiltrates many aspects of this work: *Commonwealth Bank of Australia v Barker*. His Honour is one of Australia's most brilliant legal minds and instilled in me a deeper understanding of the judicial role. My time spent working with the talented team of lawyers at MinterEllison from 2010 to 2013 allowed me to become an instructing solicitor for the Commonwealth Bank of Australia on that same case from its inception. That experience was paramount in developing the ideas behind this work.

I am thrilled to be part of a vibrant labour law research community whose support, comments, and criticisms have made this research as rigorous as possible. I am grateful to Professors David Cabrelli and Douglas Brodie, both of whom supported research visits to the Edinburgh and Strathclyde Law Schools respectively. Those experiences led to fruitful discussions and comments on my ideas for this research. Their expert feedback at various stages of the book has been critical in refining its arguments and is certainly reflected in these pages. I am equally indebted to the advice and mentorship I have received from Professor Joellen Riley Munton since commencing my academic career; it has opened my mind to the opportunities that are available to me in the fields of labour and contract law. The following people have also contributed their wisdom through stimulating discussions and comments over the course of my research: Professor Hugh Collins, Professor Gordon Anderson, Professor Guy Davidov, Professor Anthony Forsyth, Emerita Professor Rosemary Owens, Dr Rebecca Zahn, and Dr Philippa Collins. That so much of this time and attention was bestowed while universities and offices were closed due to the Coronavirus pandemic makes me even more appreciative. I have endeavoured to state the law as of 30 September 2023, and any responsibility for remaining errors lies entirely with me.

I am eternally grateful to the series editors of the *Oxford Labour Law Series* and to the anonymous referees who recommended publication of this work, as well as Rebecca Lewis, Amy Marchant, Matthew Williams, Fay Gibbons, and those working with them at Oxford University Press, for assistance at every point of the publishing journey.

Writing in the last days before submitting my final manuscript, I am deeply aware of how fortunate I have been to have the love and support of family and friends, as well as the warmth and encouragement of my colleagues. In addition to those already mentioned, special thanks are due to all my colleagues at the Adelaide Law School, particularly those who I have had the privilege of teaching with across employment and contract law, as well as my students who continually challenge my thinking and whose successes bring me immense pride.

Beyond the Law School, many dear friends have provided much-needed distraction from my writing. Githie Barrett, Lauren Russell, Ashleigh Day, Kasia Main, Stephanie Komar, Rana Kökçinar, Kalindi Benson, Chloe Symes, Aphra Lee, Dr Kerryn Brent, and Kim Hayman all deserve my deepest thanks and gratitude for their ongoing friendship. I have spent countless hours on my yoga mat thanks to Tessa Leon, Triton Tunis-Mitchell, and the entire team at Human.Kind Studios, which has kept me balanced, healthy, and mindful at all stages of my writing. My godmother, Dr Sanghamitra Guha, AM, was always willing to lend an ear when it was needed most. Every day has been filled by the generosity, laughter, and encouragement of Michael Robran.

Last, but by no means least, two of those closest to me deserve special mention: my mother and father, Carola and Jeffrey Golding. I first made the decision to pursue an academic career because of their true belief in my abilities. I have been richly rewarded by having them both as parents. All the support they have provided me over the years is the greatest gift anyone has ever given me. No handful of sentences will do justice to their role in my life. Also, for reading this book (on more than one occasion), I am endlessly thankful. I know they will be telling everyone they meet that I wrote it. Mum, Dad—this one's for you.

Gabrielle Golding
September 2023

Contents

Table of Cases xiii
Table of Legislation xxi
List of Abbreviations xxiii

Introduction: Shaping the Normative Core of Contracts for Work 1
   Advancing the Enquiry 2
   Outline of Argument and Structure 5
   Methodology 11
   Scope 13
   Rethinking the Rationale 13

PART I. TERMS IMPLIED BY LAW INTO CONTRACTS GENERALLY

1. A Legal Overview 17
   Introduction 17
   Express Terms 18
   Implied Terms 22
      A. Terms Implied in Fact 23
      B. Terms Implied by Custom and Usage 26
      C. Terms Implied by Law 28
   The Fact/Law Distinction 30
   Implication and Construction 31
   Conclusion 34

2. The Significance of Implying a Term by Law 36
   Introduction 36
   Emergence of a Powerful Judicial Technique 37
   Normative Rationalisation of Contractual Dealings 39
   Identifiable Legal Rules 42
   Wide Scope of Influence 43
   Conclusion 44

PART II. TERMS IMPLIED BY LAW INTO CONTRACTS FOR WORK

3. Origins and Current Status 49
   Introduction 49
   Duties Owed by Employers 52

A. Duty to Provide a Safe Place of Work	53
B. Duty to Indemnify Employees for Expenses Innocently Incurred	54
C. Duty to Inform Employees of their Rights	55
Duties Owed by Employees	57
A. Duty to Obey Lawful and Reasonable Instructions	57
B. Duty of Fidelity	60
C. Duty to Exercise Reasonable Care and Skill	63
D. Duty to Hold Inventions on Trust	64
E. Duty Not to Misuse or Disclose Confidential Information	66
Mutual Duties Owed by Employers and Employees	68
A. Duty of Cooperation	69
B. Duty to Provide Reasonable Notice on Termination	70
Conclusion	76
4. Mutual Trust and Confidence and Good Faith	81
Introduction	81
Mutual Trust and Confidence	83
A. Evolution and Existence in England	83
B. Rise and Fall in Australia: *Commonwealth Bank v Barker*	87
C. Application Beyond Employment	100
Good Faith	102
A. Evolution and Existence in England	102
B. Confusion as to Existence and Content in Australia	105
C. Application Beyond Employment	111
Conclusion	112

PART III. TERMS IMPLIED BY LAW INTO EMPLOYMENT CONTRACTS

5. Employment as a Class of Contract	117
Introduction	117
General Distinctive Characteristics of Employment	118
The Application of General Contract Law Principles	122
The Employee/Worker/Independent Contractor Distinction	126
The Operation of Particular Statutory Rules in Employment	136
The Courts' Imposition of Particular Duties in Employment	139
The Inability to Exclude Particular Duties in Employment	143
Employment as a Relational Contract	149
Conclusion	156
6. Necessity	159
Introduction	159
Emergence of the Necessity Test in England	160
Confusion in Applying the Necessity Test in England	163
Confusion in Applying the Necessity Test in Australia	164
Excludability and Absolute Necessity	172
Conclusion	179

7. The Judicial Role	181
Introduction	181
Examining the Judicial Role	184
A. Why Judges Should Engage in Judicial Law-making	185
B. Why Judges Should Avoid Judicial Law-making	187
Reinvigorating Coherence	189
Conclusion	196
Conclusion: Reshaping Contracts for Work	197
Summary of the Argument	197
Translating the Proposed Reshaping into Practice	200
A. Reclassifying Employment Contracts as a Class into Which Terms are Implied by Law	200
B. Defining When Terms Implied by Law are Necessary in Employment Contracts	205
C. Clarifying the Judicial Role and the Potential for a Set of Statutory Default Rules Implied into All Employment Contracts	207
D. Detailing the Precise Approach for Implying a Good Faith Term by Law into Employment Contracts	209
Rethinking the Rationale	214
Bibliography	217
Index	227

Table of Cases

A-G (NSW) v The Perpetual Trustee Company (Ltd) (1952) 85 CLR 237 (HCA).....202n.12
Abernathy v Mott, Hay and Anderson [1974] ICR 323 (CA) 26n.67
Adamson v Jarvis (1827) 4 Bing 66 (CCP) 54–55
Adventure World Travel Pty Ltd v Newsom (2014) 86 NSWLR 515 (NSWSC) 106n.174
AG Australia Holdings Ltd v Burton [2002] NSWSC 170 (NSWSC)................ 66n.82
AMEC Engineering Pty Ltd v Shanks (2001) 128 IR 116 (SASC)................. 21n.29
Armes v Nottinghamshire County Council [2018] AC 355 (UKSC)............... 132n.77
Arnold v Britton [2016] 1 All ER 1 (UKSC) 21n.22
AssetInsure Pty Ltd v New Cap Reinsurance Corp Ltd (In Liq) (2006) 225 CLR 331 (HCA) 27n.68
Attorney General of Belize v Belize Telecom Ltd [2009] 1 WLR 1988 (UKPC).........7–34
Attorney-General v Guardian Newspapers Ltd (No 2) [1990] 1 AC 109 (HL) 67n.97
Autoclenz Ltd v Belcher [2011] ICR 1157 (UKSC) 123–24, 133

Baldwin v Brighton & Hove City Borough [2007] IRLR 232 (EAT)................. 86n.24
Ball v Coggs (1710) 1 Brown PC 140 (KB) 70n.109
Barclays Bank plc v Various Claimants [2020] AC 973 (UKSC) 132n.77
Barker v Commonwealth Bank of Australia (2012) 229 IR 249 (FCA) 92
Bartlett v ANZ Banking Group Limited [2016] NSWCA 30 (NSWCA) 106
Bates v Post Office Ltd (No 3) [2019] EWHC 606 (QB)................111–12, 151–52,
152n.199, 155n.216
Baxter v Nurse (1844) 6 Man&G 935 (CCP) 71
Bedfordshire CC v Fitzpatrick Contractors Ltd (1998) 62 CmLR 64 (TCC) 101n.135
Bhasin v Hrynew [2014] 3 SCR 494 (SCC)............. 109n.205, 143n.139, 145, 210n.48
Blackmagic Design Pty Ltd v Overliese (2011) 191 FCR 1 (FCAFC) 61n.59
Blyth Chemicals Ltd v Bushnell (1933) 49 CLR 66 (HCA) 61, 88n.43
Bobux Marketing Ltd v Raynor Marketing Ltd [2001] NZCA 348 (NZCA)........ 155n.216
Bond v CAV Ltd [1983] IRLR 360 (EAT) 26–27n.68
BP Refinery (Westernport) Pty Ltd v Shire of Hastings (1977) 180 CLR 266 (HCA) ... 23–24,
30n.91, 97–98
Braganza v BP Shipping Ltd [2015] 1 WLR 1661 (UKSC) 124n.36
Breen v Williams (1994) 35 NSWLR 522 (NSWCA)............................. 166n.49
Breen v Williams (1996) 186 CLR 71 (HCA) 26nn.60,67, 28n.81, 31n.96, 166
Brennan v Kangaroo Island Council (2013) 239 IR 355 (SASCFC).....................74
Brennan v Kangaroo Island Council [2014] HCASL 153 (15 August 2014) (HCA) ..74n.136
Brian Maggs (t/a BM Builders) v Guy Marsh (2006) 150 SJLB 918 (CA) 21n.23
British Railways Board v Herrington [1972] AC 877 (HL)..........................186
British Syphon Co Ltd v Homewood [1956] 2 All ER 897 (Ch Div)................64–65
Brodie v Singleton Shire Council (2001) 206 CLR 512 (HCA) 190n.42
Brown v Merchant Ferries Ltd [1998] IRLR 682 (CA)........................... 86n.24
Burazin v Blacktown City Guardian Pty Ltd (1996) 142 ALR 144 (AIRC)...........88–89
Burn v Alder Hey Children's NHS Foundation Trust
  [2022] ICR 492 (CA) 87n.37, 172n.75, 204n.21
Butt v M'Donald (1896) 7 QLJ 68 (QSCFC) 69, 70n.105, 201–2
Byrne v Australian Airlines Ltd (1995) 185 CLR 410 (HCA) 18n.3, 23nn.35,40, 24–25,
24n.50, 26nn.60,67, 28n.81, 31n.99, 72n.124, 97–98,
144n.145, 164–71, 173n.81, 175, 179, 201n.4, 205–6

C v T Borough Council [2014] EWHC 2482 (QB)..............................153–54
Carmichael v National Power plc [1999] 1 WLR 2042 (HL).....................133n.85
Castlemaine Tooheys Ltd v Carlton & United Breweries Ltd
  (1987) 10 NSWLR 468 (NSWCA) 29nn.85–87, 194n.61
Catholic Child Welfare Society v Various Claimants [2013] 2 AC 1 (UKSC) 132n.77
Central Exchange Ltd v Anaconda Nickel Ltd (2002) 26 WAR 33 (WASC) 107n.182
CGU Workers Compensation (NSW) Ltd v Garcia (2007) 69 NSWLR 680 (NSWSC)....106n.175
Chartbrook Ltd v Persimmon Homes Ltd [2009] 1 AC 1101 (HL)...................21n.20
Cheall v Association of Professional Executive Clerical and Computer Staff
  [1983] 2 AC 180 (HL)..31n.99
Chelsfield Advisers LLP v Qatari Diar Real Estate Investment Company
  [2015] EWHC 1322 (Ch Div)..101n.135
Church of Ubuntu v Chait [2023] FWCFB 20 (FWCFB) 131n.75
Circle Freight International Ltd v Medeast Gulf Exports Ltd
  [1988] 2 Lloyd's Rep 427 (CA) 20n.18
Codelfa Construction Pty Ltd v State Rail Authority of New South Wales
  (1982) 149 CLR 337 (HCA).........................19n.9, 22n.31, 23n.35, 97n.114
Commonwealth Bank of Australia v Barker (2013) 214 FCR 450 (FCAFC)..........83n.7,
                                                                    92–94, 140–41
Commonwealth Bank of Australia v Barker (2014) 253 CLR 169 (HCA)........... vii, 3–4,
         10, 24–25, 31n.99, 32–33, 43, 73–74, 81–83, 87–101, 105–6,
         108, 109n.207, 112–13, 140–41, 147–48, 152, 154, 166n.45,
         168–71, 179, 181–83, 186, 192–93, 195–96, 202n.6, 204, 206, 212–13
Commonwealth Bank of Australia v Barker [2013] HCATrans 325
  (13 December 2013) (HCA) 93n.88
Commonwealth Bank of Australia v Barker [2014] HCATrans 73
  (8 April 2014) (HCA)...............................94n.89, 106n.171, 108n.196
Commonwealth Bank of Australia v Barker [2014] HCATrans 74
  (9 April 2014) (HCA)..94n.89, 106n.171
Con-Stan Industries of Australia Pty Ltd v Norwich Wintehur Insurance
  (Australia) Ltd (1986) 160 CLR 226 (HCA) 26–27
Concut Pty Ltd v Worrell (2000) 103 IR 160 (HCA) 61, 61–62n.60, 88n.43
Connelly v Wells (1994) 55 IR 73 (HCA) 19n.10
Construction, Forestry, Maritime, Mining and Energy Union v Personnel
  Contracting Pty Ltd (2022) 312 IR 1 (HCA) 3–4n.10, 8n.22, 125,
                                                         129n.68, 130–31, 134n.91
Corporation of Sheffield v Barclay [1905] AC 392 (HL) 54
Couchman v Hill [1947] KB 554 (CA) 20n.12
Courtaulds Northern Textiles Ltd v Andrews [1979] IRLR 84 (EAT) 84–85
Cox v Bankside Members Agency Ltd [1995] 2 Lloyd's Rep 437 (CA)...............24n.46
Cox v Ministry of Justice [2016] AC 660 (UKSC).........................62n.64, 132n.77
Crema v Cenkos Securities plc [2011] 1 WLR 2066 (CA) 33n.118
Crimmins v Stevedoring Industry Finance Committee (1999) 200 CLR 1 (HCA) 175n.90
Crossley v Faithful & Gould Holdings Ltd [2004] IRLR 377 (CA) 156n.217, 205
Cussons v Skinner (1843) 11 M&W 161 (CE) 58n.36

D J Hill & Co Pty Ltd v Walter H Wright Pty Ltd [1971] VR 749 (VSC) 20n.19
Daly v General Steam Navigation Co Ltd (The "Dragon")
  (1979) 1 Lloyd's Rep 257 (QB)...20n.16
Danowski v Henry Moore Foundation (1996) 140 SJLB 101 (CA)...............26–27n.70
Darling Island Stevedoring & Lighterage Co Ltd; Ex parte Halliday and Sullivan
  (1938) 60 CLR 601 (HCA)....................................59n.43, 173n.76

TABLE OF CASES   XV

Debus v Condor Energy Services Limited [2022] FedCFamC2G 429
    (FedCFamC2G) 170–71
Del Casale v Artedomus (Aust) Pty Ltd (2007) 165 IR 148 (NSWCA) 67n.96
Devonald v Rosser & Sons [1906] 2 KB 278 (CA) 26nn.60–64, 26–27n.68
Dick Bentley Productions v Harold Smith (Motors) Ltd [1965] 2 All ER 65 (CA). 20n.14
Downe v Sydney West Area Health Service (No 2) (2008) 71 NSWLR 633 (NSWSC). ... 106n.174
Duncombe v Porter (1953) 90 CLR 295 (HCA) 29n.85
Dye v Commonwealth Securities Ltd [2012] FCA 242 (FCA). 90–91, 106n.174
Dymocks Franchise Systems (NSW) Pty Ltd v Bilgola Enterprises Ltd
    (1999) 8 TCLR 612 (NZCA) 155n.216
Dymocks Franchise Systems (NSW) Pty Ltd v Todd [2002] 2 All ER 849 (UKPC) ... 155n.216
Dysart Timbers Ltd v Nielsen [2009] 3 NZLR 161 (NZSC) 34n.127

Eastwood v Magnox Electric plc [2005] 1 AC 503 (HL). 29n.86, 85–86nn.21,25,
                                                87nn.35–36, 96n.104, 104n.157, 211n.57
Edmonds v Lawson QC [2000] EQCA Civ 69 (CA) 138n.112
Edwards v Chesterfield Royal Hospital and Botham (FC) v Ministry of Defence
    [2012] 2 AC 22 (UKSC). 87n.35
Edwards v Levy (1860) 2 F&F 94 (CE) 58n.37
Eichholz v Bannister (1864) 144 ER 284 (CCP). 38n.11
Ellul v Oakes (1972) 3 SASR 377 (SASC) 20n.14
Equitable Life Assurance Society v Hyman [2002] 1 AC 408 (HL). 23n.38
Esso Australia Resources Pty Ltd v Southern Pacific Petroleum NL
    [2005] VSCA 228 (VSCA). 106n.175, 110n.213
Evans Deakin v Allen [1946] St R Qd 187 (QSC). 26–27nn.68, 69,71, 28n.79

Fishlock v The Campaign Palace Pty Ltd (2013) 234 IR 1 (NSWSC) 22n.33
Fitzgerald v F J Leonhardt Pty Ltd (1997) 189 CLR 215 (HCA). 32n.101
Flyn v Breccia [2015] IEHC 547 (IEHC) 155n.216
Foggo v O'Sullivan Partners (Advisory) Pty Ltd [2011] NSWSC 501 (NSWSC) 106n.174
Fortis Bank SA/NV v Indian Overseas Bank [2010] Bus LR 835 (Comm) 33n.118
French v Barclays Bank plc [1998] IRLR 646 (CA) 27n.69

GAB Robins (UK) Ltd v Triggs [2008] ICR 529 (CA) 87n.36
Garbett v Midland Brick Co Pty Ltd (2003) 129 IR 270 (WASCA) 29n.89
Gardiner v Gray (1815) 171 ER 46 (KB). 38n.11
Gardiner v Orchard (1910) 10 CLR 722 (HCA). 105n.167
Garry Rogers Motors (Aust) Pty Ltd v Subaru (Aust) Pty Ltd
    (1999) ATPR 41-703 (FCA) 106n.181
GEC Marconi Systems Pty Limited v BHP Information Technology Pty Limited
    (2003) 128 FCR 1 (FCAFC). 150–52, 155n.216
George v Davies [1911] 2 KB 445 (HL). 26n.66
Gilles v Downer EDI Ltd [2011] NSWSC 1055 (NSWSC) 108n.199
GKN (Cwmbran) Ltd v Lloyd [1972] ICR 214 (NIRC) 26–27n.68
Goldman Sachs J B Were Services Pty Ltd v Nikolich (2007) 163 FCR 62
    (FCAFC). 53nn.12,14, 175n.90
Goodman Fielder Consumer Foods Ltd v Cospak International Pty Ltd
    [2004] NSWSC 704 (NSWSC) 27nn.72–73
Goss v Lord Nugent (1833) 110 ER 713 (KB) 19n.9
Grainger v Roombridge Pty Ltd [2007] QCA 276 (QCA). 21n.28
Gramotnev v Queensland University of Technology (2015) 251 IR 448 (QCA) 106n.176
Griggs v Noris Group of Companies (2006) 94 SASR 126 (SASC) 24n.48

Halawi v World Duty Free [2015] 3 All ER 543 (CA) 138n.111
Harden v Willis Australia Group Services Pty Ltd [2021] NSWSC 939 (NSWSC).... 106n.174, 170
Harmer v Cornelius (1858) 5 CB (NS) 236 (CCP)................................. 63–64
Hart v McDonald (1910) 10 CLR 417 (HCA) 145
Hawkins v Clayton (1988) 164 CLR 539 (HCA) 24–25, 97–98
Heldberg v Rand Transport (1986) Pty Ltd [2018] FCA 1141 (FCA)................... 75
Helicopter Sales (Aust) Pty Ltd v Rotor-Work Pty Ltd (1974) 132 CLR 1 (HCA) 29n.87
Helmet Integrated Systems Ltd v Tunnard [2007] IRLR 126 (CA) 86n.28
Henry Kendall & Sons v William Lillico & Sons Ltd [1969] 2 AC 31 (HL) 20n.17
Heptonstall v Gaskin and Ors (No 2) (2005) 138 IR 103 (NSWSC)........... 83n.6, 89n.51
Hickman v Turn and Wave Ltd [2011] 3 NZLR 318 (NZCA) 34n.127
Hivac Ltd v Park Royal Scientific Instruments Ltd [1946] All ER 350 (CA) 60–62
Hollis v Vabu Pty Ltd (2001) 207 CLR 21 (HCA) 129n.62, 130–31
Horkulak v Cantor Fitzgerald International [2005] ICR 402 (CA) 111n.222
Hospital Medical Group Ltd v Westwood [2013] ICR 415 (CA)................... 129n.60
Hospital Products Ltd v United States Surgical Corp
    (1984) 156 CLR 41 (HCA)... 20n.11, 61n.55

Imperial Group Pension Trust Ltd v Imperial Tobacco Ltd [1991] 2 All ER 597 (QB) 86n.24
Interfoto Picture Library v Stiletto Visual Programs Ltd [1989] 2 QB 433 (CA) 20n.16
Investors Compensation Scheme Ltd v West Bromwich Building Society
    [1998] 1 All ER 98 (HL)... 21n.23
Irish Bank Resolution Corporation Ltd (in Special Liquidation) v Camden
    Market Holdings Corp [2017] EWCA Civ 7 (CA)............................ 18n.3

J Spurling Ltd v Bradshaw [1956] 1 Lloyd's Rep 392 (CA) 20n.17
James v Redcats (Brands) Ltd [2007] ICR 1006 (EAT) 128n.57
James-Bowen v Commissioner of Police of the Metropolis
    [2018] 1 WLR 4021 (UKSC)... 176n.91
Jani-King (GB) Ltd v Pula Enterprises Ltd [2008] 1 All ER (Comm) 451 (QB)..... 100–1nn.134–35
Jivraj v Hishwani [2011] 1 WLR 1872 (UKSC) 129n.59, 138n.111
Johnson v Unisys Ltd [2003] 1 AC 518 (HL)............... 29n.85, 85–86nn.21,26, 87n.35,
                                                104n.156, 124n.36, 141–43, 144n.145, 147,
                                                152–53, 153n.204, 194n.61, 212nn.57,62
Johnstone v Bloomsbury Health Authority [1992] 1 QB 333 (CA)...................... 145
Jones v Just (1868) LR 3 QB 197 (QB)... 38n.11

Kelly v Alford [1988] 1 Qd R 404 (QSC)... 55n.22
Kilminister v Sun Newspapers Limited (1931) 46 CLR 284 (HCA) 74n.138
King v University Court of the University of St Andrews [2002] IRLR 252 (SCS) 87n.36
Kleinwort Benson Ltd v Lincoln City Council [1999] 2 AC 349 (HL)................... 185
Koehler v Cerebos (Aust) Ltd (2005) 222 CLR 44 (HCA) 88n.43
Kuczmarski v Ascot Administration Pty Ltd [2016] SADC 65 (SADC) 73–75, 201n.4

L'Estrange v Graucob [1934] 2 KB 394 (KB)... 20
La Rosa v Nudrill Pty Ltd [2013] WASCA 18 (WASC).............................. 20
Lamb v Evans [1892] 3 Ch 462 (Ch Div) 67n.89
Lamb v Evans [1893] 1 Ch 218 (CA)... 66n.84, 67
Lane v Shire Roofing Company (Oxford) Ltd [1995] IRLR 493 (CA)............... 131n.76
Laws v London Chronicle (Indicator Newspapers) Ltd [1959] 1 WLR 698 (CA) 58–59
Leach v The Office of Communication [2012] IRLR 839 (CA) 85n.20
Lee v Showmen's Guild of Great Britain [1952] 2 QB 329 (CA) 145

Lewis v Motorworld Garages Ltd [1985] IRLR 465 (CA) 86n.24
Lister v Romford Ice & Cold Storage Co Ltd [1957] AC 555 (HL) 39n.22, 53–55,
63–64, 160–63, 175n.90
Liverpool City Council v Irwin [1977] AC 239 (HL) 28n.83, 30n.90,
39n.22, 160–64, 179, 205
London Borough of Enfield v Sivanandan [2005] EWCA Civ 10 (CA) 87n.34
London Export Corporation Ltd v Jubilee Coffee Roasting Co Ltd
  [1958] 1 WLR 661 (HL)... 27n.70
Luxor (Eastbourne) Ltd v Cooper [1941] AC 109 (HL)........................ 38n.19

Mabo v The State of Queensland (No 2) (1992) 175 CLR 1 (HCA) 185n.18
Macdonald Estates plc v Regenesis (2005) Dunfermline Ltd
  (2007) SLT 791 (CSOH)..145n.153
Mackay v Dick (1881) 6 App Cas 251 (HL) 69–70
Mackie v Wienholt (1880) 5 QSCR 211 (QSC)................................... 28n.79
Mainteck Services Pty Ltd v Stein Heurtey SA (2014) 89 NSWLR 633 (NSWCA)..... 22n.30
Majeau Carrying Co Pty Ltd v Coastal Rutile Ltd (1973) 129 CLR 48 (HCA) 26n.66
Malik v Bank of Credit and Commerce International SA (in liq) [1998] AC 20 (HL) 56n.28,
84n.13, 85–90, 88n.47, 90n.68, 92, 95–96, 142–44, 163n.29, 164n.42
Market Investigations v Minister of Social Security [1969] 2 QB 173 (QB) 132n.80
Marks & Spencer plc v BNP Paribas Securities Services Trust Company
  (Jersey) Ltd [2016] AC 742 (UKSC) 23n.35, 23n.38, 33–34, 205n.26
Marmax Investments Pty Ltd v RPR Maintenance Pty Ltd
  (2015) 237 FCR 634 (FCAFC) 109n.209
Marshall v Whittaker's Building Supply Co (1963) 109 CLR 210 (HCA) 126n.51
Matthews v Kuwait Bechtel Corporation [1959] 2 QB 57 (CA) 53n.11, 175n.90
McGowan v Direct Mail and Marketing Pty Ltd [2016] FCCA 2227 (FCCA) 74–75
McInerney v McDonald [1992] 2 SCR 138 (SCC)...............................166–67
McMahon v National Foods Milk Ltd (2009) 25 VR 251 (VCA) 70n.107
McManus v Scott-Charlton (1996) 70 FCR 16 (FCA)............................ 59n.42
Mediterranean Salvage & Towage Ltd v Seamar Trading & Commerce Inc
  (The Reborn) [2009] 2 Lloyd's Rep 639 (CA)................................33n.118
Meridian Retail Pty Ltd v Australian Unity Retail Network Pty Ltd
  [2006] VSC 223 (VSC)..109n.209
Merryweather & Sons v Master [1892] 2 Ch 518 (CA) 66–67, 66n.84
Mid Essex Hospital Services NHS Trust v Compass Group UK and Ireland
  Ltd (t/a Medirest) [2013] BLR 265 (CA) 103n.146, 209–10n.44
Mohamud v WM Morrison Supermarkets plc [2016] AC 677 (UKSC)............. 132n.77
Montreal v Montreal Locomotive Works Ltd [1947] 1 DLR 161 (UKPC) 133
Morley v Attenborough (1849) 154 ER 943 (Exch) 38n.11
Morley v Royal Bank of Scotland plc [2020] EWHC 88 (Ch Div)................. 210n.49
Mosvolds Rederi A/S v Food Corp of India (The Damodar General T J Park)
  [1986] 2 Lloyd's Rep 68 (Comm) 24n.46
Moult v Halliday [1897] 1 QB 125 (QB)............................. 26n.66, 26–27n.68
Mount Bruce Mining Pty Ltd v Wright Prospecting Pty Ltd
  (2015) 256 CLR 104 (HCA)... 22n.30
Mr H TV Ltd v ITV2 Ltd [2015] EWHC 2840 (Comm)........................ 101n.135
Mulcahy v Hydro-Electric Commission (1998) 85 FCR 170 (FCA) 56–57

Nationwide Mutual Insurance Co v Darden (1992) 503 US 318 (SCOTUS) 127n.54
Neale v Atlas Products (Vic) Pty Ltd (1955) 94 CLR 419 (HCA) 20n.17
Nelson v Dahl (1879) 12 Ch D 568 (CA) 26n.66, 26–27n.68

xviii   TABLE OF CASES

New South Wales v Shaw (2015) 248 IR 206 (NSWCA) 106n.176, 107n.183
Nottingham University v Fishel [2000] ICR 1462 (QB).......................... 86n.28

O'Kelly v Trusthouse Forte plc [1983] ICR 728 (CA)................................134
Oceanic Sunline Special Shipping Co Inc v Fay (1988) 165 CLR 197 (HCA).......... 20n.16
Official Trustee in Bankruptcy v Concut Pty Ltd (1999) 45 AILR ¶9–146 (AIRC) 61–62n.60
Oscar Chess Ltd v Williams [1957] 1 WLR 370 (CA) 20nn.11,14

Pacific Brands Sport & Leisure v Underworks Pty Ltd (2005) 12 Aust Contract
    Reports 90-213 (FCA).............................. 106n.181, 107n.186, 110n.218
Pappas v P&R Electrical Pty Ltd [2016] SADC 132 (SADC) 73n.130
Park v Brothers (2005) 222 ALR 421 (HCA) 32n.101
Parkinson v Lee (1802) 102 ER 389 (KB) 38n.11
Pearce v Foster (1886) 17 QBD 536 (CA) 60n.48
Pimlico Plumbers Ltd v Smith [2018] ICR 1511 (UKSC) 111–12, 128n.57
Price v Mouat (1862) 11 CBNS 508 (CCP)..58
Priestley v Fowler (1837) 3 M&W 1 (CE) 53
Printing Industry Employees Union of Australia v Jackson and O'Sullivan
    (1957) 1 FLR 175 (FCA) 64n.73
Proforce Recruit Ltd v Rugby Group Ltd [2006] EWCA Civ 69 (CA).............. 145n.153

Queensland Meat Export Co Pty Ltd t/as Smorgon Meat Group v Hawkins
    (unreported, Industrial Relations Court of Australia, Wilcox CJ,
    Spender and Moore JJ, 6 December 1996) (IRCA)........................ 74n.139

R v Foster; Ex parte Commonwealth Life (Amalgamated) Assurances Ltd
    (1952) 85 CLR 138 (HCA).. 126n.52, 129n.67
Re Famatina Development Corporation [1914] 2 Ch 271 (Ch Div).....................54
Re Porter (1989) 34 IR 179 (FCA)... 130n.71
Staffordshire Sentinel Newspapers Ltd v Potter [2004] IRLR 752 (EAT) 133n.86
Ready Mixed Concrete (South East) Ltd v Minister for Pensions and
    National Insurance [1968] 2 QB 497 (QB)............................. 133nn.84,86
Realestate.com.au Pty Ltd v Hardingham (2022) 170 IPR 1 (HCA) 25
Regulski v State of Victoria [2015] FCA 206 (FCA)............................ 106n.176
Reid v Rush and Tompkins Group plc [1990] 1 WLR 212 (CA) 144n.145
Renard Constructions (ME) Pty Ltd v Minister for Public Works
    (1992) 26 NSWLR 234 (NSWCA) 107
Republic of Nauru v Reid (unreported, Victorian Court of Appeal,
    23 October 1995) (VCA)... 20n.17
Reynolds v Southcorp Wines Pty Ltd (2002) 122 FCR 301 (FCA) 20n.17
Richardson v Koefod [1969] 3 All ER 1264 (Ch Div)................... 71n.112, 71n.114
Rickless v United Artists Corporation [1988] QB 40 (CA)........................ 26n.66
Rihan v Ernst & Young Global Ltd [2020] EWHC 901 (QB) 53n.14
Rinaldi & Patroni Pty Ltd v Precision Mouldings Pty Ltd [1986] WAR 131 (WASC) 20n.19
Robb v Green [1895] 2 QB 315 (CA)..................................... 60, 66n.84
Rogan-Gardiner v Woolworths Ltd [2010] WASC 290 (WASC) 104n.156,
                                                                106n.174, 211n.57
Rosenhain v Commonwealth Bank of Australia (1922) 31 CLR 46 (HCA)........... 27n.71
Royal Botanic Gardens and Domain Trust v South Sydney City Council
    (2002) 240 CLR 45 (HCA)..................................... 105n.167, 106n.173
Rugby Group Ltd v ProForce Recruit Ltd [2006] EWCA Civ 69 (CA) 21n.25
Russell v Cartwright [2020] EWHC 41 (Ch Div)............................... 210n.49

Russell v Trustees of the Roman Catholic Church for the Archdiocese of Sydney
  (2007) 69 NSWLR 198 (NSWCA) 59n.44, 104n.156, 108nn.194–95,
                                                  123, 140, 147–48, 211n.57
Russo v Westpac Banking Corporation [2015] FCCA 1086 (FCCA) 106n.176
Ryan v Textile Clothing and Footwear Union of Australia (1996) 66 IR 258 (VCA). . . . 26–27n.68

Sagar v Ridehlagh & Sons Ltd [1931] 1 Ch 310 (CA) 27n.74
Scally v Southern Health & Social Services Board [1992] 1 AC 294 (HL) 28n.82, 40n.26,
                                              55–57, 144n.145, 163n.28, 177, 200n.2
Secretary of State for Employment v ASLEF (No 2) [1972] 2 WLR 1370 (CA) 70n.106
*Secretary, Department of Education, Employment, Training and
  Youth Affairs v Prince* (1997) 82 FCR 154 (FCA) 106n.179
Secured Income Real Estate (Australia) Ltd v St Martins Investments Pty Ltd
  (1979) 144 CLR 596 (HCA)............................. 32n.101, 70n.104, 93n.81
District Council of Barunga West v Hand (2014) 202 LGERA 415 (SASCFC)....... 74n.136
Service Station Association Ltd v Berg Bennett & Associates Pty Ltd
  (1993) 45 FCR 84 (FCA) 110n.218
Shaw v New South Wales [2012] NSWCA 102 (NSWCA) 29n.87
Sheffield Corporation v Barclay [1905] AC 392 (HL) 55n.22
Sheikh Al Nehayan v Kent [2018] 1 CLC 216 (Comm)...................... 151n.194
Shepherd v Felt & Textiles of Australia Ltd (1931) 45 CLR 359 (HCA) 88n.43
Shirlaw v Southern Foundries (1926) Ltd [1940] AC 701 (HL) 23n.37
Singh v Members of the Management Committee of the Bristol Sikh Temple
  [2012] All ER (D) 68 (May) (EWHC) 128n.57
Smythe v Thomas (2007) 71 NSWLR 537 (NSWSC) 20n.14
Société Générale (London Branch) v Geys [2013] 1 AC 523 (UKSC)............... 125n.44
Solectron Scotland Ltd v Roper [2004] IRLR 4 (EAT) 27–28, 27n.69
Spain v Arnott (1817) 2 Stark 256 (CCP) 57–58
Spring v Guardian Assurance plc [1995] 2 AC 296 (HL)................. 53n.14, 144n.145
State of New South Wales v Lepore (2003) 212 CLR 511 (HCA) 53n.13
State of South Australia v McDonald (2009) 104 SASR 344 (SASCFC) 90–91, 140, 152,
                                                              169, 192–93
Stena Line Ltd v Merchant Navy Ratings Pension Fund Trustees Ltd
  [2011] Pens LR 233 (CA)... 33n.118
Sterling Engineering Company Limited v Patchett [1955] AC 534 (HL) 65
Stevens v Birmingham University [2016] 4 All ER 258 (EWHC)....................... 147
Stevens v Brodribb Sawmilling Co (1986) 160 CLR 16 (HCA)..................... 129–30
Stratton Finance Pty Ltd v Webb (2014) 245 IR 223 (FCAFC)................. 22nn.30,32
Summers v The Commonwealth (1918) 25 CLR 144 (HCA) 26–27nn.68–69
Summers v The Commonwealth (1919) 26 CLR 180 (HCA) 27n.69
Sutcliffe v Hawker Siddley Aviation Ltd [1973] ICR 560 (NIRC).................... 27n.69
Swindells v State of Victoria [2015] VSC 19 (VSC) 106n.176, 107n.183

Tai Hing Cotton Mill Ltd v Liu Chong Hing Bank Ltd [1986] AC 80 (HL) 144n.145
Takacs v Barclays Services Jersey Ltd [2006] IRLR 877 (QB) 87n.36
*TCL Air Conditioner (Zhongshan) Co Ltd v Judges of the Federal Court
  of Australia* (2013) 251 CLR 533 (HCA) 30n.91
Teesside Gas Transportation Ltd v CATS North Sea Ltd [2019] EWHC 1220 (Comm) 210n.49
The Basildon Academies v Amadi (UKEAT/0342/14/RN, 27 February
  2015) (EAT) 61–62n.60
The HMW Accounting and Financial Group v McPherson
  (2020) 292 IR 198 (QSC)....................................... 98, 171n.73

The Moorcock (1889) 14 PD 64 (CA) 23n.35, 23n.36, 163n.31
Thompson v ASDA-MFI Group plc [1988] Ch 241 (HC) 31n.99
Thornley v Tilley (1925) 36 CLR 1 (HCA) 26–27n.68
Tibaldi Smallgoods (Australasia) Pty Ltd v Rinaldi (2008) 172 IR 86 (VSC) 28n.78
Ticehurst v BT [1992] ICR 383 (CA)... 86n.30
Toll (FGCT) Pty Ltd v Alphapharm Pty Ltd (2004) 219 CLR 165 (HCA) 20n.15, 21n.20
Tote Tasmania Pty Ltd v Garrott (2008) 17 Tas R 320 (TASSC)................. 106n.175
Triplex Safety Glass v Scorah [1937] 55 RPC 221 (Ch Div) 64–65
Tullet Prebon plc v BGC Brokers LP [2011] IRLR 420 (CA) 62–63
Turner v Australasian Coal and Shale Employee Federation
 (1984) 6 FCR 177 (FCAFC)... 28n.79
Turner v Mason (1834) 14 M&W 112 (CE) 57–58

Uber BV v Aslam [2021] ICR 657 (UKSC)...............................59–60, 78, 173
University of Western Australia v Gray (2009) 179 FCR 346 (FCAFC)....... 65, 66n.83, 67,
 144n.145, 165, 167–71, 178–79, 200n.3, 205–6
Uszok v Henley Properties (NSW) Pty Ltd [2007] NSWCA 31 (NSWCA) 27n.69
UTB LLC v Sheffield United Ltd [2019] EWHC 2322 (Ch Div).................... 210n.49

Van den Esschert v Chappell [1960] WAR 114 (WASC) 20n.12
Various Claimants v Institute of the Brothers of the Christian Schools
 [2013] 2 AC 1 (UKSC)... 62n.64
Victoria University of Technology v Wilson [2004] VSC 33 (VSC).................. 65n.79
Video Ezy International Pty Ltd v Mobile Innovations Ltd [2014] NSWSC
 143 (NSWSC) 109n.209
Vodafone Pacific Ltd v Mobile Innovations Ltd [2004] NSWCA 15 (NSWCA) 18n.4,
 107n.182, 110n.217, 145–46

Wallace v United Grain Growers Ltd (1997) 152 DLR (4th) 1 (SCC) 109n.204, 142–43
Wallis v Day (1837) M&W 273 (CE) 70n.109
Warren v Dickson [2011] NSWSC 79 (NSWSC).....................................89
Watts v Lord Aldington [1999] L&TR 578 (HL) 24n.46
Western Excavating (ECC) Ltd v Sharp [1978] ICR 221 (CA) 84
Westpac Banking Corporation v Wittenberg (2016) 256 IR 181 (FCAFC) 74
Williams v Leeds United [2015] IRLR 383 (QB) 86n.30
Wilsons & Clyde Coal Co Ltd v English [1938] AC 57 (HL) 53
Woods v WM Car Services (Peterborough) Ltd [1981] ICR 666 (CA) 84–85, 84n.13, 86n.24
Workpac Pty Ltd v Rossato (2021) 309 IR 89 (HCA).................. 3–4n.10, 8n.22, 125
Worthington Pumping Engine Co v Moore (1902) 20 RPC 41 (Ch Div) 64–65

X v Mid Sussex Citizens Advice Bureau [2013] ICR 249 (UKSC)................. 138n.112
X v The Commonwealth (1999) 200 CLR 177 (HCA)........................... 64n.71

Yam Seng Pte Ltd v International Trade Corporation Ltd [2013] 1 All ER
 (Comm) 1321 (QB) 102–3, 103n.146, 151n.194, 209, 209–10n.44
Yousif v Commonwealth Bank of Australia (2010) 193 IR 212 (FCAFC) 21n.20

Zedra Trust Co (Jersey) Ltd v Hut Group Ltd [2019] EWHC 2191 (Comm) 210n.49
ZG Operations Australia Pty Ltd v Jamsek (2022) 312 IR 74 (HCA).............. 3–4n.10,
 8n.22, 125, 130, 134n.91
Zujis v Wirth Brothers Pty Ltd (1955) 93 CLR 561 (HCA)....................... 121n.16

Table of Legislation

UNITED KINGDOM

Consumer Rights Act 2015 (UK) 120–21
Copyright, Designs and Patents
    Act 1988 (UK).................... 65
Employment Relations Act
    1999 (UK) 136
Employment Rights Act 1996 (UK) ...18–19,
    29–30, 71–72, 127–28, 147
Equality Act 2010 (UK) 29–30, 128, 138
Health and Safety at Work etc.
    Act 1974 (UK)................175–78
Industrial Relations Act 1971 (UK)...83–84
Management of Health and Safety at
    Work Regulations 1999 (UK)... 175–76
National Minimum Wage Act
    1998 (UK) 29–30, 128, 137
Patents Act 1977 (UK) 65–66, 79
Poor Law Amendment Act
    1834 (UK) 70–71
Sale of Goods Act 1979 (UK) 29–30,
    37–38, 194
Statute of Artificers 1563 (UK).......70–71
Supply of Goods (Implied Terms)
    Act 1973 (UK)................29–30
Supply of Goods and Services
    Act 1982 (UK)................29–30
Working Time Regulations
    1998 (UK) 29–30, 128

AUSTRALIA

Building Work Contractors Act
    1995 (SA)....................18–19
Fair Work Legislation Amendment
    (Closing Loopholes) Bill
    2023 (Cth)....2–3, 126–27, 129, 137, 157
Competition and Consumer Act
    2010 (Cth)...................18–19
Corporations Act 2001 (Cth) 55, 66
Fair Work Act 2009 (Cth)...... 72–73, 125,
    127, 136–37, 173–74
Goods Act 1958 (Vic) 29–30
Independent Contractors Act 2006 (Cth)... 136
Industrial Relations Reform Act
    1993 (Cth) 72–73
Law of Property Act 1936 (SA).......18–19
Minimum Conditions of
    Employment Act 1993 (WA) 29–30
National Consumer Credit
    Protection Act 2009 (Cth) 18–19
Occupational Health and Safety
    Act 2004 (Vic) 175–76
Sale of Goods Act 1895 (SA).........29–30
Sale of Goods Act 1895 (WA).........29–30
Sale of Goods Act 1896 (Qld) 29–30
Sale of Goods Act 1896 (Tas) 29–30
Sale of Goods Act 1923 (NSW).......29–30
Sale of Goods Act 1954 (ACT) 29–30
Sale of Goods Act 1972 (NT) 29–30
Second-hand Vehicle Dealers Act
    1995 (SA)....................18–19
Work Health and Safety (National
    Uniform Legislation) Act
    2011 (NT) 175–76
Work Health and Safety Act
    2011 (ACT) 175–76
Work Health and Safety Act
    2011 (Cth) 73–74, 175–78
Work Health and Safety Act
    2011 (NSW) 175–76
Work Health and Safety Act
    2011 (Qld) 175–76
Work Health and Safety Act
    2012 (SA)...................175–76
Work Health and Safety Act
    2020 (WA)..................175–76
Workplace Health and Safety Act
    2012 (Tas).................. 175–76

List of Abbreviations

ABLR	Australian Business Law Review
ACLN	Australian Construction Law Newsletter
AIRC	Australian Industrial Relations Commission
AJIL	American Journal of International Law
AJLL	Australian Journal of Language and Literacy
ALJ	Australian Law Journal
Alta L Rev	Alberta Law Review
Am J Juris	American Journal of Jurisprudence
Am Soc Rev	American Sociological Review
Aust Bar Rev	Australian Bar Review
Aust J L & Soc	Australian Journal of Law & Society
Aust J Leg Philos	Australian Journal of Legal Philosophy
Can Bar Rev	Canadian Bar Review
CA	Court of Appeal
Cath U L Rev	Catholic University Law Review
CCP	Court of Common Pleas
CE	Court of Exchequer
Ch (Div)	Court of Chancery
CLELJ	Canadian Labour and Employment Law Journal
CLJ	Cambridge Law Journal
CLWR	Common Law World Review
Comm	Commercial Court
Comp Labour Law	Comparative Labour Law Journal
Comp LL & PJ	Comparative Labour Law and Policy Journal
Con LR	Construction Law Reports
Crit Inq	Critical Inquiry
CSOH	Court of Session Outer House
CUP	Cambridge University Press
Curr Leg Probl	Current Legal Problems
Deakin L R	Deakin Law Review
EAT	Employment Appeal Tribunal
Edin L R	Edinburgh Law Review
Exch	Court of Exchequer
FCA	Federal Court of Australia
FCAFC	Full Court of the Federal Court of Australia
FCCA	Federal Circuit Court of Australia
FedCFamC2G	Federal Circuit and Family Court of Australia (Division 2)
Fla LR	Florida Law Reports
FWCFB	Full Bench of the Fair Work Commission

Geo Wash L Rev	George Washington Law Review
Griffith L Rev	Griffith Law Review
HCA	High Court of Australia
HL	House of Lords
IEHC	Irish High Court
IJCLL&IR	International Journal of Comparative Labour Law and Industrial Relations
ILJ	Industrial Law Journal
IRCA	Industrial Relations Court of Australia
IRLR	Industrial Relations Law Reports
J Legal Educ	Journal of Legal Education
JBL	Journal of Business Law
JCL	Journal of Contract Law
JCULR	James Cook University Law Review
JITE	Journal of Institutional and Theoretical Economics
JSPTL	Journal of the Society of Public Teachers of Law
KB	Court of King's Bench
KCL	King's Law Journal
Leg S	Legal Studies Journal
LQR	Law Quarterly Review
MLR	Modern Law Review
Mon L Rev	Monash University Law Review
MULR	Melbourne University Law Review
NIRC	National Industrial Relations Court
NSWCA	New South Wales Court of Appeal
NSWSC	Supreme Court of New South Wales
N W L Rev	Northwestern University Law Review
NZCA	New Zealand Court of Appeal
OJLS	Oxford Journal of Legal Studies
OUCLJ	Oxford University Commonwealth Law Journal
OUP	Oxford University Press
QB	Court of the Queen's Bench
QCA	Queensland Court of Appeal
QSC	Supreme Court of Queensland
QSCFC	Full Court of the Supreme Court of Queensland
S Ac LJ	Singapore Academy of Law Journal
SADC	District Court of South Australia
SASC	Supreme Court of South Australia
SASCFC	Full Court of the Supreme Court of South Australia
S Cal L Rev	Southern California Law Review
SCC	Supreme Court of Canada
SCS	Scottish Court of Session
SCOTUS	Supreme Court of the United States
SLR	Sydney Law Review
Stan LR	Stanford Law Review

TASSC	Supreme Court of Tasmania
TCC	Technology and Construction Court
Theor Inq Law	Theoretical Enquiries in Law
UKEAT	UK Employment Appeals Tribunal
UKPC	UK Privy Council
UKSC	Supreme Court of the United Kingdom
UNSWLJ	University of South Wales Law Journal
UQLJ	University of Queensland Law Journal
UTas LR	University of Tasmania Law Review
UWALR	University of Western Australia Law Review
VCA	Victorian Court of Appeal
VSC	Supreme Court of Victoria
VUWLR	Victoria University of Wellington Law Review
WASC	Supreme Court of Western Australia

Introduction

Shaping the Normative Core of Contracts for Work

Terms implied by law shape the normative core of contemporary work relationships. Once implied by law, a term will impact all contracts within the class into which it is implied. That is a significant and influential outcome, particularly in the context of contracts for work. Over time, these terms, developed by judges, have come to fill gaps in and consequently mould work relationships.[1] The question of whether a term ought to be implied by law in the context of a contract for work has therefore become a critical issue in determining not only the nature of a work relationship, but also the application of norms in employment law. In exploring the ways in which terms implied by law have come to influence not just contracts of employment, but also the broader category of contracts for the performance of work, this present work adopts a unique perspective: its holistic analysis of the law, in England and Australia, assesses the extent to which terms implied by law have normatively influenced contracts for work in the common law world. The core values of working relationships have evolved significantly over time in response to the economic and industrial relations environments in both countries—so too have terms implied by law in shaping those relationships. It is argued that terms implied by law are the primary judicial mechanism for shaping contracts for work.[2] A move towards improved conceptualisation of circumstances in which such terms are implied represents an important development in generating a greater understanding of the normative core of contracts for work.

This introduction canvasses a selection of contemporary drivers and contradictions associated with how terms implied by law shape and influence contracts for work. It recommends that each of these components be thoroughly analysed so as to understand how the common law in two similar, yet different, jurisdictions have responded to these central questions and issues, and how both jurisdictions will

---

[1] On terms implied by law as 'gap fillers', see, eg, H Collins, *Regulating Contracts* (OUP 1999) 160–61; H Collins, *Employment Law* (2nd edn, OUP 2010) 9–11; H Collins, 'Legal Responses to the Standard Form Contract of Employment' (2007) 36 ILJ 2, 7–10; S Deakin and F Wilkinson, 'Labour Law and Economic Theory: A Reappraisal' in H Collins, P Davies, and R Rideout (eds), *Legal Regulation of the Employment Relation* (Kluwer Law International 2000) 42, 42–47. See further, Chapter 2.

[2] Cf M Freedland, *The Personal Employment Contract* (OUP 2003) 197–99, 251–52, where it is argued that the common law regulating the termination of the contract of employment is the most central component of employment law, as it dictates the rules governing the content, performance, suspension, and variation of the contract of employment.

continue to respond in the face of rapidly evolving work practices that continue to reshape the context of work.

Subsequent sections describe the central argument and overarching structure of this work, as well as its methodological approach and scope. A final section discusses the broader effects of generating this more thorough understanding of the influence of terms implied by law for the scope of protective norms of employment in English and Australian law.

Advancing the Enquiry

In his 2016 exploration of 'Implied Terms in the Contract of Employment', Hugh Collins wrote that:

> [T]erms 'implied by law' provide a legal expression of elements of the structural principles that shape the normative core of the legal institution of the contract of employment.[3]

In *Deakin and Morris' Labour Law* it was similarly noted that terms implied by law into employment contracts constitute a 'highly significant source of regulation'.[4] The authors of *Smith & Wood's Employment Law* have suggested that existing terms implied by law are now so deeply entrenched in all employment agreements that 'it could well be argued that the phrase "implied term" should be discarded and these duties simply viewed as incidents of the law of employment'.[5] Each view demonstrates that employment law assumes the steady continuation of existing terms implied by law, as well as an assumption that common law courts will consider the recognition of new terms from time to time.

Despite their primacy in contracts of employment, terms implied by law are not exclusive in influencing those agreements alone; substantially similar terms have been (or, at least, have the potential to be) implied into contracts for the performance of work more broadly,[6] thereby effectively blurring the boundaries between employment and other personal work contracts. To an extent, these same presumptions could extend in their application to not just an employment contract between an employer and employee, but also a contract between a principal and a self-employed contractor, and even other intermediate categories of personal work

---

[3] H Collins, 'Implied Terms in the Contract of Employment' in M Freedland (ed), *The Contract of Employment* (OUP 2016) 471, 472.
[4] Z Adams and others, *Deakin and Morris' Labour Law* (7th edn, Hart Publishing 2021) 238.
[5] I Smith, A Barker, and O Warnock, *Smith & Wood's Employment Law* (14th edn, OUP 2019) 145–46.
[6] See further, Chapter 3, which examines the potential for terms typically implied by law into employment contracts to operate in respect of contracts for the broader performance of work.

relationships.⁷ While terms implied by law are most obviously core components of contracts of employment, they are increasingly shaping work relationships in the broader sense. They have come to shape more than employment alone; in recognition of labour markets not remaining static, employment contract law has responded to those changes by driving the legal development of terms implied by law to suit a broader context in personal work contracts. Terms implied by law now have the capacity to shape a growing nomenclature of 'atypical' and 'non-standard' work relationships, apart from commonly used categories such as temporary, part-time, contracting, and self-employed work, and including terms such as 'reservist', 'on-call', 'as and when' contracts, as well as 'regular casuals', 'key-time' workers, 'min-max', and 'zero-hours' contracts.⁸

By focussing on the effects of terms implied by law into employment contracts in the main, but also considering how such terms are likely to be similarly implied in respect of other contracts for the performance of work, this work makes a significant contribution to the fields of employment and contract law, and in the intersection between those two disciplines.

This work identifies that common law courts have not fully explored the idea of employment contracts as a distinctive class of contract into which terms are implied by law. Nor have they clearly articulated when it is truly necessary to imply such terms. The judicial law-making role, with respect to when courts should make rules for employment, has been left unclear. The matter of whether a duty of good faith should operate as a term by law in employment has also received haphazard judicial attention across common law jurisdictions.⁹ Following the High Court of Australia's decision in *Commonwealth Bank of Australia v Barker*,¹⁰ the role of

---

⁷ As elaborated on in Chapter 5, in England, for example, there are two intermediate categories of personal work relationships which attract some employment rights; these two concepts are the 'worker' contract and the 'contract personally to do work'. They sit somewhere in between the contract of employment and the commercial contract for services. In Australia, the Fair Work Legislation Amendment (Closing Loopholes) Bill 2023 (Cth), Part 16, purports to expand the powers of the Fair Work Commission—Australia's national workplace relations tribunal—to set minimum pay and conditions for platform workers performing 'employee-like' work. At the time of writing, that Bill awaits further parliamentary debate, and may be the subject of substantial amendment. Mark Freedland and Nicola Kountouris develop a new central organising idea for modern employment protection systems in *The Legal Construction of Personal Work Relations* (OUP 2011) in the form of 'the personal work relation', the concept of which aids understanding the relationship between the standard contract of employment and other work relationships. See also R Owens, J Riley, and J Murray, *The Law of Work* (2nd edn, OUP 2011) 165–66, which frames considerations of the 'law of work' beyond the standard contract of employment to include broader work relationships.

⁸ See, eg, L Dickens, 'Exploring the Atypical: Zero Hours Contracts' (1997) 26 ILJ 262, 263; J Prassl, *The Concept of the Employer* (OUP 2015) 4.

⁹ See, eg, the further discussion on the variable treatment of the good faith duty across jurisdictions in Chapter 4.

¹⁰ (2014) 253 CLR 169 (High Court of Australia (HCA)). Three further recent High Court authorities have also generated significant upheaval in the way that work relationships are classified in Australia. Where the type of work relationship is recorded in a written contract between the parties, the consensus is now that it is the contract's express terms that determine that relationship, not how the relationship operates in reality following its formation: *Workpac Pty Ltd v Rossato* (2021) 309 IR 89 (HCA); *Construction, Forestry, Maritime, Mining and Energy Union (CFMMEU) v Personnel Contracting Pty Ltd*

implied terms in employment is now more ambiguous than ever. The decision in *Commonwealth Bank v Barker*—the most recent, leading Australian authority concerning terms implied by law, but which ruled out the implication of a mutual trust and confidence term into Australian employment contracts[11]—confirms that the time is ripe for this thorough examination, not just in the Australian context, but also more broadly.

The examination undertaken in this work involves probing the principle and policy-based considerations underpinning terms implied by law into contracts generally. It then takes the same approach with respect to employment contracts, with additional references to other contracts for the performance of work. For example, it is commonly understood that terms implied by law underpin the following principle and policy-based considerations that are imperative to the norms of employment; these being mutuality and reciprocity, care and cooperation, trust and confidence, loyalty and freedom of economic activity, as well as fair management and performance.[12] In that sense, terms implied by law, as the title of this book suggests, shape the normative order of what it means to be employed, or to be otherwise subject to another type of contract for the performance of work. Here, the idea of the normative order reflects the ways in which right from wrong in relation to the way that work is performed, and having common or overlapping conceptions of what ought to occur in the case of contracts of employment, as distinct from contracts for the performance of work.[13]

However, there is a clear challenge in reconciling whether these same principle and policy-based considerations are even exclusive to employment, or whether they could be similarly applied to other contracts for the performance of work—most obviously, contracts for work performed by independent contractors, and perhaps even further to contracts for the personal performance of work—acknowledging that there may be debates concerning the distinction between employment and contracting, particularly with work performed in the gig economy.[14] It is therefore timely and more critical than ever to examine the normative role of terms implied by law into contracts for work. It is this examination the current work hopes to pursue, presenting an enquiry into terms implied by law into contracts for work; both as they have been historically received in the common law and

---

(2022) 312 IR 1 (HCA); and *ZG Operations Australia Pty Ltd v Jamsek* (2022) 312 IR 74 (HCA). See further, Chapter 5.

[11] The existence of the mutual trust and confidence term (or a substantially similar term) has support in a range of other common law jurisdictions. See further, Chapter 4.
[12] See, eg, Freedland (n 2) 127–28.
[13] See further, N MacCormick, *Institutions of Law* (OUP 2007) 20. For a reflection on what principles of justice should apply to work, including in respect of employment and the personal performance of work more broadly, see H Collins, 'Relational and Associational Justice in Work' (2023) 24 Theor Inq Law 26.
[14] See generally, J Prassl, *Humans as a Service: The Promise and Perils of Work in the Gig Economy* (OUP 2018).

how they could develop in future within that legal framework. A comprehensive discussion of this nature is long overdue. As already highlighted, terms implied by law have had—and continue to have—a normative effect on shaping contracts for work. However, this effect is yet to be recognised by a scholarly work that probes it extensively.[15] From an overarching perspective, as the common law continues to shape contracts for work by way of the implication of terms by law, this work comprises a unique and important reference point in informing that development. It seeks to deepen and reinforce the understanding of how the common law, through the mechanism of terms implied by law, is among the most influential of avenues to shape contracts for work.

Outline of Argument and Structure

The central argument in this work is that the current rationale for implying a term by law into contracts for work needs to be rethought, the result of which is that the nature and scope of the common law employment contract, as distinct from other contracts for the performance of work, will become better understood. Indeed, in discussing the implied duties of mutual trust and confidence and good faith, Joellen Riley Munton expressed a desire for '[t]he articulation of clear and bounded principles' to encourage '[g]reater certainty in employment contract law'.[16] This work's deeper exploration of the rationale for implying terms by law into contracts for work endeavours to generate that greater certainty.

It is divided into four main parts, each reflecting a particular step towards that endeavour. Part I involves an assessment of the overarching influence of terms implied by law on the common law of contract across Chapters 1 and 2. The purpose of this discussion is to provide a standpoint from which to view the more detailed exercise that occurs in subsequent chapters, which assesses the effects of terms implied by law into contracts for work.

Chapter 1 provides an overarching survey of the law from both jurisdictions governing express and implied terms in contracts generally. In doing so, it considers the interplay between general contractual principles and their regulation of contracts for work. It also considers the relationship between implication and construction of contractual terms in each jurisdiction, including an examination of the policy considerations for the distinction between implication and construction.[17]

---

[15] Particular attention has been paid to the implied terms of mutual trust and confidence. However, detailed attention is yet to be paid to the broader range of terms implied by law into employment contracts, as well as to how those terms may impact contracts for the performance of work more broadly, including the effect that this impact may have on distinguishing between employment and other modes of work. The jurisdictional comparison present in this work is yet to be engaged in.

[16] J Riley, 'Siblings but Not Twins: Making Sense of "Mutual Trust" and "Good Faith" in Employment Contracts' (2012) 36 MULR 521, 521.

[17] As to the distinction between implication and construction, see, eg, W Courtney and J Carter, 'Implied Terms: What is the Role of Construction?' (2014) 31 JCL 151.

The chapter further considers the relationship between implication and interpretation, noting the significance of the notion that the process of implying a term into a contract is no more than a facet of interpreting its 'true meaning'; in that sense, it is acknowledged that it may sometimes be necessary to imply a term into a contract in order to make the contract work as the parties must have intended.[18] It is a brief summary, reflective of the fact that many, but certainly not all, of the legal propositions in this area are relatively straightforward. This analysis serves as an informative background and functions as a lens through which to view the remaining content of this work.

Continuing in the context of the general law of contract, Chapter 2 assesses the effects of the judicial act of implying a term by law into a contract and how that action, irrespective of the contractual context, has the potential to fundamentally guide, shape, and alter the nature of the relationship between the contracting parties. As in Chapter 1, the analysis is brief in comparison to the chapters that follow. This brevity is in recognition of the introductory nature of the debates identified, and their function as a backdrop for the remaining content.

Part II provides a comparative, historical, and legal overview of terms implied by law into employment contracts, with added reference to other contracts for the performance of work across Chapters 3 and 4. Chapter 3 provides an historical and comparative analysis of a selection of well-recognised terms implied by law into employment contracts. It conducts that same analysis in respect of those implied by law into the broader category of contracts for the non-standard performance of work. It traces the origins and current status of each select term in both jurisdictions, across employment contracts and other non-standard contracts for the performance of work (particularly in the context of independent contracting).

This exercise is significant, both in terms of the depth of analysis required and the unique nature of the contribution it makes to the literature. It does not appear that a similar exercise has been undertaken before in respect of these terms, save for the author's initial investigation in respect of terms implied into employment contracts only,[19] leaving aside consideration of non-standard contracts for the performance of work. Hence, this chapter offers a new and original analysis of the origins of the terms that are assessed, including the framework in which they operate.

---

[18] This discussion is engaged in the context of Lord Hoffman's judgment in *Attorney General of Belize v Belize Telecom Ltd* [2009] 1 WLR 1988 (Privy Council (UKPC)), which had been considered to mean that a term could or should be implied if it is reasonable to do so, and that implying a term is part of the process of interpretation of a contract. However, Lord Hoffmann's approach of conflating interpretation and implication in the decision in *Belize* was reversed by Lord Neuberger's later recognition that the processes of interpretation and implication constituted 'different processes governed by different rules' in *Marks and Spencer plc v BNP Paribas Securities Services Trust Company (Jersey) Ltd & Anor* [2015] UKSC 72 (Supreme Court (UKSC))—an authority which supports the proposition that only once the court has construed the express terms of the contract will it consider whether to imply a term.

[19] See, eg, G Golding, 'The Origins of Terms Implied by Law into English and Australian Employment Contracts' (2020) 20 OUCLJ 163.

In terms of the comparative and historical methods used, Chapter 3 traces the English origins followed by the current status of a selection of key terms implied by law into English and Australian contracts for work, dividing these key terms into three broad categories: the duties owed by the provider of work, by those performing the work, and mutually. The selection of key terms is on the basis that they are repeatedly referred to in employment law textbooks as well-established terms implied by law into employment contracts, noting their potential broader application in the context of contracts for the non-standard performance of work. The chapter traces the initial origins of those terms up to a case (or cases) cited in recent times, leaving aside incidental decisions in between. It highlights tensions between certain current terms implied by law and legislation. Ultimately, the analysis demonstrates that, in each instance of implication, there is an arbitrary judicial decision classifying the particular term as one implied by law as an apparently necessary incident in the context of the performance of work, or at least one in which the legal logic for that implication is not adequately articulated.

Chapter 3 demonstrates that most terms implied by law into both employment contracts and other contracts for the performance of work have their origins in English employment law. In most cases, while many of those terms now operate as terms implied by law, that is typically not how they originated. The majority are derived from equity, tort, and the former master and servant regime. Only later did they become accepted as terms implied by law.

The difficulty with this historical path is that it avoids adequate consideration of why the terms are necessary incidents. Their application to some, or all, instances of employment, and—in certain cases—to the broader category of contracts for the performance of non-standard work, is simply presumed. This continuance of the implied terms reflects their gestation within the womb of the 'law of persons'; it is reflective of the former characterisation of the employment relationship as one of status—rather than contract—within the context of the master and servant regime, followed by the slow, yet gradual, movement towards the recognition of the relationship as a contract.[20] As becomes apparent, there is a clear carry-over of obligations that underpinned the former master and servant regime, which have now found their way into the shaping and definition of the employment contract, and—in certain cases—the broader category of contracts for the performance of work, thereby contributing to a blurring of the distinction between employment and other non-standard modes of work.

Chapter 4 concentrates on the implied duties of mutual trust and confidence and good faith, primarily in respect of employment contracts, but with some reference to other contracts for the performance of work. Given the controversy

---

[20] See, eg, A Merritt, 'The Historical Role of Law in the Regulation of Employment: Abstentionist or Interventionist?' (1982) 1 Aust J L & Soc 56, in which she traces the presence of terms implied by law in the modern employment contract back to nineteenth-century master and servant legislation.

surrounding both duties—particularly in Australia—it makes sense to consider them separately in this chapter. As with Chapter 3, this chapter traces the historical origins and current status of both duties, in both jurisdictions.

Part III turns to the task of analysing some more nuanced issues associated with implying terms by law into employment contracts alone, across Chapters 5 to 7. There is a transition at this point from the analytical-descriptive to the normative—in other words, to an exploration of the common or overlapping conceptions of what ought to be part of all employment contracts.[21] Chapter 5 considers the first element of the test for implying a term by law as a necessary incident of employment contracts: that the term must be necessary in the 'class' of employment contracts. It undertakes a comprehensive analysis of employment contracts as a 'class' into which terms are implied by law, which, by its nature, includes an assessment of what separates that class of contract from other types of personal work contract.

The discussion in Chapter 5 demonstrates that, in the context of implying terms by law, the class of employment contracts is not easily identifiable. In fact, the so-called 'class' is an overly generalised and inconsistently defined category into which terms have been, and are, implied by law. The employment contract does not necessarily confine itself to an entirely unique definition or understanding. It retains an entire range of characteristics that are also present in other types of contracts, including the broader category of contracts for the performance of work. Courts have paid sparse attention to identifying and understanding employment contracts as a distinctive class of contract when they imply terms by law. Recent Australian case law has even gone so far as to stymie the notion that a contract of employment is unique at all from other types of contracts.[22] There is clearly scope for judges to develop that understanding. Doing so will assist them in developing the common law that regulates employment contracts. It will enable more accurate predictions of how the common law is likely to develop in respect of those agreements.

Chapter 6 focuses on the second element of the test for implying a term by law into a particular class of contract: that the term must be 'necessary'. It assesses the interpretations of the necessity test for implying a term by law that have emerged, and the confusion caused in relation to which understanding of the test should be adopted. At one end of the spectrum, courts are concerned with a narrow application of the necessity test, such that the term implied by law must be necessary for the employment contract's strict functionality alone. At the other end of the spectrum, the view is that courts ought to take into account broader principle and policy-based reasons associated with employment in deciding on a term's necessity. There is a clear fluctuation between these two approaches, which is analysed

---

[21] See further, MacCormick (n 13) 20.
[22] See generally, *Workpac v Rossato* (n 10); *CFMMEU v Personnel Contracting* (n 10); and *ZG Operations v Jamsek* (n 10).

in the chapter. Moreover, notwithstanding the existence of a necessity test, in some instances it appears that the main judicial reason for implying a term by law was simply that it had been implied previously. That reasoning seems insufficient and the chapter probes why. Attention is also paid to the emerging obligations arising under statute, tort, and equity, and their potential to stymie the development of implied terms; arguably, where a corresponding obligation exists in another area of law, it is no longer necessary as a term implied by law in the contractual context.

Chapter 6 also highlights that while certain terms are deemed necessary to the strict functionality of an employment agreement,[23] others are not. Consequently, they ought to be capable of exclusion or modification. The question of excludability therefore has the potential to generate a political and policy-based assessment for the judiciary to grapple with. Consideration is given to the proper role of terms implied by law in potentially being cut down by express terms. This is an important discussion; there is a clear political and policy-based challenge as to whether such intervention ought to be permitted to allow the judiciary to shape employment contracts, or whether the law ought to function to facilitate the autonomy of parties to agree on their own terms. Therefore, this chapter endeavours to understand the 'true' necessity test being utilised when a term is sought to be implied by law.

The question of whether a term implied by law can be excluded by a contrary express term is inextricably linked with the concept of necessity. As such, in Chapter 6, both excludability and necessity are discussed in conjunction with one another. The rationale behind this dual discussion is paradoxical: terms implied by law into employment contracts will have been implied in the first place because they are deemed 'necessary'. This purported necessity therefore raises the question of how express terms could permissibly exclude an obligation normally implied by law into a contract of employment that serves to constitute the basic elements of that relationship. Terms implied by law may not be as easily excluded as is commonly supposed; arguably, throughout this process, courts are forced to make policy-based judgements as to the desired shape of employment contracts. Perhaps, if certain terms were to be excluded, then the contract may cease to be one of employment, and potentially could be transformed into some other type of contract. The resulting question of which terms implied by law ought to be incapable of exclusion due to their absolute necessity to the employment relationship constitutes a key component of this chapter's exploration.

---

[23] In terms of the orthodox rules of contract law, this assertion is a heresy—more specifically, the notion that certain implied terms are impervious to disapplication through the use of an express clause in an employment contract. As such, any proposal that certain terms implied by law are mandatory will have a suitably strong justification, as well as addressing doctrinal problems that would inevitably arise. On the extent to which it is possible to state that certain implied terms constitute irreducible core obligations in employment contracts that cannot be removed by an express term and the challenges around that understanding, see, eg, Adams and others (n 4) 241.

Chapter 7 assesses the overarching judicial role in implying terms by law into employment contracts. Considering the High Court of Australia's comments in *Commonwealth Bank v Barker* that the implication of the mutual trust and confidence term is a matter best left to parliament (rather than the courts), it questions the future judicial role in making law with respect to employment. The chapter considers the general debate as to whether the courts or parliament should make laws with respect to employment contracts, and then offers a view as to how this debate ought to be resolved in the future, in respect of enabling the regulation of employment contracts through terms implied by law.[24] Specifically, it makes an argument for greater coherence between statute and the common law to ensure the continuation of a judicial law-making role, even where there are defensible policy positions on both sides of an argument. While academic attention is increasingly being paid to the capacity for implied terms to develop in a way that ensures human rights are respected in the workplace in England,[25] it does not appear that the courts' law-making power with respect to implying terms by law into employment contracts has been considered to date in this light.

Conclusions and recommendations are offered. In so doing, the final chapter maps a series of methods through which the courts might rethink the rationale for implying terms by law into employment contracts primarily and makes some reference to the broader category of contracts for the performance of work. In response to the analyses of the previous chapters, it suggests four options for reform.

These options include, first, that there is a need for the courts to better articulate their understanding of what constitutes the 'employment contract' as a distinctive class of contract into which terms are implied by law, separate from the broader notion of 'contracts for the performance of work'. Secondly, courts must clarify when it is 'necessary' to imply a term by law into the class of employment contracts. Thirdly, the judicial role must be clarified in relation to the regulation of employment. Lastly, there ought to be greater clarity regarding the interrelationship, if any, between a duty of good faith and mutual trust and confidence. Each of these claims is expanded on in this concluding chapter. Overall, an argument is made for reform to the legal test for implying terms by law: a test that to date the courts have applied haphazardly. It makes this argument for reform not only in respect of terms implied by law into contracts for work but also in relation to contracts generally.

The main proposals in this final chapter are for parliament to intervene, and for common law courts to reform and clarify the common law in respect of terms implied by law into contracts for work. However, that is not to say that the common

---

[24] On the fraught relationship between the common law and statute (i) in the case of labour law and (ii) in general, see Chapter 7.
[25] See, eg, J Atkinson, 'Implied Terms and Human Rights in the Contract of Employment' (2019) 48 ILJ 515. As to the broader impact of the existence of an employment relationship on the human rights of workers, see generally, P Collins, *Putting Human Rights to Work: Labour Law, the ECHR, and the Employment Relation* (OUP 2022).

law ought to take on an overly or unnecessarily expansionary role. In recognition of the need for greater coherence between statute and the common law, such legislative and judicial reforms ought to coincide, with one branch of law-making informing the other.[26]

A case is made for legislative intervention by way of statutory default minimum rules to be applied to all employment contracts, combined with an assessment of the potential costs and benefits of this mode of codification. A mirror proposal is made with respect to contracts for the performance of work. These proposals are put forward with the equal and opposite acknowledgement that there will always remain new and developing gaps to fill and particular issues in which the common law will continue to play an important regulatory role. Therefore, with precision, and while observing the need to maintain a separation between judicial and legislative power, these proactive proposals can be compatible, with each influencing the development and continuity of the other.

As such, normative conclusions are drawn on the proper role of statute in operating alongside the development and continuing recognition of terms implied by law into contracts for work. It postulates a systematic quality as to the norms that underlie an aspiration to order in respect of such contracts.[27] This work offers insight into the ways in which the legal test for implying terms by law could be refined in respect of employment contracts, other contracts for the performance of work, and even contracts generally.

Methodology

A triangulation of research methodologies is adopted throughout this work; all are well known to legal scholars and are deployed at different points. Each chapter is informed by the doctrinal research undertaken in Chapters 1 and 2, in which the general law governing express and implied terms is explained. This research method has been described as one that 'provides a systematic exposition of the rules governing a particular legal category, analyses the relationship between rules, explains areas of difficulty and, perhaps, predicts future developments'.[28] Questions regarding the historical development of select terms implied by law into contracts for work in Chapters 3 and 4 are informed by traditional historical and comparative

---

[26] In relation to the interrelationship between statute and the common law as they concern the contract of employment, see further, ACL Davies, 'The Relationship Between the Contract of Employment and Statute' in M Freedland and others (eds), *The Contract of Employment* (OUP 2016) 73.

[27] See, eg, MacCormick (n 13) 11.

[28] D Pearce, E Campbell, and D Harding ('Pearce Committee'), *Australian Law Schools: A Discipline Assessment for the Commonwealth Tertiary Education Commission* (Australian Government Publishing Service 1987) 312. See also T Hutchinson and N Duncan, 'Defining and Describing What We Do: Doctrinal Legal Research' (2012) 17 Deakin L R 83.

research methodologies;[29] understanding the legal framework in which each of these implied terms now operates is achieved through doctrinal research.

Chapters 5 to 7 build on the earlier analyses across Chapters 1 to 4, generating a more contextual understanding of the test for implying a term by law into contracts of employment specifically; that is, what that common law test *could* be and, in light thereof, what it *should* be—rather than solely concentrating on an analysis of what the law presently *is*.[30] In considering the overarching research question of this work—specifically, how the rationale for implying terms by law ought to be reconsidered in the context of contracts for work—it is important to analyse such broader consequences beyond a strict application of the existing law alone. In doing so, the discussion and analysis of the law in Chapters 5 to 7 consciously move through the principle and policy-based underpinnings upon which the key arguments of this work are based.

The research presented throughout draws on comparisons between English and Australian law, as well as primary and secondary sources across employment and contract law, including the intersection between those two areas. A comparative analysis between jurisdictions must be exercised carefully. As Sir Otto Kahn-Freund observed, 'any attempt to use a pattern of law outside the environment of its origin continues to entail the risk of rejection',[31] and that comparative analysis should not adopt a 'legalistic spirit which ignores the context of the law'.[32] In adopting a comparative methodology, the spirit of this work is not to ask which country's approach is superior, but rather to challenge contemporary understandings of how those different jurisdictions, in their specific context, approach terms implied by law into contracts for work. But to stop at a description of those terms in England and Australia would fall short of the vocation of the legal comparatist to expand knowledge, which is to understand that comparative law is an *école de vérité* that extends and enriches the 'supply of solutions'.[33] In endeavouring to supply those solutions, the work does more than simply outline the different approaches across jurisdictions; rather, it draws normative conclusions from the comparison undertaken. To be clear: a comparison of the descriptive laws across jurisdictions provides a means through which to identify convergences and divergences in respect of terms implied by law and, in turn, makes recommendations as to how terms implied by law ought to continue to shape contracts for work.

---

[29] See generally, K Zweigert and H Kötz, *An Introduction to Comparative Law* (3rd edn, Clarendon Press 1998).

[30] See, eg, A V Dicey, *Introduction to the Study of the Law of the Constitution* (Macmillan 1885) Preface to the First Edition vii, as cited by C Harlow, 'Changing the Mindset: The Place of Theory in English Administrative Law' (1994) 14 OJLS 419, 426: 'possible weakness [of purely doctrinal legal analysis] as applied to the growth of institutions, is that it may induce men to think so much of the way in which an institution has come to be what it is, that they cease to consider with sufficient care what it is that an institution has [—and therefore *could* and *should*—] become'. See also, Prassl (n 8) 9.

[31] O Kahn-Freund, 'On Uses and Misuses of Comparative Law' (1974) 37 MLR 1, 27.

[32] ibid.

[33] Zweigert and Kötz (n 29) 15.

Scope

To facilitate analytical clarity, two limitations in scope are necessary. The first of these concerns the range of relationships under examination: the focus of the present work in Chapters 1 and 2 is on parties to contracts generally. That focus then shifts to parties to contracts for work in Chapters 3 to 5 and, more specifically, to parties to employment contracts in Chapters 6 and 7. As mentioned, the emphasis is on the effects of terms implied by law into employment contracts in the main, but, at certain points, considers how such terms are implied in respect of other contracts for the performance of work; most obviously a contract for services between a principal and independent contractor, and with some consideration to other atypical work arrangements mentioned in this introduction. The enquiry following Chapters 1 and 2 therefore concentrates mostly on the contract of employment and the parties to it. However, it is vital to look briefly beyond this paradigm, to investigating how certain concepts are applied similarly to contracts for the personal execution of work. Several of the concepts discussed apply to *all* personal work contracts, and in certain instances, to all contracts in the broadest sense.

The second limitation of scope arises from the focus on the common law contract of employment: for present purposes, the jurisdictions of England and Australia. Over more than a century, stemming from developments in English law in particular, a considerable body of case law and scholarship has been built up to develop, adapt, and refine the common law concerning terms implied by law in both jurisdictions. Such developments have been universally responsible for shaping contracts for work. While the focus in the present work is firmly on the developments across these two jurisdictions, that is not to suggest that either jurisdiction is analytically distinct from the other or, indeed, from other common law jurisdictions. As demonstrated, many aspects are shared across all contracts to personally execute work in common law jurisdictions. With a large and dynamic collective body of judicial reasoning and academic commentary, this study's concentration on developments across two select common law jurisdictions provides the most appropriate core basis from which to embark on an analysis of terms implied by law and their capacity to shape contracts for work. The enquiry that follows therefore concentrates on developments in England and Australia only.

Rethinking the Rationale

In concluding this introduction, the final question to consider is that of the broader implications of the overarching aim of this work; that is, the effects of rethinking the rationale behind terms implied by law into contracts for work. As the preceding discussion suggests, normative conclusions are drawn as to how statute ought to operate alongside the development and continuing recognition of existing terms implied by law into contracts for work, so as to achieve a desired sense of 'orderliness'.[34] This work suggests ways in which the legal test for implying terms by law could be refined in future, not just in a manner that will influence employment contracts, but in a manner that will also affect other contracts for the performance of work and potentially, contracts more broadly.

As a result, the effect of rethinking the rationale behind implying terms by law into contracts for work is multifaceted. It represents an attempt to clarify the complexity associated with the context in which it is appropriate for a court to intervene and shape a contract for work by means of recognising an existing or new term implied by law. By considering the overarching influence of terms implied by law in the realm of contracts generally, as well as in the more specific context of employment contracts primarily, but with reference to other contracts for the performance of work across two common law jurisdictions, this work provides a thorough doctrinal assessment of the applicable law.

That detail generates an ideal framework from which to analyse the perennial problems associated with the task of implying terms by law into employment contracts, as well as the broader category of contracts for personal work, and even contracts generally. It enables a consideration of the principle and policy effects of the doctrinal approach taken in each jurisdiction, which, in turn, leads to suggestions as to the best approach to the rationale for implying terms by law into contracts for work into the future. The suggestions offered in Part III are therefore designed to drive clarity and coherence in the common law. In building on its descriptive core, this work provides a seminal consideration of how, through the mechanism of terms implied by law, the common law can continue to operate and develop meaningfully in the inexorably diverse and complex setting of the world of work. After all, terms implied by law are intrinsic to contracts for work; they serve as a regulatory framework that is responsible for shaping those relationships.

---

[34] See, eg, MacCormick (n 13) 16–8.

PART I
TERMS IMPLIED BY LAW INTO CONTRACTS GENERALLY

1
A Legal Overview

Introduction

This chapter introduces implied terms, as distinct from express terms. It focuses on the general law of contract as it applies to all contracts, including employment contracts[1] and contracts for the performance of work. The overarching purpose is to establish a legal framework for the remainder of the work, which focuses specifically on terms implied by law into employment contracts and contracts for the performance of work in Chapters 3 to 5, and employment contracts exclusively in Chapters 6 and 7. It also functions as a precursor to a deeper exploration in Chapter 2 of the significance of the judicial act of implying a term by law into contracts generally. The broad overview presented in this chapter reflects the fact that the general law on express and implied terms is relatively straightforward. As demonstrated from Chapter 3 onwards, however, there are challenges in respect of how terms implied by law normatively shape employment contracts as distinct from contracts for the performance of work, which warrant separate discussion. This chapter, alongside what follows in Chapter 2, provides the legal framework for the discussion of those more specific matters in the later chapters.

Given the primacy of express terms over implied terms, it is logical to consider them first and foremost. This discussion is also important in the broader context of this work: to fully understand whether it is appropriate to imply any term into any contract, one must first look at its express terms. The chapter then moves to consideration of the separate legal tests for the three main categories of implied terms: those implied in fact, by custom and usage, and by law. The courts' common confusion surrounding the distinction between implication of terms in fact and by law is then exposed. The next part addresses the relationship between implication of terms and construction, which is a distinction that will be briefly returned to in later parts of this work. Concluding comments are made about the state of the law concerning express and implied terms in contracts generally, in transition to Chapter 2's deeper assessment of the significant judicial act of implying a term by law.

---

[1] As discussed later in Chapter 5, there is an ongoing debate concerning the extent to which general contract principles should apply to employment contracts.

Express Terms

As suggested, the rights and obligations of parties to a contract are determined, at least in the first instance, by the contract's express terms, which are those explicitly agreed upon by the parties. Apart from the operation of any relevant statutory implied terms,[2] courts only ever imply terms that are not inconsistent with the existing express terms of the contract in question.[3] Any implied term must also operate to give effect to the contract's express terms.[4] Express terms can be oral or written, or a combination of both. Unless required by statute, express terms need not be recorded in a formal written document. They can be found in any communication relating to the making of the contract, such as email correspondence, text messages, letters, or telephone conversations.

When considering statutory requirements for the provision of express terms, it must be noted that in English law, Part I of the *Employment Rights Act 1996* (UK) requires that an employer must supply a worker (which can include an employee) with a 'written statement of [the] particulars of employment' not later than the beginning of the employment. The rationale behind this provision is to ensure that 'essential contractual information [is made] available to ... [workers] without impinging on the autonomy of the parties to conclude their own contractual bargain'. Such a written statement may be in the form of an employment contract, other worker contract, or letter of engagement. It must be provided for in a single document and must include certain particulars.[5] There is no equivalent statutory provision concerning employment contracts in Australia,[6] save for a statutory

---

[2] See the later discussion in this chapter concerning statutory implied terms.
[3] See, eg, *Irish Bank Resolution Corporation Ltd (in Special Liquidation) v Camden Market Holdings Corp* [2017] EWCA Civ 7 (Court of Appeal (CA)); *Byrne v Australian Airlines Ltd* (1995) 185 CLR 410 (High Court of Australia (HCA)), 449. For further discussion on the interrelationship between express and implied terms in English law, see further, F Wilmot-Smith, 'Express and Implied Terms' (2023) 43(1) OJLS 54.
[4] See, eg, *Vodafone Pacific Ltd v Mobile Innovations Ltd* [2004] NSWCA 15 (New South Wales Court of Appeal (NSWCA)) [201]. Hugh Collins also prefers an approach that characterises implied terms as providing a toolkit for the construction of express terms: see, eg, H Collins, 'Legal Responses to the Standard Form Contract of Employment' (2007) 36 ILJ 2, 7–10. However, more recently his views appear to have changed somewhat: see, eg, H Collins, 'Implied Terms in the Contract of Employment' in M Freedland and others (eds), *The Contract of Employment* (OUP 2016) 471, 489–90. Cf Mark Freedland, who describes implied terms as a regulatory function in restraining the powers conferred on a contracting party by express terms: see, eg, M Freedland, *The Personal Employment Contract* (OUP 2003) 127.
[5] See those particulars outlined under the *Employment Rights Act 1996* (UK) ss 1(3)–(4) and 3.
[6] Cf other contractual contexts in Australia, including the: *National Consumer Credit Protection Act 2009* (Cth) Sch 1, s 55, which requires that contracts supplying credit or consumer mortgages must be in writing; *Building Work Contractors Act 1995* (SA) s 28, which requires that contracts for the performance of domestic building work to the value of $12,000 or more must be in writing; *Second-hand Vehicle Dealers Act 1995* (SA) s 17, which requires that contracts for the sale of second-hand motor vehicles by dealers must be in writing; *Law of Property Act 1936* (SA) s 26, which provides that contracts for the sale of land, or any interest concerning land, must be in writing; *Competition and Consumer Act 2010* (Cth) Sch 2, ss 78 and 79, which provide that unsolicited consumer agreements (eg door-to-door and telephone sales) must be in writing.

requirement that all new employees must be provided a Fair Work Information Statement. This is a document produced by Australia's Fair Work Ombudsman, in which basic employment rights are outlined, along with the role of Australia's Fair Work Commission and Fair Work Ombudsman. There is a separate requirement that casual employees must also be provided with a Casual Employment Information Statement, which is another document issued by the Fair Work Ombudsman explaining the rights of casual employees. Strictly speaking, these documents amount to a requirement for the provision of information only; they do not amount to a requirement to provide written terms of engagement. Contrary to the English position, Australian employment contracts need not be committed to writing.

Express written terms might be specifically negotiated between the parties, or set out in a standard form document prepared by one party and presented to the other, often on a take-it-or-leave-it basis. In relation to employment contracts, Hugh Collins notes that because we are now in an 'era of extensive written contracts of employment',[7] this is generally how employers will present their contracts to employees. He suggests that '[t]he terms of the [employment] contract will normally have been drafted by the employer or its lawyers',[8] leaving little room for negotiation between the parties.

That said, this standardised format is not necessarily the case for all employment contracts or contracts for the performance of work, or indeed any other type of contract. It is still possible that oral terms might be verbally agreed between the parties, either in combination with written contractual terms, or as an entirely verbal agreement. The following discussion briefly considers, first, how express terms can be incorporated into a contract, depending on whether they are oral or in writing, and secondly, how express written terms are interpreted when they become part of a contract.

Provided there are no issues with the parol evidence rule,[9] a party who wants to incorporate an oral statement made during negotiations will need to establish that the statement has contractual force as a 'warranty', rather than being a 'mere representation'.[10] For an oral statement to constitute a warranty, the statement must have

---

[7] H Collins, 'Implied Terms in the Contract of Employment' in M Freedland and others (eds), *The Contract of Employment* (OUP 2016) 471, 490.

[8] ibid.

[9] The parol evidence rule limits the extrinsic evidence that may be used to vary or add to the terms of a written contract. See, eg, the explanation of the rule in *Goss v Lord Nugent* (1833) 110 ER 713 (Court of King's Bench (KB)), 716; *Codelfa Construction Pty Ltd v State Rail Authority of New South Wales* (1982) 149 CLR 337 (HCA), 347.

[10] As to the difficulties that may be encountered in establishing the terms of a purely oral contract, see, eg, *Connelly v Wells* (1994) 55 IR 73 (HCA), where the plaintiff could not prove that she had received and accepted an oral offer of employment. Nowadays, it is much more common for employees to be issued with a written employment contract, which their employer invites them to sign: see, eg, W Brown and others, *The Individualisation of Employment Contracts in Britain* (DTI, Employment Relations Research Series, URN 98/934, 1998) [6.2.7].

been intended by the parties to have contractual force. If the oral statement's contractual force is the subject of a legal challenge, the court will need to objectively assess whether a person in the parties' position would reasonably have considered the statement to be contractually binding.[11] The more significant an oral statement, the more likely it will be regarded as a warranty.[12] A statement is also more likely to carry contractual force if it uses words suggesting a promise.[13] A party's knowledge or expertise can be used to assess whether a statement amounts to a promise or mere representation; in that sense, a statement made by a party with expertise to an inexperienced a person is much more likely to be promissory than one made by an inexperienced party.[14]

Distinct from express oral statements, written terms may be incorporated into a contract in one of three main ways. The first is by signature. According to the rule in *L'Estrange v Graucob*,[15] a party is taken to be bound by any document that they sign, even if they have not read or understood it, so long as they have not been misled as to its content or effect. Secondly, reasonable notice through display or delivery of terms might also mean that the terms become contractually binding, provided that the notice is given before the contract is entered into.[16] Thirdly, where parties have contracted via a series of agreements, terms might be incorporated by way of reasonable notice through a prior course of dealing,[17] and it will not matter if the notice of the terms is given after each individual contract is formed.[18] In all of these situations, the document containing the terms must be intended to have contractual force.[19]

---

[11] See, eg, *Oscar Chess Ltd v Williams* [1957] 1 WLR 370 (CA), 375; *Hospital Products Ltd v United States Surgical Corp* (1984) 156 CLR 41 (HCA), 61.

[12] See, eg, *Couchman v Hill* [1947] KB 554 (CA); *Van den Esschert v Chappell* [1960] WAR 114 (Supreme Court of Western Australia (WASC)), 116.

[13] eg, 'promise', 'agree', 'guarantee', and 'warrant'.

[14] See, eg, *Oscar Chess v Williams* (n 11) 376, 378; *Dick Bentley Productions v Harold Smith (Motors) Ltd* [1965] 2 All ER 65 (CA); *Ellul v Oakes* (1972) 3 SASR 377 (Supreme Court of South Australia (SASC)), 381–82; *Smythe v Thomas* (2007) 71 NSWLR 537 (Supreme Court of New South Wales (NSWSC)), 552.

[15] [1934] 2 KB 394 (KB), 404, affirmed by the High Court of Australia in *Toll (FGCT) Pty Ltd v Alphapharm Pty Ltd* (2004) 219 CLR 165 (HCA) [42]–[48].

[16] See, eg, *Daly v General Steam Navigation Co Ltd (The 'Dragon')* (1979) 1 Lloyd's Rep 257 (Court of Queen's Bench (QB)), 262; *Oceanic Sunline Special Shipping Co Inc v Fay* (1988) 165 CLR 197 (HCA), 206–07, 228–29, 256, 261. If the term is particularly onerous or unusual, then special notice is required: see, eg, *Interfoto Picture Library v Stiletto Visual Programs Ltd* [1989] 2 QB 433 (CA), 445.

[17] See, eg, *Henry Kendall & Sons v William Lillico & Sons Ltd* [1969] 2 AC 31 (House of Lords (HL)); *J Spurling Ltd v Bradshaw* [1956] 1 Lloyd's Rep 392 (CA); *Republic of Nauru v Reid* (unreported, Victorian Court of Appeal, 23 October 1995) (Victorian Court of Appeal (VCA)); *Reynolds v Southcorp Wines Pty Ltd* (2002) 122 FCR 301 (Federal Court of Australia (FCA)) [56]–[62]; *Neale v Atlas Products (Vic) Pty Ltd* (1955) 94 CLR 419 (HCA), 427–28. See generally, J Swanton, 'Incorporation of Contractual Terms by a Course of Dealing' (1988) 1 JCL 223.

[18] See, eg, *Circle Freight International Ltd v Medeast Gulf Exports Ltd* [1988] 2 Lloyd's Rep 427 (CA); *La Rosa v Nudrill Pty Ltd* [2013] WASCA 18 (WASC) [81]–[90].

[19] See, eg, *D J Hill & Co Pty Ltd v Walter H Wright Pty Ltd* [1971] VR 749 (Supreme Court of Victoria (VSC)); *Rinaldi & Patroni Pty Ltd v Precision Mouldings Pty Ltd* [1986] WAR 131 (WASC). Whether or not the document is contractual will be easier to ascertain in some situations than others.

Should a dispute arise as to the meaning of an express term, it may be necessary for the court to interpret it. This process involves the court objectively determining what a reasonable person would have intended the words to mean, rather than subjectively asking what the parties intended their words to mean.[20] If an agreement is only in writing, the court's focus will be on the words used by the parties to describe their obligations.[21]

The bigger issue associated with the interpretation of written terms occurs when there is extrinsic evidence. In English law, the court must consider the contract's full background, but cannot take into account prior negotiations[22] or the parties' 'declarations of subjective intent'.[23] Therefore, the court is not permitted to take into account extrinsic evidence (including oral negotiations or exchanges of letters) that might have preceded the contract.[24] However, the Court of Appeal has held that when interpreting an unusual combination of words that are not defined in the agreement and have no obvious natural and ordinary meaning, it is permissible for a court to 'explore the factual hinterland of the agreement' so as to determine how the parties understood the words.[25] In doing so, the court is not considering the parties' 'declarations of subjective intent'; rather, the court is ascertaining the meaning shared by the parties and what was, in fact, incorporated into their contract.[26]

With regards to the way in which extrinsic evidence can be used to interpret contracts in Australia, Andrew Stewart and others provide a useful summary of the complex state of the law.[27] They suggest that where an obvious ambiguity arises, the court may look to what the parties have said or done before entering into their contract.[28] Courts may also consider the general context or circumstances in which the contract is made in order to determine its meaning.[29] Notwithstanding a series of conflicting High Court authorities, Stewart and others suggest that 'the better view would seem to be that such contextual evidence is always admissible (in the sense of being available for a court to consider) even if the written terms are not

---

[20] See, eg, *Chartbrook Ltd v Persimmon Homes Ltd* [2009] 1 AC 1101 (HL) [14]; *Toll v Alphapharm* (n 15) [40]; *Yousif v Commonwealth Bank of Australia* (2010) 193 IR 212 (Full Court of the Federal Court of Australia (FCAFC)) [93]–[95].

[21] See, eg, A Stewart and others, *Creighton and Stewart's Labour Law* (6th edn, Federation Press 2016) 279.

[22] This rule has been subjected to ongoing criticism. However, it was firmly upheld in *Chartbrook v Persimmon Homes* (n 20) and *Arnold v Britton* [2016] 1 All ER 1 (United Kingdom Supreme Court (UKSC)).

[23] *Investors Compensation Scheme Ltd v West Bromwich Building Society* [1998] 1 All ER 98 (HL). A court is only permitted to consider subsequent conduct, where a contract is partly oral and partly in writing, to determine the parties' original intentions: see, eg, *Brian Maggs (t/a BM Builders) v Guy Marsh* (2006) 150 SJLB 918 (CA).

[24] Noting that extrinsic evidence may be admissible for purposes of rectification.

[25] *Rugby Group Ltd v ProForce Recruit Ltd* [2006] EWCA Civ 69 (CA).

[26] ibid [55].

[27] See generally, Stewart and others (n 21) 279.

[28] See, eg, *Grainger v Roombridge Pty Ltd* [2007] QCA 276 (Queensland Court of Appeal (QCA)).

[29] See, eg, *AMEC Engineering Pty Ltd v Shanks* (2001) 128 IR 116 (SASC).

ambiguous on their face'.³⁰ However, it cannot be used to 'contradict the language of the contract when it has a plain meaning'.³¹ It is also not permissible to take account of what parties have said or done after making their contract, at least when interpreting agreed terms.³² However, the courts' use of such information may be allowable where the parties' subsequent conduct helps establish the subject matter of an agreement (eg the scope of an employee's duties).³³

Implied Terms

In any contractual agreement, it is not always possible for parties to foresee every matter that ought to be expressly agreed upon in the contract between them, even when their agreement is governed by a detailed written agreement. Parties may also fail to, or may find themselves unable to, agree on select terms. Certain terms might also be seen as essential to the functionality of a specific type of contract. In each of these instances, there is a gap in the contractual agreement. Implied terms may operate to fill those gaps. The notion of implied terms as 'gap fillers' has already been touched on in this work's Introduction. As also mentioned in the Introduction, employment contracts and contracts for the performance of work, in the same way as any other kind of contract, are susceptible to the implication of terms. They too can generate gaps that require filling.

There are three main categories of terms that can be implied into any type of contract³⁴ each of which has its own rules that are discussed in this part of the chapter: terms implied in fact; terms implied by custom and usage; and terms implied by law. As emphasised in the Introduction, terms implied by law are the primary focus of this work. While these terms can come into operation through the common law or statute, this work is mainly concerned with terms implied at common law into the class of employment contracts, as well as those with the potential to operate in respect of contracts for the performance of work more broadly.

---

³⁰ See, eg, *Mainteck Services Pty Ltd v Stein Heurtey SA* (2014) 89 NSWLR 633 (NSWCA) [69]-[88]; *Stratton Finance Pty Ltd v Webb* (2014) 245 IR 223 (FCAFC) [36]-[40]; *Mount Bruce Mining Pty Ltd v Wright Prospecting Pty Ltd* (2015) 256 CLR 104 (HCA) [47]-[52] and [108]-[113]. See generally, T J Acreman, 'The Long Road to a Wide Ambiguity Gateway' (2016) 42 Aust Bar Rev 12.
³¹ See, eg, *Codelfa Construction v State Rail Authority of New South Wales* (n 9).
³² See, eg, *Stratton Finance v Webb* (n 30).
³³ See, eg, *Fishlock v The Campaign Palace Pty Ltd* (2013) 234 IR 1 (NSWSC).
³⁴ Cf the suggestion that there are two additional categories of implication by way of a 'course of dealing' and 'construction' in J Carter and others, 'Terms Implied in Law: "Trust and Confidence" in the High Court of Australia' (2015) 32 JCL 203, 207. While the potential for these additional categories is noted, this work concentrates on the widely accepted categories of implication as set out in this chapter.

A. Terms Implied in Fact

Terms implied in fact are implied into the particular contract in question, based on the parties' presumed intention.[35] They are tailored and unique to the specific contract. In English law, there is a single legal test for any implication of a term in fact. In Australia, however, the applicable test for implying a term in fact differs depending on whether the contract is in writing or not.

In England, a term can be implied in fact into any contract so long as it is necessary to give business efficacy to a transaction, which is taken to have been intended by both parties to it.[36] This notion of 'business efficacy' must be understood in concert with the concept of the 'officious bystander'.[37] It must be asked whether the term set to be implied is so obvious that it goes without saying, that is, if an officious bystander had otherwise suggested it to the contracting parties, they would have both accepted it without question. Should a term be implied in accordance with these related 'business efficacy' and 'officious bystander' concepts, then it amounts to a term implied in fact, and implied only into the contract before the court, not more broadly. Such terms are routinely justified on the basis that they are required to make the specific contract between the relevant parties 'work'.[38]

In Australia, where a term is sought to be implied in fact into a contract in writing, the five cumulative tests in *BP Refinery v Shire of Hastings*[39] need to be satisfied. Therefore, for a term to be implied in fact into a written contract:[40]

> (1) it must be reasonable and equitable; (2) it must be necessary to give business efficacy so the contract is effective without it; (3) it must be so obvious that 'it goes without saying'; (4) it must be capable of clear expression; (5) it must not contradict any express term of the contract.

The combination of these individual tests sets a high threshold for the implication of a term in fact: all five must be satisfied for the implication to occur. As Stewart and others note, '[i]f applied rigorously, this is a very difficult set of conditions to fulfil'.[41] Jeff Goldsworthy has argued that this strict application of the tests is

---

[35] As to the parties' presumed intention, in England, see, eg, *The Moorcock* (1889) 14 PD 64 (CA); *Marks & Spencer plc v BNP Paribas Securities Services Trust Company (Jersey) Ltd* [2016] AC 742 (UKSC). In Australia, see, eg, *BP Refinery (Westernport) Pty Ltd v Shire of Hastings* (1977) 180 CLR 266 (HCA), 283; *Codelfa Construction v State Rail Authority of New South Wales* (n 9) 352–53; *Byrne v Australian Airlines* (n 3) 422, 441.
[36] See generally, *The Moorcock* (n 35).
[37] See, eg, *Shirlaw v Southern Foundries (1926) Ltd* [1940] AC 701 (HL).
[38] See, eg, *Equitable Life Assurance Society v Hyman* [2002] 1 AC 408 (HL); *Marks & Spencer v BNP Paribas* (n 35).
[39] *BP Refinery v Shire of Hastings* (n 35).
[40] ibid, 283, cited with approval in *Byrne v Australian Airlines* (n 3) 477. For a detailed assessment of how these tests are judicially applied, see further S Frauenfelder, 'Implied Terms—Are the *BP Refinery* Criteria Broken?: A Theoretical and Empirical Analysis' (2022) 38(2/3) JCL 103.
[41] Stewart and others (n 21) 280.

necessary because of the very rationalisation that terms implied in fact are based on the explicit intentions of the parties.[42] However, the strict application of the tests has also been criticised.[43] In particular, it has been argued that because 'terms implied in fact are premised on giving effect to the presumed intentions of the parties, the focus of inquiry in implying a term should be those intentions or expectations, not compliance with a set of formal criteria'.[44]

In addition, it has also been suggested that when seeking to imply a term in fact there are just two tests, either of which may be satisfied to justify the implication: one of 'business efficacy' and the other that the term to be implied must be 'so obvious that it goes without saying'.[45] In particular, some English decisions support this twofold classification.[46] Australian law, however, continues to rely on the application of the five cumulative tests from *BP Refinery v Shire of Hastings*.[47] However, there is one major exception, which is unique to the Australian context.

This exception is that if a term is sought to be implied in fact where there is no formal written agreement, the single, and seemingly more flexible,[48] test espoused by Deane J in *Hawkins v Clayton*[49] must be satisfied:[50]

> In a case where it is apparent that the parties have not attempted to spell out the full terms of their contract, the court should imply a term by reference to the imputed intention of the parties if, but only if, it can be seen that the implication of the particular term is necessary for the reasonable or effective operation of a contract of that nature in the circumstances of the case.

This statement specifically identifies 'reasonableness' or 'efficacy' each as a sufficient ground for implying a term in fact. Accordingly, it seems surprising that reasonableness alone is not a sufficient basis for implying a term in fact. Perhaps then,

---

[42] See, eg, J Goldsworthy, 'Implications in Language, Law and the Constitution' in G Lindell (ed), *Future Directions in Constitutional Law* (Federation Press 1994) 158, 169–70.

[43] For a criticism of the rationale for implying a term in fact in English law, see, eg, G Yihan, 'New Distinctions within Terms Implied in Fact' (2016) 33 JCL 183.

[44] See, eg, J Paterson, 'Terms Implied in Fact: The Basis for Implication' (1998) 13 JCL 103; E Peden, *Good Faith in the Performance of Contracts* (LexisNexis Butterworths 2003) Ch 4.

[45] See, eg, J Carter and W Courtney, 'Implied Terms in Contracts: Australian Law' (2015) 43 ABLR 246, 249–50.

[46] See, eg, *Mosvolds Rederi A/S v Food Corp of India (The Damodar General T J Park)* [1986] 2 Lloyd's Rep 68 (Commercial Court (Comm)), 70–71; *Cox v Bankside Members Agency Ltd* [1995] 2 Lloyd's Rep 437 (CA), 457. Cf *Watts v Lord Aldington* [1999] L&TR 578 (HL), 596–97. See also the related discussion concerning terms implied in fact in H Collins, 'Implied Terms: The Foundation in Good Faith and Fair Dealing' (2014) Curr Leg Probl 1, 19–23.

[47] See, eg, Carter and Courtney (n 45) 250.

[48] As Stewart and others note, in practice it is debatable whether this test is any easier to satisfy than the five *BP Refinery v Shire of Hastings* (n 35) tests: Stewart and others (n 21) 281, citing *Griggs v Noris Group of Companies* (2006) 94 SASR 126 (SASC) as an illustration of this point.

[49] (1988) 164 CLR 539 (HCA). For a detailed discussion on this decision, see generally, J P Swanton, 'Implied Contractual Terms: Further Implications of *Hawkins v Clayton*' (1992) 5 JCL 127.

[50] *Hawkins v Clayton* (n 49) 573, cited with approval in *Byrne v Australian Airlines* (n 3) 422, 442.

the 'better view', as expressed by Greg Tolhurst and John Carter, is that '"efficacy" is the overriding concern, and a term will not be implied into a contract effective without it even if it would lead to a more reasonable operation'.[51] Even so, in *Byrne v Australian Airlines*,[52] a case that is returned to throughout this work (particularly in Chapter 6), McHugh and Gummow JJ suggested 'that obviousness also remains an important element in implying a term [in fact] in an informal contract'.[53] The application of this test is discussed in Chapter 4 in respect of potential arguments that could have been raised by the parties in *Commonwealth Bank of Australia v Barker*.[54] As has already been noted in this chapter, most employment contracts are not fully expressed in writing,[55] so this test for implication in fact carries some significance in respect of those agreements.

That said, however, the High Court of Australia has gone on to cast some doubt over the extent to which the *Hawkins v Clayton* test will continue to be followed in instances where a term is sought to be implied in fact into an informal contract that is not wholly in writing, which could include an employment contract. Among other things, the court raised the potential for terms to be 'inferred' rather than implied in the context of such informal contracts, but neglected to settle on a clear or unified position. In *Realestate.com.au Pty Ltd v Hardingham*,[56] the court appeared to deliberately avoid distinguishing fully between the notion of implying a term in fact or inferring it in respect of an informal contract. Chief Justice Kiefel and Gageler J considered that a term could be inferred in such a context, but a fine line exists between inference and implication.[57] Justice Gordon considered that a definitional dispute between what constitutes implication versus inference would be 'wholly unproductive'.[58] Justices Edelman and Steward denied the existence of inferred terms at all, though that was not to say that inference did not have a part to play in discerning between what constitutes an express or implied term.[59] For ongoing clarity and consistency, this work continues based on the understanding that there remains a distinct test for implication in fact, derived from *Hawkins v Clayton*, where there is no formal written contract, simply noting the potential distinction between implying and inferring a term in this discrete context, which is limited to Australia only.

---

[51] See, eg, G Tolhurst and J Carter, 'The New Law on Implied Terms' (1996) 11 JCL 76, 86.
[52] *Byrne v Australian Airlines* (n 3).
[53] ibid 442, 444.
[54] (2014) 253 CLR 169 (HCA).
[55] See, eg, Stewart and others (n 21) 281.
[56] (2022) 170 IPR 1 (HCA).
[57] ibid [21]–[32].
[58] ibid [71]–[77].
[59] ibid [102]–[126].

B. Terms Implied by Custom and Usage

For terms implied by custom and usage, their implication is based on a custom or usage in a particular industry. Such terms are implied in situations where their generic usage is 'well known or acquiesced in', and 'everyone making a contract in that situation can reasonably be presumed to have imported that term into the contract'.[60] In England a party seeking to rely on a term being implied on the basis of an industry-based custom and usage is required to show that the proposed term is reasonable, notorious, and certain.[61] In considering what is reasonable, it 'must be approached in the round'.[62] As to what is notorious, it has been said that 'notoriety is no more than widespread knowledge and understanding [of the custom]; certainty relates to the nature of the arrangement'.[63] In determining what is certain, that relates to 'the nature of the arrangement'.[64] In Australia, four guiding principles for ascertaining whether a term ought to be implied by custom and usage have been outlined by the High Court in *Con-Stan Industries of Australia Pty Ltd v Norwich Winterthur Insurance (Australia) Ltd*[65] as follows:

1. 'The existence of a custom or usage that will justify the implication of a term into a contract is a question of fact'.[66]
2. While it need not be universally accepted, 'there must be evidence that the custom relied on is so well known and acquiesced in that everyone making a contract in that situation can reasonably be presumed to have imported that term into the contract'.[67] Just as in England, it must be 'notorious, reasonable, and certain'.[68]

---

[60] In England, see, eg, *Devonald v Rosser & Sons* [1906] 2 KB 728 (CA) [743]–[744]. In Australia, see, eg, *Con-Stan Industries of Australia Pty Ltd v Norwich Winterthur Insurance (Australia) Ltd* (1986) 160 CLR 226 (HCA), 236, which was endorsed in *Byrne v Australian Airlines* (n 3) 423–24, 440 and *Breen v Williams* (1996) 186 CLR 71 (HCA), 123.

[61] See, eg, *Devonald v Rosser* (n 60) [743]–[744].

[62] ibid.

[63] ibid.

[64] ibid.

[65] (1986) 160 CLR 226 (HCA).

[66] ibid 236. A custom must be strictly proved: see, eg, *Majeau Carrying Co Pty Ltd v Coastal Rutile Ltd* (1973) 129 CLR 48 (HCA), 52, 60–61; *Nelson v Dahl* (1879) 12 Ch D 568 (CA), 575; *Rickless v United Artists Corporation* [1988] QB 40 (CA). There is an argument that a custom may become so well known that the courts could simply take judicial notice of it, rather than require formal proof through evidence: see, eg, *Moult v Halliday* [1897] 1 QB 125 (QB), 130; *George v Davies* [1911] 2 KB 445 (HL). When a custom reaches this level of acceptance, it may even be best described as a term implied by law: see, eg, M Irving, *The Contract of Employment* (2nd edn, LexisNexis Butterworths 2019) 425.

[67] (1986) 160 CLR 226, 236, endorsed by the High Court in *Byrne v Australian Airlines* (n 3) 423, 440 and *Breen v Williams* (n 60) 123. The trade or profession in which the custom is applied may be defined broadly or narrowly: see, eg, *Majeau Carrying Co Pty Ltd v Coastal Rutile Ltd* (1973) 129 CLR 48 (HCA) (warehousemen); *Abernathy v Mott, Hay and Anderson* [1974] ICR 323 (CA) (civil engineers); *Evans Deakin v Allen* [1946] St R Qd 187 (Supreme Court of Queensland (QSC)) (apprentices in the metal industry); *Sagar v Ridehlagh & Sons Ltd* [1931] 1 Ch 310 (CA) (weavers in Lancashire); *Danowski v Henry Moore Foundation* (1996) 140 SJLB 101 (CA) (proof that the custom applies in one part of the trade will not support an inference that it applies to all employees across the whole trade).

[68] *Con-Stan Industries v Norwich Winterthur* (n 60) 236. See also *AssetInsure Pty Ltd v New Cap Reinsurance Corp Ltd (In Liq)* (2006) 225 CLR 331 (HCA), 353 [60]. As to 'notoriety' see, eg, *Bond*

3. 'A term is not implied on the basis of custom and usage if it is contrary to the express[69] [and perhaps implied][70] terms of the contract' and applicable statutes.[71]
4. 'A person may be bound by a custom notwithstanding the fact that he [or she] had no knowledge of it'.[72]

Jeannie Paterson and others suggest that Australian courts have tended to strictly apply these requirements, which means that there are not many examples of terms implied by custom and usage.[73]

In the context of employment, the implied terms based on custom and usage has become a rarity in both England and Australia.[74] 'A century ago, however, 'such terms were a significant source of employment obligations, but are now in practice almost a dead letter'.[75] In England, reluctance to imply a term by reason of custom and usage into an employment contract was evidenced by *Solectron Scotland Ltd v Roper*,[76] where it was held that the employer had failed to establish a custom and practice that circumvented a predecessor employer's contractual enhanced

---

v CAV Ltd [1983] IRLR 360 (Employment Appeals Tribunal (EAT)); *Summers v The Commonwealth* (1918) 25 CLR 144 (HCA), 148; *Ryan v Textile Clothing and Footwear Union of Australia* (1996) 130 FLR 313 (FCA), 340. As to 'reasonableness', see, eg, *Nelson v Dahl* (1879) 12 Ch D 568 (CA), 575; *Evans Deakin v Allen* (n 67) 19; *Moult v Halliday* (n 66) 128, 130; *GKN (Cwmbran) Ltd v Lloyd* [1972] ICR 214 (National Industrial Relations Court (NIRC)), 219–20; *Thornley v Tilley* (1925) 36 CLR 1 (HCA), 8. As to 'certainty', see, eg, *Devonald v Rosser* (n 60), 741; *Thornley v Tilley* (n 68), 8, both approved by the High Court of Australia in *Con-Stan Industries v Norwich Winterthur* (n 60) 236.

[69] *Con-Stan Industries v Norwich Winterthur* (n 60) 236–37. See also *Summers v The Commonwealth* (n 68) 148 (later affirmed on appeal in (1919) 26 CLR 180 (HCA)); *Uszok v Henley Properties (NSW) Pty Ltd* [2007] NSWCA 31 (NSWCA) [23]; *Sutcliffe v Hawker Siddley Aviation Ltd* [1973] ICR 560 (NIRC), 567 (express power to transfer and employee was inconsistent with the alleged custom that the transferred employee was made redundant); *Solectron Scotland Ltd v Roper* [2004] IRLR 4 (EAT) (irregular practice of the employer in renegotiating redundancy agreements did not establish a custom that the expressly agreed redundancy policy was not enforceable); *French v Barclays Bank plc* [1998] IRLR 646 (CA) (express term reserving the employer a discretion as to whether a benefit was to be conferred excluded an alleged custom about the terms on which the benefit was to be conferred).

[70] See, eg, *Danowski v Henry Moore Foundation* (n 67); *London Export Corporation Ltd v Jubilee Coffee Roasting Co Ltd* [1958] 1 WLR 661 (HL), 675.

[71] See, eg, *Evans Deakin v Allen* [1946] St R Qd 187 (QSC), 201; *Rosenhain v Commonwealth Bank of Australia* (1922) 31 CLR 46 (HCA), 53.

[72] *Con-Stan Industries v Norwich Winterthur* (n 60) 236–37. These four principles were also summarised in *Goodman Fielder Consumer Foods Ltd v Cospak International Pty Ltd* [2004] NSWSC 704 (NSWSC) [64].

[73] J Paterson, A Robertson, and A Duke, *Principles of Contract Law* (5th edn, Lawbook Co 2016) 348, citing *Goodman Fielder Consumer Foods v Cospak International* (n 72).

[74] *Sagar v Ridehlagh & Sons Ltd* (n 67) is one of few English examples where a term that was implied by reason of custom and usage, having satisfied the reasonable, notorious, and certain test, included the practice of making deductions from employees' wages for careless work in the weaving industry in Lancashire.

[75] Stewart and others (n 21) 281.

[76] *Solectron Scotland v Roper* (n 69).

redundancy payment scheme. The reason for this failure was that the practice relied upon was neither certain, reasonable, nor notorious; put another way, different terms were set for each redundancy exercise depending on the employer's will, and there was no consistent application of any of the terms. Likewise, in Australia it was held in *Ryan v Textile Clothing and Footwear Union of Australia*[77] that past conduct which was exceptional, infrequent or otherwise equivocal, or had not occurred at the time the contract of employment was made, was unlikely to establish a relevant custom or usage.[78] Courts in both jurisdictions have also tended to refuse to imply a term based on custom or usage into the employment contract of an employee entering a particular custom or trade for the first time.[79]

C. Terms Implied by Law

As mentioned at the start of this part of the chapter, in both England and Australia, terms can be implied by law, either through the common law, or by operation of statute. Both possibilities are considered here in turn and in respect of both jurisdictions. At common law, terms may be implied by law as necessary incidents of a particular class or set category of contract. When performing the task of implying a term by law, the court is not directly giving effect to the parties' intentions.[80] The focus is on the particular class or category of contract into which the term is to be implied, rather than the individual contract within that class (as it would be for a term implied in fact).[81]

In terms of the legal test for implying a term by law through the common law, first, the term must be applicable to a recognised 'class' of contract.[82] Relevantly, courts query whether the contract in question belongs to a class '[w]hose inherent nature require[s], as a matter of law, inclusion of an obligation in the terms' advanced.[83] Employment contracts as an apparent 'class' into which terms are implied by law are considered further in Chapter 5. Secondly, the term must be 'necessary'. The concept of necessity is explored in detail in Chapter 6.[84]

---

[77] (1996) 66 IR 258 (VCA), 340.

[78] ibid. See also *Tibaldi Smallgoods (Australasia) Pty Ltd v Rinaldi* (2008) 172 IR 86 (VSC) [52].

[79] See, eg, *Evans Deakin v Allen* [1946] St R Qd 187 (QSC), 199, where a custom did not bind an apprentice entering the industry; *Turner v Australasian Coal and Shale Employee Federation* (1984) 6 FCR 177 (FCAFC), 182–83, where a custom did not bind a trainee entering the industry; *Mackie v Wienholt* (1880) 5 QSCR 211 (QSC), 212–3, where a custom did not bind a cook engaged in London to perform work in Goomburra, Queensland.

[80] See, eg, Collins (n 46) 3. Cf Carter and others (n 34) 210.

[81] See, eg, D Cabrelli, *Employment Law in Context: Text and Materials* (4th edn, OUP 2020) 166; *Byrne v Australian Airlines* (n 3) 448–53; *Breen v Williams* (n 60) 103.

[82] See, eg, *Scally v Southern Health and Social Services Board* [1992] 1 AC 294 (HL), 307.

[83] *Byrne v Australian Airlines* (n 3) 440. See also *Liverpool City Council v Irwin* [1977] AC 239 (HL), 254.

[84] As Chapter 6 will make clear, in England the necessity test for implying a term by law is routinely based on wider considerations of policy. However, in Australia, there are competing narrow and wide approaches to that test.

Terms implied by law at common law are significant in that are implied into *all* contracts within the identified class where they are deemed necessary, unless they have been expressly excluded from a contract,[85] are inconsistent with its express terms,[86] or the exclusion is otherwise indicated by the circumstances surrounding the making of the contract.[87] As discussed in Chapters 5 and 6, however, there are some existing terms implied by law into the class of employment contracts that appear to function as 'defining' features of employment (as distinct from contracts for the performance of work) and should arguably be deemed absolutely necessary and incapable of exclusion. Again, the judicial technique of implying a term by law is a powerful one, warranting the dedicated attention it receives in Chapter 2.

Distinct from terms implied by law through the common law, terms implied by law through the operation of statute can come into effect through parliament's passing of relevant legislation. In that sense, parliament intervenes to introduce terms directly into contracts by the operation of legislation. The effect of such intervention is that, by virtue of being statutorily imposed terms, such terms are contractual in nature and give rise to damages for breach of contract if breached (as opposed to a breach of the relevant statute). There are also limits on the ability to contract out of these imposed terms. The most obvious examples exist in respect of contracts for the sale of goods, whereby Sales of Goods Acts across both jurisdictions operate to imply terms by law directly into those contracts.[88] In relation to employment contracts, however, there are relatively few statutorily implied terms.[89] Statutory rules and statutory-based regulations that regulate employment are far more common. These rules and regulations impose obligations outside of, and in addition to, the contractual relationship. They typically establish minimum entitlements in employment. They operate alongside employment contracts as a form of legislative regulation of the employment arrangement. Unlike statutorily implied terms, a breach of a statutory rule or regulation typically gives rise to a

---

[85] See, eg, *Johnson v Unisys Ltd* [2003] 1 AC 518 (HL) [18] and [24]; *Duncombe v Porter* (1953) 90 CLR 295 (HCA), 306, 311; *Castlemaine Tooheys Ltd v Carlton & United Breweries Ltd* (1987) 10 NSWLR 468 (NSWCA), 492D.

[86] See, eg, *Eastwood v Magnox Electric plc* [2005] 1 AC 503 (HL) [12] and [14]; *Castlemaine Tooheys v Carlton & United Breweries* (n 85) [2], [58], and [80].

[87] See, eg, *Shaw v New South Wales* [2012] NSWCA 102 (NSWCA) [45]–[46], citing *Helicopter Sales (Aust) Pty Ltd v Rotor-Work Pty Ltd* (1974) 132 CLR 1 (HCA), 17; *Castlemaine Tooheys v Carlton & United Breweries* (n 85) 492.

[88] In England, see, eg, *Sale of Goods Act 1979* (UK); *Supply of Goods and Services Act 1982* (UK); *Supply of Goods (Implied Terms) Act 1973* (UK). In Australia, see, eg, *Sale of Goods Act 1923* (NSW) ss 17–20; *Sale of Goods Act 1954* (ACT) ss 17–20; *Sale of Goods Act 1972* (NT) ss 17–20; *Sale of Goods Act 1896* (Qld) ss 15–18; *Sale of Goods Act 1895* (SA) ss 13–15; *Sale of Goods Act 1896* (Tas) ss 17–20; *Goods Act 1958* (Vic) ss 17–20; *Sale of Goods Act 1895* (WA) ss 12–15.

[89] In England, see, eg, *Equality Act 2010* (UK) s 66; *Working Time Regulations 1998* (UK) reg 4; *National Minimum Wage Act 1998* (UK) s 17; *Employment Rights Act 1996* (UK) ss 86–91. See further, ACL Davies, 'Terms Implied into the Contract of Employment by Legislation' in M Freedland and others (eds), *The Contract of Employment* (OUP 2016) 427. In Australia, see, eg, *Minimum Conditions of Employment Act 1993* (WA) s 5(1), considered in *Garbett v Midland Brick Co Pty Ltd* (2003) 129 IR 270 (Western Australia Court of Appeal (WASCA)).

breach of the relevant statute, not a breach of the employment contract itself. The notion of statutory rules operating to regulate employment contracts is returned to in this work's Conclusion.

The Fact/Law Distinction

Despite the clearly separate legal tests to be utilised, courts in both England and Australia have been known to confuse the implication of terms in fact and by law, often applying the wrong test for implication. In English law this confusion appears to have first originated in *Lister v Romford Ice & Cold Storage Co Ltd*,[90] where the court denied (or perhaps conveniently forgot) the possibility of a term implied by law as a standardised incident, insisting that all terms must conform to the presumed intentions of the parties, as terms implied in fact, and that in this case those tacit intentions probably did not coincide. This tendency for confusion has infected English and Australian contract law ever since.[91]

Such confusion resonates with what Collins coined 'metamorphosis' and 'instrumental misclassification'.[92] In relation to 'metamorphosis', in both jurisdictions, courts have, at times, suggested that a term implied in fact often enough may simply become a term implied by law into every contract of the relevant class. In relation to 'instrumental misclassification', courts have repeatedly confused the tests for implication of a term in fact and by law. However, if the distinction between factual and legal implication is continually muddled, it is questionable whether it truly matters, and indeed, whether terms implied by law are even necessary incidents of that class of contract at all. In commenting on the challenges associated with distinguishing between legal and factual implication, John Carter and Wayne Courtney have explained that 'there has always been debate as to the content of the legal requirements'.[93] Carter has even gone so far as to say that '[w]hether each represents a separate category is regarded as doubtful',[94] and separately, that once implied, it can often be difficult to tell whether the court's decision is based on legal or factual implication'.[95]

---

[90] [1957] AC 555 (HL). Later in *Liverpool City Council v Irwin* (n 83), however, the court claimed that it was being invited to create a term implied by law for a broad class of contracts, for which it would be inappropriate to legislate. See further, Collins (n 46) 11–12.
[91] In Australian law, see, eg, *TCL Air Conditioner (Zhongshan) Co Ltd v Judges of the Federal Court of Australia* (2013) 251 CLR 533 (HCA), in which the appellant's argument was one seeking implication of a term into all arbitration agreements. The High Court minority of French CJ and Gageler J dealt correctly with the proposed implied term as one to be implied by law (at [16]). However, the majority of Hanye, Crennan, Kiefel, and Bell JJ rejected the implied term with reference to the five tests in *BP Refinery v Shire of Hastings* (n 35) (at [74]).
[92] Collins (n 7) 480.
[93] W Courtney and J Carter, 'Implied Terms: What is the Role of Construction?' (2014) 31 JCL 151, 151.
[94] J Carter, *The Construction of Commercial Contracts* (Hart Publishing 2013) 89.
[95] J Carter, *Contract Law in Australia* (6th edn, LexisNexis Butterworths 2013) 235.

Nevertheless, what has been made clear from the earlier discussion in this chapter is that there remain two well-established distinctions between implication in fact and by law: one concerns itself with the presumed intention of the parties, and the other does not; one affects the particular contract in question, and the other affects all contracts in a broader class. Given that the distinction between the two forms of implication is clear, there should be no possibility for confusion. The idea that they tend to 'merge imperceptibly into each other'[96] on the same spectrum surely cannot be correct.

Many courts simply imply terms with some disregard or perhaps a lack of true understanding of the nuanced tests to be applied on the basis of generalised outcomes that they view as desirable. This uncertainty is problematic. Maintaining the distinction between the two types of implication is vital. The parties to any contract share an interest in being able to predict how courts will imply a term, whether it is in fact, or by law. The ability to predict such outcomes is important because the parties' insight into the court's approach may well influence the ways in which they form and later perform obligations under their contract. The alternative approach of basing terms on generalised outcomes without consistently applied tests for implication is shrouded in uncertainty. That is not to say that a mechanistic view towards the implication of terms is desirable. Rather, the court's approach to implying terms should be as certain as possible. If it is too uncertain, it will create a risk to the parties in contracting and participating in a contractual relationship at all. Therefore, this work continues on the assumption that, despite the potential for confusion between the two categories of implication, the distinction between them is critical and must continue to be recognised.

Implication and Construction

Construction is the process whereby courts determine the meaning and legal effect of contractual terms. The orthodox legal approach has been to treat construction and implication as separate applications of contract doctrine.[97] Nevertheless, there are some implied terms that have the potential to be implied into a very large number of contracts, if not all contracts. One obvious example is an implied term of cooperation,[98] the content of which is discussed in Chapter 3. On the one hand, such a term may be viewed as one implied by law into *all* classes of contract.[99] On

---

[96] *Breen v Williams* (n 60) 103.
[97] Courtney and Carter (n 93) 151.
[98] It has also been suggested that a duty of good faith could be construed as a rule of construction: see generally, Peden (n 44) Ch 6, and the further discussion on good faith in Chapter 4 of this work.
[99] See, eg, *Thompson v ASDA-MFI Group plc* [1988] Ch 241 (High Court of Justice (HC)), 266; *Cheall v Association of Professional Executive Clerical and Computer Staff* [1983] 2 AC 180 (HL), 188–89; *Commonwealth Bank v Barker* (n 54) [21]; *Byrne v Australian Airlines* (n 3) 449–50.

the other hand, it can be argued that, by definition, such a term does not form part of 'a coherent category, with dedicated implication criteria',[100] and instead arises as a matter of construction of the contract.[101] Indeed, while a universal term of this kind might state a default rule, that is not because its implication is referrable to a particular class of contract. As John Carter and others suggest, 'whether such implications actually exist as implied terms, rather than as common law duties or rules which are applied in construction, is open to debate'.[102]

This debate was touched on by the High Court of Australia in *Commonwealth Bank v Barker*, the facts of which are discussed in Chapter 4. For present purposes, the joint judgment of French CJ and Bell and Keane JJ referred to a 'duty to co-operate' as illustrating a category of 'universal implication'.[103] The court conceded that such a duty could 'arguably be characterised as a rule of construction',[104] and, more generally, that prior decisions of the High Court support the view that such 'universal implications' may also be 'characterised as rules of construction'.[105] At another point, the joint judgment agreed that this alternative characterisation of implied duty could well be correct.[106] Nevertheless, French CJ and Bell and Keane JJ concluded that the debate reflects 'taxonomical distinctions which do not necessarily yield practical differences'.[107] As such, the relationship between implication and construction in Australian contract law remains unclear.[108]

In England, the Privy Council challenged the distinction between implication and construction in *Attorney General of Belize v Belize Telecom Ltd*[109] 'if not generally, then at least in relation to terms implied in fact'.[110] Curiously, the joint judgment of the High Court in *Commonwealth Bank v Barker* cited *Attorney General of*

---

[100] Carter and others (n 34) 208.
[101] See, eg, *Southern Foundries v Shirlaw* (n 37) 717, 723; *Secured Income Real Estate (Aust) Ltd v St Martins Investments Pty Ltd* (1979) 144 CLR 596 (HCA), 607–08; *Park v Brothers* (2005) 222 ALR 421 (HCA), 432; *Fitzgerald v F J Leonhardt Pty Ltd* (1997) 189 CLR 215 (HCA).
[102] Carter and others (n 34) 208. See also P O'Grady, 'Nothing Implied: Construction as a Means of Curbing the Excessive Use of Power in Employment Contracts' (Paper presented at the Eight Biennial National Conference of the Australian Labour Law Association, 4 and 5 November 2016), where it is suggested that to constrain the power exercised by the employer over the employee, the implication of terms ought to be approached as a matter of construction.
[103] *Commonwealth Bank v Barker* (n 54) [29].
[104] ibid [37]. As discussed later in Chapter 4, this terminology is separate from classifying the duty as a principle of construction. It refers to the classification of the duty as one implied by law into all classes of contract.
[105] *Commonwealth Bank v Barker* (n 54) [25].
[106] ibid [29] ('whether or not such implications are characterised as rules of construction').
[107] *Commonwealth Bank v Barker* (n 54) [24].
[108] For further consideration of the distinction between implication and construction, see, eg, Courtney and Carter (n 93); Carter and others (n 34); J Riley, *Employee Protection at Common Law* (Federation Press 2005) Ch 3; Peden (n 44) Ch 2; E Peden, '"Cooperation" in English Contract Law—To Construe or Imply?' (2000) 16 JCL 56; and in the context of employee remuneration, M Moir, 'Discretion, Good Faith and Employer Control Over Executive Remuneration' (2011) 24 AJLL 121, 132–36. That said, 'both conceptions seem maintainable': M Hogg, *Promises and Contract Law: Comparative Perspectives* (CUP 2012) 272.
[109] [2009] 1 WLR 1988 (Privy Council (UKPC)).
[110] See, eg, Courtney and Carter (n 93) 151.

Belize v Belize Telecom,[111] but this reference was later labelled as 'quite perplexing', given that *Commonwealth Bank v Barker* contains 'no clear statement ... about the role of construction in implication'.[112] In *Attorney General of Belize v Belize Telecom*, Lord Hoffman held that 'the implication of the term [in question was] ... not an addition to the instrument. It only spells out what the instrument means'.[113] He went on to find that the 'proposition that the implication of a term is an exercise in ... construction' was a 'matter of logic (since a court has no power to alter what the instrument means)'.[114] In his view, it was 'also well supported by authority'.[115] For Lord Hoffman, this understanding meant that:

> [I]n every case in which it is said that some provision ought to be implied in an instrument, the question for the court is whether such a provision would spell out in express words what the instrument, read against the relevant background, would reasonably be understood to mean.[116]

Under this '*Belize* approach',[117] the rules governing the implication of terms are those which regulate construction of contracts. Therefore, the implication of a term (or at least one implied in fact), of itself, is an exercise of construction.

While support for *Attorney General of Belize v Belize Telecom* in England initially appeared to be growing,[118] this soon changed because of the United Kingdom Supreme Court's 2015 decision in *Marks & Spencer plc v BNP Paribas Securities Services Trust Company (Jersey) Ltd.*[119] As a consequence of that decision, whether the '*Belize* approach' remains a statement of English law (as Lord Hoffman obviously thought) is now doubtful. In *Marks & Spencer v BNP Paribas*—a case concerning the question of whether a tenant could, on the exercise of a break clause, recover rent paid in advance for the period after the break date—Lord Neuberger conducted an analysis of the state of the law on implied terms. His Lordship held that, prior to *Attorney General of Belize v Belize Telecom*, a 'clear, consistent and principled approach'[120] existed with respect to implied terms. In Lord Neuberger's view *Attorney General of Belize v Belize Telecom* was *not* to be treated as having

---

[111] *Commonwealth Bank v Barker* (n 54) [22].
[112] Carter and others (n 34) 216.
[113] *Attorney General of Belize v Belize Telecom* (n 109) 1993.
[114] ibid.
[115] ibid.
[116] ibid 1994.
[117] This terminology is adopted by the authors throughout Courtney and Carter (n 93).
[118] The proposition 'that the implication of a term is an exercise in ... construction of the instrument as a whole' was adopted in *Mediterranean Salvage & Towage Ltd v Seamar Trading & Commerce Inc (The Reborn)* [2009] 2 Lloyd's Rep 639 (CA), 641. See also *Fortis Bank SA/NV v Indian Overseas Bank* [2010] Bus LR 835 (Comm); *Crema v Cenkos Securities plc* [2011] 1 WLR 2066 (CA); *Stena Line Ltd v Merchant Navy Ratings Pension Fund Trustees Ltd* [2011] Pens LR 233 (CA) [36] and [44].
[119] *Marks & Spencer v BNP Paribas* (n 35).
[120] ibid [21].

changed the law on implied terms,[121] and should be treated as 'a typically inspired discussion rather than authoritative guidance'.[122] Clearly, his Lordship's judgment signifies a reassertion of the traditional approach to implied terms; it reaffirmed the test for implying a term as a matter of fact and re-established implication of a term as a matter of fact, separate from construction.

The remaining question in *Marks & Spencer v BNP Paribas* stems from the separate judgments of Lords Carnwath[123] and Clarke,[124] both of whom were more tolerant of *Attorney General of Belize v Belize Telecom*. While this outcome permits some degree of academic debate as to the future application of *Attorney General of Belize v Belize Telecom*, the vital point is that neither judge was prepared to fully accept a broad reading of that earlier decision. Therefore, in practice, both Lords Carnwath and Clarke ended up with much the same conclusion as Lord Neuberger. Overall, in the words of Lord Carnwath, *Attorney General of Belize v Belize Telecom* 'is not to be read as involving any relaxation of the traditional, highly restrictive approach to implication of terms'.[125] According to Lord Clarke, 'the critical point is that in *Belize* the Judicial Committee was not watering down the traditional test of necessity'.[126]

While the *Attorney General of Belize v Belize Telecom* approach has since been accepted in New Zealand,[127] it 'does not [appear to] represent the law in Australia',[128] and continues to remain in doubt in England. Henceforth, this work will proceed on the basis that, notwithstanding the possibility of certain implied terms being categorised as arising by reason of construction (rather than implication), the implication of terms remains a separate and valid means through which gaps in contracts can be filled.

Conclusion

This chapter has established an understanding of the general legal rules that are relevant to the remainder of this work. It began by discussing express contractual terms, which take primacy over any implied terms. The chapter then considered the legal tests for implying terms in fact, by custom and usage, and by law, including mention of the challenge routinely faced by courts in distinguishing

---

[121] ibid [24].
[122] ibid [31].
[123] ibid [57]–[74].
[124] ibid [75]–[77].
[125] ibid [66].
[126] ibid [77].
[127] See, eg, *Dysart Timbers Ltd v Nielsen* [2009] 3 NZLR 161 (Supreme Court of New Zealand (NZSC)), 168; *Hickman v Turn and Wave Ltd* [2011] 3 NZLR 318 (New Zealand Court of Appeal (NZCA)), 371–72.
[128] Courtney and Carter (n 93) 152.

between implication in fact and by law. It also addressed the concept of implying terms as it relates to construction. Considering each of these matters provides a foundation for exploring the central question of this work: how do terms implied by law shape the normative core of contracts for work? As an extension of this discussion, Chapter 2 examines the significance of the judicial act of implying a term by law, concentrating more deeply on why the implication of a term by law is a critical weapon in the judicial armoury.

2
The Significance of Implying a Term by Law

Introduction

Contractual dealings occur within a legal landscape, which is sometimes vast and complex; at other times, it can be limited and relatively straightforward. Regardless of the size or complexity of that landscape, however, terms implied by law flow continually throughout it, like streams, with their edges sculpted by the common law and statute. Insofar as the common law is concerned, such streams are made judicially to fill gaps in the landscape.[1] Yet, despite this deliberate intervention, terms implied by law are taken to have always existed as naturally occurring phenomena, irrespective of the parties' intentions.[2] Terms implied by law may exist in isolation, or may overlap with one other, or they may run alongside 'estuaries' of law, such as tort, equity, and statute.[3] Parties may attempt to block the stream of a term implied by law by contracting out of it altogether by using express terms.[4] The implication of a term by law in any contractual landscape is complex, yet it ensures the steady and harmonious flow of dealings between the contracting parties as they navigate the terrain of which they are a part.

This chapter's purpose is to pay homage to the significant judicial act of continuing to recognise an existing term implied by law, or to imply a new one altogether. It does so in respect of contracts generally, with certain references to employment contracts and contracts for the performance of work, where useful. The point of conducting such an exercise at the start of this work is to demonstrate that the judicial act of implying a term by law is not one to be taken lightly; if anything, it is one of the most influential steps a court can take in normatively shaping a contractual arrangement.[5] This chapter explains why, in a general manner, this influence is applicable across both England and Australia. It is brief in comparison to the chapters that follow. Yet, its overarching message is paramount in the context

---

[1] Understanding implied terms as 'gap fillers' has been mentioned in Chapter 1 and is briefly returned to later in this chapter.
[2] The absence of a parties' intention for implying a term by law has been mentioned in Chapter 1 and is revisited briefly in this chapter.
[3] The connection between terms implied by law and those areas of law is expanded upon later in Chapter 3 in respect of the origins of each of the terms selected for examination, which typically stem from these other areas.
[4] The question of parties' ability to contract out of certain terms is part of the assessment undertaken in Chapter 6.
[5] This proposition raises the question as to the suitable limits of the courts' role in implying terms by law—a question returned to in detail in Chapter 7.

of this work as a whole: the implication of a term by law is a dynamic judicial technique, worthy of the dedicated attention it receives in this work.

The significance of terms implied by law is evident throughout the four parts of this chapter. To begin, there is an historical analysis of how terms implied by law have emerged over time to gather the power they have amassed as a judicial technique. The second component of discussion concerns the normative effects of such terms on entire classes or categories of contracts. Next, it considers the importance of maintaining a set of identifiable legal rules by virtue of terms implied by law. That consideration is followed by an acknowledgement of the wide scope of influence of terms implied by law in respect of the sheer number of contracts that they can permeate. Its conclusion seeks to consolidate the fact that terms implied by law are not an ordinary judicial apparatus. Their influence on contractual dealings is unparalleled by any other judicial law-making function in the field of contract law.

Emergence of a Powerful Judicial Technique

Over time, terms implied by law have emerged as an integral mechanism in contracts generally, as well as in employment contracts[6] and in contracts for the performance of work specifically.[7] In her historical account of the development of implied terms, Elisabeth Peden explains that the community and its regulatory bodies (eg the church and trade organisations) engaged in the earliest form of contractual regulation.[8] For example, '[t]he church had strong views about the sale of goods and markets, the natural home of rules which developed into what

---

[6] For discussion of the historical development of the employment contract (as distinct from contracts for the personal performance of work), see generally, S Deakin, 'The Evolution of the Contract of Employment, 1900–50' in N Whiteside and R Salais (eds), *Governance, Industry and Labour Markets in Britain and France* (Routledge 1998) 212; D Hay, 'Master and Servant in England: Using the Law in the Eighteenth and Nineteenth Centuries' in Willibald Steinmetz (ed), *Private Law and Social Inequality in the Industrial Age* (OUP 2000) 227; W Cornish, 'Law and Organised Labour' in W Cornish and others (eds), *The Oxford History of the Laws of England: Volume XIII* (OUP 2010) 623–84; J Cairns, 'Blackstone, Kahn-Freund and the Contract of Employment' (1989) 105 LQR 300; S Jacoby, 'The Duration of Indefinite Employment Contracts in the United States and England: An Historical Analysis' (1982) 5 Comp Labour Law 85; B Veneziani, 'The Evolution of the Contract of Employment' in B Hepple (ed), *The Making of Labour Law in Europe* (Mansell Publishing 1986) 31, 31–72; A Merritt, 'The Historical Role of Law in the Regulation of Employment: Abstentionist or Interventionist?' (1982) 1 Aust J L & Soc 56; M Quinlan, 'Pre-Arbitral Labour Legislation in Australia' in S Macintyre and R Mitchell (eds), *Foundations of Arbitration* (OUP 1989) 29; J Howe and R Mitchell, 'The Evolution of the Contract of Employment in Australia: A Discussion' (1999) 12 AJLL 113. Similarly, the unitary notion of employment (ie a 'classless' concept common to all classes of wage-earner) really only emerged in the twentieth century in both England and Australia: Howe and Mitchell (n 6) 116.

[7] Examples of terms that are routinely implied by law into employment contracts, which carry the dual potential to operate in contracts for the performance of work, are the subject of detailed consideration across Chapters 3 and 4.

[8] E Peden, 'Contract Development Through the Looking-Glass of Implied Terms' in J T Gleeson, J A Watson, and E Peden (eds), *Historical Foundations of Australian Law* (Federation Press 2013) 201, 201–02.

we now call "contract"... Individuals were encouraged out of moral and religious conviction, to behave ethically'.[9] At that early stage, certain obligations were also recognised as attaching to certain types of commercial relationships. Through recognition of custom and trade usage, these obligations became the very first 'implied terms'.[10] Some of the earliest examples include implied warranties in the sale of goods.[11] These evolved as a '"natural part" of the relationship between purchaser and seller',[12] and are now regulated by legislation derived from the *Sale of Goods Act 1893* (UK).[13]

By the nineteenth century, the notion of the parties' intentions came to dominate all areas of contract law, including in respect of the implication of terms.[14] The focus was then on the parties' 'presumed intentions'—a concept that was often viewed as 'fictitious', although that view was not universally accepted.[15] On the one hand, implied terms were seen to represent what the parties must have 'actually' agreed, and according to 'will theory', the obligations placed on the parties were what they 'willed' them to be.[16] On the other hand, objective theorists argued that the parties could not will legal consequences since they did not know the law. In fact, 'it was circular to say that the parties willed what the law prescribed, since the law prescribed what the parties willed'.[17] Put otherwise, an intention imputed to the parties is not necessarily a reflection of their real intention. Despite the continuing conflict between will theorists and objective theorists,[18] since the beginning of the twentieth century the courts have come to discard the fictitious use of intention in respect of implied terms.[19] As Hugh Collins explains, since courts

---

[9] ibid 202.
[10] ibid 210–17.
[11] ibid 205. See especially, *Morley v Attenborough* (1849) 154 ER 943 (Court of Exchequer (Exch)), concerning an implied warranty of title; *Eichholz v Bannister* (1864) 144 ER 284 (Court of Common Pleas (CCP), concerning an implied warranty of title; *Parkinson v Lee* (1802) 102 ER 389 (Court of King's Bench (KB)), concerning an implied warranty as to fitness for purpose; *Gardiner v Gray* (1815) 171 ER 46 (KB), concerning an implied warranty to inspect goods; *Jones v Just* (1868) LR 3 QB 197 (Court of Queen's Bench (QB)), concerning an implied warranty of merchantable quality.
[12] Peden (n 8) 210.
[13] See, eg, *Sale of Goods Act 1979* (UK). See further, the remaining Sale of Goods legislation across England and Australia discussed in Chapter 1.
[14] Peden (n 8) 217–25.
[15] On the competing approaches to fictions and implied terms, see generally, E Peden, *Good Faith in the Performance of Contracts* (LexisNexis Butterworths 2003) §§2.2–2.6.
[16] See, eg, P Atiyah, *The Rise and Fall of Freedom of Contract* (Clarendon Press 1979) 213, 398–419; A Bogg, 'Good Faith in the Contract of Employment: A Case of the English Reserve' (2011) 32 Comp LL & PJ 729, 753–55.
[17] Peden (n 8) 203.
[18] See, eg, J Gordley, *The Philosophical Origins of the Modern Contract Doctrine* (Clarendon Press 1991) 230; H Collins, *The Law of Contract* (4th edn, CUP 2003) 222–23; A Mason and S Gageler, 'The Contract' in P Finn (ed), *Essays in Contract* (The Law Book Company 1987) 1.
[19] See, eg, Peden (n 15) §2.2. See also *Luxor (Eastbourne) Ltd v Cooper* [1941] AC 109 (House of Lords (HL)), 137: 'Sometimes [implied term] denotes some term which does not depend on the actual intention of the parties but on a rule of law, such as terms, warranties or conditions which, if not expressly excluded, the law imports, as for instance under the *Sale of Goods Act* ... But a case like the present is different because what is sought to imply is based on an intention imputed to the parties from their actual circumstances'.

cannot read minds to find out intent, the law uses 'proxies' of proof of intent found in ostensible intention.[20]

The judiciary has gradually come to acknowledge that some terms are consistently implied because they are part of a particular type of contractual relationship (eg an employment relationship), rather than based on the particular facts of an individual case alone.[21] These are what we now refer to as 'terms implied by law'. As explored further in Chapter 6, only in the past sixty-five years have they been classified as a distinct category of implied terms with their own unique legal test for implication.[22] It follows that these terms are now implied not based on the parties' intentions (as with terms implied in fact), but as default rules imposed by law.[23] For the reasons that follow, that default rule status is of the utmost significance in terms of normatively influencing contractual dealings.

Normative Rationalisation of Contractual Dealings

As this work's Introduction proposes, terms implied by law have a normative function. This quality is the pinnacle of their significance. By virtue of the common law, judges possess the unique ability to make decisions about the ideal nature of a certain type of contractual relationship when they continue to recognise an existing term implied by law, or decide to imply a new one, into a class or category of contract. In doing so, they rationalise the internal structure and normative core of entire cohorts of contractual dealings, shaping and moulding the foundation of those relationships.

In essence, courts imply terms by law into classes or categories of contract with the inevitable outcome that they are imputing a desired set of values or principles to govern relationships of that kind. In the context of employment, it has been said that the judiciary has elected to adopt such terms as instruments 'to project a modern vision of the employment relationship and to forge the behavioural standards against which the conduct of the contracting parties will be judged'.[24] A substantially similar role no doubt exists in respect of the broader context of contracts for the performance of work.[25]

---

[20] Collins (n 18) 225.
[21] Peden (n 8) 225.
[22] ibid. This distinction arose out of *Lister v Romford Ice & Cold Storage Co Ltd* [1957] AC 555 (HL) and *Liverpool City Council v Irwin* [1977] AC 239 (HL). See also the discussion in Chapter 1, which sets out the distinct tests for implying a term in fact and by law, as well as the importance of maintaining that distinction.
[23] Peden (n 8) 225–31.
[24] D Cabrelli, *Employment Law in Context: Text and Materials* (4th edn, OUP 2020) 174.
[25] Again, this potential broader application is examined in more detail across Chapters 3 and 4.

Returning to contracts generally, the judicial influence of terms implied by law has been articulated as being predicated on 'necessity, not reasonableness'.[26] Again, the complex notion of determining what is truly 'necessary' for implication by law in respect of employment contracts is the focus of Chapter 6. For now, in relation to contracts generally, it is noted that implication of a term by law has the potential to occur as a matter of policy, with the ability to become fundamental to the general norms of entire classes of contract, the totality of those contracts, or even the totality of all types of contracts.[27] The difficulty is, however, that we remain 'none the wiser as to the nature of the relevant policy considerations, which remain firmly concealed'[28] in judicial reasoning.

In view of this apparent judicial avoidance, several academic attempts have been made to explain the policy-fuelled processes in which the judiciary engage when implying a term by law and why that process is such an influential one. Concentrating on the implication of terms by law into employment contracts, which typically take a standard form, Collins has identified three core roles performed by terms implied by law that make them particularly dynamic in nature. A broader application (eg to contracts for the performance of work) makes it apparent that these three roles also appear able to be applied beyond the context of employment. Collins says they possess:[29]

1. a traditional gap-filling function to plug gaps in contracts, which are incomplete by design;
2. an interpretive role to generate guiding principles for the interpretation of the contract's written express terms; and/or
3. a regulatory function whereby they operate as mandatory norms with a view to monitoring and constraining the exercise of powers conferred by express contractual terms.

Collins appears to prefer the second approach, whereby terms implied by law are used in the construction of express terms.[30] This preference can be contrasted with that of Mark Freedland who uses the language of 'interpretation and construction', yet in outlining the task undertaken by the judiciary when implying a term by law, sees that there is an additional regulatory function (ie the second approach).[31]

---

[26] *Scally v Southern Health and Social Services Board* [1992] 1 AC 294 (HL), 306G–307F (Viscount Simonds).
[27] An example of such a universally applicable term includes the duty of cooperation, the origins and current status of which are examined in detail in Chapter 3. Its universal application is also touched on briefly below.
[28] Cabrelli (n 24) 169.
[29] H Collins, 'Legal Responses to the Standard Form Contract of Employment' (2007) 36 ILJ 2, 7–10.
[30] Noting that Collins' view appears to have altered more recently: H Collins, 'Implied Terms in the Contract of Employment' in M Freedland and others (eds), *The Contract of Employment* (OUP 2016) 471, 489–90.
[31] M Freedland, *The Personal Employment Contract* (OUP 2003) 127.

In that sense, terms implied by law operate to restrain powers conferred on contracting parties by the contract's express terms. David Cabrelli also favours this blended function of terms implied by law (ie a combination of Collins' second and third approaches).[32] In the context of this work, it is accepted that any or all of those three roles could be performed when a term is implied by law. It largely depends on the case argued, as well as the nature of the proposed term in the context of the class of contracts into which it is set to be implied.

Irrespective of which of the three functions are being performed when implication by law occurs, the terms ultimately implied by law remain paramount in assisting the courts to shape entire classes or categories of contracts from a normative standpoint. They stand to articulate open-textured standards about the parties' behaviour and provide a guidepost for the parties' expected behavioural norms. Their content is made up of broadly framed evaluative criteria against which the contracting parties' conduct is to be assessed. Terms implied by law therefore project a particular vision of the ideal contractual relationship within a broader category or class of contract into which they are implied. To that end, Cabrelli labels them 'an elaborate form of judicial legislation', which raises the question of whether it is even appropriate for courts to maintain such a potent law-making capability, or whether such a role ought to be performed by the legislature instead.[33] As suggested in this work's Introduction, this question is explored in Chapter 7, which considers the ambit of the judicial role when courts are asked to imply a term by law into the class of employment contracts specifically. Additionally, the question of whether parties should even be permitted to contract out of such terms is debatable and is examined in detail in Chapter 6 in respect of employment contracts, when the question of the necessity is examined.

Beyond the abovementioned three possible functions, in the context of employment contracts and contracts for the personal performance of work, Freedland also explains that there is a core group of 'guiding principles' for courts asked to imply a term by law into such contracts.[34] The first three guiding principles are closely tied to the broad notion of 'mutuality of obligation'.[35] They include: (1) mutuality and reciprocity; (2) care and cooperation; and (3) trust and confidence, noting that in the Australian context, this third principle is tenuous, since an implied duty of mutual trust and confidence was found to be non-existent in Australian employment contract law. Again, more is said about that non-existence in Chapter 4.

Freedland goes on to list two further principles, applicable to employment contracts and those for the personal performance of work.[36] They are identified as more 'regulatory' in nature and include: (4) loyalty and freedom of economic

---

[32] Cabrelli (n 24) 171.
[33] ibid.
[34] Freedland (n 31) 127–28.
[35] ibid.
[36] ibid.

activity; and (5) fair management and performance. In summary, he explains that these five core principles underpin the main judicial goals or values sought to be achieved when a term is implied by law in the contractual context of employment or the personal performance of work.[37] They are responsible for underpinning the policy-based shape of those relationships.

In the context of the current work, Freedland's five principles serve as a reminder of the common law's influential role in shaping the modern face of both employment contracts and contracts for the personal performance of work, with the curious observation that each of the five principles can be applied similarly to employment and the broader performance of work, thereby suggesting that employment may not be quite as distinctive as one might otherwise suspect—a notion that is revisited in Chapter 5, where the distinctive nature of employment contracts is examined in detail. For now, discussion moves to examining how terms implied by law can generate clarity in contracts generally through the creation of an identifiable set of legal rules.

Identifiable Legal Rules

Terms implied by law generate further significance because they can be seen as comprising an identifiable and routinely recognised set of legal rules that govern particular categories or classes of contracts. Once recognised, these terms may become so well known in the contractual context in which they apply that they form a recognisable set of rules. The predictability of applicable terms that are typically implied by law into contracts of the same kind can serve parties and the judiciary well by promoting certainty and a widely understood set of norms that routinely shape the class or category of contracts of which they are a part. This certainty and predictability are also particularly important in ensuring the development of the law in a way that is transparent and within the limits of judicial power.

Taking employment contracts, for example, there are several well-established terms implied by law that routinely operate in such contracts, each of which are the subject of dedicated examination across Chapters 3 and 4. Those terms are commonly referred to in employment law textbooks as deeply entrenched terms implied by law into all employment contracts, or at least into employment contracts of a certain type. Taking one obvious example, it is likely well understood by many that employees owe their employers a duty to obey their lawful and reasonable instructions.[38] In addition, a mutually implied duty requiring parties to cooperate, for example, is so ingrained across all types of contracts that it is routinely accepted

---

[37] ibid.
[38] This duty receives dedicated attention in Chapter 3.

as a universal term implied by law into all contracts.[39] As elaborated in Chapter 3, it is difficult to imagine how any contract would be able to operate without such a duty.

Of course, the challenge is that despite these terms being relatively well known, particularly in legal circles, parties may still find themselves unaware of certain terms that are typically implied by law into their category or class of contract. This lack of knowledge may arise when a term implied by law is newly developed, limited in its application, nuanced, or complex in nature. It could also be the case that, if buried within the depths of the common law, parties without legal training may be unaware of the existence of terms implied by law. In such situations, there is arguably merit in such terms being recognised as more readily accessible statutory-based rules, rather than as contractual terms implied by law—a possibility that is examined in this work's Conclusion. For now, their predictability and identifiability as common law terms are acknowledged as being of paramount importance.

Wide Scope of Influence

Accompanying the ability of terms implied by law to create a set of identifiable legal rules that routinely operate in contracts of a particular category or class, through their application to entire categories or classes of contract, they are significant in terms of their wide scope of influence. As mentioned, certain terms implied by law are so far-reaching that they are implied into all contracts, evincing the capacity to influence all contractual dealings, rather than those in a particular category or class alone. Given their broad application, terms implied by law could well be considered more influential than terms implied in fact, which, as explained in Chapter 1, only operate in relation to the single contract in question before the court. Not only do terms implied by law affect parties to the particular contract in question, but they also infiltrate every other contract within the class or category into which they are implied. Where implication by law occurs, the sheer breadth of effect could span a large (perhaps immeasurable) number of contractual agreements contained within a particular category or class, and the number of parties affected by their implication has the potential to be immense.

The High Court of Australia recognised this possibility in its refusal to imply a term of mutual trust and confidence into all Australian employment contracts in *Commonwealth Bank of Australia v Barker*[40] when it held that the duty amounted to:[41]

---

[39] It is worth mentioning here that such universal application might mean that the duty is instead a rule of construction, noting that, as discussed in Chapter 1, this status remains debatable.
[40] (2014) 253 CLR 169 (High Court of Australia (HCA)).
[41] ibid [38].

an implication apposite to the disposition of a particular dispute in which an employee complains of an employer's conduct. Yet it is an implication which would impose obligations not only on employers but also on employees, whose voices about that consequence of the implication are not heard in this appeal.

The court leveraged the duty's scope of application to all employment contracts as a reason to *not* imply it by law into those agreements at all. Consequently, any decision to imply it should remain 'in the province of the legislature'.[42] Again, the question of whether judicial law-making of this nature should occur in respect of employment contracts is the subject of consideration in Chapter 7. However, at this point, it must be highlighted that where a term is implied by law into a class or category of contracts, its reach is wide, conceivably affecting many parties to contracts whose voices will not be heard, but who will be just as affected by its implication.

Conclusion

This chapter has presented an analysis of the salient features of terms implied by law, which make them significant legal mechanisms. It has yielded the observation that they are a judicial technique worthy of the dedicated attention they receive in this work. The opening scrutiny of the historical emergence of terms implied by law into contracts generally demonstrated their evolution into a powerful common law mechanism. The result of that development has been that terms implied by law now rationalise the normative foundations of the classes or categories of contract into which they are implied. In effect, they permit courts to shape the very foundations upon which entire categories or classes of contract are based. Judges are anointed with the policy-driven role of creating an ideal internal structure and normative underpinning for entire categories or classes of contract each time they decide to imply an existing or new term by law.

It also emerged that the capability of terms implied by law to generate an identifiable set of legal rules applicable to the categories or classes of contract into which they are implied added further weight to their significance as a legal mechanism. Likewise, their potentially wide scope of influence across many contracts that may comprise a particular category or class further contributes to their significance beyond the contract in question, as would be the case for a term implied in fact.

With each of these attributes in mind, Chapters 3 and 4 give a dedicated consideration to specific terms implied by law into employment contracts, as well as their potential implication in contracts for the performance of work. As an extension of the examination that has taken place in this chapter, those chapters collectively

---

[42] ibid.

demonstrate the significance of terms implied by law in shaping both employment contracts, and contracts for the performance of work. Given the potential for terms implied by law to infiltrate both contractual groupings, there is an inherent challenge in identifying their true regulatory coverage in the world of work—a challenge that drives the remainder of this work.

PART II
TERMS IMPLIED BY LAW INTO CONTRACTS FOR WORK

3
Origins and Current Status

Introduction

Terms implied by law into employment contracts have a rich and diverse history. The same can arguably be said of those terms that have the potential to be similarly implied by law into contracts for the performance of work. With that sentiment in mind, this chapter is dedicated to examining the origins and current status of terms implied by law into both employment contracts and contracts for the performance of work.

As described in this work's Introduction, contracts for the performance of work encapsulate an increasing number of 'atypical' or 'non-standard' work relationships, including those performing work outside the category of employment contracts—a category, which, as explained in Chapter 5, is difficult to describe and define. It is true that '[t]he common law has always approached the task of classifying contracts with one hand tied behind its back'.[1] This chapter, therefore, refers to the category of 'contracts for the performance of work' in the general sense, noting that the label applies to more nuanced atypical and non-standard work relationships. The terminology used in respect of contracts for the performance of work is similarly general in nature, in that it refers generally to principals, hosts, and hirers who would engage a worker or independent contractor, noting that the applicable terminology would vary depending on the type of work performed.

It becomes apparent that terms implied by law into contracts for the performance of work are yet to be fully articulated in case law. The reasons behind this lack of judicial attention are largely unknown. However, it is suspected to be a consequence of those engaged under such contracts typically lacking the means to pursue the legal action needed to assert the existence or non-existence of such terms. The complex nature of the arguments needed to mount a successful case to imply a term by law makes this lack of attention unsurprising. It remains anticipated that many of the terms with the potential to be implied by law into contracts for the performance of work would mirror those already implied by law into in employment contracts, effectively blurring the distinction between the two modes of engagement. In essence, both modes of engagement can be characterised by, or be

---

[1] H Collins, 'Dependent Contractors in Tax and Employment Law' in G Loutzenhiser and R de la Feria (eds), *The Dynamics of Taxation: Essays in Honour of Judith Freedman* (Bloomsbury Publishing 2020) 117, 130.

the product of, inequality of bargaining power involving relationships of subordination. It is implicit that the terms with the potential to be implied by law into contracts for the performance of work would derive from the same historical origins as applicable in the context of employment contracts, drawing the similarity between employment and the performance of work ever closer.

Despite their potential applicability, doubt remains as to whether certain terms implied by law into employment contracts are even suitable in the context of contracts for the performance of work. Some terms are arguably so exclusive to employment that they ought not to be capable of implication in the broader realm of contracts for the performance of work. To do so would be contrary to the normative core of employment. In considering the beginnings and present operation of a series of key terms implied by law, both in respect of employment contracts and contracts for the performance of work, this chapter examines how certain terms have come to be identified as truly unique to employment.

The chapter investigates the English origins and current status of key terms that are routinely implied by law into English and Australian employment contracts.[2] It gives an historical context for the present terms by tracing their origins up to a case (or cases) cited more recently, all the while ignoring incidental decisions made in between. The terms selected for analysis are divided into three main categories: those owed by employers, those owed by employees, and those owed mutually. These terms have been chosen on the basis that they are routinely acknowledged in labour law texts as those that are well established in the employment contract.[3] Given the controversy surrounding the implied duties of mutual trust and confidence and good faith, especially in Australia, those duties are subject to a separate and dedicated discussion in Chapter 4. Perhaps the most vexed outcome of this initial inquiry is that each instance of implication of a term by law has arisen out of an arbitrary judicial decision, wherein the term in question is deemed as one to be implied by law as an apparently necessary incident of employment, absent fully articulated logic for that outcome.

For each term selected for analysis, discussion involves a transition to an examination of the origins and current status of terms that have the potential to be implied by law into the broader category of contracts for the performance of work. As demonstrated, 'the answer, as so often in relation to those workers [engaged under contracts for the performance of work], is a matter of speculation and reasoning from general principles in the absence of decided cases'.[4] It is unclear whether

---

[2] A preliminary historical analysis began in G Golding, 'The Origins of Terms Implied by Law into English and Australian Employment Contracts' (2020) 20 OUCLJ 163. This chapter presents an extension of that analysis, examining the potential for those same terms to operate in the broader realm of contracts for the performance of work.
[3] In the English context, see generally Z Adams and others, *Deakin and Morris' Labour Law* (7th edn, Hart Publishing 2021) 238–43 and 327–59; in the Australian context, see generally A Stewart and others, *Creighton and Stewart's Labour Law* (6th edn, Federation Press 2016) 496–535.
[4] M Freedland, *The Personal Employment Contract* (OUP 2003) 177.

parties to contracts for the performance of work are able to benefit from common law terms implied by law;[5] indeed, there has been no case that directly considers the potential application of terms routinely implied by law into employment contracts and their potential to apply similarly in contracts for the performance of work.

In view of that uncertainty, leading labour law scholars have begun questioning the implication of certain discrete terms typically implied by law into employment contracts in the context of contracts for the performance of work.[6] This chapter builds on those examinations, considering each of the select key terms already implied by law into employment contracts, and arrives at a view as to their potential application, or non-application, in the broader realm of contracts for the performance of work. This path enables a better understanding of the ways in which certain terms implied by law could shape both employment contracts and contracts for the performance of work, effectively muddying the waters between what constitutes employment and the performance of work.

The position ultimately arrived at in this chapter's conclusion is that some terms implied by law are coextensive and correlative across both categories of contracts. Others are unique to employment. It is problematic that for both categories of contract, however, there has been no proper justification at all for the implication of those terms by law. In the case of employment contracts, this lack of justification seems to have arisen out of the fact that the terms implied by law originated from English law, and have been supplanted as norms from the former master and servant regime, fiduciary obligations, and tort law. In some instances, they have been simply presumed as norms of employment, absent meaningful justification for being necessary incidents of employment.

For contracts for the performance of work, while speculative, it appears that the terms that have the potential to be implied into those contracts by law would share the same historical background as those implied by law into employment contracts. That fact alone draws both categories of contracts towards a substantially similar genesis. Again, if formally recognised in case law, the consequence of their implication would arguably be the same: they would become implied as terms by law, but would lack sufficient rationale to justify that outcome.

The overarching result of this chapter's analysis is that ascertaining what constitutes the normative core of employment contracts, as distinct from contracts for the performance of work, is nebulous. This outcome makes it inherently difficult to predict whether any existing, or new, terms will be implied to shape either type of

---

[5] D Cabrelli and J D'Alton, 'Furlough and Common Law Rights and Remedies' (*UK Labour Law Blog*, 8 June 2020) <https://uklabourlawblog.com/2020/06/08/furlough-and-common-law-rights-and-remedies-by-david-cabrelli-and-jessica-dalton/> accessed 20 December 2022.

[6] See, eg, ibid; H Collins, 'Employment as a Relational Contract' (2021) 137 LQR 426, 448–49.

contract. Such a result is problematic in terms of predicting the outcome of cases, not to mention determining the common law protections afforded (or not afforded) to the parties to the contract itself. The purpose of this chapter is to identify those challenges, with proposed solutions returned to in this work's Conclusion.

Duties Owed by Employers

Discussion now turns to three key duties owed by employers to their employees as terms implied by law, these being a duty to: (A) provide a safe place of work; (B) indemnify employees for expenses innocently incurred during the performance of their duties; and (C) inform employees of their rights. The following historical analysis demonstrates that, despite all now existing as contractually implied terms at common law, only one of the duties originated in that way.

Tort law is responsible for the development of an employer's duty to provide an employee with a safe place of work. An employer's duty to indemnify their employees for expenses innocently incurred began as a contractual entitlement, but was not originally understood as a term implied by law. The only duty that appears to have strictly begun as a term implied by law was an employer's duty to inform employees of their rights. However, that duty is only applicable in a discrete subclass of employment contracts, apparently having originated and continued in operation more like a term implied in fact, despite being labelled as a term implied by law.

The overarching consensus is therefore that none of these prominent duties owed by employers now routinely implied by law into the general class of employment contracts actually originated in that way. None of the authorities recognising the current implication of these terms explains why they are now apparently necessary instances of all employment. This outcome is problematic; as explained in Chapter 1, the test for implying a term by law requires that it be deemed necessary in that class of contract.

For each of the terms selected for examination, their purported existence in work relationships beyond employment is also considered. As transpires, only an employer's duty to inform employees of their rights is unable to be mirrored in contracts for the performance of work. The purported duties owed by a principal, host, or hirer to provide a worker or independent contractor with a safe place of work, and to indemnify workers or independent contractors for expenses innocently incurred, have the potential to dually operate in contracts for the performance of work. This outcome obscures what is understood as employment, as opposed to the broader performance of work.

A. Duty to Provide a Safe Place of Work

The 1837 decision, *Priestley v Fowler*,[7] seems to be the first identifiable decision in which a servant was able to recover damages from his master after suffering personal injury. The plaintiff, Priestly, was injured when a van that had been overloaded by other workers fell on him. At this stage, it was not possible for the employer's obligation to provide employees with a safe place of work to be understood as a term implied by law. Indeed, the notion that the employment relationship was actually contractual in nature was only just gaining traction. As such, in keeping with the time in which the case was decided, the court instead held that a tortious (not contractual) duty was owed by a master (not an employer) to 'provide for the safety of his servant in the course of his employment'.[8] Only later in *Wilsons & Clyde Coal Co Ltd v English*[9] was it recognised that an employer owed a non-delegable duty to provide a safe place of work for its employees (not servants). Still, just as in *Priestly v Fowler*, the duty was recognised as tortious not contractual in nature.

It was not until 1957 that the House of Lords in *Lister v Romford Ice & Cold Storage Co Ltd*[10] first labelled the duty as a contractual one implied by law, as well as tortious. More is said about this decision in Chapter 6 in relation to its role in formulating the current necessity test for a term to be implied by law. For present purposes, however, it must be noted that *Lister v Romford Ice* gave rise to a well-established duty implied by law into all employment contracts, in both England[11] and Australia,[12] requiring employers to provide their employees with a safe place of work. The duty now also operates in a contractual sense, despite originating in tort, and its continuing existence in that form has never been questioned judicially. Nowadays, an employer's non-delegable[13] tortious and contractual duties to provide employees with a safe place of work are understood as coextensive and correlative.[14]

In the broader context of contracts for the performance of work, a duty owed by principals, hosts, and hirers to provide workers and independent contractors with a safe place of work must be similarly capable of being implied by law into that class of contract. The duty appears far from unique to employment. With its origins in tort, it would be counterintuitive for the duty to cease to apply to contracts that are

---

[7] (1837) 3 M&W 1 (Court of Exchequer (CE)).
[8] ibid.
[9] [1938] AC 57 (House of Lords (HL)).
[10] [1957] AC 555 (HL).
[11] See, eg, *Matthews v Kuwait Bechtel Corporation* [1959] 2 QB 57 (Court of Appeal (CA)), 67.
[12] See, eg, *Goldman Sachs J B Were Services Pty Ltd v Nikolich* (2007) 163 FCR 62 (Full Court of the Federal Court of Australia (FCAFC)) [31] and [324].
[13] See, eg, *State of New South Wales v Lepore* (2003) 212 CLR 511 (High Court of Australia (HCA)) [257] and [265].
[14] See, eg, *Goldman Sachs v Nikolich* (n 12) [326]. See also *Spring v Guardian Assurance plc* [1995] 2 AC 296 (HL), 341F–H (Lord Woolf); *Rihan v Ernst & Young Global Ltd* [2020] EWHC 901 (QB) [573] (Kerr J).

beyond the bounds of an employment relationship. For work to be performed in any capacity, surely the place in which that work is performed must be required to be safe, for both contractual and tortious reasons. To require otherwise appears counterintuitive to the work being able to be performed at all. Absent such a duty, it is difficult to see how a contract for the performance of work could continue in operation. In that sense, the duty remains just as paramount in non-standard work settings as it does in employment. However, as is expanded upon in Chapter 6, doubt remains as to the absolute necessity of the contractual duty to provide a safe place of work where tortious and statutory duties operate concurrently.

B. Duty to Indemnify Employees for Expenses Innocently Incurred

One of the first references to a requirement to indemnify in relation to liabilities (rather than expenses) innocently incurred in contract law generally occurred in the 1827 case, *Adamson v Jarvis*.[15] At that time, however, the duty was not understood as a term implied by law, but as a 'contractual entitlement'.[16] In 1905, an implied right to reimbursement was identified in *Corporation of Sheffield v Barclay*.[17] Just as before, the right was identified in this commercial case as one occurring in relation to liabilities, not expenses. It presented what is said to be the earliest 'clear authority for an implied right to an indemnity in respect of liabilities innocently incurred'.[18]

Just a few years later, in 1914, the court in *Re Famatina Development Corporation*[19] cited the earlier decision of *Adamson v Jarvis* with approval in relation to an indemnity provided by an employer to their employee. It so happened, however, that the court only recognised the need for the indemnity due to the parties' concurrent fiduciary relationship as principal and agent, rather than their relationship as employer and employee.[20]

In 1957, in the aforementioned decision of *Lister v Romford Ice*, the court again applied *Adamson v Jarvis*, this time identifying that given the parties' relationship as employer and employee (not agent and principal), the employee was not entitled to be indemnified by their employer in respect of liability for their negligent conduct during their employment.[21] At this stage, however, there was no suggestion

---

[15] (1827) 4 Bing 66 (Court of Common Pleas (CCP)).
[16] ibid 695.
[17] [1905] AC 392 (HL).
[18] A Stewart and B Nosworthy, 'Employees and Indemnity' (2011) 27 JCL 18, 19.
[19] [1914] 2 Ch 271 (Court of Chancery (Ch Div)).
[20] ibid 280.
[21] *Lister v Romford Ice* (n 10) 595.

that a general duty to indemnify was necessary to become implied by law into all employment contracts.

In both England and Australia, an employer now owes a contractually implied duty to employees to indemnify them for expenses innocently incurred.[22] Even though this implication has occurred by reason of a term implied by law into all employment contracts in both jurisdictions, it lacks any judicial justification as to why that ought to be the case. The term's implication by law into all employment contracts has simply become the unquestioned and accepted approach across both jurisdictions, with the duty extended to unlawful acts committed by an employee during their employment, so long as they are unaware that the particular act is, in fact, unlawful.[23] However, it does not extend to cover an employee's negligent conduct, loss, or liability that would be governed by the common law,[24] or statute.[25] It is perplexing that courts across both jurisdictions have repeatedly presumed the implied term's existence in the general class of employment contracts, despite a lack of meaningful justification as to why its implication is necessary in all instances of employment.

Given the above, a duty to indemnify workers and independent contractors for expenses innocently incurred must also be capable of implication by law into contracts for the performance of work. Taking into account its origins as a fiduciary duty owed between a principal and agent, at its inception, the duty had already gathered its basis in a relationship beyond employment alone. Without such a duty operating in contracts for work, the performance of that work has the potential to be hindered significantly. Most obviously, depending on the circumstances, the work could be impossible to perform due to the sheer expense it would create for affected independent contractors and workers. It therefore appears necessary to make certain contracts for the performance of work financially viable. However, as is explained further in Chapter 6, the duty can hardly be said to be absolutely necessary in all instances of employment, since not all will necessarily attract expenses. The same could arguably be said in respect of every contract for the performance of work.

C. Duty to Inform Employees of their Rights

In 1992, the House of Lords in *Scally v Southern Health & Social Services Board*[26] decided to imply a term by law requiring employers to inform employees of their

---

[22] See, eg, *Kelly v Alford* [1988] 1 Qd R 404 (Supreme Court of Queensland (QSC)) 411; *Sheffield Corporation v Barclay* [1905] AC 392 (HL) 397.
[23] ibid.
[24] See, eg, E Peel, *Treitel: The Law of Contract* (13th edn, Sweet & Maxwell 2011) 480, 483.
[25] See, eg, *Corporations Act 2001* (Cth) ss 199A and 199B.
[26] [1992] 1 AC 294 (HL).

rights, but only in relation to a narrow category of employment contracts. The case involved a disagreement regarding standard clauses in an employment contract, which had been negotiated between the employees' representative and the employer prior to the beginning of the employment period. One of the clauses related to superannuation. It contained a beneficial provision that would allow for employees to purchase more 'years', giving rise to financial benefits, but only if they made that purchase within twelve months of beginning in their employment. The affected employees were not aware that they had such a right under their contracts, and argued that if they had been aware, they would have exercised the right.

Therefore, the House of Lords found that if an employer and representative body negotiate employment contracts containing a clause conferring a valuable benefit dependent upon employees taking a specific action to obtain that benefit, then a term implied by law exists to the effect that the employer needs to take reasonable steps to bring the clause to the employees' attention.[27] This outcome presents a rare situation of a term implied by law into employment contracts originating as such. The implied term of mutual trust and confidence presents another such example.[28] Again, that duty is the subject of dedicated discussion in Chapter 4.

The point is that this position is rare. As is made apparent in this chapter, most of the current terms implied by law into the general class of employment contracts originated in areas of the law other than employment contract law. However, they are simply presumed to be necessary across all employment contracts as necessary incidents to be implied by law. There is routinely no justification as to why that should be the case, which is problematic due to the uncertainty it creates. Courts have done little to apply consistently or meaningfully the current test for implying a term by law in respect of those terms. As time progresses, courts simply presume that they are necessary instances of employment, without questioning their origins or continued utility in the employment relationship.

It is worth mentioning that the Federal Court of Australia, in *Mulcahy v Hydro-Electric Commission*,[29] distinguished *Scally v Southern Health*.[30] The court identified that, given the outcome in *Scally v Southern Health*, an implied duty requiring employers to notify employees of changes to their contributory pension scheme had the potential to operate, but decided against its implication in this particular instance, given the facts of the case.

The duty has since not been implied into any other employment contracts in either England or Australia. Therefore, it can be said that the term derived from *Scally v Southern Health* (and later acknowledged in *Mulcahy v Hydro-Electric*) has evolved in such a way that it will only ever operate in relation to the narrow

---

[27] ibid 307.
[28] See, eg, *Malik v Bank of Credit and Commerce International SA (In Liq)* [1998] AC 20 (HL).
[29] (1998) 85 FCR 170 (Federal Court of Australia (FCA)), 210.
[30] ibid 210–11.

sub-class of employment contracts identified in *Scally v Southern Health*. If anything, this status makes it seem less akin to a term implied by law and more like one implied in fact, for the reason that its implication is in such a specific and nuanced contractual context that it lacks general application in the broader class of all employment contracts.

As to a proposed duty for principals, hosts, and hirers to inform workers or independent contractors of their rights, there does not appear to be a necessity for such a duty to extend beyond employment. As discussed, it is one of the few terms implied by law that has its origins in the law of employment as a contractually implied term. It is peculiar to limited instances of employment, in the sense that it is now applicable only in the case of a very narrow sub-class of employment contracts. Again, it seems more akin to a term implied in fact and consequently lacks application and utility outside its original context. The duty is revisited in Chapter 6 in the context of its limited necessity in employment.

Duties Owed by Employees

In converse to the above duties owed by employers, the origins and current status of five key duties owed by all employees as terms implied by law are examined in the following discussion, these being a duty: (A) to obey lawful and reasonable instructions; (B) of fidelity; (C) to exercise reasonable care and skill; (D) to hold inventions on trust (so long as there exists a duty to invent); and (E) not to misuse or disclose confidential information. As above, the potential application of each of the duties owed by employees is considered in respect of whether they would have the potential to be owed in a similar manner by independent contractors or workers in a non-standard work relationship. As is explained in this section, duties similarly owed by an independent contractor or worker to a principal, host, or hirer may include a duty to obey (at least in respect of limb (b) workers in English law), of fidelity in limited circumstances, to exercise reasonable care and skill, and not to misuse or disclose confidential information.

A. Duty to Obey Lawful and Reasonable Instructions

An employee's duty to obey the orders of their employer began in the previous context of employment as a status-based relationship between master and servant. The 1817 decision of *Spain v Arnott*[31] was one of the earliest instances in which a purported duty to obey owed by a servant was recognised. The decision involved a

---

[31] (1817) 2 Stark 256 (CCP).

master who had engaged a servant in husbandry on a twelve-month contract. The master had ordered the servant to take his horses a mile before dinner. However, the servant refused. The master proceeded to discharge the servant before seeking the magistrate's permission to do so. The servant was unsuccessful in suing the master to recoup his lost wages. The court found that the master had the right to dismiss the servant, owing to the duty to obey his master.[32] In another early decision, *Turner v Mason*,[33] a menial servant sought her master's leave to attend her dying mother's bed. The master refused, but the servant attended anyway and was later dismissed. The servant's wrongful dismissal claim failed since she was found to have disobeyed an order.

These early cases demonstrate that a servant owed a duty to obey all orders of their master, even those orders were unreasonable. This former duty was founded on the basis of a servant's complete subordination. Rather than being formulated as a contractual term implied by law, the duty originated as a norm of the master and servant relationship. Indeed, at the time, employment was not yet formulated as a contractual relationship, and the notion of a term being able to be implied by law had not yet come to fruition.

It was not until sometime later in the 1862 decision of *Price v Mouat*[34] that a duty to obey began to attract contractual force. The decision concerned an employee engaged to purchase lace, with it being suggested that 'if he was hired as a buyer, he was not bound to perform services not properly appertaining to that character'.[35] Around the same time, a one-off act of disobedience or neglect could not justify the dismissal of a manager[36] or journalist.[37]

Since these earlier English decisions, the law has developed substantially. Following the 1959 decision in *Laws v London Chronicle (Indicator Newspapers) Ltd*,[38] the duty to obey has been understood as a contractual one applying to all employees, obliging them to obey only lawful and reasonable orders of their employer. In that case, the duty was identified as a 'condition essential to the contract of service'[39] and 'one act of disobedience can justify dismissal only if it is of a nature which goes to show (in effect) that the servant is repudiating the contract'.[40] While the relevant worker was referred to as a 'servant' in the judgment, the court's rationale has continued in application in many more English cases involving employees.[41]

---

[32] It 'remains a mystery' as to how the servant was able to bring an action at common law: W Cornish, 'Law and Organised Labour' in W Cornish and others (eds), *The Oxford History of the Laws of England: Volume XIII* (OUP 2010) 644.
[33] (1834) 14 M&W 112 (CE).
[34] (1862) 11 CBNS 508 (CCP).
[35] ibid.
[36] See, eg, *Cussons v Skinner* (1843) 11 M&W 161 (CE).
[37] See, eg, *Edwards v Levy* (1860) 2 F&F 94 (CE).
[38] [1959] 1 WLR 698 (CA).
[39] ibid 700.
[40] ibid 701.
[41] See, eg, Adams and others (n 3) 330–32 (and the authorities cited therein).

Australian employees now also owe what is effectively the same duty to obey their employer's lawful and reasonable instructions,[42] with Dixon J first articulating the duty in the Australian context during 1938, finding that 'the lawful commands of an employer which an employee must obey are those which fall within the scope of the contract of service and are reasonable'.[43]

Despite this continued recognition across both jurisdictions, there exists no judicial explanation as to how the duty has come to be recognised as one that ought to be routinely implied by law in either jurisdiction, extending itself beyond a norm from the earlier master and servant regime. This result lacks due consideration of the necessity test for implying a term by law. It has simply been presumed that the duty's necessity is, without question, a part of all contemporary employment.

What the above discussion makes clear is that a duty to obey lawful and reasonable instructions originated when employment was understood as a status-based relationship between master and servant. This element of control of the employee has been said to be one of the 'defining features'[44] of modern employment, as distinct from other performance of work.

On the surface, its potential to become an equivalent duty owed by independent contractors and workers in respect of those who engage them seems implausible, if not contrary to what is intended in the creation of a contract for the performance of work. Until very recently, it has been routinely articulated in case law that rather than being required to obey lawful and reasonable instructions of a principal, host, or hirer, a worker or independent contractor attracts a much greater level of control over the work they perform, their hours, the location at which they work, and how they perform their work.[45]

However, that is not to say that, at least in English law, the duty does not have the potential to operate in respect of limb (b) workers. The United Kingdom Supreme Court, in *Uber BV v Aslam*,[46] was at pains to suggest that even though drivers who were classified as limb (b) workers and had been performing work for Uber in London were free to choose when and where they worked, they were still subject to direction and control by Uber in the performance of their work in five key ways.[47]

---

[42] See, eg, *McManus v Scott-Charlton* (1996) 70 FCR 16 (FCA).
[43] *Darling Island Stevedoring & Lighterage Co Ltd; Ex parte Halliday and Sullivan* (1938) 60 CLR 601 (HCA) 621–22.
[44] *Russell v Trustees of the Roman Catholic Church, Archdiocese of Sydney* (2007) 69 NSWLR 198 (New South Wales Court of Appeal (NSWCA)) [91]–[94] (Rothman J). Cf N Countouris and V De Stefano, 'The Future Concept of Work' in K Arabadjieva and others (eds), *Transformative Ideas—Ensuring a Just Share of Progress for All* (European Trade Union Institute 2023) 93, where the authors argue that subordination, embedded in work arrangements by the law and originated in its current form at the outset of industrialisation, is incompatible with modern polities based on the rule of law. They say that the justification for this subordination is often claimed to be in contract law (as it applies to employment) but does not explain the extent and intensity of employers' power over employees.
[45] Adams and others (n 3) 124–26.
[46] [2021] ICR 657 (Supreme Court of the United Kingdom (UKSC)).
[47] ibid [93]–[100].

First, Uber fixed their remuneration, and the drivers had no say in it. Secondly, Uber dictated their contractual terms in a standard form. Thirdly, a driver's choice about whether to accept requests for rides was constrained by Uber. Fourthly, Uber exercised a significant degree of control over the way in which drivers deliver their services. Fifthly, Uber restricted communication between passenger and driver to the minimum necessary to perform a particular trip and took steps to prevent drivers from establishing any relationship with a passenger capable of extending beyond an individual ride.

Taking all of these factors into account, the inference that can be drawn, at least for limb (b) workers, is that a duty to obey lawful and reasonable instructions of their employer has the potential to operate in respect of the work they perform. While at one stage, contractual autonomy and control may have been at the heart of all non-standard contracts for work, that notion is fast becoming eroded. Given the duty's potential broader operation, the distinction between non-standard work and employment is becoming increasingly nebulous.

B. Duty of Fidelity

The law regarding an employee's duty of fidelity originated in a blend of statute, equity,[48] and contract.[49] In order to remain within the bounds of this work, this section focuses on the duty's operation in the law of contract. The terminology of 'duty of fidelity' was first used in a contractual setting in the 1895 English decision, *Robb v Green*.[50] At that point, however, the duty was applicable in the context of a relationship between a master and servant, not employer and employee. The case involved a servant who had transcribed a customer list from his master and, upon leaving that role, proceeded to use those details to entice the same customers towards his rival business. The former master later succeeded in seeking damages against the former servant for breach of an implied duty of fidelity.

It was not until much later, in the 1946 decision of *Hivac Ltd v Park Royal Scientific Instruments Ltd*,[51] that Lord Greene first articulated the duty of fidelity owed by an employee as a contractual term implied by law to their employer. *Hivac v Park Royal* concerned a group of skilled manual workers who had begun in secret to work for a competitor of their original employer. There was nothing to suggest that the group of employees had used any of their original employer's confidential information, or that they had profited from having done so. Their original employer's case questioned whether the employees had, in fact, breached a

---

[48] The earliest indication was in *Pearce v Foster* (1886) 17 QBD 536 (CA) 539.
[49] See generally, M Irving, *The Contract of Employment* (2nd edn, LexisNexis Butterworths 2019) 516–17. Cf R Flannigan, 'The (Fiduciary) Duty of Fidelity' (2008) 124 LQR 274.
[50] [1895] 2 QB 315 (CA).
[51] [1946] All ER 350 (CA).

purported implied duty of fidelity that was said to exist in their employment contracts. A duty of fidelity was ultimately implied, but a breach of that duty was said not to have been made out on the facts of the case.

Yet, it was inconclusive from the judgment delivered as to whether the duty was to be considered one implied in fact or by law.[52] Despite labelling the duty as one to be implied by law into all employment contracts, the court's reasoning suggested that it 'must be a question on the facts of each particular case', making it appear applicable only in respect of the particular contract before the court (ie as a term implied in fact).[53] Nevertheless, the duty has now become one regularly implied by law into English employment contracts, with its necessity in those agreements seemingly presumed, despite the duty's origins.

Just as in England, in Australia, a duty of fidelity is routinely implied by law into all employment contracts.[54] That said, Australian law governing the implied term is vexed, with the contractually implied duty understood as substantially similar to the fiduciary relationship that exists between an agent and principal.[55] Just as in England, when the duty was first recognised in Australia, in *Blyth Chemicals Ltd v Bushnell*,[56] it was not as a contractually implied term by law, but rather an overarching duty owed by all employees as fiduciaries.[57] Even though Dixon and McTiernan JJ in *Blyth Chemicals v Bushnell* utilised the language of conflict of interest, which typically lends itself towards a fiduciary relationship, the case turned on whether the relevant employee's dismissal was in breach of contract. It was only later, in *Concut Pty Ltd v Worrell*,[58] that the duty was truly recognised as a term implied by law into all Australian employment contracts.

Subsequent decisions have typically recognised the duty of fidelity as a contractual one that gives rise to equitable obligations, or even one that is purely contractual, but is still identical to a fiduciary duty.[59] The contractually implied duty of fidelity is also comingled with other well-established duties. In that sense, actions amounting to an employee's breach of the duties of cooperation, or not to misuse or disclose confidential information, may similarly be considered acts of disloyalty, amounting to a concurrent breach of the duty of fidelity.

Despite these crossovers in England and Australia, the contractual duty of fidelity is now understood as a unique type of loyalty. It is typically associated with acts of competition against the employer.[60] Again, when understood as a term

---

[52] ibid 174.
[53] ibid.
[54] See, eg, *Concut v Worrell* (2000) 103 IR 160 (HCA) [25]–[26] and [57].
[55] See, eg, *Hospital Products Ltd v United States Surgical Corp* (1984) 156 CLR 41 (HCA), 68–69 and 141.
[56] (1933) 49 CLR 66 (HCA).
[57] ibid 81–82.
[58] See n 54 [57].
[59] See, eg, *Blackmagic Design Pty Ltd v Overliese* (2011) 191 FCR 1 (FCAFC) [118].
[60] Where work is conducted for a competing employer, the duty is more likely to be breached where the employee is more senior or skilled: *Hivac v Park Royal* (n 51). It has been said that there is

implied by law into all contracts of employment, the duty of fidelity is routinely viewed as entirely necessary in that context, without questions as to its origins (in particular, where it was once understood more as a term implied in fact).

The applicability of a duty of fidelity, which also began during the former master and servant regime, to contracts for the performance of work is presently subject to an imprecise legal position. Given the duty's relatively narrow focus, as previously described, on the one hand, the courts could understandably be dismissive of the position that this common law implied term could apply more broadly to such relationships.[61] In that sense, such a duty now plainly serves to protect employers who have discovered that their employee is working for a competitor. Applying the same duty to a worker or independent contractor, however, appears less compelling and carries less weight for the reason that they typically are able to perform work for others.

On the other hand, in *Tullet Prebon plc v BGC Brokers LP*[62] Kay LJ of the English Court of Appeal held that a common law implied duty of fidelity in an employment contract would apply to impose the same obligation on non-employees who had signed a 'pre-employment forward agreement', committing themselves to future employment with their principal, host, or hirer. The Court of Appeal held that such an agreement was 'more akin to an employment contract than to a purely commercial agreement'.[63] Therefore, the implied term was recognised in the context of certain contracts for the performance of work (ie where workers were set to become employees at some point in the future), since they were 'more akin to employment'.[64]

It is therefore plausible (though not entirely certain) that a duty of fidelity could be implied into certain discrete contracts for the performance of work; most obviously, only in those contracts where the workers are ultimately destined for employment in any event. The reasons for this understanding are twofold: first, courts could continue to adopt the 'akin to employment' test from *Tullet Prebon v BGC Brokers*. Secondly, the courts will likely view the duty of fidelity as one that is less open-textured and more narrowly defined than other duties (eg the mutual trust and confidence implied term, the application of which to contracts for the

---

no implied duty that an employee report their own misconduct to their employer: in Australia, see, eg, *Official Trustee in Bankruptcy v Concut Pty Ltd* (1999) 45 AILR ¶9-146 (Australian Industrial Relations Commission (AIRC)), though some doubt has been cast over that view (*Concut v Worrell* (n 54)); in England, see, eg, *The Basildon Academies v Amadi* (UKEAT/0342/14/RN, 27 February 2015) (Employment Appeals Tribunal (EAT)) [20]-[21] (Mitting J).

[61] See, eg, Cabrelli and D'Alton (n 5).
[62] [2011] IRLR 420 (CA).
[63] ibid [45].
[64] In English law, this same 'akin to employment' test has been utilised in tort law to determine whether an employer will be held vicariously liable for the negligence of its non-employees: see, eg, *Various Claimants v Institute of the Brothers of the Christian Schools* [2013] 2 AC 1 (UKSC); *Cox v Ministry of Justice* [2016] AC 660 (UKSC).

performance of work is examined in Chapter 4). Perhaps the most accurate description of the potential (but still uncertain) application of a duty of fidelity to contracts for the performance of work was articulated by Mark Freedland, who wrote that: '[Independent contractors and workers may] be subject to some implied obligations of fidelity, [but] they would in general be less exacting than those of employees with contracts of employment'.[65]

C. Duty to Exercise Reasonable Care and Skill

When it first commenced in operation, only superior servants, or workers skilled in an art, owed a duty to exercise reasonable care and skill. It was not owed by menial servants.[66] The case of *Harmer v Cornelius*[67] contained what is thought to be the first reference to the duty. The case involved a master who had engaged two painters to paint a set for a play for a fixed term. However, the master neglected to assess properly whether the workers possessed the requisite skills to complete the painting well. It transpired that they did not. Therefore, the master attempted to escape the contract he had formed with them. He was successful in asking the court to recognise that there was a general duty owed by superior servants that they 'possess the requisite ability and skill' in relation to the task they had undertaken to perform.[68] Without that requisite ability and skill, they could be summarily dismissed.

Despite this duty being articulated as 'impliedly' owed by the superior servants, at the time the case was decided, the notion of a term implied by law had not yet been developed. That understanding, along with the distinction between implying terms by law and in fact, only occurred much later.[69] The understanding of employment comprising a contractual relationship was in its very early stages. As such, despite the word 'impliedly' being used, the duty seems to have originated as a norm in the relationship between masters and superior servants. It did not commence as a term implied by law into all employment contracts.

Even so, many years later, in *Lister v Romford Ice*, the House of Lords referred to *Harmer v Cornelius* in support of a contractual duty owed by an employee to exercise reasonable care and skill in the tasks they perform.[70] Respectfully, this rationale merely presumed the duty's existence, despite its origins in the master and servant regime. Just as with those terms discussed earlier in this section, it

---

[65] Freedland (n 4) 177.
[66] See, eg, W Blackstone, *Commentaries on the Laws of England* (13th edn, Dublin 1796) 164–65.
[67] (1858) 5 CB (NS) 236 (CCP).
[68] ibid.
[69] See also G Golding, 'Terms Implied by Law into Employment Contracts: Are They Necessary?' (2015) 28 AJLL 113.
[70] *Lister v Romford Ice* (n 10) 587.

disregards the term's current necessity across all employment contracts. Its necessity in modern employment has simply been presumed to be present.

In Australia, just as in England, employees now owe a contractually implied duty to exercise reasonable care and skill in the tasks they perform.[71] This duty is typically phrased as one implied by law, notwithstanding its commencement during the master and servant regime. As before, this slant neglects consideration of the duty's necessity in modern employment contexts.[72] Nowadays, its necessity could well be challenged. For example, it has no operation where an employer deliberately directs an employee to engage in work for which they do not possess the requisite expertise.[73] In such a context, if the implied duty's necessity were considered more fully in the context of all employment, then perhaps the outcome would be different.

In its existing form, a duty to exercise reasonable care and skill may translate logically to contracts for the performance of work. It is possible that without such an implied obligation contracts for the performance of work could effectively become unworkable. Thinking back to the duty's inception in *Harmer v Cornelius*, for example, it would remain illogical for a principal, host, or hirer to engage a worker or independent contractor to paint a scene if they did not possess the requisite skill to do so. Having said that, as is apparent in Chapter 6 in respect of employment contracts, the duty's existence is contingent on the work being performed actually attracting particular skill and care. In addition, under applicable work health and safety legislation in both England and Australia, workers already owe a statutory duty to take care of their own health and safety, as well as that of others who may be affected by their actions at work. Therefore, the duty's existence in instances of non-employment remains tenuous in the sense that statute may already cover the field.

D. Duty to Hold Inventions on Trust

Ownership of inventions was first founded in England as a consequence of the fiduciary relationship that was said to exist between employers and their senior employees. Taking one of the earliest examples, in *Worthington Pumping Engine Co v Moore*,[74] the company's managing director was found to hold his invention on trust for the company. In *British Syphon Co Ltd v Homewood*,[75] the same rationale applied in respect of a senior researcher. An alternative approach in *Triplex Safety*

---

[71] See, eg, *X v The Commonwealth* (1999) 200 CLR 177 (HCA) [31].
[72] ibid, where it was said that the duty is an 'implied warranty' and an 'inherent requirement' of 'every employment'.
[73] *Printing Industry Employees Union of Australia v Jackson and O'Sullivan* (1957) 1 FLR 175 (FCA), 177–78.
[74] (1902) 20 RPC 41 (Ch Div), 48–49.
[75] [1956] 2 All ER 897 (Ch Div).

Glass v Scorah[76] concerned whether an employment contract required that an employee owe a duty to invent. If such a requirement were contractual, then the employee would effectively hold on trust for their employer an invention made during the course of their employment.

Some years later, in *Sterling Engineering Company Limited v Patchett*,[77] a term became implied into every employment contract by law that an invention or discovery made during the course of employment and with the requisite connection to employment is the employer's property, not the employee's. Again, the employee effectively holds such an invention on trust for their employer. This outcome occurred despite the term being based on the fiduciary relationship between an employer and senior employee. The duty became supplanted into all employment contracts as a term implied by law, notwithstanding that originating factor. That said, from 1977, the implied term has become superfluous at common law. Now the *Patents Act 1977* (UK) contains a statutory test to ascertain whether an employee owns an invention, effectively negating any need for the implied term.[78]

However, the same statutory test does not exist in Australia. Until 2009, because of a term implied by law, employees were required to hold *any* invention created during the course of their employment on trust for their employer.[79] Just as with the duty's English beginnings, the decisive factor was once whether the employee had been contractually engaged to develop such an invention. However, the duty's scope has been dramatically curtailed since the Full Federal Court's decision in *University of Western Australia v Gray*,[80] such that it will now only operate in situations where an employee owes a duty to invent. If that is the case, then the employer will own the invention. The fact that an employee may invent will be insufficient to invoke the duty's operation.[81] The Full Court's decision in *University of Western Australia v Gray* is returned to in Chapter 6 in the context of a more detailed discussion on the necessity required for implying a term by law.

Notwithstanding *University of Western Australia v Gray*, where the duty to hold inventions on trust was confined to instances where employees owed a duty to invent, the potential to be implied by law in such situations, despite its beginnings as a fiduciary duty, is retained. Just as with other terms implied by law into employment contracts, the duty is now implied by law in the context of employment, despite originating in another context, absent meaningful consideration as to why.

An implied duty to hold inventions on trust has no application beyond employment in the context of contracts for the performance of work. It finds itself exclusive

---

[76] (1937) 55 RPC 221 (Ch Div).
[77] [1955] AC 534 (HL), 544, 547.
[78] See, eg, *Patents Act 1977* (UK) s 39(1)(a). See also *Copyright, Designs and Patents Act 1988* (UK) s 11.
[79] See, eg, *Victoria University of Technology v Wilson* [2004] VSC 33 (Supreme Court of Victoria (VSC)) [104].
[80] (2009) 179 FCR 346 (FCAFC) [152] (and the authorities cited therein).
[81] ibid [194], [206].

to discrete instances of employment. As mentioned, since 1977 in England, the implied term has been supplanted by an equivalent statutory duty under s 39(1) of the *Patents Act 1977* (UK). That provision effectively determines whether an invention belongs to an employee. It is limited to instances of employment alone. In Australia, the term still operates as one implied by law into a narrow class of employment contracts only; it crystallises only where an employee is deemed to have a duty to invent under their employment contract. Given this limited operation in a narrow sub-class of employment contracts that contain a duty to invent owed by employees, it is difficult to see how this duty could function in parallel across contracts for the performance of work. The duty's genesis resides in the fact that the contract is one of employment in which there is a specific duty owed by an employee to invent.

E. Duty Not to Misuse or Disclose Confidential Information

The law 'recognises three different ways in which … [an employee's implied duty not to misuse or disclose confidential information] obligation … might arise. The first is by express provision in a contract. The second is by an implied term in a contract. The third is as an obligation recognised in the exclusive jurisdiction of equity'.[82] Section 183 of the *Corporations Act 2001* (Cth) also provides that in Australia, where an employee is engaged by a corporation, a statutory duty of confidence exists.

Given this work's scope, the discussion here concentrates on a contractually implied duty not to misuse or disclose confidential information. Indeed, the duty's contractual and equitable scope is effectively 'the same in both cases "despite their different conceptual origins"'.[83] Case law now tends to acknowledge the duties' coexistence. However, as discussed briefly here, that understanding is not universal.

In England, a duty not to misuse or disclose confidential information emerged in the 1890s. The Court of Appeal began to find that fiduciary duties would need to be transplanted into contracts between employers and superior servants by virtue of implied terms.[84] The level of protection for those engaged in particular trade activities also increased following the repeal of the *Master and Servant Acts*.[85]

One of the first recognitions of the duty was in the 1892 decision, *Merryweather & Sons v Master*.[86] In that decision it was held that a draftsman needed to adhere

---

[82] *AG Australia Holdings Ltd v Burton* [2002] NSWSC 170 (Supreme Court of New South Wales (NSWSC)) [73]–[74].
[83] *University of Western Australia v Gray* (n 80) [161].
[84] See, eg, *Merryweather & Sons v Master* [1892] 2 Ch 518 (CA); *Lamb v Evans* [1893] 1 Ch 218 (CA); *Robb v Green* (n 50).
[85] See, eg, Cornish, 'Law and Organised Labour' (n 32) part III, 667.
[86] *Merryweather & Sons v Master* (n 84).

to the 'confidential relation' not to record the details of his former employer's engine design with a view to using that design in his new employment. At this early stage, Lord Kekewich held that 'the confidence postulates in an implied contract', which 'calls into exercise the [court's] jurisdiction'.[87] At this moment, the duty did not come into operation as a term implied by law, primarily because that notion of implication had not yet begun. However, the court's reasoning provided for an initial assumption that the notion of confidence was meant to mould the terms of an employment contract, even if it was not referred to in that way.

Another relevant early decision is *Lamb v Evans*.[88] In this case, the plaintiff published 'The International Guide to British and Foreign Merchants and Manufacturers', which comprised a collection of traders' advertisements. While working for the plaintiff, the defendant brothers' role was to prepare the advertisement for traders. Once they had finished working with the plaintiff, the defendant brothers had kept a variety of materials that they had used during their employment with the plaintiff, including notes of traders' details. Among other things, the plaintiff then made a claim for breach of contract,[89] which was successful at first instance before Lord Chitty.[90]

The defendant brothers then appealed. In their final judgment, Lords Bowen, Lindley, and Kay referred to the existence of an 'implied term' of confidence in the contract,[91] or a more general obligation of 'good faith', which 'underlies the whole of an agent's obligation to his principal',[92] or a 'confidential relation'.[93] Significantly, the court's decision related to a duty of confidence existing between an agent and principal, as opposed to between a superior servant and their employer.

In both England and Australia, following *Lamb v Evans*, an employee's duty not to misuse or disclose confidential information has been recognised both in contract and equity. In Australia, the Full Federal Court in *University of Western Australia v Gray* suggested that the duties are the same in scope.[94] However, the ability for these duties to co-exist remains 'a matter on which differing views have been expressed'.[95] Despite these challenges as to recognition, the duty has remained phrased, across both jurisdictions, as one requiring an employee 'not to divulge confidential information or to use it in a way that could be detrimental to the employer'[96] without the consent of, or against the wishes of, the employer.[97]

---

[87] ibid 522.
[88] *Lamb v Evans* (n 84).
[89] [1892] 3 Ch 462 (Ch Div), 464–65.
[90] ibid.
[91] *Lamb v Evans* (n 84) 213.
[92] ibid 226.
[93] ibid 235.
[94] *University of Western Australia v Gray* (n 80) [161].
[95] A Stewart and others, *Intellectual Property in Australia* (6th edn, LexisNexis Butterworths 2014) 88.
[96] *Del Casale v Artedomus (Aust) Pty Ltd* (2007) 165 IR 148 (NSWCA)) [32].
[97] *Attorney-General v Guardian Newspapers Ltd (No 2)* [1990] 1 AC 109 (HL). This duty may still be binding on an employee even when an employment relationship has ended.

Just as with the terms now implied by law already mentioned, a duty of confidence has become implied as a term by law into all employment contracts, despite its origins in other areas of the law. Like others, the duty commenced as a fiduciary duty in contracts of superior servants and their employers, as well as in contracts between workers who were classified as 'agents' and their 'principals'. Only more recently has the duty come to be understood as necessary to be implied by law into all employment contracts, absent justification for why they should now operate in that framework.

Turning now to the potential recognition of a duty not to misuse or disclose confidential information in contracts for the performance of work. As mentioned, the duty was first derived in England in the context of workers (classified as agents) and their principals. Over time, it became supplanted into employment contracts in both England and Australia. From its very beginnings, the duty has had the scope to apply beyond employment. It carries that same capacity today, with the duty recognised as a contractually implied term and an equitable duty. There is no reason to suggest that it now ought to become exclusive to employment alone. To do so would ignore its origins. Moreover, in the practical context of the performance of atypical work, it seems logical for principals, hosts, and hirers to be protected from having their confidential information misused or disclosed by those performing work for them. In that sense, the duty should retain the capacity to operate equivalently across contracts of employment and for the performance of work. However, as becomes apparent in Chapter 6, it remains to be seen whether the duty's concurrent existence in equity might have the effect of negating its necessity as a contractual term implied by law.

Mutual Duties Owed by Employers and Employees

Having examined the duties owed separately by employers and employees, consideration now turns to two routinely recognised duties owed mutually by both employers and employees, these being the duty of both parties to: (A) cooperate; and (B) provide reasonable notice on termination, other than for breach or where the contract contains an express term which prescribes the requisite notice period. It is acknowledged that both the duties of mutual trust and confidence and good faith may fall into the same categories as mutual duties implied by law. However, given their significance, they are considered in a separate and dedicated discussion in Chapter 4.

It is unsurprising that just as with duties owed separately by employers and employees, the duties considered here that are owed mutually also originate from an area of law that is not composite with employment. The duty of cooperation originated as a term applied generally across all contracts, arising out of a decision about a supply contract. The duty to terminate an employment contract on reasonable notice began as a norm of employment after indefinite (as opposed to yearly) hiring grew in popularity. Notwithstanding these beginnings, both terms are routinely implied by law into all employment contracts—but, as the following discussion explains, there is continuing controversy as to the necessity of a reasonable notice term in Australia, with the duty's necessity in England being mostly circumvented by the operation of statute.

When considering the potential application of these mutually owed duties in contracts for the performance of work, it is reconciled that they both have the potential to be implied similarly in that realm. At this point, it is worth noting that for most terms implied by law into employment contracts, many have the potential for dual application in contracts for the performance of work, making employment seem less unique than might otherwise appear—a sentiment that is revisited in this chapter's conclusion.

A. Duty of Cooperation

The 1881 decision of *Mackay v Dick*[98] first established a duty to cooperate in the context of a supply contract. The court held that there was a duty owed by parties in all contracts to do 'all that is necessary to be done ... for the carrying out of [what the parties had agreed was needed to be done in the contract between them]'.[99] By not permitting Mackay to complete the work under the supply contract, Dick had breached this duty to cooperate. *Mackay v Dick* was later followed by the court in *Butt v M'Donald*,[100] wherein the duty was articulated further as a 'a general rule applicable to every contract that each party agrees, by implication, to do all such things as are necessary on his part to enable the other party to have the benefit of the contract'.[101]

A duty to cooperate has since been assumed to be a necessary incident in all employment contracts in both England[102] and Australia. It is almost impossible to imagine an employment contract (indeed, perhaps any kind of contract), which lacks a requirement that the parties must cooperate in the manner originally posed in *Mackay v Dick*. The very essence of contracting in the first place is contingent on the parties cooperating with one another. That said, just as with those duties already discussed in this chapter, the duty's necessity in employment has never been questioned, despite its emergence in the general law of contract. It too has been presumed to apply to all employment.

---

[98] (1881) 6 App Cas 251 (HL).
[99] ibid 263.
[100] (1896) 7 QLJ 68 (Full Court of the Supreme Court of Queensland (QSCFC)).
[101] ibid 70–71.
[102] Cf M Freedland, *The Personal Employment Contract* (OUP 2003) 146–51, which casts doubt over the existence of the implied duty to cooperate in English employment contracts.

The duty has since been expressed in several different ways.[103] Parties are sometimes understood as owing a duty to cooperate in the doing of acts necessary for the performance of their fundamental obligations under the contract.[104] Elsewhere the duty has been understood as a general rule applicable to every contract that each party agrees 'to do all such things as are necessary on his part to enable the other party to have the benefit of the contract'.[105] It has also been said to contain a negative obligation not to prevent the further performance of the contract.[106] The duty is important in governing those contracts containing a contingent condition (ie a condition requiring that a specific event occur before the parties must continue with the contract's performance).[107] Because of these various understandings of the duty's contemporary operation, understandably there have been questions raised as to how the duty ought to arise in all contracts, including employment contracts. For example, it has been queried whether the duty could operate as a rule of construction, rather than a term implied by law.[108] It is not this work's aim to answer whether that understanding is correct, but to highlight its potential.

Given that a duty to cooperate has now come to be routinely implied by law across all contracts since its inception in *Mackay v Dick*, so too will it be implied into contracts for the performance of work. In that sense, the duty is general in its application and not exclusive to any particular class or category of contract. Its general application to every contract clearly encompasses contracts for the performance of work. Without it, there would essentially be no point in the parties contracting in the first place. To cooperate is at the core of all contracting. Therefore, a duty of cooperation is owed mutually between parties to contracts for the performance of work, as with all other contracts.

B. Duty to Provide Reasonable Notice on Termination

When the master and servant regime was still in operation, English courts would enforce contracts of an indefinite duration. This approach effectively prevented servants from giving notice, making their engagement by their master akin to one of slavery.[109] Servants in agriculture attracted a presumption of yearly hiring

---

[103] Irving (n 49) 719.
[104] See, eg, *Secured Income Real Estate (Australia) Ltd v St Martins Investments Pty Ltd* (1979) 144 CLR 596 (HCA) 607–08.
[105] *Butt v M'Donald* (n 100) 70–71.
[106] See, eg, *Secretary of State for Employment v ASLEF (No 2)* [1972] 2 WLR 1370 (CA).
[107] See, eg, *McMahon v National Foods Milk Ltd* (2009) 25 VR 251 (Victorian Court of Appeal (VCA)) [13].
[108] On the relationship between implication and construction, see, eg, J Carter and others, 'Terms Implied in Law: "Trust and Confidence" in the High Court of Australia' (2015) 32 JCL 203, 208; P O'Grady QC, 'Nothing Implied: Construction as a Means of Curbing the Excessive Use of Power in Employment Contracts' (2017) 30 AJLL 137.
[109] See, eg, *Wallis v Day* (1837) M&W 273 (CE); *Ball v Coggs* (1710) 1 Brown PC 140 (Court of King's Bench (KB)).

during the industrial revolution[110] by virtue of the *Statute of Artificers* of 1562 and the seventeenth-century's *Poor Laws*. This statutory presumption ultimately transitioned to become a presumption at common law.[111] The English Court of Appeal eventually removed the presumption of yearly hiring in 1969,[112] despite it falling into disuse during the nineteenth century in any event once indefinite hiring had become common.

In response to this new-found trend of indefinite hiring, the modern termination on notice rule emerged. The year 1844 saw the earliest recognition of that rule in *Baxter v Nurse*.[113] At that early stage, it was not understood as a contractual obligation. However, it was understood as a contractual obligation by the early twentieth century.[114] As the duty was emerging, the termination of an indefinite contract on reasonable notice was typically understood as a 'norm' of employment. What was considered reasonable usually concerned the period during which a worker's salary or wage was calculated or was dependent on the particular trade in which they worked. For example, an employee who received a weekly wage may have, for that very reason, been entitled to receive a week's notice of termination.[115] A month's notice tended to be customary for domestic servants. For professional or managerial employees, minimum notice periods tended to range from one month to one year, however a year's notice was much less common.[116]

In current English employment law, minimum notice periods are now a part of all employment contracts, whereby employees have continuity of service for at least one month, given the operation of s 86 of the *Employment Rights Act 1996* (UK).[117] An employee becomes entitled to a minimum of one week's notice of dismissal after one month's continuous service. This period rises to two weeks after two years' continuous service, increasing for every additional year of continuous employment, reaching a total of twelve weeks' minimum notice.[118] In contrast, an employee must provide their employer with at least one week's notice after one months' continuous employment.[119]

---

[110] See, eg, S Churches, 'The Presumption of Yearly Term in a General Contract of Employment and the Plight of the Modern Manager, or the Black Death and the Malady Lingers On' (1979) 10 Univ of QLJ 195, 201–06.

[111] Yearly hiring was abolished by the *Poor Law Amendment Act 1834* (UK) s 64 and the provisions of the *Statute of Artificers 1563*, which required that yearly hiring in agriculture be repealed in 1875.

[112] See, eg, *Richardson v Koefod* [1969] 3 All ER 1264 (Ch Div), 1266.

[113] (1844) 6 Man&G 935 (CCP).

[114] See the earliest reference to the reasonable notice term as a 'rule' applicable to every employment contract in *Richardson v Koefod* (n 112) 1266.

[115] See, eg, *Baxter v Nurse* (n 113) 935.

[116] See generally, S Jacoby, 'The Duration of Indefinite Employment Contracts in the United States and England: An Historical Analysis' (1982) 5 Comp Labour Law 85.

[117] This provision does not prevent the parties from agreeing to longer notice periods, waiving their right to notice, or accepting pay in lieu: *Employment Rights Act 1996* (UK) s 86(3).

[118] *Employment Rights Act 1996* (UK) s 86(1).

[119] ibid s 86(2).

It has been suggested that this statutory provision removes the necessity for an implied term of reasonable notice, effectively 'codifying' the common law.[120] However, there does not seem to be any English authority in support of that view. Statutory minimum notice provisions surely cannot feasibly be deemed to have supplanted the reasonable notice rule at common law in situations where the common law notice period exceeds the statutory minimum. For example, a senior executive would typically fall under such an exception. Put another way, 'the common law rule is restricted to contracts of employment of an indefinite period'.[121]

The need to consider common law reasonable notice requirements are now rare in England, given the operation of s 1(4)(e) of the *Employment Rights Act 1996* (UK).[122] That statutory direction requires that an employer give an employee written particulars of any notice period at the commencement of their employment. Essentially, an employer must set out an express term in any written employment contract governing the employee's notice period. This statutory notice provision is not applicable to employment contracts made in relation to the performance of a specific task that is not expected to last longer than three months, unless the employee has been continuously employed for a period greater than three months.[123] As such, there are few instances in which the common law reasonable notice term actually has scope to operate in England. The limited instance in which such an implication could occur is typically restricted to situations where the contract's terms are silent as to any notice period and the common law reasonable notice period exceeds the statutory minimum.

With regards to the Australian position, if an employment contract is formed for an indefinite period (whether that be expressly agreed by the parties, or by them fixing no end), the position at common law is like that in England. In other words, the contract can be terminated by either party on the provision of reasonable notice to the other. If the parties do not outline the circumstances in which the contract can be terminated expressly, or if there is no binding provision under statute, Modern Award, enterprise agreement, or other instrument governing their relationship, a term will be implied by law such that the contract is terminable by either party on providing reasonable notice to the other.[124]

Just as in England, statutory provisions that outline required periods of minimum notice exist in Australia. Section 117 of the *Fair Work Act 2009* (Cth) provides that all employees (save for a few exceptions)[125] must be provided with a

[120] See, eg, R Arnow-Richman, 'Mainstreaming Employment Contract Law: The Common Law Case for Reasonable Notice of Termination' (2015) 66 Fla LR 1513, 1529.
[121] D Cabrelli, *Employment Law in Context: Text and Materials* (4th edn, OUP 2020) 588.
[122] ibid 589.
[123] *Employment Rights Act 1996* (UK) s 86(5). The statutory requirements apply to employees who have been continuously employed for three months or more under a fixed-term contract of one month or less.
[124] See, eg, *Byrne v Australian Airlines Ltd* (1995) 185 CLR 410 (HCA), 429.
[125] See, eg, *Fair Work Act 2009* (Cth) s 123.

minimum notice period in writing, or pay in lieu of notice. If applicable, Modern Awards and enterprise agreements may also set out particular requirements regarding the applicable minimum notice period.[126] That said, Modern Awards only regulate the provision of notice of termination of employment by employees. They do not do so in respect of employers.[127] Section 117 mirrors an equivalent legislative provision that has been in operation since 1993.[128] Yet, despite that statutory coverage, the common law implied duty compelling the provision of reasonable notice has been mentioned repeatedly in case law.[129]

It was therefore controversial that the South Australian District Court in *Kuczmarski v Ascot Administration Pty Ltd* found that there was no 'necessity' for an implied term requiring reasonable notice on termination where s 117 is operable.[130] According to Auxiliary Judge Clayton, there remains 'no relevant "gap to fill" in light of s 117'.[131] This statement was made despite the wealth of existing authority in support of the implied term, which included a comment made in *Commonwealth Bank of Australia v Barker* by the High Court.[132]

The effect of *Kuczmarski v Ascot Administration* is to suggest that, over an extended period, courts—including the High Court in *Commonwealth Bank v Barker*—have repeatedly been making incorrect decisions regarding the reasonable notice term's existence as one implied by law. It is nonsensical for an intermediate state court to suggest now that all those earlier authorities are incorrect. Perhaps the District Court was relying on the High Court's sentiment in *Commonwealth Bank v Barker* regarding the implication of certain terms by law into employment contracts; that it was a matter better left to the legislature.[133] However, its reasoning did not reflect that position. The District Court instead suggested that the term was unnecessary, given the existence of s 117.

It is important to note that if the reasoning in *Kuczmarski v Ascot Administration* were adopted more widely, other long-standing terms implied by law may be deemed unnecessary. Taking just one example, an employer's duty to provide employees with a safe place of work (another well-established implied term, also referred to as such in *Commonwealth Bank v Barker*)[134] could be 'displaced' by the supposedly equivalent statutory provisions under the state and federal *Work Health and Safety Acts*.[135] Such an outcome would likewise contradict well-established

---

[126] *Fair Work Act 2009* (Cth) s 118.
[127] See, eg, Stewart and others (n 3) 741.
[128] See, eg, *Industrial Relations Reform Act 1993* (Cth) s 170DB.
[129] See, eg, the numerous examples given in M Irving, 'Australian and Canadian Approaches to the Assessment of the Length of Reasonable Notice' (2015) 28 AJLL 159, 160.
[130] [2016] SADC 65 (District Court of South Australia (SADC)). See also *Pappas v P&R Electrical Pty Ltd* [2016] SADC 132 (SADC) [105].
[131] *Kuczmarski v Ascot Administration* (n 130) [56]–[57].
[132] (2014) 253 CLR 169 (HCA) [30].
[133] ibid [1], [19], [40].
[134] See, eg, *Commonwealth Bank v Barker* (n 132) [30].
[135] See, eg, *Work Health and Safety Act 2011* (Cth) s 19.

common law authorities, which have routinely supported the term's existence as one implied by law.

Another curious aspect of the decision in *Kuczmarski v Ascot Administration* is that the District Court relied on the earlier decision of the South Australian Supreme Court in *Brennan v Kangaroo Island Council*.[136] That case involved an award clause, which provided that an employee 'must be given notice of termination' according to a table set out under that particular clause. The Supreme Court held that given the clause's operation, the implication of a duty to provide reasonable notice on termination was not necessary to give 'business efficacy' to the contract.[137] As explained in Chapter 1, that is part of the test for implying a term in fact, rather than by law. It also seems contrary to existing High Court authority.[138] It must be acknowledged that 'an award notice provision generally does not confer a right to terminate the employment, but merely prescribes a minimum period of notice that must be given by the employer in the event that it exercises its contractual right to terminate the employment'.[139] The same logic applies in respect of s 117. That section concerns the quantum of notice, not any conferral of the actual right to terminate. Therefore, the South Australian District Court's finding in *Kuczmarski v Ascot Administration* that a reasonable notice term was unnecessary to imply as a term by law, based on the operation of s 117, appears misconceived.

The outcome in *Kuczmarksi v Ascot Administration* is also useful to consider alongside Buchanan J's *obiter dicta* comments in *Westpac Banking Corporation v Wittenberg*.[140] His Honour agreed with the outcome in *Brennan v Kangaroo Island Council*, also finding that award notice provisions operated similarly to s 117 by fixing minimum notice periods, and that this would prohibit any implication of a term requiring reasonable notice. Buchanan J's viewed such a provision as importing a right to terminate into all employment contracts on the provision of the requisite notice period. As his Honour reasoned, there is 'no gap to be filled by the implication' of the term by law.[141]

By way of contrast, in *McGowan v Direct Mail and Marketing Pty Ltd* the Federal Circuit Court of Australia (as it then was) disagreed wholeheartedly with the finding in *Kuczmarski v Ascot Administration*.[142] In that case, the applicant claimed that he was entitled to the provision of reasonable notice at common law by virtue

---

[136] (2013) 239 IR 355 (Full Court of the Supreme Court of South Australia (SASCFC)). Special leave to appeal to the High Court was refused: [2014] HCASL 153 (15 August 2014) (HCA). See also *District Council of Barunga West v Hand* (2014) 202 LGERA 415 (SASCFC) [57]-[62], which mentioned, but did not endorse, *Brennan v Kangaroo Island Council* (n 136).

[137] *Brennan v Kangaroo Island Council* (n 136) [34].

[138] See, eg, *Kilminister v Sun Newspapers Limited* (1931) 46 CLR 284 (HCA) 289.

[139] See, eg, *Queensland Meat Export Co Pty Ltd t/as Smorgon Meat Group v Hawkins* (unreported, Industrial Relations Court of Australia, Wilcox CJ, Spender and Moore JJ, 6 December 1996) (Industrial Relations Court of Australia (IRCA)).

[140] (2016) 256 IR 181 (FCAFC).

[141] ibid [234].

[142] [2016] FCCA 2227 (Federal Circuit Court of Australia (FCCA)).

of a term implied by law, not the minimum period from s 117. The court dismissed his claim after it found that a 1999 contract containing specific terms as to notice was still in force, despite being changed later. Therefore, the implication of a term requiring reasonable notice was unnecessary. Despite this outcome, Judge McNab acknowledged that a 'genuine controversy' continued to exist in relation to whether s 117 ousted the need for a term implied by law requiring reasonable notice.[143] Upon consideration of *Kuczmarski v Ascot Administration*, the court held that the 'better view' was that s 117 only sets out a minimum notice period.[144] Judge McNab explained that the statutory provision under s 117 does not displace the necessity for a common law implied term requiring reasonable notice in the absence of an express notice period in an employment contract for a non-award employee.[145] In the court's view, it was significant that the legislature had not made reference to s 117 removing the common law right to reasonable notice when the *Fair Work Bill 2008* (Cth) was introduced into parliament.[146]

The most recent Australian decision concerning the operation of a reasonable notice implied term is *Heldberg v Rand Transport (1986) Pty Ltd*.[147] Just as in *McGowan v Direct Mail and Marketing*, White J of the Federal Court of Australia disagreed (albeit in *obiter dicta*) that s 117 could be responsible for preventing the implication of the term. Despite providing several reasons for holding such a view, his Honour limited his discussion on the issue, suggesting that it was undesirable for the court to express a concluded view in the circumstances, given the importance of the issue.[148] Absent any further judicial clarity, it is now uncertain as to how any dispute regarding the provision of reasonable notice on termination will be resolved in a situation where there is no notice period set out in an employment contract.

It should be re-emphasised at this point that even if the implied term exists at common law, and s 117 does not circumvent its operation, its beginnings in master and servant law have been overlooked over the course of judicial decision-making. Across English and Australian law, the term has simply become viewed as necessary to be implied by law in the context of modern employment, but lacks meaningful justification as to precisely why that is now the case.

Attention now turns to the duty's potential operation in contracts for the performance of work. It must be acknowledged that some non-standard work agreements may involve a discrete exchange, such as a worker's one-off performance of a specified task of limited duration for a hirer in exchange for payment. However, just as with employment contracts, some arrangements may be agreed to operate

---

[143] ibid [79].
[144] ibid [85].
[145] ibid.
[146] ibid [84]–[85].
[147] [2018] FCA 1141 (FCA).
[148] ibid [95]–[106].

indefinitely. Others may operate for a fixed-term. If a contract for a fixed-term expires, the parties may agree to create a new contract. A new contract may also be inferred where the parties continue dealing with one another despite the expiration of a previous agreement and nothing being formally agreed between them. That new contract may not contain a fixed-term. It could still be terminated at any time, if the parties mutually consent, or if one of them breaches or repudiates in a way that is sufficient to give rise to a right of unilateral termination.

The alternative is for one party to exercise a right, implied as a term by law, to provide reasonable notice of termination to the other. Given that contracts for the performance of work are not typically the subject of statutory minimum notice periods in either jurisdiction, it would be logical for a mutually owed duty of reasonable notice on termination to operate in instances in which the parties stipulate no notice period in the contract between them. Without such an implied term, the contract for performance of work could be viewed as indefinite and incapable of being brought to an end, which would be counterintuitive to the purportedly more flexible nature of such work arrangements.[149]

Conclusion

This chapter engaged in an historical analysis of the key select terms that are routinely recognised in English and Australian employment contracts. It demonstrated that each of those terms originated in some form in English law. Most terms analysed did not commence as terms implied by law at all. That said, they are now understood to be incidents of the employment relationship in either jurisdiction, having been integrated into a contractual framework as terms implied by law.

It was discovered that an employer's duty to:

1. provide employees with a safe place of work began as a duty of care in tort;
2. indemnify employees against expenses reasonably incurred began as a fiduciary duty owed between a principal and agent during the former master and servant regime; and
3. inform employees of their rights was one of the rare duties that began as a term implied by law, but only in the context of a narrow category of employment contracts, resulting in it appearing more like a term implied in fact.

An employee's duty:

---

[149] See generally, D Gallagher, 'Independent Contracting: Finding a Balance Between Flexibility and Individual Well-being' in K Näswall, J Hellgren, and M Sverke (eds), *The Individual in the Changing Working Life* (CUP 2008) 108.

4. to obey lawful and reasonable instructions originated as a consequence of employment once being understood as a status-based relationship between master and servant;
5. of fidelity is derived from a fiduciary duty between a principal and agent during the former master and servant regime;
6. to exercise reasonable care and skill in the tasks performed began as a duty owed by superior servants during the master and servant regime;
7. to hold inventions on trust (where there is a duty to invent) began as part of a fiduciary relationship between senior employees and their employer; and
8. not to misuse or disclose confidential information originated as a fiduciary duty owed between a principal and agent, again, under the former master and servant regime.

The mutual duties on both parties to:

9. cooperate began as part of the general law of contract as a term implied by law, only later being transplanted to employment when the employment became understood as a contractual relationship; and
10. provide reasonable notice on termination transpired from the former master and servant regime when the presumption of yearly hiring that once applied to servants was eliminated, and indefinite hiring became commonplace.

Even though an employer's duty to inform employees of their rights originated as a contractual term implied by law, it did so only in relation to a very narrow sub-class of contract, leading to it seeming more like a term implied in fact, and with no potential application in the broader context of contracts for the performance of work. However, other key duties implied routinely into employment contracts by law both in England and Australia are derived from equity, tort, and the former master and servant regime (noting the continuing uncertainty regarding the reasonable notice implied term's existence in Australia). No key duties originated solely as terms implied by law. However, there has been no logical explanation for this, other than that the courts have simply come to accept each as a 'norm' and so much a part of employment that they ought to operate across every employment contract as a term implied by law.

Each of the select key terms and their potential implication by law in the broader realm of contracts for the performance of work were also considered. It was accepted that if any of the select key terms already implied by law into employment contracts were to have similar operation across contracts for the performance of work, then their historical origins must be the same; only the current contractual context would change. Through that discussion it came to light that certain key terms implied by law into employment contracts could not necessarily be said to be exclusive to employment alone. They too have the potential to be implied into contracts for the performance of work, despite not having yet been formally recognised in case law as operating in that way.

Notably, a principal, host, or hirer:

1. would likely owe a duty to provide independent contractors or workers with a safe place of work because without such a duty, the contract may be unable to be performed at all, but as is examined later in Chapter 6, its necessity as a contractual term implied by law may be circumvented by concurrent tortious and statutory duties in England and Australia;
2. may owe a duty to indemnify independent contractors or workers for expenses innocently incurred during the performance of their duties, since it originated as a fiduciary duty in respect of a work relationship akin to an independent contractor or worker and, without it, it is difficult to see how work could feasibly continue to be performed. However, it must be mentioned that the duty seems only set to operate to the extent that expenses are actually incurred in the contract in question—a notion that is revisited in terms of the duty's necessity in Chapter 6; and
3. is unlikely to owe a duty to inform independent contractors or workers of their rights for the reason that such a duty is specific to a certain type of employment and only applicable in the case of a very narrow sub-class of employment contracts. A contract for the performance of work could likely continue seamlessly in operation absent such a duty.

An independent contractor or worker:

4. is unlikely to owe a duty to a principal, host, or hirer to obey lawful and reasonable instructions in the same manner as with employees. It is inherent in the very nature of their contractual relationship to retain far greater command and control over the way in which they perform work. To recognise such a duty in a non-standard working relationship would be directly contrary to the common understanding that such a duty resides at the defining core of what constitutes employment. Nevertheless, it must be acknowledged that the recent decision in *Uber BV v Aslam* in England has given rise to the possibility that the duty is, in fact, owed by those engaging limb (b) workers, thereby blurring the lines of distinction between that form of engagement and employment;
5. may owe a duty of fidelity to a principal, host, or hirer, but likely only in limited situations where the contractual arrangement is such that they are set to become employees at some point in the future;
6. may owe a duty to exercise reasonable care and skill since it appears necessary for the effective operation and function of the contract, but only to the extent that care and skill must actually be exercised in the performance of the

contract. Again, the duty's necessity will be revisited in Chapter 6, since its operation as an implied contractual term may be circumvented by an equivalent statutory duty in both England and Australia;

7. would likely not owe an implied duty to hold on trust inventions created during the course of their performance of work. Such a duty is typically exclusive to discrete instances of employment. As mentioned, in England the implied term has been supplanted by an equivalent statutory duty under s 39(1) of the *Patents Act 1977* (UK)—a provision dictating when an invention will belong to an employee. Despite the duty continuing to operate as one implied by law into Australian employment contracts, it only operates in circumstances where an employee has a duty to invent under their employment contract, making it limited to a narrow sub-class of employment contracts. It appears to have no broader application in contracts for the performance of work;

8. would likely owe a duty not to misuse or disclose confidential information belonging to the principal, host, or hirer. Indeed, from its inception, the duty has applied beyond employment and has continued to be recognised as both a contractually implied term and an equitable duty. However, as is revisited in Chapter 6, doubt may be cast regarding the duty's necessity as a contractually implied term, given its concurrent existence in equity across both English and Australian law.

The mutual duty owed by both parties to contracts for the performance of work to:

9. cooperate would be clearly recognised in such contracts because since its beginning, it has been routinely implied by law across *all* contracts as a universally implied term applicable to all contracts. Without it, there would arguably be no point in the parties contracting in the first place; and

10. provide reasonable notice of termination where no express notice period exists in the contract between the parties should arguably apply to contracts for the performance of work. Unlike employment contracts, such contracts are generally not subject to statutory minimum notice periods, therefore generating a need for such a mutual duty to operate in circumstances in which no notice period is agreed between the parties. Without it, the contract for the performance of work would be indefinite in duration and effectively unable to be ended, which seems entirely contrary to the inherent flexibility that comes with such non-standard work arrangements.

Given the number of terms that could potentially be implied across both classes of contract as necessary incidents, the distinction between employment and the broader performance of work is certainly obscure and difficult to decipher. That said, this lack of distinction might prove beneficial in a protective sense, in that atypical workers engaged under contracts for the performance of work are more likely to suffer economic hardship, be low-paid, vulnerable, and engaged on insecure contracts, and belong to groups with protected characteristics.[150] These same traits are invariably the reason the duties are largely non-existent in case law concerning contracts for the performance of work; this cohort of workers typically lack the means to pursue the litigation necessary to support or refute their existence.

Matters are complicated by the fact that several terms that are routinely implied by law into employment contracts are seemingly broad enough in scope to allow their potential implication by law into contracts for the performance of work (acknowledging that case law is still to articulate that same understanding). This outcome is problematic in the level of uncertainty it creates in relation to attempts to rationalise the implication of terms by law as necessary incidents of certain classes of contracts. It distorts understandings as to what truly shapes the employment relationship, as distinct from other contracts for the performance of work, as well as what circumstances courts may, or may not, imply a new term by law in the context of employment alone. The discussion in Chapter 4 demonstrates similar uncertainties regarding the implied duties of good faith and mutual trust and confidence.

---

[150] Cabrelli and D'Alton (n 5), citing A Adams-Prassl, 'Inequality in the Impact of the Coronavirus Shock: Evidence from Real Time Surveys' (IZA Institute of Labour Economics Discussion Paper No 13183, April 2020) in the context of the Coronavirus pandemic.

4
Mutual Trust and Confidence and Good Faith

Introduction

Following consideration of the origins and current status of the key terms implied by law in Chapter 3, this chapter examines the English and Australian emergence and the present operation of the duties of mutual trust and confidence and good faith in employment contracts, as well as contracts for the personal performance of work. It would be remiss not to open this discussion without acknowledging one of Australia's most influential employment and contract law decisions—*Commonwealth Bank of Australia v Barker*.[1] That decision stunned Australian and English labour law communities, in that it led to the High Court of Australia unanimously denying the existence of an implied duty of mutual trust and confidence in Australian employment contracts, but left open the potential for a duty of good faith.[2] This finding occurred despite English law since the 1970s recognising a duty not to destroy mutual trust and confidence in the employment relationship, as well as the potential for an interrelated duty of good faith and fair dealing at work.[3] The facts, reasoning, and effects of *Commonwealth Bank v Barker* permeate much of this chapter as it has now made the contrast so stark between the English and Australian positions.

This chapter starts by examining the beginnings and current existence of the implied term of mutual trust and confidence in England. The discussion clarifies that, unlike most of the select key terms discussed in Chapter 3, from its inception in English law, the duty was categorised as a term implied by law into all employment contracts. However, it developed there because of a specific statutory lacuna, which is not mirrored in Australia.

The chapter then recounts the possible rise of the implied term of mutual trust and confidence in Australia, followed by its definite fall after the High Court's decision in *Commonwealth Bank v Barker*. The analysis shows that while there were moments in which some Australian courts considered the term a 'necessary'

---

[1] (2014) 253 CLR 169 (High Court of Australia (HCA)).
[2] ibid [42].
[3] J Riley, 'Siblings but Not Twins: Making Sense of "Mutual Trust and Confidence" and "Good Faith" in Employment Contracts' (2012) 36 MULR 521, 521.

element of all Australian employment contracts, following *Commonwealth Bank v Barker* it is now viewed as entirely unnecessary.[4] The duty's apparent lack of necessity in employment sets Australia apart from much of the common law world. A more detailed assessment of the necessity test adopted by the High Court in *Commonwealth Bank v Barker* is undertaken later in Chapter 6.

In *Commonwealth Bank v Barker*, the High Court also considered that the implication of the term 'involved complex policy considerations'[5] should not be engaged by the courts—rather, it held that these constituted matters that were better dealt with by the legislature. That aspect of the High Court's decision is explored separately in Chapter 7 as it has the potential to be extremely problematic. It could result in the courts refusing altogether to imply any new terms by law into employment contracts, thereby leaving unfilled gaps in those contracts.

The purpose of this chapter's commentary on *Commonwealth Bank v Barker* is not to ascertain whether the High Court's decision was correct, or to resolve the debate about whether there should be an implied term of mutual trust and confidence in Australian employment contracts. As this chapter's latter discussion of the decision makes clear, that question has already been the subject of rigorous academic debate. Rather, the discussion here aims to identify some of the controversies now faced due to the High Court's decision. One such controversy includes the duty's potential application in situations beyond employment in the realm of contracts for the personal performance of work, both in England and Australia. This topic receives dedicated attention later in the chapter's discussion of mutual trust and confidence.

The chapter then engages in an historical analysis of the implied duty of good faith by considering its origins followed by discussion of its current status, both in England and Australia. That analysis reveals that the status of a general duty of good faith in all contracts in England remains unclear, and that, historically, there has been great hesitancy towards applying it. In the employment context, however, the duty appears to have originated (and continues to exist) as a term implied by law into all employment contracts by virtue of the mutual trust and confidence term. As is explained, in English law, both duties are understood as being interrelated in the context of employment.

In Australia, however, a good faith duty has not been dually recognised in the general sense or in the specific context of employment. The High Court explicitly left open the question of a good faith duty in *Commonwealth Bank v Barker*, but there is also a range of conflicting authorities as to its status, both in contracts generally and in employment contracts specifically (if it even exists). Therefore, part of the discussion outlines potential future options for the recognition of a good faith duty in Australia: as a term implied by law or in fact, as a rule of construction, or

---

[4] *Commonwealth Bank v Barker* (HCA) (n 1) [36]–[37].
[5] ibid [40].

perhaps as not existing at all. As to the separate issue of whether a good faith duty *should* be implied by law into all Australian employment contracts, that question is addressed later in this work's Conclusion. As with the discussion on mutual trust and confidence, this chapter finishes by canvassing the potential application of a duty of good faith beyond employment in contracts for the performance of work, both in England and Australia.

Mutual Trust and Confidence

This part of the chapter traverses the duty of mutual trust and confidence as a term routinely implied by law into English employment contracts, which is then contrasted with the duty's absence in Australian law. In a comparative sense, this analysis presents a fascinating, yet vexed, divergence between two common law jurisdictions that otherwise share many similar features in an historical sense, as discussed in Chapter 3. The duty's potential existence beyond employment in contracts for the performance of work across both England and Australia is discussed in the final section of this part.

A. Evolution and Existence in England

Looking back at the select key terms discussed in Chapter 3, mutual trust and confidence is one of the few terms that evolved as a term implied by law into all employment contracts when it first emerged in England. There are numerous views regarding its origins. However, the focus in this section is on the well-accepted understanding of the term's development during the 1970s, in response to changes to unfair dismissal legislation.[6] This section recounts the main steps in that developmental process.[7]

When statutory protection against unfair dismissal was first enacted in England in 1971,[8] a new problem emerged. Employers seeking to avoid liability to pay statutory compensation would stop short of terminating employees.[9] Instead, they used other techniques to encourage employees to resign. Courts grappled with determinations regarding the conduct of the employer that would enable an employee to terminate their employment contract within the statutory meaning of 'dismissal'.

---

[6] See, eg, *Heptonstall v Gaskin and Ors (No 2)* (2005) 138 IR 103 (Supreme Court of New South Wales (NSWSC)) [19]–[23].

[7] See also the historical surveys by Jessup J in *Commonwealth Bank of Australia v Barker* (2013) 214 FCR 450 (Full Court of the Federal Court of Australia (FCAFC)) [213]–[235] and G Anderson, D Brodie, and J Riley, *The Common Law Employment Relationship: A Comparative Study* (Edward Elgar 2017) 118–21.

[8] *Industrial Relations Act 1971* (UK) s 23.

[9] J Riley, *Employee Protection at Common Law* (Federation Press 2005) 70.

The basic definition of 'dismissal' under s 23(2)(a) of the *Industrial Relations Act 1971* (UK) was a 'termination of the contract of employment by the employer'. The problem under consideration was how an employer's conduct that induced an employee to resign would be encapsulated within that statutory concept of dismissal.[10] Eventually, such conduct on the part of an employer came to be regarded, for statutory purposes, as a 'constructive dismissal', as the case law applying s 23(2)(c) treated the single concept of 'dismissal' as having a constructive and literal aspect.[11]

For example, in *Western Excavating (ECC) Ltd v Sharp*,[12] it was held that in deciding whether an employee had been 'constructively dismissed' in accordance with the relevant statutory definition, one needed to consider whether the employer's conduct was sufficient to justify the employee regarding their employment contract as being discharged, giving the employee the right to terminate it. If so, the employment contract would be terminated due to the employer's conduct, despite being carried out by the employee. The employee then had access to a claim for unfair dismissal. By leaving, the employee was effectively terminating their own employment. This outcome meant there could only be a repudiation or a fundamental breach by the employer if a recognised obligation under the employment contract was breached.

As a consequence of *Western Excavating v Sharp*, the English courts' focus turned to the type of breach that could be said to have occurred where an employer had in some way treated an employee badly. Specifically, there was a concern that a practice of 'squeezing out'[13] would arise. It was feared that some employers—those keen keen to be rid of an employee without exposing themselves to a claim for wrongful dismissal—would attempt to make employment sufficiently uncomfortable for the employee to induce them to leave (albeit without going far enough to seriously breach or repudiate their employment contract). Therefore, when the employee left, they would have no access to a claim for unfair dismissal.

It was this recognition that led English courts to formulate the implied term of mutual trust and confidence. It was first couched as a term implied by law into all employment contracts in *Courtaulds Northern Textiles Ltd v Andrews*.[14] In that decision, the English Employment Appeal Tribunal held that the implied term gave rise to an obligation owed by the parties to the employment contract 'not to conduct themselves in such a manner as is intended, although not intended by itself, to destroy or seriously damage the relationship in question'.[15] Soon afterwards,

---

[10] M Freedland, *The Contract of Employment* (Clarendon Press 1976) 237.
[11] ibid 238. For an assessment of constructive dismissal from a contractual standpoint, see generally, D Brodie, 'Constructive Dismissal: The Contractual Maze' (2022) 33 KLJ 151.
[12] [1978] ICR 221 (Court of Appeal (CA)).
[13] See, eg, the concern expressed in *Woods v WM Car Services (Peterborough) Ltd* [1981] ICR 666 (CA), 671; *Malik v Bank of Credit and Commerce International SA (In Liq)* [1998] AC 20 (House of Lords (HL)), 37–38, 46.
[14] [1979] IRLR 84 (Employment Appeals Tribunal (EAT)).
[15] ibid 85.

in *Woods v WM Car Services (Peterborough) Ltd*,[16] Browne-Wilkinson P applied *Courtaulds Northern Textiles Ltd v Andrews*, again articulating the duty as a term implied by law into all employment contracts:[17]

> In our view it is clearly established that there is implied in a contract of employment a term that the employer will not, without reasonable and proper cause, conduct themselves in a manner calculated or likely to destroy or seriously damage the relationship of confidence and trust between employer and employee ...

The House of Lords later approved this same reasoning in *Malik v Bank of Credit and Commerce International SA (In Liq)*.[18] It was this decision that first unlocked the remedial potential arising from a breach of the implied term.

It later followed that any 'squeezing out' became a fundamental breach of the term, which justified the employee's termination of their employment contract and claim for damages for unfair dismissal.[19] Despite its initial purpose in filling a statutory lacuna, the mutual trust and confidence term has continued to be implied into all English employment contracts to the present day. That is not to say that its continued implication in English law has been without criticism; there has been some suggestion that it has been overused.[20]

This employment law concept is nevertheless well advanced in England, with English appellate courts having applied it for over thirty years. Extensive case law supports the implied term's existence,[21] and a there is now a wealth of academic commentary on its operation.[22] Following *Malik v Bank of Credit and Commerce*

---

[16] *Woods v WM Car Services* (n 13).
[17] ibid 670–71.
[18] *Malik v Bank of Credit and Commerce International* (n 13) 34–35, 45–46. The emergence and acceptance of mutual trust and confidence following this decision, as well as the decision's broader implications, are explored in D Brodie, '*Malik v BCCI*: The Impact of Good Faith' in ACL Davies, J Adams-Prassl, and A Bogg, *Landmark Cases in Labour Law* (Hart Publishing 2022) 245.
[19] Riley (n 3) 527.
[20] In a conference paper, former Employment Appeals Tribunal President, Brian Langstaff J, wrote that the term 'might often be overused, in particular where some perfectly good contractual right could be relied on, with a view to claiming constructive dismissal (because such breaches are inevitably repudiatory)'. He also mentioned on behalf of other judges in that Tribunal that '[t]he general experience [of those judges] ... is that parties in resignation cases ... all too often argue that the ... [implied term] has been broken by their employer. It is being slowly picked up by employers too': B Langstaff, 'Overconfidence in the Implied Term? Court Out ...' (Paper presented at the Industrial Law Society Conference, Oxford, 19 September 2014) 10, 14. See also *Leach v The Office of Communication* [2012] IRLR 839 (CA) [53], where Mummery LJ similarly warned against the term's overuse, suggesting 'it is not a convenient label to stick on any situation'.
[21] The key House of Lords decisions are: *Malik v Bank of Credit and Commerce International* (n 13); *Johnson v Unisys Ltd* [2003] 1 AC 518 (HL); *Eastwood v Magnox Electric plc* [2005] 1 AC 503 (HL).
[22] See, eg, M Freedland, *The Personal Employment Contract* (OUP 2003) 154–70; D Brodie, 'The Heart of the Matter: Mutual Trust and Confidence' (1996) 25 ILJ 121; D Brodie, 'Beyond Exchange: The New Contract of Employment' (1998) 27 ILJ 79; D Brodie, 'A Fair Deal at Work' (1999) 19 OJLS 83; D Brodie, 'Mutual Trust and the Values of the Employment Contract' (2001) 30 ILJ 84; D Brodie, *The Employment Contract: Legal Principles, Drafting and Interpretation* (OUP 2005) 63–84; D Brodie, 'Mutual Trust and Confidence: Catalysts, Constraints and Commonality' (2008) 37 ILJ 329; The Honourable Mr Justice Lindsay, 'The Implied Term of Trust and Confidence' (2001) 30 ILJ 1; M Freedland, 'Constructing

International,²³ it has been described in numerous decisions as a mutual obligation that employers and employees shall not without reasonable and proper cause conduct themselves in a manner calculated or likely to destroy the relationship of confidence and trust between them.²⁴ It has also been formulated as a positive duty upon employers to act fairly, responsibly, and in good faith in the conduct of their business and the treatment of their employees.²⁵ More is said later about the duty's links to the development of a good faith duty in employment contracts in England. Since its inception, the mutual trust and confidence term has been treated as 'an overarching obligation implied by law as an incident of the contract of employment'.²⁶

The English iteration of the term now requires that each party must have regard to the other's interests, but not to subjugate their own interests to those of the other.²⁷ In that respect, the duty is different from a fiduciary obligation.²⁸ Even though the duty is apparently mutual in operation, it has been said that '[t]he major importance of the implied duty of trust and confidence lies in its impact on the obligations of the employer'.²⁹ In practice, the duty has rarely been invoked against an employee because 'the law already sets the higher standard of requiring employees to comply with all lawful instructions of their employer'.³⁰

The rationale behind the duty is that it operates to facilitate the functioning of the employment contract; preserve the employment relationship; and protect employees from oppression, harassment, and the loss of job satisfaction.³¹ As Lizzie Barmes writes, since its recognition it has created '[a] prism ... through which to evaluate whether there has been respect for the implicit behavioural commitments made by entry into, and continuance in, working relationships'.³² A leading authority on the operation of the term in English law, Douglas Brodie, describes

---

Fairness in Employment Contracts' (2007) 36 ILJ 136; D Cabrelli, 'The Implied Duty of Mutual Trust and Confidence: An Emerging Overarching Principle?' (2005) 34 ILJ 284.

²³ *Malik v Bank of Credit and Commerce International* (n 13) 34–35, 45–46.
²⁴ See, eg, *Woods v WM Car Services* (n 13) 350, approved in *Lewis v Motorworld Garages Ltd* [1985] IRLR 465 (CA); *Imperial Group Pension Trust Ltd v Imperial Tobacco Ltd* [1991] 2 All ER 597 (High Court of Justice (QB)); *Malik v Bank of Credit and Commerce International* (n 13) 49; *Brown v Merchant Ferries Ltd* [1998] IRLR 682 (CA); *Baldwin v Brighton & Hove City Borough* [2007] IRLR 232 (EAT) (clarifying the objective nature of the test).
²⁵ See, eg, *Eastwood v Magnox Electric* (n 21) [11], [50].
²⁶ *Johnson v Unisys* (n 21) 536.
²⁷ See, eg, H Collins, K D Ewing, and A McCoglan, *Labour Law* (2nd edn, CUP 2019) 143.
²⁸ See, eg, *Nottingham University v Fishel* [2000] ICR 1462 (QB), 1493; *Helmet Integrated Systems Ltd v Tunnard* [2007] IRLR 126 (CA) [33].
²⁹ *Malik v Bank of Credit and Commerce International* (n 13) 46.
³⁰ Collins, Ewing, and McCoglan (n 27) 143, citing *Williams v Leeds United* [2015] IRLR 383 (QB) as a rare example of a breach of the mutual trust and confidence term by an employee. See also *Ticehurst v BT* [1992] ICR 383 (CA), where it was suggested that if an employee refuses to indicate, prior to the time of performance, whether they will perform their obligations, that may constitute a breach of the implied term.
³¹ See, eg, *Malik v Bank of Credit and Commerce International* (n 13) 36–38.
³² L Barmes, 'Common Law Implied Terms and Behavioural Standards at Work' (2007) 36 ILJ 35, 41.

it as an 'open textured' term and one which provides 'a conduit through which the courts can channel their views as to how the employment relationship should operate'.[33]

English authorities have consequently come to suggest that a broad range of conduct of the employer during employment will give rise to a breach of the implied term.[34] In what is commonly referred to as the '*Johnson* exclusion zone', the term does not apply at the point of dismissal. The result is that the duty cannot attach to the power to terminate the employment relationship.[35] The rationale behind this limitation was that a claim for breach of the implied term would be inconsistent with statutory unfair dismissal legislation, and it would be inappropriate to sidestep those limitations. That said, damages are recoverable if the breach occurs before termination (eg during a disciplinary process,[36] noting that a separate and distinct term implied by law may now exist in England requiring an employer to conduct a disciplinary process fairly).[37] If the term is implied and breached, this will give rise to a right to damages for breach of contract and, potentially, the right to terminate the employment contract.[38]

B. Rise and Fall in Australia: *Commonwealth Bank v Barker*

Leading up to the High Court's decision in *Commonwealth Bank v Barker*, 'there was a vigorous judicial debate about whether the mutual duty of trust and confidence was part of the common law of Australia'.[39] Indeed, just a few years before that decision, Joellen Riley Munton explained that claims for a breach of mutual trust and confidence had even become the '"abracadabra" of the plaintiff lawyer, sprinkled liberally over statements of claim, in the hope of summoning up some exceptional damages award from a mundane termination of employment claim'.[40]

---

[33] Brodie, 'The Heart of the Matter: Mutual Trust and Confidence' (n 22) 128.
[34] The implied term cannot be breached after employment has ended: see, eg, *London Borough of Enfield v Sivanandan* [2005] EWCA Civ 10 (CA).
[35] See, eg, *Johnson v Unisys* (n 21) [2], [56]–[58] and [80]; *Eastwood v Magnox Electric* (n 21) [10]–[11] and [28]; *Edwards v Chesterfield Royal Hospital and Botham (FC) v Ministry of Defence* [2012] 2 AC 22 (Supreme Court of the United Kingdom (UKSC)) [40]. For a discussion that traces the legal position of mutual trust and confidence prior to *Johnson v Unisys* (n 21), the case itself, and its ongoing legacy, see, eg, J Atkinson, '*Johnson v Unisys* Ltd (2001): A Compelling Constitutional Vision of Common Law and Statute?' in ACL Davies, J Adams-Prassl, and A Bogg, *Landmark Cases in Labour Law* (Hart Publishing 2022) 267.
[36] See, eg, *Eastwood v Magnox Electric* (n 21) [31] and [39]; *Takacs v Barclays Services Jersey Ltd* [2006] IRLR 877 (QB) [56]–[58]; *GAB Robins (UK) Ltd v Triggs* [2008] ICR 529 (CA) [32]–[39]; *King v University Court of the University of St Andrews* [2002] IRLR 252 (Scottish Court of Session (SCS)) [21]–[22].
[37] See, eg, *Burn v Alder Hey Children's NHS Foundation Trust* [2022] ICR 492 (CA) [35], where such a duty was suggested as a possibility.
[38] See the further discussion on the consequences of a breach of the implied term in Z Adams and others, *Deakin and Morris' Labour Law* (7th edn, Hart Publishing 2021) 335–38.
[39] A Stewart and others, *Creighton and Stewart's Labour Law* (6th edn, Federation Press 2016) 526.
[40] J Riley, 'The Boundaries of Mutual Trust and Good Faith' (2009) 22 AJLL 73, 73.

In addressing such claims, most Australian courts assumed either that the implied term existed, or simply conceded its existence.[41] These findings were made despite there being no appellate decision concerning the term's existence,[42] including no definitive High Court authority.[43] Many commentators also asserted that the duty ought to be implied by law into all Australian employment contracts (although not necessarily its power to generate independent damages awards).[44] To take just one example, labour law barrister and researcher, Mark Irving, explained that without a mutual trust and confidence term in Australia, 'employees who are lied to, humiliated or oppressed would have no remedy in contract or any right to terminate the contract. They would be required to continue to serve a dishonest, corrupt, morally repugnant, or untrustworthy employer for the term of their contracts'.[45] That is not to say that there were not writers who were tentative as to the term's existence,[46] or who wholly rejected it.[47]

Australian courts recognising the term as one implied by law appeared to have little difficulty in doing so.[48] However, their justifications were based largely on those given in England. To quote from one of many examples of cases assuming the application of the term on the same basis as in English law, *Burazin v Blacktown*

---

[41] See, eg, C Sappideen and others, *Macken's Law of Employment* (7th edn, Lawbook Co 2011) 162 (and the authorities cited therein).

[42] Riley (n 3) 530.

[43] Cf the High Court's loose references to the duty in *Koehler v Cerebos (Aust) Ltd* (2005) 222 CLR 44 (HCA) [24], where McHugh, Gummow, Hayne, and Heydon JJ referred to 'the implied duty of mutual trust and confidence' as part of the 'contractual position' that must be explored in determining the extent of an employer's allegedly excessive workload; *Concut Pty Ltd v Worrell* (2000) 103 IR 160 (HCA) [51](3), where Kirby J, in *obiter dicta*, described the implied duty of 'mutual trust' as one of the 'basic starting points ... for the elucidation of the applicable law'; *Blyth Chemicals Ltd v Bushnell* (1933) 49 CLR 66 (HCA), 81, where Dixon and McTiernan JJ referred to 'the necessary confidence between employer and employee'; *Shepherd v Felt & Textiles of Australia Ltd* (1931) 45 CLR 359 (HCA), 372, 378, where Starke J spoke of an employee's misconduct as being 'inconsistent with the continuance of confidence between the parties' and Dixon J of a relationship between employer and employee that 'involved some degree of mutual confidence and required a continual cooperation'.

[44] See, eg, R Owens, J Riley, and J Murray, *The Law of Work* (2nd edn, OUP 2011) 288; A Brooks, 'The Good and Considerate Employer: Developments in the Implied Duty of Mutual Trust and Confidence' (2001) 20 UTas LR 29, 38–43; J Riley, 'Mutual Trust and Good Faith: Can Private Contract Law Guarantee Fair Dealing in the Workplace?' (2003) 16 AJLL 1; K Godfrey, 'Contracts of Employment: Renaissance of the Implied Term of Trust and Confidence' (2003) 77 ALJ 764; Riley (n 9) 73–76; A Stewart, 'Good Faith and Fair Dealing at Work' in C Arup and others (eds), *Labour Law and Labour Market Regulation: Essays on the Construction, Constitution and Regulation of Labour Markets and Work Relationships* (Federation Press 2006) 579, 583–84; Riley (n 40); Riley (n 3) 523; I Neil and D Chin, *The Modern Contract of Employment* (Lawbook Co 2012) 146; M Irving, *The Contract of Employment* (LexisNexis Butterworths 2012) 487.

[45] Irving (n 44) 493.

[46] See, eg, Sappideen and others (n 41) 162; B Creighton and A Stewart, *Labour Law* (5th edn, Federation Press 2010) 431–33.

[47] See, eg, Greg McCarry who noted after the term was adopted by the House of Lords in *Malik v Bank of Credit and Commerce International* (n 13), 'the necessity which justified the implication of the term in England does not exist here [in Australia] and the English decisions cannot automatically be followed': G McCarry, 'Damages for Breach of the Employer's Implied Duty of Trust and Confidence' (1998) 26 ABLR 141, 143.

[48] See the further assessment of Australian cases prior to *Commonwealth Bank v Barker* (HCA) (n 1) in J Riley Munton, *Labour Law: An Introduction to the Law of Work* (OUP 2021) 92–93.

City Guardian Pty Ltd,[49] the Full Court of the former Industrial Relations Court of Australia indicated that there was 'ample English authority for the implication of the ... term',[50] and therefore that it should automatically be implied as one by law in Australia. Following *Burazin v Blacktown City Guardian*, many judges simply applied that authority, accepting that *Malik v Bank of Credit and Commerce International* also represented the law in Australia. This acceptance occurred without further consideration of the term's actual necessity in Australia's unique and detailed statutory context.

Some Australian courts, however, were aware that the same necessity for implying the term in *Malik v Bank of Credit and Commerce International* was unparalleled in Australia. Several courts were reluctant to find an implied duty in the face of Australia's comprehensive statutory regulation of the terms and conditions of employment. In this view, any recognition of the duty would be 'incoherent' with statutory law.[51] Taking one example, in *Warren v Dickson*[52] (a decision made by a single judge of the Supreme Court of New South Wales), it was stated that '[c]are should be taken when referring to United Kingdom authorities in this area of the law',[53] and that '[t]he modern English formulation of the ... [implied term had] evolved against a different statutory background and as a consequence of the legal recognition in the United Kingdom of arguably higher expectations on an employer'.[54]

The labour law academic Greg McCarry similarly warned against the adoption of the term by Australian courts, given that the implication of the term in England was achieved on a notion of necessity that was very different from that in Australia.[55] The basis for his argument was that Australia did not find itself in a position similar to England in the 1970s, where the statutory unfair dismissal regime provided inadequate protection to employees. If anything, the protections afforded to the majority of Australian employees under applicable industrial instruments, the provisions of the former *Workplace Relations Act 1996* (Cth), and the existing common law, were more than sufficient. As such, there was no similar necessity in Australia to allow separate claims for a breach of an implied term of mutual trust and confidence in employment as there was in England.

Justice Jessup made a substantially similar argument to McCarry in his dissenting judgment in the Full Federal Court appeal decision in *Commonwealth Bank v Barker*,[56] which (as described below) became highly influential in the High

---

[49] (1996) 142 ALR 144 (Australian Industrial Relations Commission (AIRC)).
[50] ibid 151.
[51] See, eg, *Heptonstall v Gaskin (No 2)* (n 6) [29].
[52] [2011] NSWSC 79 (NSWSC).
[53] ibid [42].
[54] ibid.
[55] McCarry (n 47) 144.
[56] *Commonwealth Bank v Barker* (FCAFC) (n 7) [161]–[371].

Court's decision on the same matter.[57] His Honour criticised the heavy reliance of English courts on *Malik v Bank of Credit and Commerce International* as a basis for the implying term. In his view, English courts never properly considered the true necessity of the term into all employment contracts in that case. The House of Lords simply assumed the term's existence.[58] Justice Jessup observed that in *Malik v Bank of Credit and Commerce International*, 'their Lordships ... were not required to rule on the primary question whether there was such a term implied into all contracts of employment, and Lord Nicholls did not deal with the subject'.[59] Only in *obiter dicta* comments was an attempt made by Lord Steyn to identify the source and jurisprudential justification of the term.[60] His Honour then went on to say that, 'the existence of the term was a "fact" in *Malik* because it was common ground as between the parties to the appeal'.[61] Therefore, in seeking an authority in support of the introduction of the implied term of mutual trust and confidence by law, 'that authority would not be *Malik*'.[62]

Prior to *Commonwealth Bank v Barker*, there was also judicial criticism of the mutual trust and confidence term in Australia with reference to the difficulty of giving it practical and effective content. For instance, in *State of South Australia v McDonald*[63] and *Dye v Commonwealth Securities Ltd*,[64] it was emphasised that any implication of the term ought not to provide an occasion for courts to review employers' 'routine management decisions'.[65] There was apparently 'no ready way of putting a limit to the range of matters which ... [could] be brought within the scope of the implied term and be said to be suitable for examination by a court'.[66] On this analysis, a general implication of the term to all employment contracts would detract from what is often referred to as 'managerial prerogative',[67] such that it would unduly limit the 'normal' employment relationship.[68] While this potential did not seem to present a problem in England, the courts in *State of South*

---

[57] In particular by Gageler J in his separate reasons: *Commonwealth Bank v Barker* (HCA) (n 1) [115]–[118].
[58] This same conclusion was later reached by the High Court majority in *Commonwealth Bank v Barker* (HCA) (n 1) [34]–[35].
[59] *Commonwealth Bank v Barker* (FCAFC) (n 7) [226].
[60] ibid.
[61] ibid [229].
[62] ibid [230].
[63] (2009) 104 SASR 344 (Full Court of the Supreme Court of South Australia (SASCFC)), a decision that will be revisited in Chapters 5 and 6.
[64] [2012] FCA 242 (Federal Court of Australia (FCA)).
[65] See, eg, *State of South Australia v McDonald* (n 63) [275]; *Dye v Commonwealth Securities* (n 64) [611]–[613].
[66] *State of South Australia v McDonald* (n 63) [275], noting that Buchanan J agreed with this proposition in *Dye v Commonwealth Securities* (n 64) [613].
[67] For further explanation of this concept, see, eg, C Sappideen and others, *Macken's Law of Employment* (9th edn, Lawbook Co 2022) 155.
[68] Cf *Malik v Bank of Credit and Commerce International* (n 13) 46, where it was held that the mutual trust and confidence term provides a means by which 'a balance [is] ... struck between an employer's interest in managing [its] business as [it] sees fit and the employee's interest is not being unfairly and improperly exploited'.

Australia v McDonald and *Dye v Commonwealth Securities* were aware that the implication could curtail an employer's ability to 'manage' its employees by impacting on its discretionary use of prerogative powers in the employment relationship (eg through changing policies, relocating employees, altering employees' working hours, awarding salary increases, and granting bonuses).[69]

As this chapter's introduction made clear, in its ruling in *Commonwealth Bank v Barker*, the High Court put a definitive end to the implied term of mutual trust and confidence in Australian employment contracts. While this decision has been labelled by one text as 'profoundly disappointing',[70] if nothing else, it 'authoritatively settled the debate'[71] on the status of the mutual trust and confidence term in Australia, which had been in a state of flux since the mid-1990s. The following discussion outlines the facts and circumstances that led to the High Court's ultimate denial of the duty's existence.

The entire dispute between Mr Stephen Barker and the Commonwealth Bank of Australia arose out of what was, at its core, a simple administrative error by the bank. Mr Barker had been employed by the bank as an Executive Manager in its Corporate Banking section in Adelaide, South Australia. He was employed under a written employment contract, which permitted the bank to terminate it, without cause, provided the bank gave him four weeks' written notice. Mr Barker had been working at the bank since November 1981, and had worked his way up to a managerial position after starting in a series of junior roles.

The bank had undergone a significant restructuring affecting Mr Barker's area. On 2 March 2009, he was handed a letter informing him that his current position was going to be made redundant, but it was the bank's preference to redeploy him to another suitable position. The letter also suggested that the bank would later consult him to explore 'appropriate options'. Clause 8 of Mr Barker's employment contract stated that if his position became redundant and the bank was 'unable to place the employee in an alternative position with the bank or one of its related bodies, in keeping with the employee's skills and experience', compensation would be payable to him. The bank also had a Redeployment Policy contained in its lengthy *HR Reference Manual*. However, the manual stated that its terms did not 'form any part of an employee's contract of employment'.

Mr Barker was required to clear out his desk, hand in his office keys and mobile phone, and not return to work. His work email and access to the bank's intranet were also terminated immediately. However, the human resources section of the bank, responsible for managing his impending redeployment, was unaware that he no longer had access to his work email or mobile phone. In fact, that section of the

---

[69] See, eg, K Godfrey, 'The Renaissance of the Implied Term of Trust & Confidence' [2003] 88 ACLN 29, 32.
[70] Stewart and others (n 39) 526.
[71] ibid.

bank had made several unsuccessful attempts to contact Mr Barker by those means to inform him that the position of 'Executive Manager – Service Excellence' within the bank, would have been suited to his skill set.

Pure human error meant that Mr Barker was not able to receive the notifications sent to his work email account or mobile phone about other vacancies for which he could have applied. Whoever was responsible for forwarding him information on those other positions ignored 'bounce-backs' from his email account and neglected to forward the relevant information to his home address. Therefore, contrary to the bank's Redeployment Policy, Mr Barker missed the necessary information about redeployment opportunities because bank staff had confiscated the tools he needed to receive the necessary communications from the bank. On 9 April 2009, Mr Barker was advised in writing that his employment would be terminated due to redundancy, with effect from close of business that day.

In 2010, Mr Barker brought proceedings against the bank for breach of his employment contract and for damages under s 82 of the former *Trade Practices Act 1974* (Cth). His claim was, in part, based upon an implied term of mutual trust and confidence that he said existed in his employment contract with the bank. This term, as described in the English case of *Malik v Bank of Credit and Commerce International*,[72] was said to oblige the bank not to, without reasonable cause, conduct itself in a manner likely to destroy its relationship of trust and confidence with Mr Barker.

When Mr Barker's claim came before Besanko J of the Federal Court of Australia at first instance, there were two main issues to be decided: first, whether Mr Barker's employment contract contained the implied term; and secondly, if it did, whether the bank's breach of its own Redeployment Policy constituted a serious breach of the relationship of trust and confidence upon which the term was founded. At first instance, Besanko J found that the bank had been almost totally inactive in complying with its policies during the period after notifying Mr Barker of his redundancy.[73] His Honour held that this inactivity amounted to a serious breach of the implied term of mutual trust and confidence.[74] While it was not factually relevant in this case, his Honour also noted the possibility that the mutual trust and confidence term could be excluded.[75] Mr Barker was awarded damages of $317,000 for the loss of the opportunity to be redeployed to a another suitable position within the bank.[76]

The bank then appealed to the Full Court of the Federal Court of Australia, where the majority of the Full Court (Jacobsen and Lander JJ) considered that, although no High Court authority had determined the question of whether the

---

[72] *Malik v Bank of Credit and Commerce International* (n 13).
[73] *Barker v Commonwealth Bank of Australia* (2012) 229 IR 249 (FCA) [352].
[74] ibid.
[75] ibid [329].
[76] ibid [369].

implied term formed part of employment contracts in Australia, it had obtained a sufficient degree of recognition, both in England and Australia, such that it ought to be accepted by an intermediate court of appeal as a term implied by law into all employment contracts.[77] They said that Besanko J was wrong in finding that a breach of the bank's policies was necessarily a breach of the implied term, given that the policies were not part of Mr Barker's employment contract.[78] Nevertheless, the majority considered that the bank was required by the implied term to take 'positive steps' to consult with Mr Barker about alternative positions, and to give him the opportunity to apply for them.[79] Instead, it failed to make contact with him for a certain period of time, which the primary judge had found to be unreasonable. Overall, that was sufficient to amount to a breach of the implied term.[80]

Alternatively, Jacobsen and Lander JJ held that the bank had breached an implied duty of cooperation, which 'requires a party to a contract to do all things necessary to enable the other party to have the benefit of the contract'.[81] They said that the relevant benefit could not be the Redeployment Policy, because it was not a term of the contract.[82] However, they held that it was sufficient that clause 8 'contemplated the possibility of redundancy and redeployment within the bank, as an alternative to termination'.[83] They dismissed the bank's appeal, as well as Mr Barker's cross-appeal against the quantum of damages (other than to correct one error in calculation by the primary judge).[84]

In a lengthy and powerful dissent, Jessup J of the Full Court held that the implied term did not form part of the common law of Australia. His Honour held that it had never been accepted as part of the *ratio decidendi* of any decision by an appellate court and there was no 'ready consensus' as to its existence.[85] Justice Jessup also said that the implied term did not meet the established requirement that the implication be necessary (and not merely reasonable) to prevent 'the enjoyment of the rights conferred by the contract [being] ... rendered nugatory, worthless, or ... seriously undermined'.[86] His Honour further considered that, even if the implied term did exist, the bank's failure to comply with its own policies did not amount to a breach of it.[87] No doubt encouraged by this dissent, the bank filed an application for special leave to appeal to the High Court, which was granted.[88] The

---

[77] *Commonwealth Bank of Australia v Barker* (2013) 214 FCR 450 (FCAFC)) [13].
[78] ibid [113]–[114].
[79] ibid [112].
[80] ibid [117].
[81] *Secured Income Real Estate (Australia) Ltd v St Martins Investments Pty Ltd* (1979) 144 CLR 59 (HCA), 607.
[82] *Commonwealth Bank v Barker* (FCAFC) (n 7) [125].
[83] ibid [127].
[84] ibid [159]–[160].
[85] ibid [281].
[86] ibid [339].
[87] ibid [349].
[88] [2013] HCATrans 325 (13 December 2013) (HCA).

High Court heard the appeal on 8 and 9 April 2014,[89] and handed down its decision on 10 September 2014.[90] It is the outcome of that decision which underpins the remainder of this section.

Having considered the facts of *Commonwealth Bank v Barker*, the following discussion explores the High Court's decision following the bank's successful special leave application.[91] The analysis of the High Court's decision is focused on the principal joint judgment of French CJ and Bell and Keane JJ, and also briefly considers the separate reasons of Kiefel J (as her Honour then was) and Gageler J, who came to the same conclusion not to imply the term. The main points of contention arising out of the High Court's decision are also identified. Again, the purpose of this discussion is to identify the controversies now faced by the courts because of the High Court's decision, rather than to provide a definitive view as to whether the decision was correct, or whether the mutual trust and confidence term should have been implied.

The implication of the term extends beyond the proper law-making role of the courts

In their joint judgment, French CJ and Bell and Keane JJ held that the implication of the contractual term was 'a step beyond the legitimate law-making function of the courts', which 'should not be taken'.[92] They stated that the primary question raised by the bank's appeal was 'whether, under the common law of Australia, employment contracts contain a term that neither party will, without reasonable cause, conduct itself in a manner likely to destroy or seriously damage the relationship of trust and confidence between them'.[93] The judges stated that the creation of a new standard of that kind was a form of 'judicial-law making'[94] and 'not a step to be taken lightly'.[95]

As mentioned earlier, a detailed assessment of this policy-based reasoning is provided in Chapter 7. This basis for avoiding the implication of the term is clearly

---

[89] [2014] HCATrans 73 (8 April 2014) (HCA); [2014] HCATrans 74 (9 April 2014) (HCA).
[90] *Commonwealth Bank v Barker* (HCA) (n 1).
[91] For other recent summaries of the decision and its implications, see, eg, J Carter and others, 'Terms Implied in Law: "Trust and Confidence" in the High Court of Australia' (2015) 32 JCL 203; L Chighine, '*Commonwealth Bank of Australia v Barker*—No Implied Term of Mutual Trust and Confidence in Employment Contracts, But Door Still Open for Good Faith' (2015) 28 AJLL 77; F Reynold QC, 'Bad Behaviour and the Implied Term of Mutual Trust and Confidence: Is There a Problem?' (2015) 44 ILJ 262; G Golding, 'Terms Implied by Law into Employment Contracts: Are they Necessary?' (2015) 28 AJLL 113; G Golding, 'The Role of Judges in the Regulation of Australian Employment Contracts' (2016) 32 IJCLL&IR 69; D Brodie, 'The Dynamics of Common Law Evolution' (2016) 32 IJCLL&IR 45; A Gray, 'Good Faith in Australian Contract Law After *Barker*' (2015) 43 ABLR 358; L Hillbrick, 'Why the High Court Went Too Far in Rejecting the Implied Term of Mutual Trust and Confidence in Its Entirety, in the Context of Constructive Dismissal Claims' (2018) 31 AJLL 45.
[92] *Commonwealth Bank v Barker* (HCA) (n 1) [1].
[93] ibid [15].
[94] ibid [29].
[95] ibid [20].

controversial. Saying that the implication of the term is a matter best left to parliament has the potential to encourage judges to avoid implying any terms by law into contracts altogether, thereby limiting their law-making function and leaving gaps in contracts that need to be filled. It is an aspect of the judgment that warrants further and distinct consideration.

The development of the implied term in England is not applicable in Australia
The majority judgment noted that the common law of the employment contract has developed in a 'symbiotic relationship' with legislation in Australia.[96] Their Honours explained that Australia's common law now differs from England's because of its different statutory protection of employment rights.[97] They stated that the history of the development of the implied term in England was linked to the concept of constructive dismissal, as it applied to particular legislation, which is not 'applicable to Australia'.[98] As detailed above, these findings accord with those of some Australian courts in earlier decisions, as well as academics like McCarry, who asserted that the term was unnecessary by reason of Australia's detailed statutory regime regulating employment.

Nevertheless, several commentators have expressed disappointment with this aspect of the High Court's judgment. In *Creighton and Stewart's Labour Law*, it is said that even though the High Court identified the differences between the Australian and English industrial relations systems, which might have distinguished *Malik v Bank of Credit and Commerce International*, it 'shed no light on why Australian employees should be different from those in most of the rest of the common law world'.[99] Moreover, in an article critiquing the High Court's decision, John Carter, Wayne Courtney, Elisabeth Peden, Joellen Riley Munton, and Greg Tolhurst commented that they found the court's reasons for rejecting mutual trust and confidence based on the statutory differences between Australian and English employment law 'unconvincing'.[100]

The implied term of mutual trust and confidence is not synonymous with the implied term of cooperation
The majority judgment also stated that the mutual trust and confidence term was not an application of the implied duty of cooperation, which prohibits conduct that would prevent the proper performance of a contract.[101] They held that as to the direct application of the implied duty of cooperation, clause 8 of Mr Barker's employment contract conferred a benefit that would apply by way of a termination

---

[96] ibid [17].
[97] ibid [18].
[98] ibid [35].
[99] Stewart and others (n 39) 526.
[100] Carter and others (n 91) 225.
[101] *Commonwealth Bank v Barker* (HCA) (n 1) [41].

payment, but did not confer a contractual entitlement to the benefit of the bank's Redeployment Policy.[102] As such, the submission on behalf of Mr Barker that 'the prospect of "redeployment was a benefit in the relevant sense"' was not accepted.[103]

Notwithstanding this apparent distinction between the implied term of mutual trust and confidence and cooperation (whether it is understood as a term implied by law into all contracts, or as a rule of construction), there is English authority for the proposition that a term of mutual trust and confidence evolved from the mutual duty of cooperation.[104] On appeal to the Full Court of the Federal Court, the majority of Jacobsen and Lander JJ also rationalised the recognition of mutual trust and confidence term in that way. Their Honours cited *Malik v Bank of Credit and Commerce International*, finding that:[105]

> One of the various bases for recognition of the implied term was stated by Lord Steyn in *Malik* at 45. He considered that the employer's obligation probably has its origin in the general duty of co-operation between contracting parties.

In a case commentary issued just before the High Court's decision, Riley Munton took a similar view that 'the implied duty of mutual trust and confidence ... is essentially a duty upon each of the parties to cooperate in allowing the other to enjoy the benefit of the contract'.[106]

In addition, in relation to the correct interpretation of clause 8, Riley Munton recognised that there are many ways in which it could be understood. In her view, and quite apart from that of the High Court majority:[107]

> In a case such as this, where the employer is a large national employer with diverse employment opportunities for thousands of people, it is reasonable to infer from a clause such as cl 8 that the parties intended Mr Barker to have the benefit of an opportunity for redeployment somewhere in the Bank's network before being dismissed for redundancy.

There is nothing in the High Court's judgment in *Commonwealth Bank v Barker* to suggest that it considered such an argument.

---

[102] ibid [25]–[27].
[103] ibid [27].
[104] See, eg, *Eastwood v Magnox Electric* (n 21) [5]; *Malik v Bank of Credit and Commerce International* (n 13) 45.
[105] See, eg, *Commonwealth Bank v Barker* (FCAFC) (n 7) [118].
[106] J Riley, 'Before the High Court—"Mutual Trust and Confidence" on Trial: At Last' (2014) 36 SLR 151, 159.
[107] ibid.

The implied term is not necessary

Drawing on the previous decision in *Byrne v Australian Airlines Ltd*,[108] the three judges stated that the implied term of mutual trust and confidence imposes mutual obligations 'wider than those which are "necessary", even allowing for the broad considerations which may inform implications in law. It goes to the maintenance of a relationship'.[109] The majority also found that while some lower courts in Australia had made 'approving references' to the recognition of the term, it was up to the High Court to 'determine the existence of the implied duty by reference to the principles governing implications of terms in law in a class of contract'.[110] This required the High Court 'to determine whether the proposed implication is "necessary" in the sense that would justify the exercise of the judicial power in a way that may have a significant impact upon employment relationships and the law of the contract of employment in this country'.[111]

This aspect of the High Court's judgment is explored in detail in Chapter 6. Unfortunately, it has not resolved what the judicial approach ought to be in relation to the necessity test that Australian courts use when asked to imply a term by law into employment contracts. There is a resulting sense of confusion and avoidance by the courts in applying the test to employment contracts, which, as elaborated in Chapter 6, is problematic because gaps in those contracts may remain and need to be filled.

The implied term could not be implied in fact into Mr Barker's employment contract

As an alternative, Mr Barker sought to argue that a duty of mutual trust and confidence ought to be implied in fact into his particular employment contract. However, the majority found that his counsel was unable to point to any particular feature of his contract that would support its implication in fact. This conclusion was drawn despite references to Mr Barker's seniority, his long and distinguished career with the bank, and the contract's silence on matters of trust and confidence.[112]

While this reasoning marked a clear rejection of the term as one implied in fact into Mr Barker's employment contract, it still left itself open to criticism. According to Carter and others commenting on the High Court's decision,[113] the High Court assumed that the five cumulative tests for implying a term in fact in *BP Refinery (Westernport) Pty Ltd v Shire of Hastings*[114] in relation to any contract in writing (or

---

[108] (1995) 185 CLR 410 (HCA), 436 (McHugh and Gummow JJ).
[109] *Commonwealth Bank v Barker* (HCA) (n 1) [37].
[110] ibid [36].
[111] ibid.
[112] ibid [43].
[113] See generally, Carter and others (n 91).
[114] (1977) 180 CLR 266 (HCA), 283. See also *Codelfa Construction Pty Ltd v State Rail Authority of New South Wales* (1982) 149 CLR 337 (HCA).

evidenced by writing) applied to this matter. As described in Chapter 1, in *Hawkins v Clayton*[115] Deane J suggested that the five *BP Refinery v Shire of Hastings* tests would not govern factual implication when 'it is apparent that the parties have not attempted to spell out the full terms of their contract'.[116] This suggestion was later approved in *Byrne v Australian Airlines*.[117] Deane J's single criterion from *Hawkins v Clayton* was that the implied term must be 'necessary for the reasonable or effective operation of a contract of that nature in the circumstances of the case'.[118] The High Court in *Commonwealth Bank v Barker* made no reference to this single criterion for implication. Carter and others believed that this was 'surprising',[119] given that many implied terms in employment contracts (including, potentially, the mutual trust and confidence term) would be implied according to Deane J's criterion. As Carter and others point out, '[c]learly, the criterion of "reasonable or effective operation" does not, in terms, match French CJ, Bell and Keane JJ's category of terms implied "in fact or ad hoc to give business efficacy to a contract"'.[120] Accordingly, '[a] term may be *necessary* for the "reasonable operation" of a contract without also being "necessary" to give it "business efficacy"'.[121]

Overall, had the High Court interpreted the test for implying the mutual trust and confidence term in fact according to the test in *Hawkins v Clayton*, this may well have resulted in the implication of the term into Mr Barker's employment contract. It has since been interesting to note that a more recent argument was put before the Supreme Court of Queensland that a mutual trust and confidence term should otherwise be implied in fact into the particular contract in question in *The HMW Accounting and Financial Group v McPherson*,[122] but was ultimately unsuccessful based on the particular facts of the case.[123]

The employees who would be affected by the implication were not heard in the appeal, therefore providing a further basis for the term's rejection

The majority judgment recognised that it was significant that the term would impose obligations on employees, whose voices were not heard in the appeal. This suggested another reason for it to remain 'in the province of the legislature'.[124] The judges concluded by finding 'the complex policy considerations encompassed by those views of the implication mark it, in the Australian context, as a matter more appropriate for the legislature than for the courts to determine'.[125] Like

---

[115] (1988) 164 CLR 539 (HCA).
[116] ibid 573.
[117] *Byrne v Australian Airlines* (n 108) 422, 442.
[118] *Hawkins v Clayton* (n 115) 573.
[119] Carter and others (n 91) 211.
[120] ibid.
[121] ibid.
[122] (2020) 292 IR 198 (Supreme Court of Queensland (QSC)).
[123] ibid [115]–[163].
[124] *Commonwealth Bank v Barker* (HCA) (n 1) [38].
[125] ibid [40].

the majority's finding that the implication of the term is beyond the proper lawmaking function of the courts, this reason for avoiding the implication of the term is informed by policy-based considerations. Again, a more detailed assessment of this aspect of the majority's judgment is conducted in Chapter 7.

In her separate reasons, Kiefel J said the Full Federal Court had concluded that the term of trust and confidence required the bank to take positive steps to consult with Mr Barker about redeployment. However, she said clause 8 of his contract left no room for the operation of the term. Her Honour found that '[a] term cannot be said to be necessary in this sense if the contract is effective without it. A contract clearly is effective where it already contains a term to the effect sought'.[126] In more general terms, she said that employment contracts would not be 'rendered futile' if they did not contain an implied term that an employer must attempt to redeploy an employee before terminating their employment.[127]

Justice Kiefel also criticised the Full Federal Court majority for 'brushing aside' the test of necessity as 'elusive'.[128] On the contrary, she said it was 'not uncertain' and 'has the advantage of providing objectivity' to the test for implying terms by law.[129] She noted that the Full Federal Court majority 'did not explain how the obligation to attempt to redeploy [Mr Barker] could arise from the term of trust and confidence'.[130] Her Honour stated that the term of trust and confidence developed from conduct that would allow the employee to terminate the relationship, but out of that context actionable conduct 'effectively becomes anything that damages the employment relationship'.[131]

Justice Gageler agreed with the reasons and orders of the majority, adding that the test of necessity meant no more than that 'a court should not imply a new term other than by reference to considerations that are compelling'.[132] His Honour also endorsed Jessup J's dissenting judgment from the Full Federal Court that the implied term of mutual trust and confidence ought not to be imported into Australia's common law. In particular, he agreed with Jessup J's view that the term was inherently uncertain and had 'the potential to act as a Trojan horse in the sense of revealing only after the event the specific prohibitions which it imports into the contract'.[133]

---

[126] ibid [90].
[127] ibid [108].
[128] ibid [85].
[129] ibid.
[130] ibid [101].
[131] ibid [102].
[132] ibid [114].
[133] ibid [117].

C. Application Beyond Employment

Having considered the mutual trust and confidence term's status in respect of English and Australian employment contracts, its application in a context broader than employment now warrants attention in respect of both jurisdictions. The above discussion has made it apparent that in England the duty is routinely implied by law in the context of employment. However, in Australia it no longer has any application in employment.

Therefore, on the one hand, it may be safe to assume that, absent any operation in the context of Australian employment contracts, the duty would, in turn, be unable to operate in the context of contracts for the performance of work in Australia. In English contracts for the performance of work, on the other hand, the duty's potential scope of operation may well be wider, based purely on its prevalence in the context of all employment.

However, this rationale seems overly simplistic. Looking more closely at Australian contracts for the performance of work, for instance, the same statutory regulation that apparently barred the duty's implication in Australia following *Commonwealth Bank v Barker* only exists in respect of employment contracts. Contracts for the performance of work are not subject to the same statutory protections as employment contracts. If anything, contracts for the performance of work are characterised, in part, by a lack of statutory regulation. Such a lack of regulation may have the flow-on effect of limiting a court's ability to suggest that the duty's implication in contracts for the performance of work ought to remain the legislature's responsibility. An Australian court may therefore choose to adopt a different approach to that of the High Court in *Commonwealth Bank v Barker* if faced with the question of whether it is necessary to imply a mutual trust and confidence term into a contract for the performance of work. It is possible that a court may take the opportunity to identify a necessary gap to be filled in the absence of adequate statutory protection. The following discussion therefore continues based on the assumption that the duty *may* be capable of operation in respect of contracts for the performance of work in Australia, as well as in England.

Despite such potential, it is unclear as to whether those engaged under contracts for the performance of work would even stand to benefit from a mutual trust and confidence term implied by law. Indeed, doubt has been expressed as to whether such a term could apply fully to contracts for the performance of work outside the common law category of employment.[134] For instance, in four English cases a claim for the existence of a mutual trust and confidence term in an instance

---

[134] See, eg, Freedland (n 22) 177; D Cabrelli and J D'Alton, *Furlough and Common Law Rights and Remedies* (*UK Labour Law Blog*, 8 June 2020) <https://uklabourlawblog.com/2020/06/08/furlough-and-common-law-rights-and-remedies-by-david-cabrelli-and-jessica-dalton/>, accessed 20 December 2022, citing *inter alia, Jani-King (GB) Ltd v Pula Enterprises Ltd* [2008] 1 All ER (Comm) 451 (QB) (regarding a franchise agreement).

of non-employment has been flatly rejected.[135] Similar cases have not arisen in Australia, no doubt due to the High Court's outright rejection of the term in respect of employment contracts in *Commonwealth Bank v Barker*. That is not to say, however, that such arguments could not be made beyond employment.

In respect of the English position, David Cabrelli and Jessica D'Alton suggest that those cases, which have rejected the mutual trust and confidence term's operation in respect of non-employment contracts, ought not to negate the possibility that courts will abandon their hesitancy, potentially recognising a mutual trust and confidence term in a contract for the personal performance of work. The rationale behind this suggestion is that, just as with employees, those engaged under personal work contracts also suffer from an imbalance of bargaining power. Policy considerations would therefore typically indicate that they should not be denied common law protection conferred by the mutual trust and confidence term. The fact that workers and independent contractors are not subject to the same kinds of protections typically afforded to employees should not prevent relevant policy considerations from being afforded the weight they deserve in the conferral of such a common law right for their benefit.[136] The same logic could arguably be applied to those engaged under a contract for the performance of work in Australia. Again, for the reasons already described, the likelihood of such arguments succeeding remains uncertain. The point is that a mutual trust and confidence term may well have an extended role in shaping contracts for the performance of work in both England and Australia, based on policy grounds. It seems illogical to suggest that its application or non-application should be contingent on the existence of an employment contract alone, particularly given the vulnerability of those performing work under contracts for the performance of work, which is common to both jurisdictions.

Nevertheless, given the potential uncertainty associated with the application of a mutual trust and confidence term as one implied by law into contracts for the performance of work, Cabrelli and D'Alton suggest that another option for those engaged under such contracts is to instead claim that it be implied as a term in fact into their particular contract. However, as described in Chapter 1, the test for implying a term in fact is not necessarily easy to satisfy. If implied in fact, such a test would also only have the effect of altering the particular contract for the performance of work in question, serving no wider purpose in shaping those contracts in a broader, more consistent sense. For that reason, the term's potential operation as

---

[135] See, eg, *Bedfordshire CC v Fitzpatrick Contractors Ltd* (1998) 62 Con LR 64 (England and Wales High Court (Technology and Construction Court) (TCC)) (highway maintenance contract); *Jani-King v Pula Enterprises* (n 134) (franchise agreement); *Chelsfield Advisers LLP v Qatari Diar Real Estate Investment Company* [2015] EWHC 1322 (High Court of Justice (Chancery Division) (Ch Div)) (property development promotion contract); *Mr H TV Ltd v ITV2 Ltd* [2015] EWHC 2840 (Commercial Court (Comm)) (reality TV production contract).
[136] Cabrelli and D'Alton (n 134).

one implied by law in select contracts for the performance of work seems unpalatable and devoid of broader policy-based effect.

Good Faith

Discussion now turns to the duty of good faith. First, attention is paid to the duty's status in England in contracts generally, and in employment contracts specifically.[137] Secondly, consideration is given to the duty's potential in Australia both in respect of contracts generally and employment contracts specifically, noting the confusion as to its existence and content, followed by a look at future options available for embracing it. Finally, the duty's application is considered beyond the scope of employment in contracts for the personal performance of work in both England and Australia.

A. Evolution and Existence in England

English courts have traditionally been highly averse to developing a general contractual duty of good faith.[138] A leading commentary on the issue notes that:[139]

> in keeping with the principles of freedom of contract and the binding force of contract, in English contract law there is no legal principle of good faith of general application, although some authors have argued that there should be.

Gunther Teubner has also described good faith as an 'irritant' in English law. He sees it as an 'infection' from European law, which does not accord with the inherent culture of the common law.[140]

Notwithstanding this defiance, the English position on a general duty of good faith appears to be evolving as a consequence of the English High Court decision concerning a distribution agreement, *Yam Seng Pte Ltd v International Trade Corporation Ltd*.[141] In that case, Leggatt J made the bold assertion that 'I respectfully suggest that the traditional English hostility towards a doctrine of good faith in the performance of contracts, to the extent it still persists, is misplaced'.[142] His

---

[137] For a summary of the English position in respect of the role of a general duty of good faith, see J Paterson, 'Good Faith Duties in Contract Performance' (2014) 14 OUCLJ 283, 285–87.

[138] This tendency in England has been described in J Beatson and D Friedmann, 'From "Classical" to Modern Contract Law' in J Beatson and D Friedman (eds), *Good Faith and Fault in Contract Law* (Clarendon Paperbacks 1995) 3, 14–15.

[139] H Beale, *Chitty on Contracts* (31st edn, Sweet & Maxwell 2012) ¶1-039.

[140] See generally, G Teubner, 'Legal Irritants: Good Faith in British Law or How Unifying Law Ends Up in New Divergences' (1998) 61 MLR 11.

[141] [2013] 1 All ER (Comm) 1321 (QB).

[142] ibid [153].

Honour ultimately held that there was a term implied in fact into the particular contract in question that the parties would deal with each other in good faith.[143] Specifically, he held that what good faith requires is 'sensitive to context', but that it included the 'core value of honesty'.[144] His Honour described the test of good faith as an objective one: whether, in the particular context, reasonable people would regard the conduct as 'commercially unacceptable'.[145]

Notwithstanding this recognition of the duty, the extent to which Leggatt J's decision will be followed in England remains unclear.[146] As Brodie has emphasised, the law surrounding a general duty of good faith across contracts generally 'is still in a decidedly embryonic stage'.[147] That said, he predicts that this approach is 'likely to change sooner rather than later where the relationship can be viewed as analogous to employment'.[148]

As to the application of the good faith duty in employment, Alan Bogg explains that 'some caution is warranted before we fix upon a characterisation of [good faith in] English contract law in general, and the English contract of employment in particular'.[149] In making this claim, Bogg draws on the work of Simon Whittaker and Reinhardt Zimmerman, who assert that any statements about the English common law's rejection of good faith often 'must be qualified to such an extent as to make these bald general statements appear little more than caricatures'.[150] Whittaker and Zimmerman go on to mention that 'the law of special contracts is far less hostile to the idea of a good faith doctrine that its general counterpart'.[151] They cite the employment contract 'as a 'leading example of such a phenomenon'.[152]

Bogg then explains that '[w]hat history discloses is how recently the contract of employment [has] displayed elements of good faith in its basic constitution'.[153] He identifies that a duty of good faith in English employment contracts came to fruition in the late 1970s following, first, the development of the concept of terms implied by law and, secondly, the emergence of the mutual trust and confidence

---

[143] ibid [131] and [146]. For further discussion on this decision, see, eg, D Campbell, 'Good Faith and the Ubiquity of the *"Relational"* Contract' (2014) 77 MLR 475; S Whittaker, 'Good Faith, Implied Terms and Commercial Contracts' (2013) 129 LQR 463.
[144] *Yam Seng v International Trade Corporation* (n 141) [141].
[145] ibid [144].
[146] See, eg, the later decision in *Mid Essex Hospital Services NHS Trust v Compass Group UK and Ireland Ltd (t/a Medirest)* [2013] BLR 265 (CA) [105], in which the English Court of Appeal cited *Yam Seng v International Trade Corporation* (n 141) but did not base its decision on the principles stated by Leggatt J.
[147] D Brodie, 'Fair Dealing and the World of Work' (2014) 43 ILJ 29, 43.
[148] ibid.
[149] A Bogg, 'Good Faith in the Contract of Employment: A Case of the English Reserve?' (2011) 32 Comp LL & PJ 729, 730.
[150] ibid, citing S Whitaker and R Zimmerman, 'Good Faith in European Contract Law: Surveying the Legal Landscape' in S Whitaker and R Zimmerman (eds), *Good Faith in European Contract Law* (CUP 2000) 7, 41.
[151] Whitaker and Zimmerman (n 150) 41.
[152] ibid.
[153] Bogg (n 149) 741.

term.[154] He specifically cites 1977 as the year in which the development of the duty of good faith as a term implied by law in employment 'coincided with the judicial articulation of the mutual trust and confidence term'.[155]

Nowadays, English authorities have tended to support the notion that there is actually a single obligation encompassing both a duty of mutual trust and confidence in employment and a duty of good faith. In that sense, both duties have come to be treated as one and the same.[156] For example, in a pair of cases concerning the abuse of an employer's disciplinary powers, Lord Nicholls invoked the language of good faith alongside the application of the mutual trust and confidence term:[157]

> The trust and confidence implied term means, in short, that an employer must treat his employees fairly. In his conduct of his business, and in his treatment of his employees, an employer must act responsibly and in good faith.

There are four key reasons for this apparent 'transformation of the contract of employment into a contract of good faith'.[158] First, it was largely the consequence of judicial thinking reconfiguring the concept of the English employment contract. Specifically, the regulatory gap left by the disappearance of collective bargaining during that time (and the good faith functions fulfilled by that system of collective bargaining) 'necessitated a creative regulatory response by the common law and the crafting of a contractual good faith duty'.[159] Secondly, the courts had developed a 'distinctive employee-protective philosophy compared with the dominant "judicial philosophy of market individualism"'.[160] Thirdly, some judicial speeches given at that time pointed to the influence of relational contract theory as underpinning the shift toward contractual good faith in employment.[161] Fourthly, there was a deep normative reconfiguration of the employment contract in the English common law, such that employment was no longer considered a mere exchange of wages for work and, due to the inherent subordination of the employee to employer, the employee was seen as especially vulnerable to abuses of power by the employer.[162] As Brodie elucidates, this focus on 'human dignity' has generated a

---

[154] ibid 742.
[155] ibid 746–47, citing B Hepple, *Rights at Work: Global, European and British Perspectives* (Sweet & Maxwell 2005) 51–52. As to the interrelationship between the two duties, see further, D Cabrelli, 'Discretion, Power and the Rationalisation of Implied Terms' (2007) 36 ILJ 194, 201–02; Collins, Ewing, and McCoglan (n 27) 147–48, 150–52; Anderson, Brodie and Riley (n 7) 135–40.
[156] See, eg, *Johnson v Unisys* (n 21) [24]; *Eastwood v Magnox Electric* (n 21) [11]; *Russell v Trustees of the Roman Catholic Church for the Archdiocese of Sydney* (2007) 69 NSWLR 198 (New South Wales Court of Appeal (NSWCA)) [32]; *Rogan-Gardiner v Woolworths Ltd* [2010] WASC 290 (Supreme Court of Western Australia (WASC)) [125]–[126].
[157] *Eastwood v Magnox Electric* (n 21) [11].
[158] Bogg (n 149) 746–47.
[159] ibid 749.
[160] ibid.
[161] ibid.
[162] ibid 750.

distinctive version of good faith in English employment contracts.[163] Separately, Brodie has commented that nowadays in England, '[g]ood faith ... has assumed a central role in the life of the employment contract and has acted, and continues to act, as a catalyst for further evolution at common law'.[164]

B. Confusion as to Existence and Content in Australia

This discussion considers the widespread confusion surrounding the existence of a duty of good faith in Australia, both in respect of contracts generally, and employment contracts specifically. The law concerning a general duty of good faith in Australia remains 'in a chaotic state'.[165] Over the past thirty years, 'despite multiple opportunities, Australian courts have failed to reach anything approaching consensus'.[166] As has already been made clear, while the High Court in *Commonwealth Bank v Barker* was firm in denying the implication of the mutual trust and confidence term across all employment contracts, it deliberately left open the possibility for a future implication of a more general duty of good faith.[167] However, the High Court did not make clear its view as to the contractual context in which the duty ought to operate, or if it should even operate at all. In their joint judgment, French CJ and Bell and Keane JJ stated that their rejection of the implied term 'should not be taken as reflecting upon the question whether there is a general obligation to act in good faith in the performance of contracts'.[168] Justice Kiefel said that the question had not been resolved in Australia, and stated that '[n]either that question, nor the questions whether such a standard could apply to particular categories of contract (such as employment contracts) or to the contract here in issue, were raised in argument in these proceedings'.[169] She noted it was therefore 'neither necessary nor appropriate to discuss good faith further, particularly having regard to the wider importance of the topic'.[170]

When reflecting on these loose references to the duty, Anthony Gray commented that there was no real need for the court to mention good faith as 'the submissions

---

[163] Brodie, 'Mutual Trust and Confidence: Catalysts, Constraints and Commonality' (n 22) 339.
[164] Brodie (n 147) 32. For an assessment of the transformative role that good faith can play in employment, see S Tsuruda, 'Good Faith in Employment' (2023) 24 Theor Inq Law 206.
[165] Stewart and others (n 39) 528.
[166] ibid.
[167] See also the earlier decision in *Royal Botanic Gardens and Domain Trust v South Sydney City Council* (2002) 240 CLR 45 (HCA) [40] and [156], where the High Court similarly declined to decide whether Australian law should recognise a general obligation to act in good faith in the performance of contracts. Cf the early reference in *Gardiner v Orchard* (1910) 10 CLR 722 (HCA), 739–40, where Isaacs J found the ability of a contracting party to exercise a termination right was limited by requirements of good faith and reasonableness.
[168] *Commonwealth Bank v Barker* (HCA) (n 1) [42].
[169] ibid [107].
[170] ibid.

in the case barely referred to good faith, and the transcripts reflect justices raising questions about good faith, rather than either advocate making substantial submissions about the doctrine'.[171] With this in mind Gray suggested that 'members of the court went out of their way to keep discussion of good faith bubbling along'.[172]

Beyond the High Court reserving its position in *Commonwealth Bank v Barker*,[173] some lower Australian courts have suggested that there is a duty of good faith in the performance of employment contracts, which is similar to an obligation found in commercial contracts.[174] Others have found that no such duty exists in either type of contract.[175] Several decisions concerning whether the duty ought to be implied into employment contracts following *Commonwealth Bank v Barker* have rejected the term.[176] In *Bartlett v ANZ Banking Group Limited*[177] the Court of Appeal mentioned the possibility of the duty in employment,[178] but failed to make a definitive ruling on its existence.

Apart from the confusion surrounding the duty's existence, there is also the question as to what its content would entail in the Australian context. This is not a simple question to answer. Justice Finn once described the concept as 'protean'.[179] Geoffrey Kuene referred to it as 'chameleonic'.[180] At the very least, it seems to require that parties act in a way that is not arbitrary or capricious in their performance of the contract.[181] However,

---

[171] Gray (n 91) 359, citing *Commonwealth Bank of Australia v Barker* [2014] HCATrans 73 (8 April 2014) (HCA); [2014] HCATrans 74 (9 April 2014) (HCA). Good faith was not argued in the lower court decisions either.

[172] Gray (n 91) 359.

[173] The High Court had also left the matter open in *Royal Botanic Gardens and Domain Trust v South Sydney City Council* (n 167) [40] and [165].

[174] See, eg, *Downe v Sydney West Area Health Service (No 2)* (2008) 71 NSWLR 633 (NSWSC) [320]–[328]; *Rogan-Gardiner v Woolworths* (n 156) [125]–[126]; *Foggo v O'Sullivan Partners (Advisory) Pty Ltd* [2011] NSWSC 501 (NSWSC) [89] and [98]; *Dye v Commonwealth Securities* (n 64) [47]–[50]; *Adventure World Travel Pty Ltd v Newsom* (2014) 86 NSWLR 515 (NSWSC) [26]; *Harden v Willis Australia Group Services Pty Ltd* [2021] NSWSC 939 (NSWSC) [26]–[32].

[175] See, eg, *Esso Australia Resources Pty Ltd v Southern Pacific Petroleum NL* [2005] VSCA 228 (Victorian Court of Appeal (VSCA)) [2]–[5] and [22]–[28]; *CGU Workers Compensation (NSW) Ltd v Garcia* (2007) 69 NSWLR 680 (NSWSC) [132], [143], and [168]; *Tote Tasmania Pty Ltd v Garrott* (2008) 17 Tas R 320 (Supreme Court of Tasmania (TASSC)) [16].

[176] See, eg, *Swindells v State of Victoria* [2015] VSC 19 (Supreme Court of Victoria (VSC)) [172]; *Russo v Westpac Banking Corporation* [2015] FCCA 1086 (Federal Circuit Court of Australia (FCCA)); *Regulski v State of Victoria* [2015] FCA 206 (FCA) [219]–[223]; *New South Wales v Shaw* (2015) 248 IR 206 (NSWCA); *Gramotnev v Queensland University of Technology* (2015) 251 IR 448 (Queensland Court of Appeal (QCA)). See further, the discussion about the potential scope for a good faith duty post-*Commonwealth Bank v Barker* (HCA) (n 1) in Riley Munton (n 48) 93–94.

[177] [2016] NSWCA 30 (NSWCA).

[178] ibid [38]–[49] and [106]–[107].

[179] *Secretary, Department of Education, Employment, Training and Youth Affairs v Prince* (1997) 82 FCR 154 (FCA), 130.

[180] G Kuehne, 'Implied Obligations of Good Faith and Reasonableness in Performance of Contracts: Old Wine in New Bottles?' (2006) 33 UWALR 63, 64.

[181] See, eg, *Garry Rogers Motors (Aust) Pty Ltd v Subaru (Aust) Pty Ltd* (1999) ATPR 41-703 (FCA); *Pacific Brands Sport & Leisure v Underworks Pty Ltd* (2005) 12 Aust Contract Reports 90-213 (FCA), 104.

it cannot operate in a manner inconsistent with 'the express terms of the contract',[182] 'or with rights granted by statute'.[183]

Beyond these understandings, courts and academics remain divided on the duty's content. For some, it is restricted to a notion of honesty,[184] but for others, it includes a broader obligation to act reasonably.[185] There is also the circular argument that good faith includes an obligation not to act in bad faith,[186] but this hardly progresses an understanding of what good faith itself entails.

The broader view of good faith finds support in *Renard Constructions (ME) Pty Ltd v Minister for Public Works*.[187] In that case, a subclause in the contract between Renard Constructions (the contractor) and the Minister for Public Works (the principal) provided that upon default, the contractor could be required to show cause as to why the contract should not be terminated. After the contractor commenced work, delays occurred. The principal then gave notice under the subclause calling on the contractor to show cause as to why it should not take over the work or cancel the contract. In his judgment in the Court of Appeal, Priestley JA observed:[188]

> The contract can in my opinion only be effective as a workable business document under which the promises of each party to the other may be fulfilled, if the subclause is read ... as subject to requirements of reasonableness.

However, Elisabeth Peden has described this approach, which equates an obligation of reasonableness with one of good faith, as 'misconceived'.[189] Peden contends that it cannot be argued that for a party to a contract to act in good faith, it must discharge a positive obligation to act reasonably.[190] On this understanding, if acting reasonably involves 'subjective reasonableness, then this description really goes no further than requiring "honesty"'.[191] She goes on to say that reasonableness in this subjective sense 'can be used when considering the exercise of rights', and that this approach sits 'comfortably with a more limited concept of good faith'.[192] For some

---

[182] Stewart and others (n 39) 531, citing *Vodafone Pacific Ltd v Mobile Innovations Ltd* [2004] NSWCA 15 (NSWCA); *Central Exchange Ltd v Anaconda Nickel Ltd* (2002) 26 WAR 33 (Supreme Court of Western Australia (WASC)).
[183] Stewart and others (n 39) 531, citing *Swindells v State of Victoria* (n 176) [172]; *New South Wales v Shaw* (n 176) [135].
[184] For a discussion on authorities which mention good faith and honesty, see, eg, Gray (n 91) 366–68.
[185] For a discussion on authorities which mention good faith and reasonableness, see, eg, Gray (n 91) 368–69.
[186] See, eg, *Pacific Brands Sport & Leisure v Underworks* (n 181) [65].
[187] (1992) 26 NSWLR 234 (NSWCA).
[188] ibid 258.
[189] E Peden, 'When Common Law Trumps Equity: The Rise of Good Faith and Reasonableness and the Demise of Unconscionability' (2005) 21 JCL 226, 236.
[190] See, eg, ibid. See also J Carter and E Peden, 'Good Faith in Australian Contract Law' (2003) 19 JCL 155, 157.
[191] Peden (n 189) 236.
[192] ibid.

time, in fact, 'courts have held that discretions or powers must be exercised honestly or in a way that no reasonable person would consider is unreasonable'.[193]

Legitimate questions also exist as to whether good faith differs from the mutual trust and confidence term rejected in *Commonwealth Bank v Barker*. There may actually be no distinction between an implied duty of mutual trust and confidence and one of good faith.[194] In the lead up to *Commonwealth Bank v Barker*, 'there was little effort or reason to distinguish between … [the two duties]'.[195] During oral submissions in *Commonwealth Bank v Barker*, however, French CJ pondered: 'How does the implication found here differ from an implication of good faith? Is that just a subset or is it just a manifestation?'[196] Bret Walker SC, for the bank, responded that he could not discern 'any factor which would distinguish the supposed implied term in this case from something that is as broad as a notion of good faith'.[197] That said, there remains a view to the contrary, whereby the mutual trust and confidence and good faith duties are separate and able to coexist.[198] In support of this view, Riley Munton argues that '[t]he two concepts … describe closely related but nevertheless distinct obligations arising in an employment relationship, and perhaps perform different functions in resolving employment contract disputes'.[199]

Riley Munton's reasons for viewing mutual trust and confidence and good faith as two separate (albeit related) duties include that 'just like siblings, they are derived from the same source',[200] such that they are part of a relationship of employment, but perform different functions.[201] She explains that it '[i]t is useful to reserve the terminology of "mutual trust and confidence" to describe a particular characteristic of an employment contract that distinguishes it from, say, a contract of sale or other transient contractual arrangement'.[202] The terminology of 'good faith' most appropriately describes a distinct 'governing principle in the construction and interpretation of relational contracts such as employment'.[203]

---

[193] ibid 237 and the cases discussed from 237–40. See also the discussion below in relation to how a duty of good faith (if it is recognised) might operate in respect of an employer's exercise of a discretionary power.
[194] See, eg, *Russell v Trustees of the Roman Catholic Church* (n 156) [32], where Basten JA stated: 'Although there were said to be two implied terms, it is probably sufficient to identify them as a single obligation'.
[195] Stewart and others (n 39) 529, citing *Russell v Trustees of the Roman Catholic Church* (n 156) 567.
[196] [2014] HCATrans 73 (8 April 2014) (HCA) [365].
[197] ibid [370].
[198] See generally, Riley (n 3).
[199] ibid 523, citing *Gilles v Downer EDI Ltd* [2011] NSWSC 1055 (NSWSC) [78]–[79], in which Rothman J supports this proposition.
[200] Riley (n 3) 529.
[201] ibid.
[202] ibid.
[203] ibid. As to the relationship between implication and construction, see Chapter 1. For a discussion on employment contracts as 'relational', see Chapter 5.

With these differing views in mind, both the existence and content of a duty of good faith—whether in employment contracts or contracts generally—remains unclear. The Supreme Court of Canada's concession that the obligation is 'incapable of precise definition'[204] provides little encouragement in the search for a more exacting description.[205] Catherine Mitchell has also suggested that trying to contract for such a behavioural value 'may at best appear contrived and, at worst, may empty cooperative behaviour of much of ... [the contract's] value by interfering with its natural development'.[206] That is not to say that there are not options that might enable the duty to be embraced in some capacity in the future, which are canvassed directly below.

The latest edition of *Creighton and Stewart's Labour Law* lists 'three different views as to how a standard of good faith might be embraced in Australia'[207] in the future. The first is that a good faith term will be implied by law into all contracts, or at least into all commercial contracts. Whether employment contracts should be treated as commercial for this purpose remains unclear.[208] Again, the specific question of whether a good faith duty *ought* to be implied as a term by law into all employment contracts is returned to in this work's Conclusion.

For now, it is worth noting that there are some recent cases recognising an implied duty of good faith and fair dealing as one implied by law, which have involved franchisors who are said to owe the duty to their franchisees.[209] The authors of *Creighton and Stewart's Labour Law*, as well as Brodie, make the argument that, because of shared characteristics between employment and franchise agreements, 'the franchisee is vulnerable in very similar ways to the employee'.[210] It is difficult to see why the same protection ought not to be given to an employee.[211]

The second view rejects the existence of any general good faith duty. This rejection is:[212]

---

[204] See, eg, *Wallace v United Grain Growers Ltd* (1997) 152 DLR (4th) 1 (Supreme Court of Canada (SCC)) [98].
[205] Cf the more recent decision in *Bhasin v Hrynew* [2014] 3 SCR 494 (SCC) [63]–[64], where the Supreme Court of Canada unanimously accepted that good faith was an 'organising principle' of Canadian contract law. The court also attempted to explain what it meant by good faith, emphasising its flexible nature depending on individual circumstances. For a more detailed discussion on this decision, see generally, C Mummé, '*Bhasin v. Hrynew*: A New Era for Good Faith in Canadian Employment Law, or Just Tinkering at the Margins?' (2016) 32 IJCLL&IR 117.
[206] C Mitchell, 'Behavioural Standards in Contracts and English Contract Law' (2016) 33 JCL 234, 234.
[207] Stewart and others (n 39) 528. See also the range of options discussed as to the potential future application of a good faith duty following *Commonwealth Bank of Australia v Barker* in Gray (n 91) 370–77.
[208] Stewart and others (n 39) 528.
[209] See, eg, Stewart and others (n 39) 529, citing *Video Ezy International Pty Ltd v Mobile Innovations Ltd* [2014] NSWSC 143 (NSWSC) [72] and *Marmax Investments Pty Ltd v RPR Maintenance Pty Ltd* (2015) 237 FCR 634 (FCAFC) [122]. Cf *Meridian Retail Pty Ltd v Australian Unity Retail Network Pty Ltd* [2006] VSC 223 (VSC) [210]–[212].
[210] Brodie (n 147) 34.
[211] Stewart and others (n 39) 529.
[212] ibid 528.

[O]n the basis of a lack of necessity for its implication, a lack of clarity about the class of contract into which it would be implied, uncertainty about its content, or the lack of coherence between a judicial imposition of such a broad normative standard and the statutory imposition of more limited obligations.

That said, 'those who adopt this [second] view appear to accept that, in some cases at least, a duty of good faith may be a term implied in fact'[213] into the specific contract in question. Jeannie Paterson has noted that this has been the most common way in which the obligation has been treated in Australian case authorities.[214]

The third view is that a duty of good faith is not implied as a term at all—rather, it functions as a rule of construction,[215] applicable to all contracts.[216] As discussed in Chapter 1, on this understanding, the good faith term would constitute 'a principle or value that informs the meaning and application of express terms in the contract, or at least express written terms'.[217] If this becomes the accepted view, then 'the duty is not an independent term of the contract' capable of being breached and giving rise to a remedy. Instead, 'it operates as a fetter upon the exercise of the discretions and powers created by the contract'.[218]

Overall, while there are several possibilities as to how the duty could be embraced in Australia, these have not yet been 'scrutinised in any meaningful way in employment cases considering the matter'.[219] If anything, a 'resolution of the debate about the role of good faith in contracts generally will [likely] determine (or at least substantially resolve) the role of good faith in employment contracts'.[220] Assuming the duty is recognised in the context of employment, based on a collection of recent authorities,[221] it will most likely operate where it applies to a particular power, discretion, or obligation conferred by the employment contract. Should the duty attach to a discretionary power of the employer (rather than all

---

[213] ibid 529, citing *Esso Australia Resources v Southern Pacific Petroleum* (n 175) [2]–[5] and [22]–[28]; *CGU Workers Compensation v Garcia* (n 175) [132], [143] and [168]; *Tote Tasmania v Garrott* (n 175) [16].

[214] Paterson (n 137) 287, citing W M Dixon, 'Good Faith in Contractual Performance and Enforcement—Australian Doctrinal Hurdles' (2011) 39 ABLR 227.

[215] See, eg, E Peden, 'Incorporating Terms of Good Faith in Contract Law in Australia' (2001) 23 SLR 223, 230; P O'Grady, 'Nothing Implied: Construction as a Means of Curbing Excessive Use of Power in Employment Contracts' (2017) 30 AJLL 137; M Warren, 'Good Faith: Where Are We At?' (2010) 34 MULR 344, 948–49.

[216] As referred to in Chapter 1, the duty has also been characterised as a 'universal term' (ie a term implied by law into all contracts, and distinct from a rule of construction): see, eg, N C Seddon, R A Bigwood, and M P Ellinghaus, *Cheshire and Fifoot's Law of Contract* (10th edn, LexisNexis Butterworths 2012); J Paterson, A Robertson, and A Duke, *Principles of Contract Law* (5th edn, Lawbook Co 2016) 338; Paterson (n 137) 288.

[217] Stewart and others (n 39) 529, citing E Peden, *Good Faith in the Performance of Contracts* (LexisNexis Butterworths 2003). Cf *Vodafone Pacific v Mobile Innovations* (n 182) [204]–[206].

[218] *Pacific Brands Sport & Leisure v Underworks* (n 181) [64]. Cf *Service Station Association Ltd v Berg Bennett & Associates Pty Ltd* (1993) 45 FCR 84 (FCA), 91–8.

[219] Stewart and others (n 39) 529.

[220] ibid.

[221] See, eg, those authorities discussed in Stewart and others (n 39) 529–31.

acts of the employer under the contract) in this way, then the duty would apply when the exercise of that discretionary power affects an employees' enjoyment of the contract's essential benefits.[222]

C. Application Beyond Employment

The preceding discussion has highlighted the complexities associated with recognising a duty of good faith in both English and Australian contracts generally, and employment contracts specifically. It remains to be seen whether the same complexities plaguing the duty's existence and content in employment would extend to its potential application to contracts for the performance of work. If nothing else, in English law, there is arguably a clearer path for the potential operation of good faith duty in contracts for the performance of work (given its purported interrelationship with a duty of mutual trust and confidence) than in Australia, where the duty's existence and content remain in a heightened state of flux.

For this discussion, it is presumed that a good faith duty has the potential to operate in both jurisdictions as a term implied by law, and that this operation is not necessarily exclusive to employment contracts alone. Given the present uncertainty associated with the duty in Australia in particular, this presumption is clearly speculative in nature. However, it is adopted for the sake of examining the duty's potential application beyond employment in broader work relationships.

It must again be emphasised that it remains unclear whether those engaged under contracts for the performance of work would stand to benefit from common law terms implied by law, including a duty of good faith. Just as with the implied term of mutual trust and confidence, good faith may attach itself to contracts for the performance of work as a term implied by law for substantially similar policy-based reasons. An imbalance of bargaining power, coupled with greater vulnerability and economic hardship suffered by those engaged under contracts for the performance of work similarly point towards the duty's potential recognition as one implied by law into those contracts.

Apart from the potential influence of these policy-based factors, Hugh Collins has separately posited that understanding contracts for the performance of work as 'relational' in nature—which, he suggests, would usually be the case—may mean that those contracts automatically attract a duty of good faith.[223] (More is said about classifying contracts as 'relational' in Chapter 5.) Collins refers to *Bates v Post Office Ltd (No 3)*,[224] in which the sub-postmasters that had been classified

---

[222] See, eg, *Horkulak v Cantor Fitzgerald International* [2005] ICR 402 (CA). See generally, Cabrelli (n 155). For a discussion as to how the duty might operate in respect of the exercise of discretionary powers, see, eg, Stewart and others (n 39) 529–31.
[223] H Collins, 'Employment as a Relational Contract' (2021) 137 LQR 426, 448–49.
[224] [2019] EWHC 606 (QB).

as independent contractors held many similar traits to employees in respect of their work arrangements. Importantly, their contracts were classified as relational in nature. Collins also cites *Pimlico Plumbers Ltd v Smith*,[225] suggesting that the court's interpretations placed on the statutory concept of 'worker' emphasised a need for similar features to those of employment, including subordination to their employer, a requirement to work exclusively for that employer, as well as being engaged under a relational contract. Essentially, if this trend of closely approximating workers and independent contractors to employees continues, it follows that a term implied by law requiring performance in good faith will be applicable to those workers, so long as they are engaged under a relational contract.

Conclusion

Notwithstanding the English recognition of a duty of mutual trust and confidence, which exists alongside an interrelated duty of good faith in all employment contracts, Australia's position on both duties is unique. It does not flow naturally from the position in English law, as with many of the other key terms discussed in Chapter 3. As an extension of the historical analysis undertaken in Chapter 3, this chapter first explored the origins of both duties in England and then considered their current status in Australia. That inquiry shows that, from its inception, in the employment context the duty of mutual trust and confidence originated in England as a term implied by law. Later, the good faith term in employment was recognised as existing alongside the now well-established mutual trust and confidence term. These origins are unlike those of most of the other key terms analysed in Chapter 3, which stem from a combination of equity, tort, and the former master and servant statutory regime.

Despite these English origins, the High Court in *Commonwealth Bank v Barker* refused to recognise the duty of mutual trust and confidence as one implied by law into the class of employment contracts. It also left open the question as to the existence of a duty of good faith, both in respect of contracts generally and employment contracts specifically. Therefore, as with the select terms discussed in Chapter 3, the historical analysis undertaken in this chapter causes one to question the rationale that Australian courts should use when faced with the question of whether to imply a new term by law into the class of employment contracts. That rationale is reflexive, in the sense that the basis for English courts continuing to imply new terms by law could be similarly questioned. Broader debates are also raised in relation to the High Court's reasons not to imply the mutual trust and confidence term, particularly in respect of its obscure application of the necessity test, as well as its

---

[225] [2018] ICR 1511 (UKSC).

policy-based reasoning that any implication of the term would be better handled by the legislature. Given their significance, these matters are set to receive further attention in Chapters 6 and 7, respectively.

In relation to good faith in the Australian context, while the future of the duty (if it does exist) remains in doubt, it has the potential to come into operation as a term implied by law or in fact, or as a rule of construction. The question of whether the duty of good faith ought to be implied as a term by law into the class of employment contracts in Australia is returned to in this work's Conclusion. It makes sense to consider this question later to enable further consideration of the appropriate rationale for the courts to adopt when deciding whether to imply a term by law into the class of employment contracts.

A key hypothesis of this chapter was that in both England and Australia a duty of mutual trust and confidence and good faith have the potential to operate as terms implied by law into contracts for the performance of work, and beyond the scope of the employment relationship alone. This suggestion is speculative only as no case law exists in either England or Australia to suggest that this ought to be the widely accepted approach. Indeed, in Australia, the existence of either duty as one implied by law into contracts for the performance of work is particularly tenuous, given the challenges associated with the status of both duties in the realm of employment. It is nevertheless reconciled that contracts for the performance of work typically have several traits that lend themselves to being similar to employment, in the sense that workers and independent contractors also are subject to subordination and imbalances in bargaining power, and there is greater likelihood of their vulnerability and economic hardship. As such, for policy-based reasons, those engaged under contracts for the performance of work arguably ought to have the benefit of the duties of mutual trust and confidence and good faith. It is apparent from this hypothesis that contracts for the performance of work may possess many similar traits to employment contracts, in some ways suggesting that they may be more similar than they are different. It is therefore appropriate to examine, in Chapter 5, the distinctiveness of the employment contract as opposed to other contracts for the performance of work.

PART III

TERMS IMPLIED BY LAW INTO EMPLOYMENT CONTRACTS

5
Employment as a Class of Contract

Introduction

Understanding precisely what constitutes employment, as distinct from other contracts for the performance of work, is surprisingly inconsistent across English and Australian law. This chapter therefore aims to explore employment as a class of contract, surveying a series of understandings that have shaped its composite strands.[1]

As described in Chapter 1, at common law, terms may be implied by law as necessary incidents of a particular class or category of contract, including employment contracts. This chapter supports the proposition that, in the context of implying terms by law, the class of employment contracts is not easily identifiable. The so-called 'class' has evolved into an overly generalised and inconsistently defined category into which terms have been and continue to be implied by law. The result is that there is widespread confusion about what makes employment contracts distinct from other types of contracts, and particularly from those for the broader performance of work, a result caused by the obfuscation between what does and does not constitute employment. In turn, courts have struggled to identify when it is appropriate to imply new terms by law into employment contracts. This chapter identifies the problems that inevitably arise in response to such inconsistencies.

First, it describes recent academic approaches to identifying the distinctive characteristics of employment contracts. Secondly, the chapter addresses the extent to which general contract law principles have become applicable to employment contracts. Thirdly, the focus turns to the distinction between employees, workers in the middle category between employees and independent contractors, and independent contractors. Fourthly, following that discussion, the chapter provides assessment of the operation of statutory rules that are specific to employment, or contingent on there being an employment contract. Fifthly, attention moves to a consideration of the courts' imposition of duties that are exclusive to employment. Sixthly, the focus turns to the courts' reluctance to exclude particular duties in employment. Lastly, there is an assessment of recent academic and judicial classifications of employment as a relational contract.

Seen from the perspective of these seven sections, competing understandings emerge about what constitutes employment as a separate and distinct class of

---

[1] This chapter builds on preliminary explorations into what makes the employment contract distinctive in G Golding, 'The Distinctiveness of the Employment Contract' (2019) 32 AJLL 170.

contract. Various distinguishing factors are identified, with no single, universally applicable definition or understanding evident. The employment contract is clearly capable of some description, albeit based on a wide range of factors which need not apply universally to every instance of employment. It may also be the case that there is no single or distinct feature of an employment contract that is not shared by any other contract.

A brief conclusion shows how the resulting tension caused by a lack of unified understanding is brought to the fore in relation to generating a better understanding of employment as distinct from the performance of work, especially when courts choose to shape them through the mechanism of implying a new term by law. It presents a case for generating greater judicial clarity about what makes employment contracts a distinct class of contract into which terms may be implied by law. In sum, it is suggested that there is scope for the courts to generate greater clarity in their understanding of what makes employment contracts distinctive in order to give rise to more accurate predictions of when new terms may be implied by law in shaping employment contracts. It remains possible and preferable for courts to explain more consistently and comprehensively their understanding of what constitutes the employment contract, without necessarily generating an exhaustive, 'catch-all' definition.

General Distinctive Characteristics of Employment

Despite doubts expressed on the potential for courts to generate a comprehensive understanding of what constitutes an employment contract, this does not mean that leading labour law writers have not made convincing attempts to do it. The present section canvasses four recent approaches. Ways in which the judiciary and the legislature have attempted to understand and differentiate the employment contract are covered in the remaining sections.

First, Mark Freedland has argued that the employment contract could be envisaged as containing, or even as being built around, three core structural principles: exchange, integration, and reciprocity.[2] Taking each of these principles in turn, under the 'exchange principle' an employment contract 'should be regarded as essentially consisting of an exchange, or more usually a series of exchanges, of work and remuneration taking place in the context of a personal work relationship'.[3] The 'integration principle' provides that where the exchange principle operates, 'the worker should be regarded and treated as integrated into the organisation of the employer or employing enterprise'.[4] Finally, the 'reciprocity principle'

---

[2] See generally, M Freedland, 'The Legal Structure of the Contract of Employment' in M Freedland and others (eds), *The Contract of Employment* (OUP 2016) 28, 28–51.
[3] ibid 42.
[4] ibid.

provides that 'the employer or employing enterprise and the worker should be regarded and treated as being committed to reciprocal cooperation in the conduct of that contractual relationship'.[5] According to Freedland, these three principles 'can be expanded in such a way as to provide a normative critique or underpinning of the structure of the contract of employment'.[6] They can be used to 'both frame and evaluate the functioning of the law of the contract of employment',[7] and are said to represent a 'normative' view of the employment contract as they present 'a set of ideas' that 'constitute the normative commitments or purposes of the law of the contract of employment because they implement or fulfil the functions of labour law'.[8]

Whether these three principles can be used to set out a distinctive understanding of employment contracts remains to be considered. Certain employment contracts will not have all three features. For instance, the reciprocity principle in zero hours contracts is clearly different in continuing contracts, given that there is no mutuality of obligation. The hirer is under no irrevocable obligation to offer the zero hours' worker any work, and there is no corresponding irrevocable commitment imposed on the zero hours' worker to accept any work offered by the hirer. Some contracts for services have all three features. Absent any implied duty of mutual trust and confidence, the reciprocity feature in Australian employment contracts, in contrast with English employment contracts,[9] is substantially curtailed.

Secondly, Clyde Summers has written of the similarities and differences between employment and civil or commercial contracts.[10] In the process of doing so, he identified that there is much less freedom of contract in employment contracts than in commercial contracts.[11] However, that is not to say that employment contracts are entirely without the element of freedom of contract. Freedom to contract is curtailed in the context of employment due to the nature of the terms that an employer can lawfully impose, with employment contracts being designed to balance the bargaining power between employees and their employer in the labour market.[12] In reaching this overarching conclusion, Summers lists six characteristics, which he says in combination and in their totality, set employment contracts apart from other types of contract:[13]

---

[5] ibid.
[6] ibid.
[7] ibid 41.
[8] ibid.
[9] As to the existence of the mutual trust and confidence term in England and its non-existence in Australia, see Chapter 4.
[10] See generally, C Summers, 'Similarities and Differences between Employment Contracts and Civil or Commercial Contracts' (2001) 17 IJCLL&IR 5.
[11] ibid.
[12] ibid.
[13] ibid 7–8.

1. Employment contracts are relational contracts, as contrasted with transactional or spot contracts. However, as will be elaborated on later, other types of contracts also have the potential to be classified as relational in nature, so this feature is certainly not unique to employment.
2. The employment contract creates and governs a dominant–servient relationship, with the employer empowered to give orders, and the employee obligated to obey. Yet, it can hardly be said that this imbalance of power in the contractual relationship is unique to employment; such imbalances are common to many different types of commercial contract.
3. The employment contract establishes a personal human relationship, with special personal rights and duties on either side. As is revisited below in this chapter, it may be that this notion that one of the parties needs to be human is one of the truly unique and identifiable features of the employment contract.
4. The employment contract is generally a contract of adhesion, in which the employer prescribes terms without negotiation between the parties. Again, however, this same principle could be applicable in many instances of commercial contracting.
5. The employment contract is commonly one between parties with marked inequality of bargaining power. Again, as already suggested, this is hardly an identifying and unique feature exclusive to employment alone. Such imbalances exist in many different types of commercial contract.
6. The individual employment contract may be legally subordinate to another contract, the collective agreement, which has not been personally agreed to by the employer. While this feature may be applicable to some employment contracts, it is certainly not common to all of them as not all employees are covered by an overarching collective agreement.

Summers concludes his assessment of these six characteristics with the recognition that they are far from unique to employment and that various civil contracts may have one or more of them. For Summers, the unique nature of the employment contract comes from the curtailing of the scope of the freedom to contract. Yet again, as mentioned, that curtailing also has the potential to arise in other contractual contexts.

Thirdly, Mark Irving has identified what he views as several 'key features' common to 'almost all' employment contracts,[14] including that:

1. Employment contracts are personal contracts, such that employment contracts involve personal relationships and the personal performance of work.

---

[14] M Irving, 'What is Special about the Employment Contract?' (Paper presented at the Industrial Relations Society of South Australia Conference, Adelaide, 19 October 2012) 6–7.

Interestingly, Irving identifies that an employment contract is the only type of contract that requires one of the parties to be human.[15]
2. Employment contracts are contracts of control, meaning that they involve the control of one party by another. The right to control remains one of the identifying features of employment.[16]
3. There is freedom to contract, which means that employment contracts are almost always formed voluntarily.
4. Employment is a fiduciary relationship, whereby all employees (regardless of status or position) are in a fiduciary relationship with their employer.[17]
5. The individual contract exists in a social context, in which many employees are performing similar work and many of the principal terms of their employment are not negotiated individually.
6. The contract exists within a statutory context.

Irving goes on to refer to four additional characteristics that he has identified as present in most (but not all) employment contracts. Briefly, that:[18]

7. Work often provides a sense of dignity, self-esteem, and an opportunity to further one's career.
8. Employment contracts tend to be long term in nature and tend to evolve.
9. Employment relationships tend to be regulated by express terms.
10. Employment relationships tend to involve economic dependence and a disparity of power.

Despite the existence of these ten common characteristics, Irving acknowledges that none are exclusive to employment contracts. Taken individually, they all have the potential to exist in other types of contracts, such as contracts for services. Each feature may therefore be present in, but is not exclusive to, an employment contract. On assessment of each of these common, but far from unique characteristics, as with Summers' assessment of the identifying features of the employment contract, it may be that the only distinctive feature of an employment contract is that one of the parties to the contract must be human.

---

[15] 'Marriage, for instance, no longer succumbs to contract principles when disputes arise, although we may still occasionally speak of the "marriage contract"': J Riley, 'The Future of the Common Law in Employment Regulation' (2016) 32 IJCLL&IR 33, 40. Cf consumer contracts in English law, which demand that the consumer be an 'individual': *Consumer Rights Act 2015* (UK) s 2(3).
[16] See, eg, *Zujis v Wirth Brothers Pty Ltd* (1955) 93 CLR 561 (High Court of Australia (HCA)) [2].
[17] Cf the doubt cast upon this proposition in L Clarke, 'Mutual Trust and Confidence, Fiduciary Relationships and Duty of Disclosure' (1999) 30 ILJ 348; V Simms, 'Is Employment a Fiduciary Relationship' (2001) 30 ILJ 101; R Flannigan, 'The (Fiduciary) Duty of Fidelity' (2008) 124 LQR 274; D Brodie, 'The Employment Relationship and Fiduciary Obligations' (2012) 16 Edin L R 198; A Fraser, 'The Employee's Contractual Duty of Fidelity' (2015) 131 LQR 53; R Flannigan, 'Employee: Fiduciary' (2016) 19 CLELJ 509; D Brodie, *The Future of the Employment Contract* (Edward Elgar 2021) Ch 2.
[18] Irving (n 14) 7.

Fourthly, in his monograph, *The Future of the Employment Contract*,[19] Douglas Brodie noted that in reflecting on the future of the employment contract, it would be remiss not to address the foundational question of who should be afforded the protections associated with the norms of an employment relationship[20]—in other words, consideration must be given to what is distinctive about being employed under an employment contract. Brodie concurs that the existing framework in which the employment contract sits is insufficiently inclusive,[21] leading the courts to view themselves as imposing a singular set of rules when presented with any employment contract. He recognises that it may be seen as an improvement on the current position, should a more inclusive and less unitary approach be taken to understanding what constitutes an employment relationship.[22] In saying that, he acknowledges indications that courts tend to impose a singular set of rules when presented with an employment contract, and that, increasingly, a more extensive range of working relationships could fall under the 'employment banner'.[23] However, he finds it conceivable that there may be some further and potentially unexpected consequences for the content of employment contracts should there be an increase in the type of relationships captured within that classification.[24] Brodie reiterates that those found to be working under an employment contract could range 'from a chief executive to a labourer'.[25] With that example in mind, he says that '[i]t is not axiomatic that the common law should take a singular view of the appropriate rights and obligations arising under the contract', apparently suggesting that it may actually be inappropriate to arrive at a single understanding of what constitutes an employment contract at all.

The Application of General Contract Law Principles

In addition to academic attempts to identify the distinctive characteristics of employment contracts, there is debate as to whether employment contracts should attract more of their own specific contractual rules or should continue to borrow from the general law of contract.[26] Discussion now turns to that debate. It is logical to argue that the more distinctive employment contracts are, the less they should be regulated by general contractual principles. As Brodie points out, the extent to which employment contracts should be regulated by their own specific contractual

---

[19] Brodie, *The Future of the Employment Contract* (n 17).
[20] ibid 34
[21] ibid.
[22] ibid 55.
[23] ibid.
[24] ibid.
[25] ibid.
[26] For a summary of the early academic literature dealing with this debate, see, eg, M Freedland, *The Contract of Employment* (Clarendon Press 1976) 3–7.

rules has become a 'paramount question'.²⁷ Hugh Collins explains that this question raises a 'central dilemma'.²⁸ He identifies ambiguity as to:²⁹

> the extent to which [the] ... law should, on the one hand, borrow from the general law of contract applicable to commercial and consumer contracts, and on the other, differentiate itself from those general rules in order to tailor a special law for the contract of employment.

Following the recognition of employment as 'contractual' over the last century, it could easily be assumed that the general principles of contract law will continue to apply to employment contracts as a matter of course. This appears to be the view Rothman J took in *Russell v Trustees of the Roman Catholic Church, Archdiocese of Sydney*,³⁰ when his Honour held that: '[T]o the extent that the particular and peculiar features of a contract of employment do not require differentiation, *a contract of employment should be treated no differently from any other type of contract*'.³¹ His Honour qualified this statement, outlining that even where differentiation is required because of the 'special nature' of the employment contract, there needs to be:³²

> coherence between the principles adopted in relation to a contract of employment and other contracts. Some of the matters of differentiation will be such that the contract of employment will be treated identically with some other special contracts.

A separate approach exists whereby the law applying to employment contracts ought to be regulated to a greater extent by specifically tailored contractual rules. After all, other types of contracts (eg contracts for the sale of goods, insurance contracts, and contracts for the sale of land) similarly attract their own specific statutory and common law rules. In support of this approach, Matthew Boyle argues that: 'Not one of ... [the] features of classical contract law is an accurate description of the reality of the employment relationship'.³³ Collins has also called for an 'abandonment' of the 'simple view that the [employment] relation comprises a

---

²⁷ D Brodie, 'The Autonomy of the Common Law of the Contract of Employment from the General Law of Contract' in M Freedland and others (eds), *The Contract of Employment* (OUP 2016) 124, 124.
²⁸ H Collins, 'Contractual Autonomy' in A Bogg and others (eds), *The Autonomy of Labour Law* (Hart Publishing 2015) 45, 46.
²⁹ ibid.
³⁰ (2007) 69 NSWLR 198 (New South Wales Court of Appeal (NSWCA)), a decision also referred to later in this chapter as part of the discussion concerning the inability to exclude particular duties in employment.
³¹ ibid [103] (emphasis added).
³² ibid [104].
³³ M Boyle, 'The Relational Principle of Trust and Confidence' (2007) 27 OJLS 633, 634.

contract governed by the ordinary principles of private [contract] law'.[34] Moreover, in *Autoclenz Ltd v Belcher*,[35] Lord Clarke emphasised that employment contracts were to be treated as a specific kind of contract and not the same as commercial contracts.[36] On this understanding, employment should arguably be regulated to a greater extent according to specific and exclusive contractual rules.

Notwithstanding these conceptual challenges, Brodie has reminded us that 'the general principles of the law of contract will continue to play a pivotal role in the development of the law of the employment contract and the resolution of hitherto unresolved controversies'.[37] He argues that the dynamic rule-making process across contract law in general and other nominate contracts can lead to 'cross-fertilisation across a wider range of contracts or even contract law as a whole'.[38] Brodie views this 'cross-fertilisation' process as beneficial to employment contracts in the sense that it has the potential for 'further evolution of the employment contract in a manner consonant with contemporary judicial recognition of its nature'.[39] With this understanding in mind, he states that it would be 'foolish to restrict the extent of the contractual doctrine to the creation of solutions to problems that arise in the industrial relations context'.[40] Accordingly, Brodie sees that there is room for further specialised development in the law of the employment contract, but that 'prudent recourse to general principles'[41] of contract law remains crucial to the successful development of that area of law. What is required, however, is a 'proper understanding [of the rules specific to employment contracts, which] can only be gained through consideration of the way in which the law of the employment contract also interacts with the law of other nominate contracts'.[42] In making rules with respect to employment contracts, the common law should continue to respond to this 'need for change by drawing not only on general principles but also on developments in all areas of contract law'.[43]

Brodie's approach demonstrates the belief that a general contractual framework can 'cope' with the pressures placed upon it by the changing notion of the

---

[34] H Collins, 'Market Power, Bureaucratic Power and the Contract of Employment' (1986) 15 ILJ 1, 10.

[35] [2011] ICR 1157 (Supreme Court (UKSC)). For a comprehensive discussion of this decision and its broader implications, see further, J Adams-Prassl, '*Autoclenz v Belcher* (2011): Divining "The True Agreement Between the Parties"' in ACL Davies, J Adams-Prassl, and A Bogg, *Landmark Cases in Labour Law* (Hart Publishing 2022) 299.

[36] ibid [21]. See also *Johnson v Unisys Ltd* [2003] 1 AC 518 (House of Lords (HL)), 539A–D (Lord Hoffmann); *Braganza v BP Shipping Ltd* [2015] 1 WLR 1661 (UKSC) 1673C (Lady Hale) and 1677F–1678C (Lord Hodge); B Langstaff, 'Changing Times, Changing Relationships at Work … Changing Law?' (2016) 45 ILJ 131, 141 for an interesting discussion of this broader issue.

[37] Brodie (n 27) 141.
[38] ibid 130.
[39] ibid 131.
[40] ibid 141.
[41] ibid 143.
[42] ibid 144.
[43] ibid.

employment relationship. At least in the near future, general contract law principles will continue to play a major role as the central organising concept of the individual employment relations system. As such, the general rules of contract should continue to apply to employment, albeit with relevant adaptations specific to employment for policy-based reasons,[44] rather than reasons of principle alone.

In support of this proposition, it so happens that three sequential decisions of the High Court of Australia have since drawn heavily on the general law of contract to inform the development of the employment contract specifically.[45] The first decision, *Workpac Pty Ltd v Rossato*,[46] involved Mr Rossato who argued against his purported status as a casual employee, asserting that he was instead permanently employed and entitled to paid annual, personal, and compassionate leave under Australia's *Fair Work Act 2009* (Cth), as well as other entitlements afforded to permanent employees under the relevant enterprise agreement. However, the High Court disagreed, finding that Mr Rossato was truly a casual employee, as that is what had been originally agreed in his employment contract, and that to find otherwise would 'not accord with elementary notions of freedom of contract'.[47] In the second and third decisions, *Construction, Forestry, Maritime, Mining and Energy Union (CFMMEU) v Personnel Contracting Pty Ltd*[48] and *ZG Operations Australia Pty Ltd v Jamsek*,[49] the High Court similarly held that where parties have committed the terms of their relationship to a written contract, then the characterisation of their relationship as one of employment (ie employer and employee), or otherwise (ie principal and independent contractor), must proceed by reference to the rights and obligations of the parties set out under that contract. These two decisions are discussed in more detail in the next section; for now, it is important to note that just as in *Workpac v Rossato*, they stand for the proposition that the wording of the contract is what counts in determining a worker's status. In *CFMMEU v Personnel Contracting* the majority of the High Court went as far as to suggest that:[50]

> The employment relationship with which the common law is concerned must be a *legal* relationship. It is not a social or psychological concept like friendship. There is nothing artificial about limiting the consideration of legal relationships to legal concepts such as rights and duties.

---

[44] Lord Sumption clearly preferred this policy-based approach in *Société Générale (London Branch) v Geys* [2013] 1 AC 523 (UKSC), 567D.
[45] It is important to note that these decisions are only reflective of the position in Australia. They do not represent the approach taken in England, which is examined below in the discussion of the employee/worker/independent contractor distinction.
[46] (2021) 309 IR 89 (HCA).
[47] ibid [99]; see also [62]–[63].
[48] (2022) 312 IR 1 (HCA).
[49] (2022) 312 IR 74 (HCA).
[50] *CFMMEU v Personnel Contracting* (n 48) [44].

It is evident that, across all three decisions, the primacy of the general law of contract has been robustly reinforced, with the High Court's reasoning disregarding the reality of arrangements between parties, including the natural evolution and progression of working arrangements that can occur over time.

With this collection of decisions in mind, there is little question that the notion of employment as a contractual relationship needs better understanding and further articulation. While employment contracts clearly can have both general and specific contractual rules, there is an increasing number of judicial statements suggesting that employment contracts ought not to be regulated to such a great extent by more specific rules. Curiously, the latest developments from the High Court of Australia suggest that greater weight ought to be placed on the general law of contract than on any nuanced rules peculiar to employment. Such statements generate considerable doubt as to whether employment contracts are indeed an appropriate general (or distinctive) class into which terms ought to be implied by law at all.

The Employee/Worker/Independent Contractor Distinction

Another way to understand the employment contractual relationship is in terms of the distinction between working individuals as 'employees' engaged under an employment contract or contract of service,[51] as 'workers' constituting a middle category between employees and independent contractors, or as 'independent contractors' engaged under an independent contract or contract for services.[52] Importantly, the intermediate statutory concept of 'worker' is currently exclusive to English law and does not yet form part of Australian law, though this may be subject to change with the recent introduction of the Fair Work Legislation Amendment (Closing Loopholes) Bill 2023 (Cth) to Australian Federal Parliament. As mentioned in this work's Introduction, Part 16 of that Bill purports to allow Australia's Fair Work Commission to set minimum standards for some (but not all) gig economy and road transport industry workers through the inclusion of an 'employee-like' category of worker. At the time of writing, the Bill remains the subject of parliamentary debate. It is consequently in doubt if, when, and to what extent this proposed amendment may be passed in to legislation. Therefore, this chapter continues its assessment with the existing Australian legal position in mind, albeit on the proviso that legislative change may be in the offing. Nevertheless, the current definitions as they apply in each jurisdiction remain important because they stand for different levels of protection in the scope of employment law. In both jurisdictions, employees are afforded all the protections the law has to offer, while

---

[51] See, eg, *Marshall v Whittaker's Building Supply Co* (1963) 109 CLR 210 (HCA) [7].
[52] See, eg, *R v Foster; Ex parte Commonwealth Life (Amalgamated) Assurances Ltd* (1952) 85 CLR 138 (HCA) [6].

independent contractors receive almost no protection. In English law, workers receive some protection. With the importance of these distinctions in mind and their relevance to the central thesis of this chapter, the focus is now on the divergence between employees, workers (in the English context), and independent contractors.

An employee engaged under a contract for service is subservient to their employer—as a servant to a master in past times—working under their control and direction, and within a hierarchical organisational structure determined by the demands of the employer's business interests.[53] As employees, they are an integral part of the employer's enterprise.

In English law, s 230(1) of the *Employment Rights Act 1996* (UK) provides that an 'employee' is 'an individual who has entered into or works under ... a contract of employment', with the 'contract of employment' being a common law concept (s 230(2)). The statute makes no attempt to define a contract of employment or a contract of service. As Souter J so aptly described, because statute defines 'employee' as someone with a 'contract of service', but does not provide any further definition, like in other common law jurisdictions, it 'explains nothing'.[54]

In Australian law, perhaps the closest thing to a definition of 'employee' is contained under s 15 of the *Fair Work Act 2009* (Cth), 'which helpfully explains that any reference to the "ordinary meaning" of employee or employer includes someone who is "usually" an employee or employer'.[55] As Andrew Stewart and others note, however, there is no doubt that the Act is to be 'taken as using these terms in their common law sense'.[56] Unfortunately, ascertaining whether someone constitutes an 'employee' through the mechanism of the common law has proved problematic—a point that will be expanded on later in this section. Such a difficulty has undoubtedly given rise to section 237 of the Fair Work Legislation Amendment (Closing Loopholes) Bill 2023 (Cth), which, if passed into legislation, purports to insert a definition of 'employee' into the *Fair Work Act 2009* (Cth). Again, however, with that Bill remaining the subject of parliamentary debate, this chapter continues its assessment with the current Australian legal position in mind.

Attention now turns to the category of 'worker' in English law, which straddles the juncture between employees and independent contractors. Even more nuanced is the fact that English labour law contains two different definitions of 'worker': the 'worker definition' and the 'broad worker definition'. The broad worker definition includes some self-employed people (ie independent contractors), whereas

---

[53] J Riley, 'The Definition of the Contract of Employment and its Differentiation from Other Contracts and Other Work Relations' in M Freedland and others (eds), *The Contract of Employment* (OUP 2016) 321, 324.
[54] See, eg, *Nationwide Mutual Insurance Co v Darden* (1992) 503 US 318 (Supreme Court of the United States (SCOTUS)).
[55] A Stewart and others, *Creighton and Stewart's Labour Law* (6th edn, Federation Press 2016) 196.
[56] ibid.

the worker definition does not. The 'worker definition' under s 230(3) of the *Employment Rights Act 1996* (UK) is:

> ... an individual who has entered into or works under ...
> (a) a contract of employment, or
> (b) any other contract, whether express or implied and (if it is express) whether oral or in writing, whereby the individual undertakes to do or perform personally any work or services for another part to the contract whose status is not by virtue of the contract that of a client or customer of any profession or business undertaking carried on by the individual ...

The first point to note is that this definition includes employees in paragraph (a), meaning that if a statute gives a right to 'workers', employees will also benefit from that right. However, so do those who fall within the ambit of paragraph (b). As such, if a right is granted to workers, it will aide more people than one granted to employees only. To fall within paragraph (b), the claimant must fulfil the following three criteria:

1. There must be mutuality of obligation between the parties to the contract, in the sense of a basic work-wage bargain.[57]
2. They must be under a duty to perform the work personally.
3. The recipient of their services must not be a client or customer (ie they must not be running a business).

This larger group of workers have rights under the *National Minimum Wage Act 1998* (UK) in terms of s 54(3) of that Act, the *Working Time Regulations 1998* (UK) in terms of reg 2(1), and under the *Trade Union and Labour Relations (Consolidation) Act 1992* (UK) in terms of s 296(1)(b).

Independent contractors only have the chance of legislative protection when the 'broad worker definition' is used. The following quotation encapsulates that definition well:[58]

> 'Employment' means employment under a contract of service or apprenticeship or contract personally to execute any work or labour.

---

[57] See, eg, *James v Redcats (Brands) Ltd* [2007] ICR 1006 (Employment Appeal Tribunal (EAT)), 1022C–1025C (Elias J); *Pimlico Plumbers Ltd v Smith* [2018] ICR 1511 (UKSC); *Singh v Members of the Management Committee of the Bristol Sikh Temple* [2012] All ER (D) 68 (May) (EWHC).

[58] *Equality Act 2010* (UK) s 83 (2).

This broad worker definition includes employees because they are employed under a contract for service. The requirements of mutuality of obligation in the sense of a work/wage bargain and of a duty to perform the work personally remain applicable to employees as well. It is significant, however, that there is no exclusion for those running their own business, which means that self-employed people can fall within the 'broad worker definition', but only where they perform the work personally and are in a subordinate position *vis-à-vis* the hirer.[59] Such a definition extends the coverage of employment law protection to its widest possible scope. To take a working example: a self-employed medical doctor who carries out hair restoration procedures for the clients of a private clinic using the premises of that clinic would be a worker under this definition.[60] However, the owner of the clinic who employs staff to carry out that same work would not.

The focus now shifts to independent contractors, which exist in both England and Australia. An independent contractor engaged under a contract for services provides labour to others while in pursuit of their own discrete enterprise.[61] It has been judicially emphasised that employment contracts and contracts for services are mutually exclusive; a contract can be one of them, but it cannot be both.[62] To repeat a point made at the beginning of this section concerning the significance of the employee/independent contractor dichotomy, it is 'the emblematic regulatory device deployed to decide whether an individual supplier of labour is entitled to the protection of employment laws'.[63] This definition is critical to whether an employer is vicariously liable for the tortious acts of its employees.[64] It also has a bearing on other rights and liabilities that affect the relationship between the parties under statute.[65] With this in mind, there is a 'persistently challenging problem'[66] in defining whether a contract should be categorised as one of service or one for services.[67]

In the Australian context, the original common law approach to distinguishing between these two types of work arrangement provided for a multifactorial test that required scrutiny of indicia. This test was set out in *Stevens v Brodribb Sawmilling Co*,[68] and included consideration of:[69]

---

[59] See, eg, *Jivraj v Hishwani* [2011] 1 WLR 1872 (UKSC).
[60] See, eg, *Hospital Medical Group Ltd v Westwood* [2013] ICR 415 (Court of Appeal (CA)).
[61] Stewart and others (n 55) 196. An examination of the wider legal regulation of independent contractors is beyond the scope of this chapter.
[62] See, eg, *Hollis v Vabu Pty Ltd* (2001) 207 CLR 21 (HCA) [39] and [72].
[63] D Cabrelli, *Employment Law in Context: Text and Materials* (OUP 2014) 61.
[64] *Hollis v Vabu* (n 62) [32].
[65] See, eg, the later discussion concerning the operation of particular statutory rules in employment.
[66] Riley (n 53) 322.
[67] See, eg, *R v Foster* (n 52) [6].
[68] (1986) 160 CLR 16 (HCA). Curiously, the proposed definition of 'employee' under Fair Work Legislation Amendment (Closing Loopholes) Bill 2023 (Cth) seeks to mirror this pre-existing common law definition in response to the decisions in *CFMMEU v Personnel Contracting* (n 48) and *ZG Operations v Jamsek* (n 49), the impact of which is described further below in this part.
[69] *Stevens v Brodribb Sawmilling Co* (n 68) 23–9.

- the employer's right of control in the relationship;
- a person's integration into the hirer's organisation;
- a person's responsibility for the supply of tools or equipment;
- whether remuneration occurs by time or task;
- whether a person is free to work for others; and
- whether a person has the right to delegate or subcontract to others.

As emphasised by the High Court of Australia in *Hollis v Vabu*, this multifactorial test was to be applied by reference to the 'totality of the relationship'[70] between the parties and an employment relationship may be found to exist, even if the parties intend otherwise.[71]

However, the test had become problematic as there was nothing conclusive about how it was to be applied. The multitude of factors were not counted and applied on balance. Instead, the court needed to make an impressionistic judgement. Consequently, the application of the multifactorial test had become inherently uncertain, and it perhaps became an overstatement to label it as a 'test' at all, given the fluidity with which the courts applied it. Certain Australian authorities had further muddied the waters in relation to understanding what the 'totality of the relationship' meant. In fact, it was possible to distinguish at least three different ways of applying that test.[72]

In the related decisions of *CFMMEU v Personnel Contracting* and *ZG Operations v Jamsek*, the majority of the High Court of Australia has since held that where parties have committed the terms of their relationship to a written contract, the characterisation of their relationship as one of employment (or otherwise) must proceed by reference to the rights and obligations set out under that contract. As such, where a written contract stipulates that a worker is an independent contractor, the previous indicia will no longer apply as justification that they are an employee. The wording of the contract is what counts. This approach is said to apply, so long as the written contract in question is not challenged on the basis that it is a sham[73] or otherwise ineffective under general law or statute.

Therefore, so long as a written contract exists, the High Court's approach does away with the former 'multifactorial' test, with the court stating that 'without guidance as to the relative significance of the various factors the multifactorial test is

---

[70] *Hollis v Vabu* (n 62) [44].

[71] As Gray J once famously held: '[T]he parties [to a work relationship] cannot create something which has every feature of a rooster, but call it a duck and insist that everybody else recognise it as a duck': *Re Porter* (1989) 34 IR 179 (Federal Court of Australia (FCA)) [13].

[72] See, eg, A Stewart and S McCrystal, 'Labour Regulation and the Great Divide: Does the Gig Economy Require a New Category of Worker?' (2019) 32 AJLL 4, 7–8.

[73] If an employer incorrectly represents a worker as an independent contractor when, in fact, they are an employee, this could constitute a sham contracting arrangement, which is prohibited by the *Fair Work Act 2009* (Cth) Part 3-1 Division 6, exposing the employer to the possibility of substantial civil remedies under the *Fair Work Act 2009* (Cth) Part 4-1.

"distinctly amorphous" in its application, is "necessarily impressionistic", and thereby is "inevitably productive of inconsistency".[74] Priority is instead given to the rights and duties established under the written contract between the parties in determining a worker's status as either an independent contractor or employee. Only in situations in which there is no written contract will the multifactorial test become determinative of a worker's status, and it is anticipated that such situations will be rare.[75] It is therefore key to consider a worker's designation under any written contract that they are engaged under (ie as an employee or independent contractor), assuming one exists.

The effect of the High Court's decisions is that whatever a worker agrees to be engaged as in writing is what matters; that agreed status will be the status of their engagement, irrespective of how their work relationship operates in reality. The so-called delving deeper into determining the 'totality of the relationship' between the parties ascribed from the earlier High Court decision in *Hollis v Vabu* has no further application where there is a written employment contract. This approach now puts Australia in a very conservative position. To repeat a point made earlier, the wording of the contract is paramount, and the High Court's reasoning deliberately overlooks the reality of arrangements between parties, which is concerning, given the typical evolution and progression of working arrangements over time. In fact, a strict reading of these Australian decisions gives the impression that there is nothing overly distinctive about employment at all. What matters is the label applied to the relationship in the applicable written contract, rather than how it operates.

Turning now to English law, various tests have been used to interpret the application of employment law protections. The 'control test' asks:[76]

> [W]ho lays down what is to be done, the way in which it is to be done, the means by which it is to be done, and the time when it is done? Who provides (ie, hires and fires) the team by which it is done, and who provides the material, plant and machinery and tools used?'

If the employer decides these matters, or at least has the right to do so, then a contract of employment will exist (or vice versa).

Claims for personal injuries often turn on whether the worker is an employee or an independent contractor. The predominant test used to establish vicarious liability for that purpose is concerned with the application of the control test. However, the scope of vicarious liability has been now expanded. In four recent

---

[74] *CFMMEU v Personnel Contracting* (n 48) [33] (citations omitted).
[75] See, eg, the unique situation in *Church of Ubuntu v Chait* [2023] FWCFB 20 (Full Bench of the Fair Work Commission (FWCFB)) where the Fair Work Commission upheld the relevance of the multifactorial test when the parties have not comprehensively set out their relationship in a written agreement.
[76] See, eg, *Lane v Shire Roofing Company (Oxford) Ltd* [1995] IRLR 493 (CA).

decisions,[77] the Supreme Court has recognised that vicarious liability may be imposed in respect of the acts of persons who are in a position 'akin to employment', but who are not strictly employees. It is not surprising that uncertainty has now emerged as to the true reach of that test to traditionally understood independent contractors, rather than employees alone.[78] What these decisions demonstrate is that the significance of the distinction between a contract for service and a contract for services has been diminished. Such diminishing has arisen through the application of a recent test of whether the imposition of vicarious liability would be 'fair, just and reasonable', considering factors such as whether the employer created the risk of the tort being committed by entering the contract for services as an integrated part of its business.

To encapsulate certain workers within the duty of care and vicarious liability, English courts have also sometimes referred to an 'organisation test'. That test asks whether workers are members of the employer's organisation, considering factors such as the application of dress and grooming codes, supply of infrastructure including office accommodation and communication facilities, as well as the application of the employee's rulebook or staff handbook. Even a senior manager with considerable autonomy and who is paid exclusively by a profit-sharing arrangement could be viewed as an employee by reference to the organisation test because it only requires a formal legal subordination, rather than actual subordination, to a managerial authority.[79]

There also exists a 'business risk' or 'economic reality' test in English law, which asks:[80]

> [I]s the person who has engaged himself to perform these services performing them as a person in business on his own account? ... Factors, which may be of importance are such matters as whether the man performing the services provides his own equipment, whether he hires his own helpers, what degree of financial risk he takes, what degree of responsibility for investment and management he has, and whether and how far he has an opportunity for profiting from sound management in the performance of his task.

---

[77] For the most recent Supreme Court case on extension of vicarious liability to those working who are in a position or relationship that is 'akin to employment', see, eg, *Barclays Bank plc v Various Claimants* [2020] AC 973 (UKSC), 988C–F (Baroness Hale). See also *Catholic Child Welfare Society v Various Claimants* [2013] 2 AC 1 (UKSC); *Cox v Ministry of Justice* [2016] AC 660 (UKSC); *Mohamud v WM Morrison Supermarkets plc* [2016] AC 677 (UKSC); *Armes v Nottinghamshire County Council* [2018] AC 355 (UKSC).

[78] See further, S Silink and D Ryan, 'Vicarious Liability for Independent Contractors' (2018) 77 CLJ 458.

[79] See further, H Collins, K D Ewing, and A McCoglan, *Labour Law* (2nd edn, CUP 2019) 204–05 and the authorities cited therein.

[80] See, eg, *Market Investigations v Minister of Social Security* [1969] 2 QB 173 (High Court of Justice (QB)).

If the worker takes on these risks, the more likely it is that a contract for services exists (or vice versa).

A similar multifactorial test to that which was once prominent in Australia also operates in England, which Lord Clarke reaffirmed in *Autoclenz v Belcher*.[81] His Lordship held that, within the overall duty of courts to construe who is an employee, in light of the relative bargaining power of the parties, multiple factors are to be taken into account. Lord Wright in *Montreal v Montreal Locomotive Works Ltd*[82] took this approach when he held that 'in many cases the question can only be settled by examining the whole of the various elements which constitute the relationship between the parties'.[83]

With regards to the multifactorial test, English courts have said that there exists three basic ingredients (or irreducible minimum criteria) for the establishment of a contract of employment: (1) control;[84] (2) mutuality of obligation;[85] and (3) personal service.[86] If any one of these three basic ingredients is missing, then the courts will hold that there is no contract of employment. If each of them is present, then there is a strong case that there is a contract of employment, but the court will then need to go on to adopt the multifactorial approach, checking for the other factors indicative of employment. Mutuality of obligation is the most significant of the three criteria mentioned and accounts for many cases where an individual is held not to qualify as an employee.[87] It is a requirement that the hirer has an ongoing commitment to provide a reasonable and minimum amount of work in the future and to pay for it, with a corresponding obligation imposed on the individual to perform that reasonable and minimum amount of work when offered by the hirer in the future.

On an assessment of the case law adopting the multifactorial test, Collins and others have identified that indicative factors that favour the finding of a contract of employment include: [88]

- the employer's control over the content of the work and the manner in which it is done;
- the employer agreeing to pay wages and accepting the business risk of profit and loss;
- the worker being integrated into the organisation;

---

[81] [2011] UKSC 41 (UKSC).
[82] [1947] 1 DLR 161 (Privy Council (UKPC)).
[83] ibid 169.
[84] See, eg, *Ready Mixed Concrete (South East) Ltd v Minister for Pensions and National Insurance* [1968] 2 QB 497 (QB).
[85] See, eg, *Carmichael v National Power plc* [1999] 1 WLR 2042 (HL).
[86] See, eg, *Ready Mixed Concrete* (n 84); *Staffordshire Sentinel Newspapers Ltd v Potter* [2004] IRLR 752 (EAT).
[87] See, eg, *O'Kelly v Trusthouse Forte plc* [1983] ICR 728 (CA); *Carmichael v National Power* (n 85).
[88] See, eg, Collins, Ewing, and McCoglan (n 79) 207.

- the employer supplying capital, raw materials, tools, and equipment;
- the worker usually being required to perform work personally rather than using substitutes;
- the business accepting the allocation of other risks such as sickness and health and safety responsibility.

While this multiplicity of factors provides a good example of the balancing act in which English courts and tribunals must engage, just as was once the case in Australia, there has been substantial judicial confusion surrounding their application. For example, in *O'Kelly v Trusthouse Forte plc*,[89] the Court of Appeal produced a list of no less than eighteen relevant factors in finding that the worker was an independent contractor, some of which were explicitly considered consistent with the existence of a contract of employment, ultimately finding that the parties' own designation of status tipped the balance.[90]

In recognition of the unsatisfactory state of the common law test for distinguishing employees from independent contractors in England in particular, several academic proposals have been made with reference to reframing the operation of employment law.[91] For example, Collins proposed that there be a presumption that *any* person working for another is an employee unless they are working under a task performance contract and no badges of membership to the firm's organisation are used.[92] While not explicitly stated, it appears that Collins' suggestion is that this proposal should occur through the development of a relevant statutory provision (ie through the development of 'a test suitable for application by the courts').[93]

Separately, suggestions have been made for the transcending of the concept of employment. Specifically, Mark Freedland and Nicola Kountouris have articulated a multifaceted view of the personal employment relation, which includes not only 'contracts', but also a wider range of 'arrangements' under which work is performed by individuals rendering service personally to others under a 'personal work nexus'.[94] As Freedland wrote separately, there[95]

---

[89] *O'Kelly v Trusthouse Forte* (n 87).
[90] ibid 745.
[91] Each of these suggestions were made prior to the High Court of Australia's conservative approach in *CFMMEU v Personnel Contracting* (n 48) and *ZG Operations v Jamsek* (n 49).
[92] H Collins, 'Independent Contractors and the Challenge of Vertical Disintegration' (1990) 10 OJLS 353, 379. See further, the Taylor Review, which reported in 2017, recommending such a shift in the onus of proof: M Taylor and others, *Good Work: The Taylor Review of Modern Working Practices* (July 2017) <https://www.gov.uk/government/uploads/system/uploads/attachment_data/file/627671/good-work-taylor-review-modern-working-practices-rg.pdf> accessed 20 December 2022, at 62, but the UK government rejected it, subject to their production of an online tool to clarify the employment status of individuals: see, eg, *Good Work: A Response to the Taylor Review of Modern Working Practices* (HM Government, February 2018) <https://assets.publishing.service.gov.uk/government/uploads/system/uploads/attachment_data/file/679767/180206_BEIS_Good_Work_Report__Accessible_A4_.pdf> accessed 20 December 2022, at 70.
[93] Collins (n 92) 378.
[94] See, eg, M Freedland and N Kountouris, *The Legal Construction of Personal Work Relations* (OUP 2011) 34–36. See also M Freedland, 'Contract of Employment to Personal Work Nexus' (2006) 35 ILJ 1.
[95] Freedland (n 94) 13.

is no bright-line binary divide or partly or wholly rejected out-group within this family of contracts. It becomes easier in this construct to recognise specific typologies within the contract of employment, but even more important, also to accept typologies which transcend the boundaries of the contract of employment.

Simon Deakin has added that in substance, this does not abandon the binary divide but merely draws 'that line in a different place'.[96] Jeremias Adams-Prassl suggests that another solution could lie in a renewed focus on the concept of the employer instead of on different understandings of the employee.[97] Adams-Prassl argues that we should abandon the received unitary concept, which aims to identify a single entity as the employer in all circumstances, in favour of a more openly functional concept, defining the employer as 'the entity or combination of entities, playing a decisive role in the exercise of relational employing functions, as regulated or controlled in each particular domain of employment law'.[98]

Nevertheless, there is now a substantial divergence in approaches between England and Australia insofar as determining what constitutes an employment contract as distinct from a contract for services. In Australia, where a written contract exists, the wording of the contract is determinative of a worker's status, irrespective of how their working relationship operates in reality. This conservative approach is to be contrasted with the multitude of tests used to differentiate between employees and independent contractors where no written contract exists in Australia, and in determining the status of all independent contractors as distinct from employees in England (irrespective of whether their contract is in writing). In those instances, the multitude of tests used to differentiate between employees and independent contractors focus more on the differences between the two types of contracts than the distinctive features peculiar to employment contracts alone. It is also unclear whether the application of the relevant tests tends to support the purpose of protecting employment rights where they are needed and appropriate. It is axiomatic that many types of jobs sit on the boundary between the legal categories. All that is truly highlighted is that there is a highly variable distinction between employment contracts and contracts for services, and that in Australia this variability has the potential to be entirely ignored in situations where a contract is reduced to writing.

---

[96] S Deakin, 'Does the 'Personal Employment Contract' Provide a Basis for the Reunification of Employment Law?' (2007) 26 ILJ 68, 77.
[97] See, eg, J Prassl, The Concept of the Employer (OUP 2015).
[98] ibid 155.

The Operation of Particular Statutory Rules in Employment

While this chapter is looking to expose what is distinctive about the employment contract for common law purposes, it is evident that the common law has shortcomings. As this section demonstrates, one cannot simply rely on parliament to fill that void of understanding—a shortcoming that is expanded upon in Chapter 6. Parliament has also not sought to generate further clarity about what is distinctive about the employment contract. Statutes across both jurisdictions have adopted the common law meaning and tests concerning the definition of employment, notwithstanding the associated flaws identified in the discussion in the previous section. Statutes extending beyond the common law meaning, deeming certain workers to be employees for the purpose of the particular statute, have generated added uncertainty.[99]

There are many statutory rules, which are contingent on the existence of an employment contractual relationship.[100] Collins explains that '[s]tatutory employment rights are ... parasitic on the common law of contract'.[101] Gordon Anderson, Douglas Brodie, and Joellen Riley Munton further emphasise that '[p]arties to employment relationships have always been constrained, to some extent, in their freedom to contract over terms and conditions of employment',[102] by reason of statutory rules. An employment contract will sometimes be described in legislation as a 'contract of service', which, as already mentioned, is distinct from a 'contract for services'.[103] However, it is apparent that that binary division does not satisfactorily serve the purposes of labour regulation, with many jobs straddling the boundaries of the two legal categories.

In Australia there are also probably more than 100 statutes that impose various rights and liabilities according to whether a person is an 'employee' at common law.[104] While the term 'employee' has been defined in more than fifty Commonwealth statutes,[105] in those statutes, 'employee' is generally given its

---

[99] In the Australian context, see, eg, A Clayton and R Mitchell, *Study on Employment Situations and Worker Protection in Australia: A Report to the International Labour Office* (Centre for Employment and Labour Relations Law, University of Melbourne, 1999) 29–46. In English law, see, eg, *Employment Relations Act 1999* (UK) s 23, which permits the conferral upon individuals the rights that were guaranteed by a variety of employment statutes, as distinct from rights granted under various discrimination statutes. Section 23 effectively allows, *inter alia*, the deeming of individuals as 'parties to workers' contracts or contracts of employment', and the declaration of persons as the employers of individuals.

[100] As to the interaction between statute and common law in the characterisation of work contracts, see, eg, P Bomball, 'Statutory Norms and Common Law Concepts in the Characterisation of Contracts for the Performance of Work' (2019) 42 MULR 370.

[101] Collins (n 28) 60.

[102] G Anderson, D Brodie, and J Riley, *The Common Law Employment Relationship* (Edward Elgar 2017) 70.

[103] See, eg, the *Independent Contractors Act 2006* (Cth) s 5 and the *Fair Work Act 2009* (Cth) ss 357–59, which utilise this distinction.

[104] Irving (n 14) 39.

[105] ibid 36.

common law meaning as a 'term of art'.¹⁰⁶ English legislation defines the scope of many labour law rights by reference to the presence of an employee engaged under a contract of service. Among those statutory rights are the right to minimum periods of notice prior to the termination of employment; the right to claim unfair dismissal; the right to claim a redundancy payment; and the right to a written statement of the particulars of employment, maternity leave, and parental leave. To re-emphasise, determining who is an employee at common law is particularly significant in assigning many statutory rights and liabilities in employment. The employee/independent contractor dichotomy is clearly not without its own challenges.

Beyond these understandings, in Australia there are many statutes that extend protection beyond the common law meaning to a broader class of 'workers' by effectively redefining employment contracts and deeming independent contractors to be employees for the purpose of a particular statute.¹⁰⁷ These extended statutory definitions of 'employee' appear in laws covering matters as diverse as workers' compensation, anti-discrimination, work health and safety, superannuation, annual and long service leave, as well as taxation liabilities (eg payroll and fringe benefits tax).¹⁰⁸ As Riley Munton points out, 'the enactment of the *Fair Work Act 2009* (Cth) provided an opportunity to consider a more expansive definition of worker for the purposes of Australia's general industrial regulation, but this opportunity was ignored'.¹⁰⁹

In England, to address the problem of borderline cases, legislation sometimes extends a particular employment right to identifiable groups of workers. For example, the *National Minimum Wage Act 1998* (UK) explicitly includes agency workers and home workers, even if they may not be workers under the general provision governing the scope of the legislation. Even though most civil servants and public sector workers are now regarded as working under ordinary contracts of employment governed by the ordinary law of contract, special rules and exclusions will sometimes apply to certain categories of public sector jobs, such as the police, armed services, workers in the Houses of Parliament, judges, and office holders.¹¹⁰

Some statutes, such as the *King's College London Act 1997* (UK) s 15 distinguish between different employees or 'staff' for the purpose of granting direct participation rights in governance. Many partnership agreements and company constitutions also achieve this, meaning that certain subgroups of employees will have rights beyond statute. As described above, legislation may also extend the

---

[106] See also, ibid.
[107] ibid 39.
[108] ibid.
[109] Riley (n 53) 338. As mentioned above, some gig economy and road transport industry workers may come to receive some protection under the *Fair Work Act 2009* (Cth), should the Fair Work Legislation Amendment (Closing Loopholes) Bill 2023 (Cth) be passed in its current form.
[110] See further, Collins, Ewing, and McCoglan (n 79) 226.

employment law right beyond employees to a broader class of 'workers', including some independent contractors who are in practice economically dependent on a core business.

To add further to this tangle of statutory provisions regarding the personal scope of labour law, for the purpose of English discrimination law, s 83(2) of the *Equality Act 2010* (UK) defines its scope as 'employment' and a 'contract personally to do work':

> Employment means –
> (a) employment under a contract of employment, a contract of apprenticeship or a contract personally to do work…

While this provision uses the common law definition of employment, it differs from the statutory definition of 'worker' because it does not contain the explicit exclusion of professionals and independent businesses. Unfortunately, this situation has resulted in outright ambiguity. On one reading, the word 'employment' is a preliminary condition for the entire definition, making it arguable that discrimination laws cover only employees (or employees in an extended sense). On another reading, because it differs from the statutory definition of employment (and worker), the formulation seems to have the purpose of extending coverage beyond contracts of employment to *any* persons who have a contract personally to do work. That second interpretation could include independent contractors, including professionals, if the contract requires the individual to perform the work personally, rather than manage a business that provides the service. Consequently, the precise scope and meaning of this statutory concept, along with the application of anti-discrimination laws, is contested.[111] To take one example, in an anomalous case involving a volunteer for the Citizens Advice Bureau, a person who appeared vulnerable was held to be outside the scope of discrimination protection.[112]

Separately, the *Pensions Act 2008* (UK) s 1 states that a 'jobholder' (which draws a linguistic analogy to a 'shareholder' in a corporation) is a 'worker', but only those ordinarily working in Great Britain, aged between 16 years and under 75 years, and with qualifying earnings. Jobholders have a right to be automatically enrolled by the employer in a defined contribution occupational pension plan.

Overall, while certain statutes may be applicable in the context of employment, the fact that the common law provides the substratum for that regulation

---

[111] See further, ibid 221–22. This is the approach that was adopted in *Jivraj v Hishwani* (n 59); *Halawi v World Duty Free* [2015] 3 All ER 543 (CA).

[112] See, eg, *X v Mid Sussex Citizens Advice Bureau* [2013] ICR 249 (UKSC). See also *Edmonds v Lawson QC* [2000] EQCA Civ 69 (CA) where it was held that a seemingly vulnerable pupil barrister was similarly outside the scope of minimum wage protection. However, it should be emphasised that it is unclear whether either decision still represents good precedent.

does little to assist in understanding what actually constitutes an instance of an employment contractual relationship in either jurisdiction. Even though the employment contract defines the scope of a great number of statutes, those statutes tend to adopt the common law meaning of employment, which is not without its flaws. This uncertainty is further emphasised by the fact that some statutes extend the understanding of employment beyond the common law meaning by deeming certain people to be employees in certain statutory contexts, or by extending or diminishing their rights as employees in certain ways.

The Courts' Imposition of Particular Duties in Employment

As this chapter has already made clear, purely by characterising a contract as one of employment (as opposed to an ordinary commercial contract, or any other kind of contract), the common law triggers the application of certain terms implied by law.[113] As terms implied by law into the general class of employment contracts, they are said to 'not infect a regular commercial contract'.[114] Collins explains that the operation of these implied terms as 'default' rules inserted into all employment contracts gives them 'another considerably more ambitious role than [just] interpretation or gap-filling'.[115] Citing Freedland,[116] Collins goes on to assert that '[t]hese terms "implied by law" provide a legal expression of elements of the structural principles that shape the normative core of the legal institution of the contract of employment'.[117] Essentially, terms implied by law into the class of employment contract help to make up 'the legal framework for the contract of service or contract of employment'.[118] They allow courts to prescribe 'the ground rules for typical [employment contracts]'.[119]

Employment contracts are more susceptible to the implication of terms by law than any other type of contract. Collins agrees with this sentiment, saying that the practice of implying terms by law is 'particularly evident in relation to the contract of employment. These implied terms serve as a regulatory framework that normally applies to and shapes an employment relationship.'[120] Brodie suggests

---

[113] Cf S Honeyball and D Pearce, 'Contract, Employment and the Contract of Employment' (2006) 35 ILJ 30, where it is argued that the subsistence of implied terms is not necessarily coterminous with the employment relationship. This argument is reflective of the fact that the employment relationship and the employment contract arguably do not necessarily coexist simultaneously.
[114] Riley (n 53) 339–40. This statement ignores duties that are implied into all classes of contract, including employment contracts (eg the duty of cooperation).
[115] H Collins, 'Implied Terms in the Contract of Employment' in M Freedland and others (eds), *The Contract of Employment* (OUP 2016) 471, 472.
[116] See, eg, M Freedland, *The Personal Employment Contract* (OUP 2003) 119.
[117] Collins (n 115) 472.
[118] ibid.
[119] ibid 477.
[120] ibid 472.

that one of the reasons that employment contracts are so prone to the implication of terms by law is that such terms 'offer a judicial vision of the obligations which ought to be inherent in employment relations'.[121] By utilising terms implied by law as default rules, courts are able to effectively shape the employment relationship.

As has already been established in this chapter, the problem is that common law understanding of the general class of employment contracts lacks clarity and the result is that the courts struggle to determine whether new terms should be implied by law into employment contracts. In deciding whether to imply new terms by law into the class of employment contracts, both English and Australian courts have done relatively little to express a clear and consistent judicial view on the nature of employment contracts.

The following four authorities concerning whether a term of mutual trust and confidence ought to be implied by law into Australian employment contracts assist in illustrating this point:

1. Following an historical account of the contract of employment,[122] Rothman J in *Russell v Trustees of the Roman Catholic Church* emphasised that the element of control of the employer was one of the defining features of modern employment.[123] Among other things, his Honour noted: 'The employee contracts to devolve to the employer the right to control the manner in which the employee shall work'.[124]
2. In *State of South Australia v McDonald*,[125] the Full Court of the South Australian Supreme Court found that the 'contemporary view' of the employment relationship involves 'elements of common interest and partnership [between employee and employer], rather than conflict and subordination [between master and servant]'.[126]
3. Jessup J's lengthy dissent in the Full Federal Court in *Commonwealth Bank of Australia v Barker*[127] represented a rare attempt by an Australian judge to articulate the distinctive features of an employment relationship to see whether they justified the implication of a mutual trust and confidence term. In doing so, his Honour set out what he saw as the 'relevant features' of an employment contract that would make an implied term of mutual trust and confidence necessary. These included, first, that employment must involve 'a relationship, not merely a contractual exchange of work for remuneration'.[128] Second, his

---

[121] D Brodie, *The Employment Contract: Legal Principles, Drafting and Interpretation* (OUP 2005) 49.
[122] *Russell v Trustees of the Roman Catholic Church* (n 30) [84]–[90].
[123] ibid [91]–[94].
[124] ibid [91].
[125] (2009) 104 SASR 344 (Full Court of the South Australian Supreme Court (SASCFC)).
[126] ibid [231].
[127] (2013) 214 FCR 450 (Full Court of the Federal Court of Australia (FCAFC)) [161]–[371]. This dissent was supported by members of the High Court on appeal, particularly by Gageler J in his separate reasons: (2014) 253 CLR 169 (HCA) [115]–[118].
[128] *Commonwealth Bank v Barker* (FCAFC) (n 127) [294].

Honour held that there was a requirement that 'the relationship of employer and employee ... [must be] one of trust and confidence' and concluded that '[i]f this premise is not valid, the case for the existence of the implied term is seriously compromised if not mortally wounded'.[129] It is worth noting that Jessup J's judgment was contingent on there being a mutual trust and confidence term. As such, whether his articulation of the distinctive features of employment could apply more broadly is unclear.

4. Most recently, on appeal to the High Court in *Commonwealth Bank v Barker*, the joint judgment of French CJ and Bell and Keane JJ added:[130]

> Today it would be unusual to find an employment relationship defined purely by contract. Large categories of employment relationships are governed, at least in part, by statutory obligations expressed in awards and agreements ... The relationship also has a fiduciary aspect.

Their Honours acknowledged 'the suggestion that the contract of employment could be described in modern times as a "relational contract,"'[131] but did not confirm whether they viewed the employment contract as being truly relational in nature. Further discussion on classifying employment contracts as relational is presented in the following section. Other than recognising *Johnson v Unisys Ltd*[132] and *McDonald* as prior authorities dealing with how the employment relationship ought to be viewed,[133] the High Court did not elaborate further as to its own view.

Despite the existence and continuing recognition of a mutual trust and confidence term, English courts have achieved relatively little in articulating what they deem to be the true nature of the employment contract in the context of implying terms by law. It would be impractical to survey every decision in which the term is recognised, particularly because English appellate courts have applied it routinely for over twenty-five years. However, the following snapshot of two seminal authorities responsible for key developments in respect of the mutual trust and confidence term illustrate the same point:

---

[129] ibid [295].
[130] *Commonwealth Bank v Barker* (HCA) (n 127) [16]. See further, J Murray, 'Conceptualising the Employer as Fiduciary: Mission Impossible' in A Bogg and others, *The Autonomy of Labour Law: Essays in Honour of Mark Freedland* (Hart Publishing 2015) 337, 337–66.
[131] Citing *Johnson v Unisys* (n 36) [20], as well as the work of I Macneil and S Macaulay: see, eg, I Macneil, *The New Social Contract: An Inquiry into Modern Contractual Relations* (Yale University Press 1980); S Macaulay, 'Non-Contractual Relations in Business: A Preliminary Study' (1963) 28 Am Soc Rev 55, as discussed in D Brodie, 'How Relational is the Employment Contract?' (2011) 40 ILJ 232.
[132] *Johnson v Unisys* (n 36), a case referred to in relation to the '*Johnson* exclusion zone' and the operation of the mutual trust and confidence term in the United Kingdom.
[133] *Commonwealth Bank v Barker* (HCA) (n 127) [16]–[18].

1. Couched in the context of justifying the need to imply and find a breach of the mutual trust and confidence term, in *Malik v Bank of Credit and Commerce International SA (In Liq)*, Lord Nicholls (with other members of the House concurring) wrote the following brief note of what constitutes the employment relationship:[134]

   > Employment, and job prospects, are matters of vital concern to most people. Jobs of all descriptions are less secure than formerly, people change jobs more frequently, and the job market is not always buoyant. Everyone knows this. An employment contract creates a close personal relationship, where there is often a disparity of power between the parties. Frequently the employee is vulnerable.

   Through this passage, his Lordship highlights the importance of employment in people's lives, particularly given the diminishing security of work. The close personal relationship between employer and employee espoused from the employment contract also warrants a mention, as does the power imbalance that exists in the context of that relationship with the employee's vulnerability being brought to the fore. Beyond these comments, at no further point in the judgment is the nature and content of the employment relationship examined or critiqued further for the purpose of implying the term. That is not to say that his Lordship's comments are unhelpful; rather, they demonstrate that, similar to the Australian position, little attention has been given to what is perhaps the most critical component of the need to imply the term at all.

2. Later in *Johnson v Unisys*, Lord Millett of the House of Lords added that '[c]ontracts of employment are no longer regarded as purely commercial contracts entered into between free and equal agents'. Quoting from *Wallace v United Grain Growers Ltd*,[135] his Lordship added that '[i]t is generally recognised today that "work is one of the defining features of people's lives"; that "loss of one's job is always a traumatic event"; and that it can be "especially devastating" when dismissal is accompanied by bad faith'.[136] Just as in *Malik v Bank of Credit and Commerce International*, his Lordship's description of employment focussed on the importance and status it embeds in people's lives, coupled with an emphasis on the fact that it extends beyond a mere exchange of wages for work; the employment relationship has far more significance than that. Beyond these two key points, his Lordship did not expand on the explicit factors of the employment relationship, instead relying

---

[134] *Malik v Bank of Credit and Commerce International SA (In Liq)* [1998] AC 20, 77.
[135] (1997) 152 DLR (4th) 1 (Supreme Court of Canada (SCC)), 33, cited with approval in *Johnson v Unisys* (n 36) [39].
[136] *Malik v Bank of Credit and Commerce International* (n 134), 77.

on what, at face value, are all-encompassing and general statements about the importance and status of employment in our lives. Through this judgment it becomes apparent that the House of Lords was not concerned with being expansive about what constitutes 'employment' for the purpose of implying the term.

These examples collectively demonstrate that across both jurisdictions there is no consistent thread in case law to assist in understanding what an employment contract is. This selection of authorities supports the proposition that both Australian and English courts have offered relatively sparse and inconsistent judicial guidance on how they view the employment contractual relationship when they decide whether to imply terms by law into the general class of employment contracts.

These collective approaches are problematic as they create ambiguity as to when and how an implied term will operate in the class of employment contracts. It is further complicated by the fact that for certain terms implied by law into the class of employment contracts, substantially similar terms may also be implied into other types of contracts, particularly into contracts for services.[137] This implication further blurs the understanding of employment contracts as a separate and distinct class into which terms can be implied by law.

The Inability to Exclude Particular Duties in Employment

Apart from implying terms by law as apparently exclusive incidents of employment, the converse is that certain terms implied by law into employment contracts ought to be incapable of exclusion. As borne out in the following discussion, this is largely an academic argument. In most instances, it appears that courts have not considered the inability of certain terms to be excluded. Consequently, Brodie has emphasised that '[t]he issue of contracting-out throws up a number of questions that remain unanswered ... '.[138]

While a lack of excludability might mean certain terms are considered 'defining features' of employment,[139] it has not been without controversy. The authors of *Deakin and Morris' Labour Law* have recognised this challenge and posed the question: 'To what extent is it possible to go further and state that certain implied terms are an irreducible core of obligation in the context of employment, which cannot be removed by express agreement?'[140]

---

[137] See, eg, Stewart and others (n 55) 197.
[138] Brodie, *The Future of the Employment Contract* (n 17) 15.
[139] For instance, in Canada, since *Bhasin v Hrynew* [2014] 3 SCR 494 (Supreme Court of Canada (SCC)), the Canadian courts have viewed good faith as an 'organising principle', thereby pointing away from any ability to contract out of such a core term.
[140] Z Adams and others, *Deakin and Morris' Labour Law* (7th edn, Hart Publishing 2021) 241.

In general, parties to a contract should be able to exclude any term implied by law. The existing common law is clear that terms implied by law can be excluded. Case authority exists to support the proposition that a term will not be implied by law if it is expressly excluded, or altered by the parties.[141] In *Malik v Bank of Credit and Commerce International*, for example, Lord Steyn referred to the derogable (ie *ius dispositivum*) nature of implied terms when he remarked that they are 'default rules [and] the parties are free to exclude or modify them'.[142] On this understanding, implied terms are not entrenched (ie *ius cogens*). Instead, they may be ousted by the express terms in the sense that 'the latter will always supplant the former'.[143] It is this approach that 'chimes with general principles of contract law'.[144]

The paradox is that these terms will have been implied into contracts of a particular type because they are deemed 'necessary' for ensuring that the enjoyment of the rights conferred by the contract are not rendered worthless, nugatory, or seriously undermined.[145] Despite acknowledging that the notion of inalienable implied terms would amount to a 'legal heresy',[146] Collins says that they will have been 'devised primarily with a view to constructing an efficient, functioning exchange and a fair balance of obligations between the parties to the relationship constituted by this kind of transaction'.[147]

This understanding therefore raises the question of how express terms could possibly 'purport to exclude an obligation normally implied by law in a contract of employment that serves to constitute the basic elements of that relationship'.[148] With this question in mind, '[i]mplied terms may not be so easily excluded as is commonly supposed'.[149] Perhaps, if certain terms were capable of exclusion, then the contract may even cease to be one of employment and potentially be transformed into some other type of contract altogether.[150]

---

[141] In the Australian context, see, eg, *Byrne v Australian Airlines* (1995) 185 CLR 410 (HCA) [64]–[66].
[142] *Malik v Bank of Credit and Commerce International* (n 134), 108.
[143] Cabrelli (n 63) 232.
[144] ibid.
[145] See, eg, *Byrne v Australian Airlines* (n 141) [73] and [81]. Cf the wider policy-based approach to the necessity test derived from *University of Western Australia v Gray* (2009) 179 FCR 346 (FCAFC) discussed in Chapter 6. In the English context, see also, *Scally v Southern Health and Social Services Board* [1992] 1 AC 294 (HL) [12] (Lord Bridge); *Spring v Guardian Assurance plc* [1995] 2 AC 296 (HL), 339H–340A and 354B (Lords Slynn and Woolf respectively); *Johnson v Unisys* (n 36) 539B (Lord Hoffmann); *Reid v Rush and Tompkins Group plc* [1990] 1 WLR 212 (CA), 220A (Gibson LJ); *Tai Hing Cotton Mill Ltd v Liu Chong Hing Bank Ltd* [1986] AC 80 (HL), 104H–105C (Scarman LJ). In *James-Bowen v Commissioner of Police of the Metropolis* [2018] 1 WLR 4021 (UKSC), 4032A–B, Lord Wilson (somewhat controversially) equated the relevant policy considerations for implying terms in law to 'precisely the same [involved in the] question as to whether the proposed term is fair and reasonable as arises if the claim is put in tort …'.
[146] See, eg, H Collins, 'Legal Responses to the Standard Form Contract of Employment' (2007) 36 ILJ 2, 9–10.
[147] Collins (n 115) 483.
[148] ibid.
[149] ibid.
[150] ibid.

It should be mentioned that there are different ways in which an exclusion of an implied term might occur through express terms. The most obvious is where an express term excludes either 'all implied terms' in a sweeping manner,[151] or a particular implied term in very explicit terms. An express term may also reiterate the effect of, or even extend the reach of, a particular implied term. The result of this kind of exclusion is that the implied term is effectively excluded because it is no longer necessary.

An employer may also attempt to insert an 'entire agreement' clause under which the parties agree that the written terms of the contract comprise all their rights and obligations to each other with a view to excluding further implied terms. According to *Hart v McDonald*,[152] however, implied terms are generally not excluded by operation of an entire agreement clause.[153]

The resulting question of which terms implied by law ought to be incapable of exclusion due to being absolutely 'necessary' to the employment relationship has been explored elsewhere.[154] The implied duty on an employee to obey their employer's lawful and reasonable instructions is one such duty.[155] In the Canadian context, since *Bhasin v Hrynew*,[156] the Canadian courts have viewed good faith as an 'organising principle', turning away from any ability to contract out of what is viewed as a core term in that jurisdiction.

In the English context, the issue of whether a term implied by law could be contracted out of arose in *Johnstone v Bloomsbury Health Authority*[157] in respect of an employer's implied obligation to take reasonable care for the health and safety of its employees. In this case, an express term regarding working hours was relied upon to restrict the employer's liability for personal injury. However, the Court of Appeal held that the *Unfair Contract Terms Act 1977* (UK) prevented the employer from relying on that express term as a means of excluding any claim arising out of the implied obligation. It is also open to English courts to deem an implied term mandatory on the grounds of public policy, as was the case in *Lee v Showmen's Guild of Great Britain*.[158]

At this point it is worth noting the New South Wales Court of Appeal's finding in the commercial contract decision, *Vodafone Pacific Ltd v Mobile Innovations Ltd*.[159]

---

[151] This potential exclusion is elaborated on later in this section.
[152] (1910) 10 CLR 417 (HCA).
[153] ibid 427, 430. For English and Scottish authorities making the same point, see, eg, *Proforce Recruit Ltd v Rugby Group Ltd* [2006] EWCA Civ 69 (CA) [39]–[41] (Mummery LJ); *Macdonald Estates plc v Regenesis (2005) Dunfermline Ltd* (2007) SLT 791 (Court of Session Outer House (CSOH)).
[154] See, eg, D Brodie, 'The Employment Contract and Unfair Contracts Legislation' (2007) 27 Leg S 95, 103–05.
[155] Collins agrees with this proposition, asserting that any attempt to exclude it 'would begin to turn the proper classification of the contract towards a contract for services': Collins (n 115) 483.
[156] *Bhasin v Hrynew* (n 139).
[157] [1992] 1 QB 333 (CA), 346–47.
[158] [1952] 2 QB 329 (CA).
[159] [2004] NSWCA 15 (NSWCA).

This decision concerned a contract that granted Vodafone the power to set the sales levels for its distributor, Mobile Innovations. The power was expressed to be 'in the sole discretion of Vodafone'.[160] The contract also provided that: 'To the full extent permitted by Law and other than as expressly set out in this Agreement *the parties exclude all implied terms ....*'[161] The Court of Appeal held that the combination of these provisions was sufficient to exclude any implied duty of good faith.[162] In essence, the court's decision revolved around the fact that no duty could be implied unless it was consistent with the contract's express terms, which, in that case, it was not.[163]

Reflecting on the finding in *Vodafone v Mobile Innovations* more closely, it is hardly feasible to exclude a duty of cooperation, as the court seems to have done by recognising an express exclusion of 'all implied terms'. As discussed elsewhere,[164] the duty of cooperation also ought to be considered absolutely necessary to all contracts, including employment contracts, because without the duty, it would be difficult—if not impossible—for the contract to properly function. However, in making its decision, the court in *Vodafone v Mobile Innovations* did not consider this issue at all. It is worth mentioning that the court was under no obligation to engage in such a consideration, though it was arguably appropriate to do so. Without such a consideration, the court's assessment seems incomplete.

For now, it is sufficient to note, for at least some standard default rules in employment, if they are excluded expressly, this will raise 'complex questions' about whether the contract will remain one of employment.[165] Where this is the case, it is obvious that the terms ought to be deemed absolutely necessary to employment and incapable of exclusion. Writing extrajudicially, Lord Bingham has gone so far as to say that an attempt to contract out of terms already implied by law into all employment contracts using an express term would unlikely be 'sympathetically interpreted'.[166] Brodie has similarly adopted this selective approach to the entrenchment of terms implied by law in employment, whereby only 'fundamental' implied terms would be treated as inderogable.[167]

Both Brodie and Freedland floated the idea that the implied term of mutual trust and confidence is one such 'fundamental term', in that it cannot be excluded by the express terms of an employment contract.[168] Collins recently agreed with this

---

[160] ibid [83], referring to clause 18.4 of the contract.
[161] ibid [95] (emphasis added), referring to clause 24.1(a) of the contract.
[162] See, eg, ibid [184], [191], and [198].
[163] See the further discussion concerning this decision in J Paterson, A Robertson, and A Duke, *Principles of Contract Law* (5th edn, Lawbook Co 2016) 359.
[164] See, eg, G Golding, 'Terms Implied by Law into Employment Contracts: Are they Necessary?' (2015) 28 AJLL 113.
[165] Collins (n 115) 483.
[166] T Bingham, 'Singapore Academy of Law Annual Lecture 2001: From Servant to Employee: A Study of the Common Law in Action' (2001) 13 S Ac LJ 253, 266.
[167] See, eg, Brodie (n 154) 103–05.
[168] See, eg, Freedland (n 116) 119.

approach, saying that despite the orthodox view being against it, the idea that an employer cannot exclude the implied term of mutual trust and confidence is undoubtedly attractive'.[169] Brodie repeated this sentiment in his latest monograph, re-emphasising that he views mutual trust and confidence as 'an obligation which is fundamental to the modern employment relationship and expresses the essence of the bargain', suggesting that any attempts to establish an employment relationship without it would be a 'sham'.[170]

An English decision, *Stevens v Birmingham University*,[171] is relevant in this context. The terms of Professor Stevens' employment contract provided that he was entitled to be accompanied by a colleague or trade union official to any disciplinary hearings held in relation to his employment (a term that also duplicated his statutory right for the same).[172] Professor Stevens, however, had no suitable colleague to accompany him to such a hearing, and he was also not a member of a trade union. Nonetheless, the university did not allow him to be accompanied by anyone else— in this case a member of the Medical Defence Union, as it is not a trade union. The English High Court held that it was unable to imply a term permitting Professor Stevens to be accompanied by any person of his choosing at the relevant hearing; that would be inconsistent with the express terms of his contract, which needed to be interpreted consistently with the 'overriding obligation of trust and confidence'.[173] In this context, the duty of mutual trust and confidence required that he be permitted to be accompanied by a support person. Apart from using the implied term of mutual trust and confidence to modify the express terms of Professor Stevens' employment contract, the court also rejected the argument endorsed by the majority in *Johnson v Unisys* that the common law should not circumvent restrictions on statutory rights.[174] As Collins rightly encapsulates: 'This decision illustrates how [English] courts will be extremely reluctant to permit express terms to exclude aspects of the requirement of good faith or mutual trust and confidence in relational contracts including employment'.[175]

Reflecting on the Australian position, it is worth mentioning that prior to the High Court's decision in *Commonwealth Bank v Barker*, in the first instance decision of *Russell v Trustees of the Roman Catholic Church*, Rothman J held that a duty of mutual trust and confidence could not be expressly excluded, as it formed an 'essential ingredient' of the employment relationship: 'Without trust and confidence there is no contract of employment'.[176] Since then, in the Australian context, the mutual trust and confidence term was viewed as entirely unnecessary by

---

[169] Collins (n 115) 489.
[170] Brodie, *The Future of the Employment Contract* (n 17) 17.
[171] [2016] 4 All ER 258 (EWHC).
[172] *Employment Rights Act 1996* (UK) s 10.
[173] *Stevens v Birmingham University* (n 171) [88] (Andrews J).
[174] A Sanders, 'Fairness in the Contract of Employment' (2017) 46 ILJ 508, 521.
[175] H Collins, 'Employment as a Relational Contract' (2021) 137 LQR 426, 448.
[176] *Russell v Trustees of the Roman Catholic Church* (n 30) [127]–[128] (emphasis added).

the High Court in *Commonwealth Bank v Barker*—a finding that occurred, despite clear assertions by Rothman J and British academics in respect of its apparent non-excludability. Essentially, in one jurisdiction, the mutual trust and confidence term is now understood by leading academics as so necessary that it is incapable of exclusion, whereas in another, it is viewed by the judiciary as wholly unnecessary. This outcome is significant because of 'the range of workplace situations where employees are now denied a right against the employer'[177] in Australia, but not in other common law jurisdictions, including England, where the duty is recognised[178]—a point that has already received thorough attention in Chapter 4. This judicial non-recognition raises some doubt over the extent to which the courts' reluctance or unwillingness to exclude certain terms implied by law in employment contracts is truly indicative of the nature of employment contracts as a class. The courts have never needed to explore what would occur if a term implied by law is excluded and nothing is put in its place. What would follow from that circumstance is unclear, and this is problematic due to the uncertainty it creates.

The preceding discussion has shown that the debate concerning whether terms currently implied by law as necessary incidents of employment contracts are capable of exclusion is extremely complex. There are tangible views from both academics and judges, which give rise to conflicting results as to a term's potential excludability by the parties to an employment contract. The crux of the debate is that, on the one hand, terms implied by law into the class of employment contracts have only come to be because they have been understood as entirely necessary to that class of contract. On the other hand, parties to an employment contract surely ought to be capable of deciding for themselves what does and does not form part of the contract between them, meaning that, in theory, all terms implied by law should be capable of exclusion. What is proposed here, however, is that rather than approaching the potential excludability of terms implied by law into the class of employment contracts in an overly simplistic and binary fashion, a more nuanced approach is required. Put another way, some terms are absolutely necessary to shaping employment contracts, and if they are excluded by the parties, the relationship would cease to be one of employment at all. Therefore, some terms are capable of exclusion, whereas others are not. Those terms implied by law that are incapable of exclusion are considered in detail in Chapter 6, where which of those terms ought to be deemed absolutely necessary to the employment relationship are closely examined.

---

[177] D Brodie, 'The Dynamics of Common Law Evolution' (2016) 32 IJCLL&IR 45, 48.

[178] These jurisdictions include the United Kingdom, Bermuda, South Africa, Hong Kong, Tonga, Vanuatu, Fiji, New Zealand, and Canada (at least to some extent). See the related discussion in Chapter 3.

Employment as a Relational Contract

Examining employment as a relational contract here is useful in the sense that it provides added confirmation that, despite the applicability of that classification in the context of employment, it is by no means unique to the employment relationship. The consequence is that understanding employment as an apparently unique mode of contracting becomes even more disparate and difficult to reconcile. Indeed, it is commonplace that various types of contracts, including employment contracts, can be understood as more than a discrete exchange affecting the social relationship between contracting parties—an approach that is generally understood as 'relational contract theory'. Following on from a ground-breaking empirical study conducted by Stewart Macaulay in the 1960s,[179] Ian Macneil and other relational contract theorists have since argued that contract law suffers from too strong a focus on discrete contractual exchanges,[180] and that there ought to be a greater focus on the relationship between the contracting parties.

At this moment, it is necessary to highlight that often a simplistic distinction between what Macneil coined the 'discrete' and the 'relational' contract is drawn, with the contract of employment obviously falling into the latter category.[181] Often, Macneil's work strikes the reader as advocating for a specific class of relational contracts,[182] which would encompass employment contracts. Such a reading is overly simplistic; Macneil endeavoured to shift his position during the course of his work, coming to realise that theoretical consistency meant that he needed to deny explicitly that there were any 'truly' discrete contracts at all.[183] Those arrangements would have amounted to amoral bargains of a type envisaged in neoclassical economics.[184] This developed view of contractual relations does not simply identify the relational elements in only one particular 'class' of contracts.

Curiously, Macneil never sought to deny that discrete contracts had a fixed place on the 'spectrum' of contracts, even after relational contracts had been adequately

---

[179] This study revealed that in certain circumstances, business people have little regard to the law of contract when they enter into business transactions, make adjustments, and resolve disputes. Instead, it is their relationships that typically have a significant impact on the way in which they deal with one another: see, eg, S Macaulay, 'Non-Contractual Relations in Business: A Preliminary Study' (1963) 28 Am Soc Rev 55.

[180] See generally, I Macneil, 'Contracts: Adjustment of Long-Term Economic Relations Under Classical, Neoclassical, and Relational Contract Law' (1978) 72 N W L Rev 854; I Macneil, 'Values in Contract: Internal and External' (1983) 78 N W L Rev 340; D Campbell (ed), *The Relational Theory of Contract: Selected Works of Ian Macneil* (Sweet & Maxwell 2001).

[181] Campbell (ed) (n 180) 15–16.

[182] See generally, J M Feinman, 'Contract After the Fall' (1987) 39 Stan LR 1537. Cf I Macneil, 'A Brief Comment on Farnsworth's "Suggestions for the Future"' (1988) 38 J Legal Educ 301.

[183] See, eg, I Macneil, 'Barriers to the Idea of Relational Contracts (The Complex Long-Term Contract, Structures and International Arbitration)' in F Nicklisch (ed), *Der Komplexe Langzeitvertrag. Strukturen und Internationale Schiedsgerichtsbarkeit* (Müller Juristischer Verlag 1987) 277.

[184] See, eg, I Macneil, 'Contract Remedies: A Need for a Better Efficiency Analysis' (1988) 144 JITE 6, 9.

recognised.[185] His later work therefore became a sophisticated and elaborate attempt to analyse the different combinations of discrete and relational values in all contracts.[186] Unfortunately, interest in his work began to wane just at the time that this improvement happened.

In view of this development, rather than seeking to use relational contract theory in a somewhat 'bipolar' manner that Macneil eventually abandoned, this section is prefaced on the understanding that the full notion of 'relational' contracting cannot be appreciated in isolation from its opposite in Macneil's understanding of 'discrete' contracting. Homage is also paid to Macneil's proposition that discrete exchanges and relational contracts form an axis,[187] and within that axis there lies a spectrum of contractual phenomena.[188] At one end of this spectrum is the discrete transaction, triggering the application of the classical law. At the other end, there exists a deeply intertwined relationship, typically exemplified by a long-term relationship between the contracting parties. It is self-evident that at that most relational end lies the pure application of relational contract theory.[189]

It is possible that, depending on their duration and nature, employment contracts may be situated at various points along the spectrum; in essence, it depends on how 'relational' the contract between the particular employer and employee truly is, and that is subject to variability, which has been explored in detail elsewhere.[190] It is worth briefly adding here that other contracts for the performance of work (eg a contractor engaged by a principal under an independent contract) would most likely find themselves further away from that relational end of the spectrum. In the interests of simplicity and consistency, this section continues with this nuanced understanding in mind, referring to employment contracts as 'relational' throughout, noting that this label is not to be applied in the simplistic and dichotomous manner that it seems to suggest on an initial reading.

Stemming from the early theoretical work, in the Australian context, Finn J listed the following core features of a relational contract in *GEC Marconi Systems Pty Limited v BHP Information Technology Pty Limited*:[191]

---

[185] 'Exchange occurs in various patterns along a spectrum ranging from highly discrete to highly relational': I Macneil, 'Relational Contract Theory as Sociology: A Reply to Professors Lindenberg and de Vos' (1987) 143 JITE 272, 275.
[186] See generally, I Macneil, 'Exchange Revisited: Individual Utility and Social Solidarity' (1986) 96 Ethics 567.
[187] I Macneil, 'The Many Futures of Contract' (1974) 47 S Cal L Rev 691, 736–37.
[188] Macneil (n 184) 12.
[189] See generally, Macneil (n 185).
[190] See generally, Collins (n 175); D Brodie, 'How Relational Is the Employment Contract?' (2011) 40 ILJ 232.
[191] (2003) 128 FCR 1 (FCAFC). Many of these features are also highlighted in academic texts on relational contracts: see, eg, Campbell (ed) (n 180).

- the difficulty of reducing important terms to well defined obligations;
- the impossibility of foretelling all the events which may impinge upon the contract;
- the need to adjust the relationship over time to provide for unforeseen factors or contingencies which cannot readily be provided for in advance;
- the commitment, likely to be extensive, which one party must make to the other, including significant investment; and
- that they are in an economic sense likely to be incomplete in failing to allocate, or allocate optimally, the risk between the parties in the event of certain future contingencies.[192]

Importantly, these factors were not listed in the context of an employment contract dispute specifically, but were rather framed generally, and in the context of a matter concerning a contract for the development of complex communication network software. Nevertheless, the factors provide a useful judicial attempt to articulate what is meant by a 'relational contract'. As Brodie has suggested, the factors articulated in *GEC Marconi Systems v BHP Information Technology* also have the potential to operate as a guide in the context of employment contracts.[193]

Arguably, the factors listed more recently by Fraser J of the English High Court in *Bates v Post Office Ltd (No 3)* operate in the same way.[194] In that decision, which concerned a dispute over certain contracts between the Post Office Ltd and sub-postmasters, his Honour held that the following non-exhaustive list of characteristics, not dissimilar to those separately put forward in *GEC Marconi Systems v BHP Information Technology*, are relevant to the analysis of whether a contract is relational in nature:[195]

- a mutual intention for there to be a long-term relationship;
- an intention for the parties' roles to be performed with integrity and fidelity to their bargain;
- a commitment to collaboration;
- the spirits and objectives of the venture being incapable of exhaustive expression in a written contract;
- trust and confidence, but not of the kind involved in fiduciary relationships;
- a high degree of communication, co-operation and predictable performance based on mutual trust, confidence, and expectations of loyalty;

---

[192] *GEC Marconi Systems v BHP Information Technology* (n 191) 63–65.
[193] See, eg, D Brodie, 'Relational Contracts' in M Freedland and others (eds), *The Contract of Employment* (OUP 2016) 146.
[194] [2019] EWHC 606 (QB). See also, the earlier decision in *Yam Seng Pte Ltd v International Trade Corporation Ltd* [2013] 1 All ER (Comm) 1321 (QB) where the High Court had suggested that certain types of long-term contract were relational in nature, meaning that the court would be more willing to imply a duty of good faith. Lord Justice Leggatt later reiterated this same stance in *Sheikh Al Nehayan v Kent* [2018] 1 CLC 216 (Commercial Court (Comm)).
[195] *Bates v Post Office* (n 194) [725].

- a degree of significant investment or substantial financial commitment by one or both parties; and
- exclusivity of the relationship.

While the potential for the recognition of common law employment contracts as relational may well have increased following *GEC Marconi Systems v BHP Information Technology* and *Bates v Post Office*, this presumption does not necessarily hold true in respect of the High Court of Australia's decision in *Commonwealth Bank v Barker*. The potential for employment contracts to be classified as relational was mentioned dismissively in that decision. In making their decision not to imply a mutual trust and confidence term, French CJ and Bell and Keane JJ held that: '[These] ... observations were linked to the suggestion that the contract of employment could be described in modern terms as a "relational contract".[196] Their Honours later observed that:[197]

> [The implied duty of mutual trust and confidence] ... appears, at least in part, to be informed by a view of the employment contract as 'relational', a characteristic of uncertain application in this context and not one which was advanced on behalf of Mr Barker.

Therefore, while common law employment contracts have the obvious potential to continue to be 'categorised as relational in nature ... it is [now] less than clear whether that [classification] is sufficient to provide a deeper understanding of legal doctrine'.[198] Collins has also emphasised this same point, raising the question of whether a relational contract is even a legal concept at all, but providing a caveat that the 'blocks of a legal concept' do 'seem to be in place'.[199]

As also mentioned in *Commonwealth Bank v Barker*, the High Court of Australia acknowledged 'the suggestion that the contract of employment could be described in modern times as a "relational contract"', [200] but did not confirm whether it viewed the employment contract as being truly relational in nature. Other than recognising *Johnson v Unisys* and *State of South Australia v McDonald* as prior authorities dealing with how the employment relationship ought to be viewed,[201] the court did not elaborate further as to its own view.

---

[196] *Commonwealth Bank v Barker* (HCA) (n 127) [33].
[197] ibid [37].
[198] Brodie (n 190) 145.
[199] See, eg, H Collins, 'Is a Relational Contract a Legal Concept?' in S Degeling, J Edelman, and J Goudkamp (eds), *Contract in Commercial Law* (Thomson Reuters 2016). See also Collins' later contribution as to the categorisation of employment contracts as relational following the decision in *Bates v Post Office* (n 194) in Collins (n 175).
[200] Citing *Johnson v Unisys* (n 36) [20], as well as the work of Ian Macneil and Stewart Macaulay: see, eg, Macneil (n 180); Macaulay (n 179).
[201] See, eg, *Commonwealth Bank v Barker* (HCA) (n 127) [16]–[18].

Separately, it is worth noting that in the earlier English decision in *Johnson v Unisys*, Lord Steyn had previously accepted the description of an employment contract as 'relational'. This appears to be the very first time that the employment contract was labelled as relational as part of a judicial decision. Appropriately, his Lordship held that:[202]

> it is no longer right to equate a contract of employment with commercial contracts. One possible way of describing a contract of employment in modern terms is as a relational contract.

At this point, it is worth noting that Lord Steyn did not go so far as to say that the employment contract was to be unequivocally understood as 'relational'; his Lordship stopped short of making that assertion, rather emphasising that it was but one 'possible' way in which such contracts may be described.

Attention should also be given to *C v T Borough Council*,[203] wherein the English High Court demonstrated some sensitivity in translating the potential relational norms of an employment contract into doctrine. The case involved a teacher and his employer (a local authority running the school), who had reached a compromise agreement to terminate his employment because of allegations regarding his inappropriate use of force against students. The agreement incorporated a letter of reference to be provided to any third party who might request a reference, and provided that any oral reference should be given in the terms and spirit of the reference. When the police requested information on the teacher for a criminal record, the local authority provided them with a detailed chronology, which was reproduced in the criminal record. This led to the teacher being terminated from his employment at another school.

Ultimately, the court rejected the teacher's argument that the employment relationship was a 'relational contract', the consequence of which ought to be that the local authority owed a duty not to misrepresent that it would limit disclosure to any third party, including the police. The court held that this was 'an entirely adversarial situation', where both parties had been represented in an 'arms-length negotiation' leading to the compromise agreement and had 'agreed that remaining at the school was not a possible option'.[204] In drawing these conclusions, the court was conscious of not allowing the rhetoric of relational contracting to enter the realm of this particular last moment of the employment relationship. In a sense, this case was unique; unlike an ongoing employment relationship governed by cooperative norms, at the stage close to termination (arising from misconduct), such

---

[202] *Johnson v Unisys* (n 36) [20].
[203] [2014] EWHC 2482 (QB).
[204] *C v T Borough Council* (n 203) [71]–[72], noting that the reasoning in this decision is very similar to that in the abovementioned decision *Johnson v Unisys* (n 36).

norms, while operative to facilitate a compromise agreement, did not support an enhanced duty to limit disclosure of publicly relevant information to safeguarding authorities.[205]

Apart from the abovementioned, to date, there have been few other explicit judicial indications that the employment contract constitutes a relational contract. Even so, it is worth noting that in a separate part of the judgment in *Commonwealth Bank v Barker*, the High Court of Australia noted the influence of relational contract theory in underpinning the shift towards the recognition of a contractual duty of good faith in employment.[206] In that context, the terminology of 'good faith' most appropriately describes a distinct 'governing principle in the construction and interpretation of relational contracts such as employment'.[207]

While courts are clearly beginning to expressly recognise employment contracts as relational, most of the support for the classification resides in academic commentary. To take one example, Matthew Boyle has made a compelling case for understanding the implied duty of mutual trust and confidence as a 'quintessentially relational norm' of the employment contract.[208] Even though that implied duty is recognised as existing in some form or another across most common law jurisdictions, as already mentioned, it was explicitly held not to be necessary in the Australian context by the High Court of Australia in *Barker*.[209] Even so, it may be that an implied duty of mutual trust and confidence bears little resemblance to an implied duty of good faith,[210] such that Boyle's thesis may still hold true in the Australian context in respect of that duty. However, that is a controversial suggestion. The debate surrounding the potential similarities of and differences between those two duties, if any, is beyond the scope of the present exercise and is considered in further detail elsewhere.[211]

To take another academic example, Collins has suggested that the label of an employment contract as relational comprises three dimensions. The first dimension is that it would require a court to consider the express terms in any written contract in such a way that they could be impacted by any necessary additional implications or interpretations arising from the employment relationship if it were expected to last for a certain period, or indefinitely. The second is put with a view to matching the obligations of the contract with the long-term payoffs that were anticipated for a long-term contract or relationship (eg exemplified by bonuses,

---

[205] See further, Z X Tan, 'Disrupting Doctrine? Revisiting the Doctrinal Impact of Relational Contract Theory' (2019) 39 Leg S 98, 117–18.
[206] See, eg, *Commonwealth Bank v Barker* (HCA) (n 127) [16]–[18].
[207] ibid. For further consideration of the distinction between implication and construction, see Chapter 1.
[208] M Boyle, 'The Relational Principle of Trust and Confidence' (2007) OJLS 27 633
[209] *Commonwealth Bank v Barker* (HCA) (n 127) [36]–[37].
[210] ibid [42].
[211] For a separate consideration of these two duties, including a discussion as to their controversy and potential similarity, see Chapter 3.

a pension entitlement, or promotions). Collins' third dimension concerns trust, or the preservation of the employment relationship itself, or what is sometimes coined the 'psychological contract'.[212]

Overall, despite the concept being an overwhelmingly academic one, it appears that judicial recognition of the employment contract as one that is relational in nature is gaining momentum. This momentum has no doubt been driven by the concept having received more detailed academic attention, stemming from the initial studies conducted by Macaulay and Macneil. The extent to which the relational conception will influence the future development of the employment contract remains to be seen;[213] in fact, Brodie has since labelled himself a 'relational sceptic', expressing doubt as to whether this classification will be as influential as he once expected.[214] It is also worth re-emphasising for the overarching purpose of this chapter, that the potential classification of employment contracts as relational (or, to be more precise, as existing on the highly relational end of the spectrum) is by no means unique to employment. The mere fact that a relational classification is possible does not present a distinguishing feature of what it means to be engaged under an employment contract. As Bill Dixon explains in the context of considering whether a duty of good faith should be implied into *all* relational contracts, the judicial recognition of such contracts is becoming 'increasingly common'[215] in respect of a whole range of contractual contexts. There exists a swathe of other contracts beyond employment that have typically been regarded by courts as relational, including distributorships, agency relationships, partnerships, joint ventures, long-term leases, and franchise agreements.[216] The relational classification

---

[212] See, eg, H Collins, 'The Contract of Employment in 3D' in D Campbell, L Mulcahy, and S Wheeler (eds), *Changing Concepts of Contract* (Palgrave Macmillan 2013) 65. Again, see further, Collins (n 175).

[213] See the future projections arising out of the relational classification in Brodie, *The Future of the Employment Contract* (n 17) Part IV. As to the potential influence of the relational classification where an employment contract is breached, see, eg, G Golding, 'Employment as a Relational Contract and the Impact on Remedies for Breach' (2021) 30 Griffith L Rev 270.

[214] Brodie, *The Future of the Employment Contract* (n 17) vii. See also, D Brodie, 'The Demise of the Relational Contract of Employment' (Paper presented at the Phillipa Weeks Lecture in Labour Law, ANU College of Law, Australian National University, Canberra, 16 November 2022).

[215] B Dixon, 'Common Law Obligations of Good Faith in Australian Commercial Contracts—A Relational Recipe' (2005) 33 ABLR 87, 94.

[216] See, eg, the following scattered examples concerning such commercial transactions in the common law world: *Dymocks Franchise Systems (NSW) Pty Ltd v Bilgola Enterprises Ltd* (1999) 8 TCLR 612 (New Zealand Court of Appeal (NZCA)) [236] (regarding a retail business franchise), affirmed on other grounds in *Dymocks Franchise Systems (NSW) Pty Ltd v Todd* [2002] 2 All ER 849 (UKPC); *Flyn v Breccia* [2015] IEHC 547 (Irish High Court (IEHC)) (regarding an agreement between shareholders for the acquisition of shares in a business); *Bobux Marketing Ltd v Raynor Marketing Ltd* [2001] NZCA 348 (NZCA) [42] (regarding a distribution agreement); *GEC Marconi Systems v BHP Information Technology* (n 191) [351] (regarding a software development contract); *Bates v Post Office* (n 194) [725] (regarding contracts between the Post Office Ltd and sub-postmasters). The notion of a relational contract has also been used in scholarly literature concerning certain kinds of commercial agreements, including franchises, distributorships, and other long-term business arrangements: see, eg, D Campbell, 'Good Faith and the Ubiquity of the *"Relational"* Contract' (2014) 77 MLR 475.

is by no means exclusive to employment, and can hardly be touted as a unique identifying feature of employment.

Conclusion

A careful analysis of the various factors defining the scope of the employment contract as opposed to contracts for the performance of work through the preceding seven sections has yielded the observation that there is nothing inherent in generating a consistent or universal judicial understanding of employment contracts as a class. This results in a deep tension between when it is appropriate for courts to imply terms by law into the class of employment contracts and when it is not.

Upon closer investigation it emerged that, in fact, there may be no single feature of an employment contract that is not shared by any other contract. However, it remains possible and preferable for the courts to have a sound understanding of what constitutes the 'employment contract', without necessarily generating an exhaustive definition. Such an understanding will make courts more comfortable to perform their role in implementing appropriate default rules in the context of employment, hopefully avoiding a situation like that in *Barker* where the court felt ill-equipped to imply a term into the general class.[217]

There is an entire range of factors that make employment contracts appear substantially similar to other types of contractual agreement and, therefore, less distinctive. There is also inconsistency in relation to the way in which employment contracts are presently understood as a class. In particular, the seven sections of this chapter indicate that:

1. Recent academic attempts to define the general distinctive characteristics of employment contracts are inconsistent. The definitions put forward also contain characteristics that could equally apply to other types of contractual arrangement, particularly to contracts for services, thereby making employment contracts appear less distinctive.
2. There is an ongoing debate about the extent to which general contract law principles should be applied to employment contracts specifically. While some contractual rules applicable to employment contracts are more nuanced, the consensus remains that general contract law principles will continue to underpin employment contracts. Arguably, the continuing

---

[217] In the English context, see, eg, *Crossley v Faithful & Gould Holdings Ltd* [2004] IRLR 377 (CA), wherein the Court of Appeal rejected the case for an implied term in law enjoining the employer to exercise reasonable care for the economic and financial wellbeing of their employees. For commentary on this decision, see, eg, C Wynn-Evans, 'Of Portmanteaux and Bridgeheads' (2004) 33 ILJ 355.

application of those general principles, absent further development of more specific rules, makes employment contracts less distinctive.
3. While an employment relationship is commonly understood at common law as being distinct from an independent contractor relationship, present case authorities enunciating that distinction are difficult to reconcile. This irreconcilability is problematic, due to the uncertainty it creates in understanding the scope of the employment relationship and what makes it distinctive.
4. While the operation of many statutory rules is reliant upon the existence of an employment contract, this is complicated by the fact that the relevant statutes tend to rely on the common law definition of employment (as distinct from an independent contract) to dictate when particular provisions will operate. Moreover, under certain statutes, independent contractors are deemed employees for the purpose of statutory protections. This situation further blurs the understanding of what constitutes an employment contractual relationship, also making it appear less distinctive. In English law, there is the added complexity of a third category of 'worker', who, in certain statutory circumstances, is afforded the same statutory labour law rights as an employee. The potential for similar complexity in Australia looms, should the Fair Work Legislation Amendment (Closing Loopholes) Bill 2023 (Cth) passed in its current form, generating statutory protections for certain workers performing 'employee-like' work.
5. When implying terms by law into employment contracts, the courts have done little to generate an understanding of employment contracts as a class into which the particular default rule will operate. This lack of understanding is complicated by the fact that certain terms implied by law into employment contracts also have the potential to operate in respect of other types of contracts, particularly contracts for services, thereby making employment contracts seem less distinctive.
6. There is a tension arising out of the apparent ability for parties to exclude terms implied by law and the rationale justifying the implication of those terms as necessary. It is possible that if they are excluded, then the contract may become less like one of employment, once again making it appear less distinctive. It is especially peculiar that in Australia, an implied term of mutual trust and confidence has been viewed as unnecessary, but in England, it has been repeatedly implied by law and deemed entirely incapable of exclusion.
7. There is relatively little understanding as to what classifying an employment contract as relational may mean for that class of contract. It may not comprise a distinctive feature at all. Other types of contracts can equally be classified as relational, making any such classification in employment less of a distinct or defining feature.

Finally, this chapter has established that the situation remains just as Lord Wedderburn put it in 1986: just like an 'elephant', the employment contract remains 'an animal too difficult to define, but easy to recognise when you see it'.[218] There is scope for the courts to develop their understanding of the employment contract as a class into which terms are implied by law. There need not be an all-encompassing definition of what constitutes the 'employment contract', but it is abundantly clear that the common law understanding of such contracts needs further articulation and understanding. Generating this further understanding will assist courts in developing the common law that shapes employment contracts, as opposed to other contracts for the personal performance of work. It will also enable greater certainty and consistency and, in turn, more accurate predictions of how the common law is likely to develop and shape those agreements in the future. It will also show when it is necessary to imply an existing or new term by law into such agreements. With that potential in mind, an exploration of when it is truly necessary to shape employment contracts through the mechanism of terms implied by law is the focus of Chapter 6.

[218] Lord Wedderburn, *The Worker and the Law* (3rd edn, Penguin 1986) 116.

6
Necessity

Introduction

Apart from being implied into contracts of a particular category or class, terms implied by law must also be 'necessary' within that category or class. A great deal of confusion has emerged over time as to when it is truly necessary to imply a term by law, in both England and Australia.[1] This chapter examines the reasons for this confusion in the specific context of employment contracts, with many of the preliminary concepts applying to contracts generally.

In traversing the challenges associated with determining when it is truly necessary to imply terms by law into employment contracts—and, conversely, which of those terms ought to be incapable of exclusion—this chapter commences with an historical account of the emergence of the 'necessity test' for implying a term by law into contracts generally in England. Following discussion of the emergence of that test, the chapter's focus turns to the difficulties associated with its application in England. Attention is then paid to the narrow (ie functional) and wide (ie political or policy-based) interpretations of that test in Australia, and the complications that those interpretations have generated, which have been surprisingly unparalleled in English law.

The final part of this chapter questions whether, in either jurisdiction, a term implied by law into the class of employment contracts could, or should, be capable of exclusion by a contrary express term, or as a consequence of concurrent statutory, tortious, and equitable obligations. Arguably, throughout the process of considering a term's potential excludability, courts must make a political or policy-based judgement as to the desired shape of the employment contract's normative core. Perhaps if certain terms were capable of exclusion, the contract may even cease to be one of employment and potentially transformed into some other type of contract.

The resulting question of which terms implied by law ought to be incapable of exclusion due to absolute necessity to the employment relationship is a key component of this chapter's final exploration. The chapter's ultimate conclusion is that the

---

[1] In the Australian context, see the preliminary discussion in G Golding, 'Terms Implied by Law into Employment Contracts: Are they Necessary?' (2015) 28 AJLL 113. This chapter presents an extension of that article, focussing on a comparison between the English and Australian interpretations of the necessity test, as well as questioning the potential excludability and absolute necessity of certain terms implied by law in the class of employment contracts.

so-called necessity test, as presently applied, must be better articulated and understood when the question arises of whether to imply a term by law. Rather than being restricted by the narrow operation of the test, the decision as to a term's necessity ought to be based on a wider approach, which must be better articulated by the judiciary than at present. To assist in better articulating that wider approach, it seems a holistic value judgement is required, contingent on how the implied term will sit with existing law; how a decision to imply it into a class or category of contracts will affect the parties to those types of contractual relationships; and more expansive notions of what is fair and acceptable as a societal norm. To simply label the necessity test as narrow or wide seems nebulous and ignores the intricate level of decision-making that is required to change an entire category or class of contract through the creation of a new term implied by law.

Emergence of the Necessity Test in England

In an effort to understand the complexities associated with what is necessary to imply as a term by law in the context of employment contracts, it is useful to trace the development of the necessity test back to its emergence in England. The reason this exercise is helpful is that the development of terms implied by law in England gave rise to what is now commonly referred to as the 'necessity test', both in England and Australia. As detailed in Chapter 1, the test for implication of terms was once based on the parties' intentions.[2] Over time, the courts acknowledged that some terms were consistently implied because of the type of relationship between the parties, rather than the facts of the case in question.[3] This development of implication by law as a separate category occurred as a consequence of cases decided over the past seventy years.[4] As Richard Austen-Baker remarks, '[i]t is by no means easy to attempt to fix the date or method of entry' for implied terms in English contract law.[5] Nevertheless, there are two key English decisions which enunciated this distinction and the first application of the necessity test for a term implied by law: *Lister v Romford Ice & Cold Storage Co Ltd*[6] and *Liverpool City Council v Irwin*.[7]

Lister v Romford Ice revealed the first indication by the House of Lords of the necessity test to ascertain whether it was appropriate for a new term to be implied by law. The case involved Lister, who drove a lorry for Romford Ice. Lister was

---

[2] E Peden, 'Contract Development Through the Looking-Glass of Implied Terms' in J T Gleeson, J A Watson, and E Peden (eds), *Historical Foundations of Australian Law* (Federation Press 2013) 201, 203–10.
[3] ibid 225.
[4] ibid.
[5] R Austen-Baker, *Implied Terms in English Contract Law* (2nd edn, Edward Elgar 2017) 11.
[6] [1957] AC 555 (House of Lords (HL)).
[7] [1977] AC 239 (HL).

reversing the lorry when his father (also an employee of Romford Ice) was injured; Lister had been negligent in carrying out the manoeuvre. His father sued Romford Ice, which, in turn, sued Lister on behalf of the company's insurer. Romford Ice tried to recover from Lister in tort, as well as contract.

In reaching their conclusion not to imply a term that an employer must insure their employee for damage caused by the employee's negligence, the majority (comprising Viscount Simonds and Lords Tucker and Morton) used a variety of tests. Lord Morton used a business efficacy test,[8] which has been described in Chapter 1 as one of the five cumulative tests for implying a term in fact. Lord Tucker used an obviousness test,[9] which has similarly been described in Chapter 1 as one of the tests for implying a term in fact. Viscount Simonds used a test that is similar to the current necessity test for implying a term by law.[10] He thought that a 'wider view' had to be taken of the question of implication and that the question to be asked was whether 'in the world in which we live today it is a necessary condition of the relation of master and man that the master should ... look after the whole matter of insurance'.[11] He rejected the familiar test of business efficacy, but on the facts, applied the obviousness test.[12] Unfortunately, Viscount Simonds did not take the opportunity to explain why. Again, as discussed in Chapter 1, the business efficacy and obviousness tests are but two of five cumulative requirements for implying a term in fact. Overall, these variances in judicial opinion as to the 'correct test for implication and its future application' left the ratio from the case unclear.[13] Even though the decision in *Lister v Romford Ice* is unhelpful for that reason, it did at least generate an initial sense of distinction between terms implied in fact and by law, as well as some reference to a necessity test.[14]

The House of Lords later sought to apply *Lister v Romford Ice* in the classic English authority about implied terms, *Liverpool City Council v Irwin*.[15] This case concerned the obligations of a landlord council in relation to the common areas of the stairs, lifts, and rubbish chutes in a fifteen-storey apartment block. The Irwins were tenants in the building. They withheld rent payable to the council in response to the conditions of the premises. They claimed that the council was in breach of a

---

[8] *Lister v Romford Ice* (n 6) 583. His Lordship thought that if a term were to be implied it would have to be implied into all contracts where an employee drove a vehicle. However, he felt that the appropriate test to imply terms for a particular type of contract, rather than a specific one, was still the business efficacy test. On that basis, he concluded that there should be no implied term.

[9] ibid 594. His Lordship thought that the law should not introduce 'some quite novel term' into the master and servant relationship and refused to imply a term.

[10] ibid 576-79. The minority judgments also differed. Lord Radcliffe believed that the implication could be justified on the basis that the common law has to develop in response to society's development (at 591). Lord Somervell relied on the business efficacy test (at 599).

[11] ibid 576.

[12] ibid.

[13] Peden (n 2) 225.

[14] ibid 226.

[15] This decision is discussed in detail in Peden (n 2) 227-31.

duty to repair and maintain the common parts of the building. Furthermore, since the council was a public authority under statute, it was responsible for providing housing at subsidised rent for members of the public, selected because of their specific needs. However, there was no express mention of any obligations owed by the council in the relevant lease.

Unfortunately when making their decision, their Lordship's speeches were again 'unclear on the question of the legal principles involved in the implication of the proposed term'.[16] Lord Wilberforce's speech is cited regularly as providing the necessity test for implying terms by law.[17] His Lordship thought of each of the categories of implied term as shades 'on a continuous spectrum',[18] but did not explain the differences between the different types of implication. Instead, he considered the test for implication to be applied to the case in question, finding that 'such obligation should be read into the contract as the nature of the contract itself requires, no more, no less: a test, in other words, of necessity'.[19]

Lord Cross agreed with Lord Wilberforce's decision to imply the proposed term.[20] He discussed implied terms in general, adopting the distinction between the two types of implied terms as explained by Viscount Simonds and Lord Tucker in *Lister v Romford Ice*.[21] Unfortunately, Lord Cross did not acknowledge which test for implication was to be used, but appeared to have applied the test for all contracts of a particular type.[22] However, it seems that in doing so, he was concerned with what the parties themselves would have agreed to, had they been asked. This contradicts his earlier reasoning, as such an approach is substantially similar to the test for implication in fact.[23]

Giving briefer reasons, Lord Salmon concluded that while the proposed implied term had to be reasonable, it also had to be necessary, as reasonableness alone was not enough.[24] Lord Edmund-Davies reached the same conclusion as Lord Salmon,[25] but 'was the only judge to stress the justification of the implication'.[26] Ultimately, the House of Lords found in favour of implying the term in question and emphasised a test of 'necessity' in doing so.[27] Despite this result, it remains difficult to determine a clear test of implication from their speeches.

---

[16] Peden (n 2) 228.
[17] Lord Fraser agreed with Lord Wilberforce (at 269). See also Peden (n 2) 228.
[18] *Liverpool City Council v Irwin* [1977] AC 239 (HL), 254. See also the discussion of Lord Wilberforce's judgment in Peden (n 2) 228–29.
[19] *Liverpool City Council v Irwin* (n 7) 254.
[20] ibid 257. See also the discussion of Lord Cross' judgment in Peden (n 2) 228.
[21] *Lister v Romford Ice* (n 6) 576–79, 594.
[22] Peden (n 2) 228.
[23] ibid 230.
[24] *Liverpool City Council v Irwin* (n 7) 262.
[25] ibid 269.
[26] Peden (n 2) 230.
[27] ibid.

Confusion in Applying the Necessity Test in England

Since *Liverpool City Council v Irwin*, English decisions have supported the idea that a court is making rules to regulate a contract when it settles on an implied term by law and that the court is informed by a notion of necessity,[28] as well as making a policy-based decision[29] about how best to regulate a certain type of contract. However, English support for the necessity test has not been unequivocal. The courts have undergone what Hugh Collins calls 'collective amnesia' during which they have forgotten the distinction between legal and factual implication and the separate tests to be applied.[30] At times, they have fallen into the trap of assuming that all implied terms must be necessary for the effective operation of the particular contract in question (ie applying the 'business efficacy' test).[31]

In other words, English courts had developed an erroneous pattern for implying terms using a test for implication in fact when they were really dealing with an implication by law, and having realised their mistake they have fixed it. For example, as Collins explains, in *Lister v Romford Ice* the court denied (or perhaps conveniently forgot) the possibility of a term implied by law as a standardised incident.[32] The court insisted that all terms must conform to the presumed intentions of the parties, as terms implied in fact, and that in that particular case, those tacit intentions probably did not coincide.[33] Later, in *Liverpool City Council v Irwin*, however, the court claimed that it was being invited to create a term implied by law for a broad class of contracts, for which it would be inappropriate to legislate.[34]

In explaining why English courts have routinely confused the implication of terms in fact and by law, Collins has identified two separate sources for the courts' confusion: 'the possibility of a metamorphosis, and an instrumental misclassification'.[35] In relation to metamorphosis, after a succession of similar cases involving a term implied in fact, the courts may begin to assume that the term has become one implied by law, such that 'in the absence of express terms to the contrary, it will be binding on both parties as a standardised default rule'.[36] Separately, an

---

[28] See, eg, *Scally v Southern Health and Social Services Board* [1992] 1 AC 294 (HL), where Lord Bridge (with Lords Roskill, Goff, Jauncey, and Lowry agreeing) attempted to summarise the English position by drawing a distinction between *Lister v Romford Ice* (n 6) and *Liverpool City Council v Irwin* (n 7), confirming that the test for implication was one of necessity.

[29] See, eg, *Malik v Bank of Credit and Commerce International SA (In Liq)* [1998] AC 20 (HL), 45–46.

[30] H Collins, 'Implied Terms: The Foundation in Good Faith and Fair Dealing' (2014) Curr Leg Probl 1, 10.

[31] As already mentioned in Chapter 2, this business efficacy test is derived from *The Moorcock* (1889) 14 PD 64 (Court of Appeal (CA)). See further, the discussion concerning the application of the test in A Phang, 'Implied Terms, Business Efficacy and the Officious Bystander—a Modern History' [1998] JBL 1.

[32] Collins (n 30) 11–12.

[33] ibid.

[34] ibid 12.

[35] H Collins, 'Implied Terms in the Contract of Employment' in M Freedland et al (eds), *The Contract of Employment* (OUP 2016) 471, 480.

[36] ibid 481.

instrumental misclassification may occur in situations in which the court has described a term as one implied by law, 'when in reality it only applied to the interpretation of that particular contract of employment';[37] in other words, as a term implied in fact. Overall, with this potential for confusion in mind, while *Liverpool City Council v Irwin* was a breakthrough in the development of the implication of terms by law, it was also limiting. In Andrew Phang's opinion, it is 'rather surprising that the ... case has been cited with such confidence', given its ambiguities.[38]

Confusion in Applying the Necessity Test in Australia

Liverpool City Council v Irwin left the Australian courts with a similar problem to that faced in England: the process of determining necessity was vague and unclear. Once the *Liverpool City Council v Irwin* test was adopted in Australia by virtue of the High Court of Australia's decision in *Byrne v Australian Airlines Ltd*[39] (a case briefly referred to in earlier chapters), the lack of clarity was transferred and distorted even further.

In *Byrne v Australian Airlines*, the plaintiff employees argued that it was necessary to imply a term into their employment contracts, in accordance with clause 11(a) of the Transport Workers (Airlines) Award 1988, stating that they would not be harshly, unjustly, or unreasonably dismissed. As part of its assessment of whether it was necessary to imply such a term by reason of custom and usage, the High Court took into account the statutory context of the employees' contracts. It did not agree that it was necessary to imply a term, as the issue was already covered by clause 11(a) of the award.[40]

The judgment in *Byrne v Australian Airlines* was mostly concerned with arguments as to whether the particular term ought to be implied in fact, or by custom and usage. However, in their joint judgment, McHugh and Gummow JJ took the opportunity to mention that a term will be implied as a matter of law where it is necessary to ensure that the enjoyment of the rights conferred by the contract will not be 'rendered nugatory, worthless, or ... seriously undermined'.[41] This approach represented a very narrow and functional view of necessity that contains no reference to any broader notions, such as justice and policy. It is contrary to the wider political and policy-based approach inherent in English decision-making on the existence of terms implied by law.[42]

---

[37] Collins (n 35) 482.
[38] A Phang, 'Implied Terms Revisited' [1990] JBL 394, 403.
[39] (1995) 185 CLR 410 (High Court of Australia (HCA)).
[40] ibid 422–23, 453.
[41] ibid 450.
[42] See, eg, *Malik v Bank of Credit and Commerce International* (n 29) 45–46.

While the formulation of the *Byrne v Australian Airlines* necessity test appears narrow in its wording, it has the potential to be applied more widely, just as in England. Essentially, the test can be read and interpreted in a strict and functional sense, but its application could still incorporate broader political and policy-based reasoning. The Full Court of the Federal Court of Australia in *University of Western Australia v Gray* recognised this possibility when it observed that:[43]

> It doubtless is the case that this necessity test [(specifically, the *Byrne v Australian Airlines* formulation of the test)]—and its characteristic concern with whether the enjoyment of contractual rights could be rendered nugatory or worthless, or be seriously undermined if no implication is made—has been invoked to address the *broad* range of instances where the issue of such an implication ordinarily arises ...

Despite the potential for a wider application of an apparently narrowly worded test, this work operates on the presumption that the narrow wording used in *Byrne v Australian Airlines* similarly means that the necessity test derived from that case is to be applied in a strict and functional sense: that is, by allowing for a term to be implied by law only where it is necessary to make the contract work, without taking broader considerations into account, as would otherwise be the case in English law.

Practically speaking, a contract remains workable without certain terms implied by law. However, there may still be good political and policy-based reasons as to why a particular term *should* still be recognised as one implied by law. For example, there is nothing unworkable about an indefinite employment contract that is set to continue until an employee dies or if there is some serious breach by either party. To put it another way: there is no absolute need to imply a term by law requiring reasonable notice on termination to make the contract function. However, a term requiring reasonable notice on termination *is* absolutely necessary in a wider sense because if it does not exist, then the contract will cease to be classified as one of employment. Instead, it will be a contract for slavery, potentially requiring the employee to work indefinitely. This example is returned to below in the context of discussing which terms implied by law are absolutely necessary to employment and incapable of exclusion. The overarching point is that while certain terms implied by law may not be necessary to make a contract work, they may still be necessary for broader political and policy-based reasons.

The narrowness of the *Byrne v Australian Airlines* necessity test for implying a term by law is akin to the business efficacy requirement that the term must be necessary to 'enable the contract to operate in a businesslike manner'.[44] The similarity

---

[43] (2009) 179 FCR 346 (Federal Court of Australia (FCA)) [140] (emphasis added).
[44] J Paterson, A Robertson, and A Duke, *Principles of Contract Law* (5th edn, Lawbook Co 2016) 340.

between these two tests contributes to a blurring of the distinction between implying terms in fact and by law; a confusion already considered in Chapter 1.

The comments made by McHugh and Gummow JJ in *Byrne v Australian Airlines* were later applied by the High Court in *Breen v Williams*.[45] This application meant that McHugh and Gummow JJ's narrow necessity test became the accepted position for the implication of a term by law in Australian contracts. *Breen v Williams* considered whether a term ought to be implied by law into a contract between a doctor and a patient that would allow a patient the right of access to their medical records. In deciding that it was not necessary to imply such a term by law, the High Court in *Breen v Williams* noted that a doctor was subject to an implied obligation to exercise reasonable care in treating patients.[46] Specifically:[47]

> [I]t could not be said that unless a term relating to the access of records was implied as a matter of law, the enjoyment of the rights conferred on the patient by the contract ... would be rendered worthless or seriously undermined.

The court's reasoning in *Breen v Williams* was concentrated on the narrow view that the contract could operate effectively without the particular implied term. It did not consider whether there were good political or policy-based reasons as to whether patients should have that right. For instance, in his dissenting judgment in the New South Wales Court of Appeal for the same matter, Kirby P (as his Honour then was) cited with approval the decision of the Supreme Court of Canada in *McInerney v McDonald*,[48] which held that the doctor–patient relationship was fiduciary in nature and that a patient is entitled to reasonable access to examine and copy the doctor's records. Justice La Forrest, writing for a unanimous court, stated:[49]

> Information about one's self revealed to a doctor acting in a professional capacity remains, in a fundamental sense, one's own. The doctor's position is one of trust and confidence. The information conveyed is held in a fashion somewhat akin to a trust. While the doctor is the owner of the actual record the information is to be used by the physician for the benefit of the patient. The confiding of the information to the physician for medical purposes gives rise to an expectation that the patient's interest in and control of the information will continue. The trust-like 'beneficial interest' of the patient in the information indicates that, as a general

---

[45] (1996) 186 CLR 71 (HCA). The same application of *Byrne v Australian Airlines* (n 39) occurred in *Commonwealth Bank of Australia v Barker* (2014) 253 CLR 169 (HCA) [29].
[46] *Breen v Williams* (n 45) 88.
[47] ibid 124.
[48] [1992] 2 SCR 138 (Supreme Court of Canada (SCC)).
[49] Quoted by Kirby P in *Breen v Williams* (1994) 35 NSWLR 522 (New South Wales Court of Appeal (NSWCA)), 545.

rule, he or she should have a right of access to the information and that the physician should have a corresponding obligation to provide it.

This alternative reasoning further supports the idea that the distinction between legal and factual implication is blurred by the approach in *Byrne v Australian Airlines*. Both types of implication have the potential to apply a narrow and functional view of necessity, focusing on whether the implication of the particular term is necessary purely to make the contract work, rather than any other broader political or policy-based notions.

The Full Court of the Federal Court later examined the issue of necessity in *University of Western Australia v Gray*, a case that has already been discussed briefly in Chapters 3 and 5. By way of reminder, the case concerned various claims by the University of Western Australia against Dr Gray, who was employed by the University as a Professor of Surgery. One of those claims was that an implied term existed in Dr Gray's employment contract to the effect that rights to any inventions developed in the course of his employment belonged to the University of Western Australia. While the Full Court did not find in favour of implying such a term, its reasoning suggested that the concept of necessity could take on a different and potentially wider meaning to that in *Byrne v Australian Airlines*:[50]

> What is clear is that necessity in this context has a different shade of meaning from that which it has in formulations of the business efficacy test ... The principal reason for this is, as Viscount Simonds indicated in *Lister* ... that implication in law rests 'upon more general considerations', a view endorsed both by Lord Wilberforce in *Liverpool City Council* ... and Lord Bridge in *Scally* ...

The Full Court observed that the necessity test adopted by the High Court in *Byrne v Australian Airlines* could cause difficulties if the 'elusive concept' of necessity was too narrowly conceived.[51] In making these findings, the Full Court was clearly suggesting that the net for implying terms ought to be cast much wider than the strict approach in *Byrne v Australian Airlines*, instead taking into account matters of 'justice and policy'.[52]

The Full Federal Court's decision in *University of Western Australia v Gray* stressed that policy concerns ought to form a significant part of the courts' decision-making process as to whether to imply a term by law. In *University of Western Australia v Gray* the court made reference to the idea that 'implication in law rests upon more general considerations ... [which] require that regard be had to the inherent nature of the contract and of the relationship thereby established'.[53]

---

[50] *Byrne v Australian Airlines* (n 39) [142].
[51] ibid [140]–[141].
[52] ibid [141]–[147].
[53] (2009) 179 FCR 346 (Full Court of the Federal Court of Australia (FCAFC)) [145].

The court highlighted that those 'very considerations themselves can raise issues of justice and policy ... as well as consideration, not only of consequences within the employment relationship, but also of social consequences'. This suggestion appears to place importance on how courts may seek to emphasise fairness between the contracting parties when implying terms by law.

Later, in *Commonwealth Bank of Australia v Barker*, the High Court applied the narrow necessity test from *Byrne v Australian Airlines*, yet, curiously, its reasoning suggested that it had not ruled out an application of the wider test from *University of Western Australia v Gray*. The relevant facts and outcomes of that case have already been discussed in Chapter 4. For present purposes, this discussion focuses on the High Court's reasoning in respect of its application of the necessity test in deciding not to imply the mutual trust and confidence term.

The High Court in *Commonwealth Bank v Barker* cited *Byrne v Australian Airlines* as a basis to refuse the implication of a term of mutual trust and confidence as a matter of law. As suggested in Chapter 4, prior to the decision, several writers had confidently asserted that a mutual obligation of trust and confidence would satisfy the *Byrne v Australian Airlines* test.[54] However, the High Court took a different view in *Commonwealth Bank v Barker*. The majority of French CJ and Bell and Keane JJ stated that the implied term imposed mutual obligations 'wider than those which are "necessary," even allowing for the broad considerations which may inform implications in law. It goes to the maintenance of the relationship'.[55] The majority also found that, while some lower courts in Australia had made 'approving references to the implied term', it was up to the High Court to 'determine the existence of the implied duty by reference to the principles governing implications of terms in law in a class of contract'.[56] This reasoning required the High Court to decide whether the proposed implication was '"necessary" in the sense that would justify the exercise of the judicial power in a way that may have a significant impact upon employment relationships and the law of the contract of employment in this country'.[57]

However, apart from applying *Byrne v Australian Airlines*, the High Court majority also cited *University of Western Australia v Gray* on two occasions to reach its conclusion that the mutual trust and confidence term was not necessary to be implied.[58] While the court did not expressly state that it was applying the wider *University of Western Australia v Gray* test, equally it did not expressly rule out its application. In denying the implication of the mutual trust and confidence term, the court's reasoning focussed on the fact that the term would involve 'complex

---

[54] See, eg, K Godfrey, 'Contracts of Employment: Renaissance of the Implied Term of Trust and Confidence' (2003) 77 ALJ 764, 766.
[55] *Commonwealth Bank v Barker* (n 45) [37].
[56] ibid [36].
[57] ibid.
[58] ibid [29] and [36].

policy considerations ... more appropriate for the legislature than for the courts to determine'.[59] The majority then recognised that it was significant that the term would impose obligations on employees whose voices were not heard in the appeal, which suggested a further reason for it to remain 'in the province of the legislature'.[60] This political and policy-informed reasoning, which is examined further in Chapter 7 in light of the judicial role in regulating employment contracts, extends beyond a strict application of the narrower considerations espoused in *Byrne v Australian Airlines*. It appears more akin to an application of the wider considerations in *University of Western Australia v Gray*, even though the majority did not expressly label it as such. There are references in *University of Western Australia v Gray* to issues of 'justice and policy', 'consequences within the employment relationship', as well as 'social consequences'.[61] However, there is no guidance as to what weight should be given to each of these factors, or how they should be applied in the employment context. If anything, the policy considerations later applied in *Commonwealth Bank v Barker* could be seen as limiting any future implication of terms by law in employment contracts, since such an implication may be similarly viewed as 'a step beyond the legitimate law-making function of the courts', which 'should not be taken'.[62]

In the earlier 2009 case of *State of South Australia v McDonald*,[63] a case discussed in Chapters 4 and 5, the Full Court of the Supreme Court of South Australia was also aware of the policy issue of not wanting to trespass into legislative territory when it was asked to imply a term of mutual trust and confidence. The Full Court concluded that 'the statutory and regulatory context in which ... [Mr McDonald's] contract of employment operated made the implication of a term concerning mutual trust and confidence unnecessary'.[64] The 'statutory and regulatory context' in *State of South Australia v McDonald* included formal procedures for dealing with teachers' grievances,[65] a statutory right of appeal against decisions of the employer,[66] and policies regulating the employer's conduct.[67] The Full Court in *State of South Australia v McDonald* therefore contemplated employees like Mr Barker who were not afforded the benefit of such statutory protections having access to the mutual trust and confidence term. In effect, the High Court's denial of the mutual trust and confidence term in *Commonwealth Bank v Barker* for the reason of not wanting to engage in complex policy considerations contradicted the Full Court's decision in *State of South Australia v McDonald*.

---

[59] ibid [40].
[60] ibid [38].
[61] *University of Western Australia v Gray* (n 53) [142].
[62] *Commonwealth Bank v Barker* (n 45) [1].
[63] (2009) 104 SASR 344 (Full Court of the South Australian Supreme Court (SASCFC)) [275].
[64] ibid [270].
[65] ibid [259].
[66] ibid [251].
[67] ibid [267]–[268].

The High Court's decision in *Commonwealth Bank v Barker* has left Australian courts at a crossroads as to how they ought to apply the necessity test to employment contracts if they are asked to imply a new term by law. As David Chin explains: '[T]he elusive nature of the criterion of "necessity" in this context is reflected in the variable application of this concept to the contract of employment'.[68] The courts remain faced with the question of whether it is strictly the narrow approach in *Byrne v Australian Airlines*, or whether it includes the wider considerations from *University of Western Australia v Gray*. There are two decisions which demonstrate why this juxtaposition of necessity tests is problematic.

First, an intermediate appellate court came to rely on a combination of the two necessity tests in *Harden v Willis Australia Group Services Pty Ltd*[69]—an outcome which is hardly surprising given the uncertainty generated by the High Court:[70]

> The test for whether a term should be implied by law is that of 'necessity'. It must be demonstrated that absent the implication the enjoyment of the rights conferred by the contract would or could be rendered nugatory, worthless, or the contract would be deprived of its substance, seriously undermined or drastically devalued. Considerations of justice and policy should be included in a consideration of 'necessity'.

Secondly, Judge Egan of the Federal Circuit and Family Court of Australia (Division 2) decided in *Debus v Condor Energy Services Limited*[71] that it was appropriate to imply a term requiring the employee to disclose his disability (Autism) prior to commencing employment, as well as during his employment. However, in making that decision, Judge Egan did not indicate whether the implication was to occur in fact into the specific employment contract in question or into all employment contracts by law, and if so, what necessity test was operative. No reference was made to the relevant test for implication at all, and the term was simply stated to be implied. Despite this lack of clarity, the decision seems to have been made with highly problematic policy-based reasoning in mind; in essence, having Autism was deemed to have such a sufficient impact upon the workplace that it ought to override employee privacy and be disclosed—a decision that seems in direct conflict with Australia's disability discrimination legislation. Should this duty to disclose apply to all employment contracts, it is especially problematic, in that it carries the

---

[68] D Chin, 'Implied Terms and the Stifling of Innovation in the Employment Contract' (Paper presented at the Eight Biennial National Conference of the Australian Labour Law Association, St Kilda, 4 and 5 November 2016) 2.
[69] [2021] NSWSC 939 (New South Wales Supreme Court (NSWSC)) [24].
[70] Citations omitted.
[71] [2022] FedCFamC2G 429 (Federal Circuit and Family Court of Australia (Division 2) (FedCFamC2G)) [26].

potential to require any employee who suffers from an invisible disability to disclose that disability if it may affect their work.

Beyond these vexed decisions, if the *University of Western Australia v Gray* test continues to be adopted for future implication of terms by law, the courts may instead find themselves avoiding the issue, or refusing to imply a term based purely on political and policy-based grounds. The result of leaving the courts to identify what is deemed reasonable to be the 'correct' approach to political and policy-informed necessity in contracts is highly variable and subjective.[72] This is perhaps even more the case for employment contracts, which may bring with them a unique set of considerations. As Chapter 5 suggests, however, the distinctiveness of employment contracts is questionable.

Another outcome of adopting the broader *University of Western Australia v Gray* approach could be that the courts actually avoid making any political or policy-based decisions at all. As Andrew Stewart suggests, a consequence of the High Court's reasoning in *Commonwealth Bank v Barker* is that '[I]t may be difficult to persuade an Australian court to recognise *any* new implied term'.[73] Australian courts might accept that they are making a political or policy-informed determination when they are asked to imply a new term by law into employment contracts, but might also maintain that such action ought to remain a matter for the legislature as a matter of course. This approach could result in the courts passing off all responsibility for regulating employment contracts through terms implied by law to parliament. Whether this shift in the courts' law-making power should occur is explored further in Chapter 7. To borrow Joellen Riley Munton's metaphor used to describe the short-comings of private law regulation in 2003, it could be that terms implied by law in employment contracts have now developed into a 'Rolls Royce with no fuel in the tank. As handsome as ... [they are, they] won't take us anywhere'.[74] Having said that, a strict reading of *Commonwealth Bank v Barker* could also result in the adoption of the narrower approach to necessity in *Byrne v Australian Airlines*, without reference to the wider interpretation of necessity *in University of Western Australia v Gray*.

It is worth noting at this point that a reliance on a political and policy-based approach to necessity in English law has not stymied the development of new terms implied by law in the context of employment contracts. Rather, the courts have embraced the opportunity to consider the broader implications of new terms they choose to imply, with the most obvious example being the routine implication of a

---

[72] According to Phang, '[w]hen policy factors are involved, legal uncertainty is perforce increased': Phang (n 38) 409.

[73] A Stewart, *Stewart's Guide to Employment Law* (7th edn, Federation Press 2021) 115. Cf *The HMW Accounting & Financial Group v McPherson* (2020) 292 IR 198 (Supreme Court of Queensland (QSC)), which left open the possibility of a new implied term that an employer ought not operate its business unlawfully in a manner that causing damage to its employees.

[74] J Riley, 'Mutual Trust and Good Faith: Can Private Contract Law Guarantee Fair Dealing in the Workplace' (2003) 16 AJLL 1, 22.

mutual trust and confidence term. More recently, a new term requiring employers to conduct disciplinary processes fairly has been suggested for implication by law into all English employment contracts, with the court's reasoning suggesting that the term arises from the very 'nature of the disciplinary process'[75]—a far broader concept that is contingent on factors extending beyond the mere functionality of the employment contract alone. Notwithstanding the pre-existing common law and statutory regulation of disciplinary action in English law, the term's necessity still appears justified for political and policy-based reasons, in that it contributes to the common law's response to the particular vulnerabilities of employees, and also in terms of achieving a fair balance between the parties to employment contracts.

Excludability and Absolute Necessity

To overcome the various difficulties associated with the application of the necessity test, both in England and Australia, rather than trying to ascertain whether a term implied by law is necessary to be implied into all employment contracts, perhaps the question that ought to be asked is why *some* existing terms implied by law are considered necessary in employment contracts while others are not. As things stand, it remains largely unclear at what point a term implied by law ceases to be necessary. It is significant that no cases have taken the step of analysing earlier terms that have been accepted as terms implied by law into employment contracts. All existing terms have been left untouched and continue to operate, despite contradictions as to the necessity test to be applied, alongside the potential for the co-existence of equivalent duties under statute, as well as in the law of equity and tort.

As already suggested in Chapter 5, while employers may just attempt to contract out of every implied obligation that they are said to owe, or to significantly modify certain terms, it seems illogical to do so in respect of some (but certainly not all) duties that have already been deemed necessary in the employment relationship. Some existing duties implied by law into employment contracts ought to be capable of exclusion or modification, and others ought not to be. The point is that those duties that are incapable of exclusion or substantial modification are, by virtue of that very status, also those that are truly necessary in shaping the normative core of employment.

Arguably, if (1) an employee's duty to obey lawful and reasonable instructions of their employer, (2) a mutual duty to provide reasonable notice of termination for an otherwise indefinite contract, and/or (3) a mutual duty to cooperate were contracted out of or significantly modified, it would mean that the employment relationship is no longer viable. In that sense, these duties ought to be understood

---

[75] *Burn v Alder Hey Children's NHS Trust* [2021] EWHC 1474 (CA) [42]; see also Underhill LJ's comments concerning the conceptual basis of procedural fairness (at [35]).

as *absolutely* necessary features of the employment relationship. The reasons surrounding the absolute necessity of these three duties are considered in more detail directly below.

As discussed, not all of these terms implied by law are necessary in the strictest sense (ie to make the contract 'work'). Specifically, a mutual duty to provide reasonable notice on termination need not be classified as necessary for the functionality of an employment contract. This classification would be particularly true in the English context, where the duty has been largely usurped by statute. Absent equivalent legislative coverage, however, an employment contract could operate without it, but it can be classified as necessary for the policy-based reason that without it, the contract would otherwise be categorised as one for slavery. However, the same cannot be said for an employee's duty to obey, or a mutual duty to cooperate. As described below, arguably both duties are strictly necessary for the proper functioning of an employment contract, even avoiding the need for political or policy-based considerations.

The duty for an employee to obey lawful and reasonable instructions ought to be considered absolutely necessary.[76] As highlighted in Chapter 5, the reason for this absolute necessity is that an employer's capacity to manage its workforce is underpinned by this duty. In support of this conclusion, it has been said that the obligation of an employee to obey their employer's orders is 'one of the identifying features of employment'.[77] In that sense, an employee's duty to obey their employer's lawful and reasonable orders is coterminous with the employment contract. Collins goes further in making the point that any exclusion or limitation on an employer's right to direct the performance of work in line with this duty begins 'to turn the proper classification of the contract towards a contract for services'.[78] Without it, 'the courts may no longer classify the contract as one of employment'.[79] That said, as noted in Chapter 3, it may well be that the duty's sanctity as an exclusive and identifying feature of employment is being gradually eroded following the United Kingdom Supreme Court's judgment in *Uber BV v Aslam*.[80] To reiterate, the duty arguably operates similarly in respect of 'limb (b) workers' in England, generating a far wider scope of application than to employment alone.

In a written employment contract that does not contain a set notice period (either as an express term or by operation of an applicable statutory provision), or is not for any fixed-term, a term implied by law provides that the contract is terminable on reasonable notice.[81] Without that term, the employment contract

---

[76] See, eg, *Darling Island Stevedoring & Lighterage Co Ltd; Ex parte Halliday and Sullivan* (1938) 60 CLR 601, 621.
[77] M Irving, *The Contract of Employment* (2nd edn, LexisNexis Butterworths 2019) 500.
[78] Collins (n 35) 483.
[79] ibid 484.
[80] [2021] ICR 657 (Supreme Court of the United Kingdom (UKSC)).
[81] *Byrne v Australian Airlines* (n 39) 429.

could actually require the employee to be available indefinitely,[82] consequently amounting to a contract for slavery. Chapter 3 has highlighted the same potential for the implied term of reasonable notice to operate in respect of contracts for the performance of work, which are not for a fixed-term and contain no set notice period. As Collins argues in the case of employment contracts, an exclusion or substantial modification of this basic liberty of 'the employee to quit by terminating the contract [would] edge the proper classification of the contract towards forced labour or a non-contractual kind of servitude'.[83] Considering the reasons already described in Chapter 3, it therefore makes little sense for the common law implied term to be displaced in its entirety. This is particularly the case in the Australian context, where the reasonable notice implied term plays an even greater gap-filling role, accepting that the 'better view' is that s 117 of the *Fair Work Act 2009* (Cth) prescribes a minimum notice period, and gives only the employer the right to terminate without affording an employee the same right.

An employment contract (or any contract for that matter) could surely not operate without a duty of cooperation.[84] This same argument is made in Chapter 3 in respect of the existence of a duty to cooperate comprising a necessary element of contracts for the performance of work. Indeed, in all contractual dealings, parties are 'unlikely to have intended the performance of their contract to be obstructed by an unreasonable lack of cooperation'.[85] The only situation that would displace the necessity for an implied term would be one in which the same duty was pitched as an identical express term (or at least an equivalent express term covering the same ground). Without such a term, it would be difficult—if not impossible—for any contract to properly function. It is highly unlikely that the parties will be able to foresee every circumstance that may arise in the future, making the term a necessary element of all contracts. If the parties were not expected to cooperate during the course of their agreement, there would be little point in them contracting in the first place.

Despite the absolute necessity of these three existing terms, which are routinely implied into employment contracts by law, there are many more that may be viewed as not necessary and capable of exclusion or modification—in other words 'less significant' to all instances of employment.[86] Indeed, as already shown in Chapter 3, a number of these duties are capable of operation in contracts for the performance of work, making them appear less pertinent to shaping employment alone. These excludable duties include: (1) an employer's duty to provide a safe place of work; (2) an employer's duty to indemnify their employees for expenses

---

[82] See further the discussion about indefinite contracts in Stewart (n 73) 382–83.
[83] Collins (n 35) 483.
[84] See the further discussion as to the content of this duty in Chapter 3. As described in Chapters 1 and 3, it may instead be categorised as a rule of construction, rather than an implied term.
[85] J Paterson, 'Terms Implied in Fact: The Basis for Implication' (1998) 13 JCL 103, 119.
[86] Collins (n 35) 484.

innocently incurred; (3) an employer's duty to inform an employee of their rights; (4) an employee's duty of fidelity; (5) an employee's duty to exercise reasonable care and skill; (6) an employee's duty to hold inventions on trust; and (7) an employee's duty not to disclose their employer's confidential information.

As the following discussion concerning each of these terms makes clear, there are two key reasons for the lack of necessity for each of these terms. The first is that the term is not necessary because there is another concurrent obligation (eg under statute, the common law, or equity). The second is that the employment contract could still function without the particular implied term. This second reason is essentially based on an application of the *Byrne v Australian Airlines* necessity test, but is also very similar to an application of the 'business efficacy' test for implying a term in fact (discussed in Chapter 1). This type of rationalisation contributes to a blurring of the distinction between terms implied by law and in fact,[87] and has most probably added to the courts' confusion when asked to imply terms by law into employment contracts. As Chin explains, conflating the different concepts of necessity in this way also has the potential to erroneously preclude the operation of a term implied by law that 'may not be necessary to give business efficacy to the contract because the contract is effective without it, but is nonetheless necessary (in the broader sense) to the class of contract to which the contract belongs, and is otherwise not inconsistent with the express terms of the contract or any applicable statutory regime'.[88] A key example Chin uses to illustrate this point is a good faith term, which has already been considered in Chapter 4, and is returned to in this work's Conclusion.

In relation to an employer's contractual duty to provide a safe place of work, concurrent statutory provisions exist under applicable work health and safety laws in both England and Australia.[89] These statutory provisions each create essentially identical duties owed by employers, in that the statutory provisions effectively cover the same ground as the common law implied term. Moreover, employers also owe an obligation in tort to take reasonable care for the safety of their employees.[90] As explained in Chapter 3, this tortious duty is concurrent with the employer's

---

[87] See the earlier discussion in Chapter 1 concerning the courts' confusion in relation to this fact/law distinction.

[88] Chin (n 68) 4.

[89] In England, see, eg, *Health and Safety at Work etc. Act 1974* (UK); *Management of Health and Safety at Work Regulations 1999* (UK); and sundry other pieces of health and safety legislation. In Australia, see, eg, *Work Health and Safety Act 2011* (Cth); *Work Health and Safety Act 2011* (ACT); *Work Health and Safety Act 2011* (NSW); *Work Health and Safety (National Uniform Legislation) Act 2011* (NT); *Work Health and Safety Act 2011* (Qld); *Workplace Health and Safety Act 2012* (Tas); *Work Health and Safety Act 2012* (SA); *Work Health and Safety Act 2020* (WA); Victoria, which continues to use its own *Occupational Health and Safety Act 2004* (Vic), as the Victorian government has confirmed that it will not be implementing the Model Work Health and Safety Act in its current form.

[90] In England, see, eg, *Lister v Romford Ice* (n 6); *Matthews v Kuwait Bechtel Corporation* [1959] 2 QB 57 (CA). In Australia, see, eg, *Crimmins v Stevedoring Industry Finance Committee* (1999) 200 CLR 1 (HCA) [61] and [226]; *Goldman Sachs JB Were Services Pty Ltd v Nikolich* (2007) 163 FCR 62 (FCAFC) [324].

contractual duty of care created by the term implied by law. While there are some differences between the two causes of action in tort and contract (eg differences in limitation periods, dates of the causes of action accruing, entitlements to an award of interest, and assessing the remoteness of damages), the fact that a concurrent duty exists in tort (in combination with an equivalent statutory duty) makes it seem much less likely that a contractually implied duty is absolutely necessary to be implied by law into all employment contracts. Put another way: because of the concurrent tortious and statutory duties, at face value, there really is no gap to fill through the operation of a contractually implied term by law into the class of employment contracts.[91] Notwithstanding these concurrent obligations, it could also be said that an employment contract could still function without a contractually implied duty owed by an employer to provide a safe place of work—unlike a duty owed by an employee to obey lawful and reasonable instructions of their employer, it is not central to the function of an employment relationship. While remaining important in a practical sense, it is arguably peripheral to the function and existence of the core of the employment relationship between the parties.

Nevertheless, a strong and perhaps more palatable counter-argument exists whereby an employer's duty to provide a safe place of work is central to employment. On this interpretation, the implied term could be viewed as necessary in both the narrow and the wide sense. Requiring an employer to provide a safe place of work could be viewed as necessary to make the employment contract work, in that it may prove physically impossible for work to be performed in an unsafe environment. From a broader policy perspective, it makes sense to require employers to provide their employees with a safe working environment; requiring any employee to work in an unsafe environment is directly contrary to maintaining the employment relationship. As Chapter 3 explained, arguably the same logic can be applied in respect of the duty's potential operation with regards to contracts for the non-standard performance of work. For work to be performed in either capacity, the environment in which the work is performed must surely be safe.

In addition, an employer's duty to indemnify employees for expenses innocently incurred during the performance of their duties is also not a necessary feature of the employment relationship. Even though, as described in Chapter 3, the duty (in its full force) requires an employer to indemnify an employee for all liabilities and

---

[91] There is also a compelling argument that where the common law has already recognised a duty of care in tort, there exists no necessity for what is effectively the same duty operating concurrently as a term implied by law in contract, including in respect of a duty derived from a previously recognised term implied by law such as the implied duty of mutual trust and confidence in English law. For example, in *James-Bowen v Commissioner of Police of the Metropolis* [2018] 1 WLR 4021 (UKSC) Lord Lloyd-Hones reasoned that the derivative duties imposed on employers, which stem from the implied duty of mutual trust and confidence, did not, and should not, extend to an employer-owed obligation to conduct litigation in a way which protects employees from reputational harm. This case presents an example of an existing term implied by law not being permitted to give rise to a derivative duty where there is no concurrent common law recognition of the same obligation in tort law.

expenses that arise from the performance of the employee's duties, it can hardly be said that the duty is absolutely necessary to all instances of employment.

As also discussed in Chapter 3, an employer's duty to inform employees of their rights will only ever apply in respect of the very narrow sub-class of employment contracts referred to in *Scally v Southern Health & Social Services Board*.[92] The duty has no broader application. Therefore, only in very limited instances of employment will an employer be required to notify their employees of changes to their contributory pension scheme. Consequently, it cannot be said to be a necessary feature of all employment contracts.

An employment contract would arguably not be rendered worthless, nugatory, or seriously undermined if it did not contain a duty of fidelity to be owed by an employee as broad as that currently implied.[93] As the discussion of the duty in Chapter 3 suggests, courts have routinely complained that the duty of fidelity is rather vague and that achieving clarity is not assisted by the diffuse manner in which some courts and texts have approached the related cases. The fact that the duty is vague and not easily identified makes it appear less necessary to employment than others. As Chapter 3 has made apparent, the same could be said of the duty's likely limited application to non-standard forms of work. However, the duty could still be viewed as necessary in particular situations of employment that are largely contingent on the employee remaining loyal to their employer. For example, the duty would arguably be more necessary for an employee working in sales who sets up a business in direct competition with their employer. In such instances, the duty would have greater scope for application and importance.

In relation to an employee's contractual duty to exercise reasonable care and skill in the tasks they perform, statute in both jurisdictions imposes equivalent obligations on employees to take care of their own health and safety and to take reasonable care that their acts or omissions do no adversely affect the health and safety of others.[94] As such, there is no absolute necessity for an equivalent contractually implied duty to operate at the same time; as a consequence of these statutory provisions, there is no gap that requires filling. Moreover, the associated obligation on an employee to exercise reasonable 'skill' in the tasks they perform will only arise in settings where the exercise of a skill is actually required. This situation is certainly not universal to all instances of employment, so it cannot be said that this aspect of the duty is a necessary feature of every employment contract either. Nevertheless, while this duty is not strictly necessary in the narrower 'business efficacy' sense, it will remain so for those employment contracts in the sub-category for which the

---

[92] [1992] 1 AC 294 (HL).
[93] The formulations of the duty of fidelity are not without 'an air of unreality or artificiality': Austen-Baker (n 5) 51.
[94] In Australia, see, eg, the *Work Health and Safety Act 2011* (Cth) s 28(a)–(b), and the equivalent sections from counterpart Acts in most state and territory jurisdictions; in England, see, eg, the *Health and Safety at Work etc. Act 1974* (UK) s 7.

term is to apply. A substantially similar argument was put in relation to the duty's potential operation in contracts for the performance of work in Chapter 3.

As also described in Chapter 3, the duty requiring employees to hold inventions created in the course of performing their employment duties on trust for their employer (at least where there is a duty to invent) will only ever apply to an employee who has a duty to invent as part of their employment. In that sense, while it is exclusive to employment, the duty can hardly be said to be necessary in all instances of employment. Again, while this duty will not be absolutely necessary across all employment contracts in the narrower 'business efficacy' sense, for contracts where an employee has a duty to invent, the term will become necessary at least in relation to contracts in that sub-category.

As the Full Court of the Federal Court noted in *University of Western Australia v Gray*, an employee's duty not to misuse or disclose confidential information is 'an unhappy mixture' of equity, contract, and statute.[95] The relationship between each of the co-existent duties has already been touched upon in Chapter 3, as has its potential application to non-standard contracts for the performance of work. As suggested there, however, given that the duty exists concurrently in areas other than contract, it surely cannot be said that it is strictly necessary to be implied as a term by law in a contractual sense alone. As above, given that the duty (or a substantially similar equivalent) exists in equity and under statute, it can hardly be said that there is any real gap to fill in relation to employment contracts. Furthermore, like the other duties mentioned above, it is reasonable to suggest that an employee's duty not to misuse or disclose confidential information is not actually a central element of the employment relationship—unlike an employee's duty to obey, the relationship would still exist without it.

Overall, the preceding discussion shows that, irrespective of the necessity test applied, only certain terms implied by law can be considered absolutely necessary features in employment contracts, and therefore incapable of exclusion or modification. Only a select few terms implied by law are 'constitutive of the concept of a contract of employment'.[96] While they might be labelled as terms implied by law, others are not necessary, or are perhaps 'less significant' to employment, despite being 'routinely incorporated' into employment contracts as apparently necessary terms implied by law.[97] Where that is the case, those terms can be freely excluded or modified by the parties. This possibility leads to a consideration of what pursuit the courts are truly engaging in when deciding on a term's necessity as one to be implied by law.

---

[95] *University of Western Australia v Gray* (n 53) [159].
[96] Collins (n 35) 491.
[97] ibid 484.

Conclusion

This chapter has shown that problems with identifying when a term is necessary to imply by law have existed for some time. These difficulties stem from the obscure development of the law in England. *Liverpool City Council v Irwin*, the seminal English case concerning terms implied by law, was lacking in clarity. The result was that when Australian courts followed the necessity test derived from *Liverpool City Council v Irwin*, the confusion continued. To add to this problem, the High Court went on to adopt a somewhat narrow interpretation of the necessity test in its decision in *Byrne v Australian Airlines*, which continues to apply in Australian contract law. That test provides that any term sought to be implied by law must be necessary to prevent rights normally conferred by contracts of the particular class from being 'rendered nugatory, worthless, or … seriously undermined'.[98] However, in *University of Western Australia v Gray*, the Full Court of the Federal Court suggested that necessity could take on a potentially wider meaning and involve consideration of matters of justice and policy in the court's determination of what is necessary. While the High Court in *Commonwealth Bank v Barker* openly applied the narrow test from *Byrne v Australian Airlines*, its policy-based reasons for denying the implication of the mutual trust and confidence term paradoxically suggest that its approach to necessity is actually wider. The necessity test for implying a term by law now remains uncertain and must be clarified. If it is not clarified, the courts may refuse to apply even the narrow necessity test from *Byrne v Australian Airlines* and avoid implying terms by law into contracts altogether.

As the last part of this chapter highlights, certain terms implied by law are seemingly absolutely necessary in employment contracts and therefore are incapable of exclusion or modification, specifically: (1) an employee's duty to obey lawful and reasonable instructions of their employer; (2) a mutual duty to provide reasonable notice of termination of an otherwise indefinite contract; and (3) a mutual duty to cooperate. Each of these terms has operated and continues to operate as a necessary incident in that class of contract to ensure that certain gaps are filled. Despite being labelled as terms implied by law, a greater number of terms that have been routinely implied by law are largely not necessary (in the narrow sense), or, in other words, are less significant incidents of employment, and therefore, are capable of exclusion or modification. The reasons for this lack of necessity to employment could be said to fluctuate between the particular duty existing through in some other format (eg under statute, in tort or equity), or that the term is not necessary for the functioning of an employment relationship. Such terms include: (1) an employer's duty to provide a safe place of work; (2) an employer's duty to indemnify their employees for expenses innocently incurred; (3) an employer's duty to inform

---

[98] *Byrne v Australian Airlines* (n 39) 450 (McHugh and Gummow JJ).

an employee of their rights; (4) an employee's duty of fidelity; (5) an employee's duty to exercise reasonable care and skill; (6) an employee's duty to hold inventions on trust; and (7) an employee's duty not to disclose confidential information of their employer.

Overall, there is uncertainty surrounding the future application of the necessity test in relation to terms implied by law into all contracts. A closer analysis of existing terms implied by law into employment contracts shows that many of those terms are actually not strictly necessary features of all employment relationships. The courts need to make further efforts to clarify which necessity test they ought to apply, as well as how that test translates to existing terms implied by law.

The present understanding of the necessity test lacks clarity and full articulation, making ambiguous the exercise that the courts are truly engaging in when applying it. It is therefore suggested that when deciding whether a term implied by law is truly needed to fill a gap in a class or category of contracts, the process the courts are undertaking is much more nuanced than simply indicating that a narrow or wide test is being applied. What seems to be happening during the process of implication by law is a decision involving the broader approach, but that must be more holistically understood and articulated. It appears that the process that the courts are truly engaging in when deciding whether to imply a term by law is based on how the implied term will coincide with existing law, whether under statute or the common law; how the parties to the particular class or category of contract will themselves be affected by the new term; and lastly, whether the implication is fair and acceptable as a societal norm that applies in respect of the agreements for which the term will become a part. This deeper understanding of the 'true' broad necessity test appears to encompass more than a label; it lends itself to a judgement based on wider policy-based considerations, which are of equal weight and importance in a court's decision-making process as whether to recognise the implied term at all. This work's Conclusion further considers ways in which that clarity might be achieved after the judicial role in shaping employment through the implication of terms by law has been examined in Chapter 7.

7
The Judicial Role

Introduction

There exists an overarching debate as to whether the courts or parliament should make laws that shape employment contracts. This chapter offers a view as to how that debate ought to be resolved in respect of allowing for employment contracts to be shaped through terms implied by law in the future.[1] This is an important exercise, as it is the employment contract that 'holds the subject of labour law together and provides its core ingredient'.[2] In the context of the employment contract, the relationship between common law and statute has been labelled 'a hugely important one'.[3] As with Chapter 6, attention in this chapter rests solely on employment contracts, rather than extending further to contracts for the performance of work.

Considering the High Court of Australia's comments in *Commonwealth Bank of Australia v Barker*[4] to the effect that the implication of the mutual trust and confidence term is a matter best left to the legislature (rather than the judiciary), the discussion throughout this chapter questions the future judicial role in shaping employment contracts through the mechanism of terms implied by law. While

---

[1] On the fraught relationship between the common law and statute in the case of labour law, see, eg, D Brodie, *The Future of the Employment Contract* (Edward Elgar 2021) Ch 7; G Golding, 'The Role of Judges in the Regulation of Australian Employment Contracts' (2016) 32 IJCLL&IR 69; J Riley, 'Uneasy or Accommodating Bedfellows? Common Law and Statute in Employment Regulation' (Paper presented at the Phillipa Weeks Lecture in Labour Law, ANU College of Law, Australian National University, Canberra, 25 September 2013); B Hepple, *Rights at Work: Global, European and British Perspectives* (Sweet & Maxwell 2005) 52, 65; A Bogg, 'Common Law and Statute in the Law of Employment' (2016) 69 Curr Leg Probl 67; S Anderman, 'The Interpretation of Protective Employment Statutes and Contracts of Employment' (2000) 29 ILJ 223; ACL Davies, 'The Relationship Between the Contract of Employment and Statute' in M Freedland and others (eds), *The Contract of Employment* (OUP 2016) 73, 75–80; M Freedland, *The Personal Employment Contract* (OUP 2003) 10–12, 155–56, 189, 339–44; M Freedland and N Kountouris, *The Legal Construction of Personal Work Relations* (OUP 2011) 101; L Barmes, 'Common Law Implied Terms and Behavioural Standards at Work' (2007) 36 ILJ 35, 37–38; S Honeyball, 'Employment Law and the Primacy of Contract' (1989) 18 ILJ 97, 105–08; S Honeyball and D Pearce, 'Contract, Employment and the Contract of Employment' (2006) 35 ILJ 30; and P Elias, B Napier, and P Wallington, *Labour Law: Cases and Materials* (Butterworths 1980) 526–27.

[2] H Collins, K D Ewing, and A McColgan, *Labour Law* (2nd edn, CUP 2019) 136. Cf Sir Otto Kahn-Freund, who once viewed the employment contract as being of marginal significance, despite providing a mechanism for the enforcement of collective agreements and some statutory rights: see, eg, M Freedland, 'Otto Kahn-Freund, the Contract of Employment and the Autonomy of Labour Law' in A Bogg and others (eds), *The Autonomy of Labour Law* (Hart Publishing 2015) 29.

[3] Brodie (n 1) 210.

[4] (2014) 253 CLR 169 (High Court of Australia (HCA)).

Commonwealth Bank v Barker is not binding in English courts, it remains influential, particularly in the sense that it raises broader questions regarding the ambit of judicial law-making powers in respect of employment contracts. Those questions are applicable across both England and Australia, as well as in respect of common law jurisdictions more broadly. This chapter therefore continues on the proviso that the ideas and arguments raised are applicable in both England and Australia, as well as in respect of common law jurisdictions in the general sense.

To revisit a point made in Chapter 4, when deciding not to imply a mutual trust and confidence term by law into all Australian employment contracts, French CJ and Bell and Keane JJ in *Commonwealth Bank v Barker*[5] jointly emphasised that the term's recognition would involve 'complex policy considerations ... more appropriate for the legislature than for the courts to determine'.[6] Their Honours found that the implication of the contractual term was a 'step beyond the legitimate law-making function of the courts', which 'should not be taken'.[7] The court also held that 'the common law ... must evolve within the limits of judicial power and not trespass into the province of legislative action'.[8]

Accordingly, French CJ and Bell and Keane JJ were not denying the judges' law-making role. Rather, they were placing limits on that role, and introducing ambiguity around those limits. The broader problem now apparent is precisely *where* to draw those limits. Specifically, it is unclear what criteria ought to be applied in determining when it is legitimate for a common law court to make law with respect to employment contracts, and when it is not. ACL Davies suggests that judicial statements like this mark employment contract law as an area in which the courts are tending to show 'a high degree of deference to statute, particularly when they are called upon to develop the common law'.[9] Sir Patrick Elias has also observed that there must be 'a limit to how far the courts can legitimately interfere with the express terms of a contract',[10] yet there remains uncertainty as to where those limits ought to be placed, and the extent to which parliament ought to intervene.

In recognition of this challenge, this chapter focuses on the broader implications of the High Court's reasoning in *Commonwealth Bank v Barker*, specifically in relation to whether English and Australian courts (or, indeed, any common law court) *should* maintain a rule-making power with respect to employment contracts. On the one hand, it can be argued that courts should not feel bound by out-of-date precedents in making decisions about employment contracts. They should arguably be able to revise, replace, and develop new rules where they view it as

---

[5] As already noted in Chapter 4, while all judges were unanimous in finding against the implied term of mutual trust and confidence, Kiefel and Gageler JJ issued separate judgments.
[6] *Commonwealth Bank v Barker* (n 4) [40].
[7] ibid [1].
[8] ibid [19].
[9] Davies (n 1) 81, citing ACL Davies, 'Judicial Self-Restraint in Labour Law' (2009) 38 ILJ 278.
[10] P Elias, 'Changes and Challenges to the Contract of Employment' (2018) 38(4) OJLS 869, 872.

necessary, based on their own judicial interpretations. On the other hand, there is an equally compelling proposition that judges should be limited to developing the common law incrementally in a manner bound by existing precedent, as well as to interpreting and applying the laws already made by parliament. To do otherwise may be seen as inherently anti-democratic, as it allows unelected and politically unaccountable judges to participate in governing employment contracts. It may also threaten the wider public respect for judges as impartial enforcers of law and adjudicators of disputes.

This chapter closely examines the role that courts ought to play in that rule-making process. It is acknowledged that parliament will always possess the primary rule-making power through the creation of either primary or delegated legislation. Indeed, the legislature can overrule any judicial decision it does not agree with by implementing amending legislation. The overarching question that remains, however, is whether the judiciary should exercise the ability to make rules with the effect of shaping employment contracts at all.

This discussion recognises that implying terms by law is but one way that judges can shape the employment relationship.[11] For example, judges can interpret the express terms of employment contracts, apply existing laws from both statute and common law, and award remedies where appropriate. But this chapter concentrates on the specific question of whether judges *should* impose new norms of conduct through terms implied by law, without touching on other potential regulatory conduct. To go further would be beyond this work's scope.

The first section of this chapter sets out the general arguments for and against judicial law-making in order to come to a more specific view about the judicial law-making role with respect to employment contracts. This discussion also contemplates that, especially since *Commonwealth Bank v Barker*, coherence between statute and the common law ought to be reinvigorated to prevent further uncertainty.

Considering those initial arguments, the final part of this chapter considers what amounts to coherence, and how that coherence might be achieved through both common law and statutory action. It suggests ways in which statute and the common law can operate symbiotically to solve the difficulty associated with determining what role judges should play in shaping employment contracts, which is briefly revisited in this work's Conclusion. While burgeoning academic attention is now being paid to the judiciary's capacity to develop implied terms in a way that ensures human rights are respected in the workplace in England,[12] it does not

---

[11] Hugh Collins appears optimistic about the courts' ability to imply terms into employment contracts, suggesting that they apparently 'permit judicial intervention whilst maintaining the appearance of conformity to respecting the parties' self-determination': H Collins, 'Implied Terms: The Foundation in Good Faith and Fair Dealing' (2014) Curr Leg Probl 1, 1.

[12] See especially, P Collins, *Putting Human Rights to Work: Labour Law, the ECHR, and the Employment Relation* (OUP 2022) Ch 7, which investigates the probability of a new function for the mutual trust and confidence term, as well as the possible development of a new implied obligation owed

appear that the courts' overarching law-making power with respect to implying terms by law into employment contracts has been considered in the manner posed by this chapter.

Examining the Judicial Role

Let us now turn to the overarching question governing this chapter: what law-making role *should* the courts play with respect to shaping employment contracts? Seeking to answer this question definitively presents an obvious challenge. There are competing arguments as to whether the courts ought to make new rules with respect to those contracts, or whether parliament should exclusively hold that role. At one time, according to what has sometimes been referred to as the declaratory theory of the common law,[13] judges simply 'found' a legal set of rules that were to apply from time immemorial. It is now accepted that judges are necessarily making choices and law when they determine the status and scope of the common law.[14] The question that follows is what role judges should play in doing so.

This part considers the arguments that have been raised in the general literature for and against the law-making power of the courts with a view to answering the more specific question asked in this work's Conclusion about what rule-making role the courts should play with respect to employment contracts. As set out directly below, arguments in favour of judicial law-making are focussed on the idea that judges are able to flexibly develop the law, as well as ensure the law's coherence and predictability. Arguments against the judicial law-making role follow. They are linked to parliament's perceived democratic legitimacy, its efficiency in developing the law, and the importance of maintaining the perception of an impartial judiciary. The importance of reinvigorating a symbiotic relationship between statute and the common law is discussed at the close of this chapter, following which an overarching conclusion is drawn.

---

by an employer to respect an employee's human rights. See also, J Atkinson, 'Implied Terms and Human Rights in the Contract of Employment' (2019) 48 ILJ 515.

[13] See, eg, D Jensen, *Theories, Principles, Policies and Common Law Adjudication* (2011) 36 Aust J Leg Philos 34, 43–48, which conducts a detailed examination of that theory.

[14] See generally, A Mason, 'The Judge as Law-Maker' (1996) 3 JCULR 1; Lord Reid, 'The Judge as Lawmaker' (1972) 12 JSPTL 22.

A. Why Judges Should Engage in Judicial Law-making

Flexibility

The courts are arguably in a better position than parliament to develop the law flexibly. The judicial role is inherently dynamic. The law is rarely clear and incontestable, therefore leaving room for judges to develop it flexibly in order to achieve important and necessary outcomes. In that respect, common law judges need not remain behind the times, unable to replace strict rules with more suitable standards. Where appropriate, they should have the opportunity to free themselves from the 'straitjacket of law as authority'.[15]

Lord Goff addressed the question of whether judges should effect this kind of developmental change in the common law in *Kleinwort Benson Ltd v Lincoln City Council*,[16] a 1999 case concerning money paid under mistake of law. His Lordship held as follows:

> In the course of deciding the case before him [the judge] may, on occasion, develop the common law in the perceived interests of justice, though as a general rule he does this 'only interstitially', to use the expression of O W Holmes J in *Southern Pacific Co v Jensen* (1917) 244 US 205, 221. This means not only that he [or she] must act within the confines of the doctrine of precedent, but that the change so made must be seen as a development, usually a very modest development, of existing principle and so can take its place as a congruent part of the common law as a whole...

Occasionally, a judicial development of the law will be of a more radical nature, constituting a departure—even a major departure—from what has previously been considered to be established principle, and leading to a realignment of subsidiary principles within that branch of the law.[17] In the context of the common law rule as to mistake of law, Lord Goff carefully considered the arguments in favour of judges making more radical changes to the English common law. His Lordship purposefully left open the opportunity for judges to make more significant developments to the law, rather than just basing their decisions on what can be drawn from the existing law under the traditional common law method. He emphasised this possibility, stating that he could not 'imagine how a common law system, or indeed any legal system... [could otherwise] operate' should the law not be capable of 'organic change'.[18]

---

[15] J Gava, 'The Rise of the Hero Judge' (2001) 24 UNSWLJ 747, 747.
[16] [1999] 2 AC 349 (House of Lords (HL)).
[17] ibid 378.
[18] ibid. Cf *Mabo v The State of Queensland (No 2)* (1992) 175 CLR 1 (HCA), 29–30, wherein Brennan J warned against judges departing from precedent 'where the departure would fracture what I have called the skeleton of principle'.

Relatedly, in the 1972 decision, *British Railways Board v Herrington*,[19] when commenting on occupiers liability legislation, Lord Wilberforce suggested that the 'common law is a developing entity'.[20] His Lordship added that 'so long as we follow the well tried method of moving forward in accordance with principle as fresh facts emerge and changes in society occur, we are surely doing what Parliament intends that we do'.[21] In acknowledging this statement and its effect on the relationship between judicial and legislative law-making, Douglas Brodie labelled it 'equally applicable where the employment contract is concerned'.[22]

With these suggestions in mind, the implication of a new term by law into all employment contracts arguably illustrates the judicial role being performed in a way that flexibly develops the common law. This flexibility arises because implying a new term by law can enable judges to take a lead from existing legislative intervention in rebalancing the employment relationship, recognising that employment is more than a contractual exchange of labour for wages, and utilising the common law tool of implying a term by law into all employment contracts accordingly.[23] As Jack Hodder explained, it is 'at the end of this incremental and progressive process' that 'fairness has been enhanced, the potential for abuse of employer power curbed, and the sum of total human happiness increased. This, it might be asserted, is the adaptive and creative genius of the common law at work.'[24] Ronald Dworkin also had a well-known vision of the common law along these lines. He described it using a metaphor of a 'chain novel', whereby judges are authors as well as critics who participate in the collaborative writing of the novel that is the law.[25] Clearly, the common law has the potential to further the aims of legislation in that regard.

Furthermore, if a court decides, as it did in *Commonwealth Bank v Barker*, not to imply a term by law into all employment contracts on the basis that such a decision 'ought to not trespass into the province of legislative action',[26] there is always the risk that parliament will not step in to clarify the issue at all. For whatever reason, parliament may not bother to make the matter part of its legislative agenda. As it stands, '[w]e only have a very limited knowledge of what demands are likely to be met with legislative action'.[27] This potential inaction on the part of the legislature is a further reason for judges to avoid a conservative approach to developing the law and to feel comfortable exercising their creative function.

---

[19] [1972] AC 877 (HL).
[20] ibid.
[21] ibid.
[22] Brodie (n 1) 210.
[23] J Hodder, 'Employment Contracts, Implied Terms and Judicial Law-Making' (2002) 33 VUWLR 475, 477.
[24] ibid 477–78.
[25] See generally, R Dworkin, 'Law as Interpretation' (1982) 9 Crit Inq 179.
[26] *Commonwealth Bank v Barker* (n 4) [40].
[27] B Reiter, 'The Control of Contract Power' (1981) 1 OJLS 347, 365.

Coherence and predictability

An additional argument in favour of judges making rules with respect to employment contracts is that the common law is often more coherent and predictable than statute. In support, Joachim Dietrich wrote that, all too often, we are ' "stuck with" (in many cases) piecemeal legislation, [and] we cannot assume that there is a "coherent whole" that is merely being obscured by such legislation'.[28] Consequently, as Roger Traynor argues, a judge's role ought to be 'greater now that legislatures fabricate laws in such volume'.[29] In keeping with this idea, Leeming JA also pointed out that 'swathes of statutory law lack the complexity brought about by decades or centuries of litigation and analysis, although there is ample scope for analysis and complexity in ... many ... areas dominated by statute'.[30] His Honour further explained that '[a]ll this is a natural consequence of a legal system whose norms are statutes of general application enacted by different levels of government, and by governments with different policy objectives'.[31] A more controversial view is that 'the elected branch, vulnerable to the felt passions of the time and prone to arbitrary and irrational action must be constrained by the calmer cooler heads of the judiciary'.[32]

B. Why Judges Should Avoid Judicial Law-making

Democratic legitimacy

Despite the above arguments in favour of judicial law-making, much has been written, both academically and judicially, about why judges ought to avoid making bold new statements of law, with legislation considered a more democratically legitimate form of law-making.[33] So much so, that it is now commonplace to speak of an 'age of statutes'.[34] The reasons for this legislative dominance have often been

---

[28] J Dietrich, 'What is Lawyering?' (2006) 65 CLJ 549, 573.
[29] R Traynor, 'Statutes Revolving in Common Law Orbits' (1968) 17 Cath U L Rev 401, 401–02.
[30] M Leeming, 'Theories and Principles Underlying the Development of the Common Law—The Statutory Elephant in the Room' (2013) 36 UNSWLJ 1002, 1006.
[31] ibid.
[32] G Huscroft, 'Romance, Realism, and the Legitimacy of Implied Rights' (2011) 30 UQLJ 35, 42.
[33] Taking just one example that encapsulates this deference to parliament due to democratic legitimacy, Lady Hale explains: 'Never say never, but I think that the judges are unlikely to create an entirely new cause of action ... This they would now regard themselves as institutionally incompetent to do so, even if they might on occasions have done so in the past, when Parliament was less active and there were no Law Commissions to show how it should be done': Baroness Hale, 'Legislation or Judicial Law Reform: Where Should Judges Fear to Tread?' (Annual Society of Legal Scholars Conference, Oxford, 7 September 2016) 17–18.
[34] There are too many examples to sensibly mention here, but, see, eg, G Calabresi, *A Common Law for the Age of Statutes* (Harvard University Press 1982); A Burrows, 'The Relationship Between Common Law and Statute in the Law of Obligations' (2012) 128 LQR 232, 233; P Finn, 'Statutes and the Common Law' (1992) 22(1) UWALR 7; A Connolly and D Stewart (eds), *Public Law in the Age of Statutes: Essays in Honour of Dennis Pearce* (Federation Press 2015). As these diverse citations indicate, the phenomenon is not limited to just one jurisdiction.

articulated by the courts as feeling reluctant or ill equipped to make policy decisions that might be called for in a particular uncertain area of the law.

One of the main justifications for this outcome is parliament's perceived political accountability. In a matter of contested policy, such as whether to imply a new term by law into all employment contracts, there is an argument that parliament is the more appropriate body to make the decision about which policy to adopt.[35] To do otherwise would effectively allow 'unelected and politically unaccountable judges to participate in government'.[36] This end result may give rise to the parties' rights in their employment contract 'taking second place to the desire of judges to create what they believe to be the best rules for the future'.[37] John Gava has gone so far as to label such actions as a 'sneaky' way for judges to change the law for political or market-oriented reasons without going through the rigours required for those who wish to become politicians.[38]

The research facilities and resources available to parliament also put it in a more advantageous position than the courts in respect of making well-informed policy decisions. Judges are not given this same access, nor can they seek out the advice of expert lobbyists. They also avoid the political accountability associated with scrutiny by the media and public. The courts are 'constrained in their ability to take part in and learn from the robust public debate that characterises normal politics'.[39] Parliament, by contrast, finds itself in the unique position of being able to conduct a broad survey of problems in the entire field of which they are a part.

Efficiency

There is arguably efficiency in parliament being able to avoid the limitations of the common law method when making rules with respect to employment contracts. Even if a court wants to make a significant change in the law, it is limited to the facts of the case before it, as well as any applicable *ratio decedendi*. The court must therefore wait for the appropriate case to be brought before the change can occur. Even then, if the court chooses to make a bold statement of law, there is always the possibility that it will be distinguished in future cases, or that the decision will be appealed. In addition to this, parliament finds itself in the unique position of being able to amend legislation to intervene and correct any 'mistakes' or undesirable decisions made by judges.

---

[35] Taking a recent example, when examining the possibility of English courts implying a new term by law requiring that an employer respect an employee's human rights, Philippa Collins cites the dominance of existing statutory regulation along with a likely cautious approach held by the judiciary as reasons for deference to legislative action: P Collins, *Putting Human Rights to Work: Labour Law, the ECHR, and the Employment Relation* (OUP 2022) 171.
[36] Gava (n 15) 747.
[37] ibid 751.
[38] ibid 752.
[39] ibid 754.

Faith in an impartial judiciary

In all common law jurisdictions, including England and Australia, there is an obvious importance in maintaining a perception of an impartial judiciary. For both practising lawyers and the public at large, there is value in being able to face a judge without the concern that they will make their decision based on political bias. This generates a sense of faith in judges as independent arbitrators of disputes. Allowing judges to determine the law of their own volition creates a risk of harming the judiciary's reputation. As Gava explains, it is important that we avoid a 'culture in which judges are seen as part of the political regime and not as impartial referees whose decisions can and should be accepted as law'.[40]

Reinvigorating Coherence

As the above arguments demonstrate, there are clearly problems assuming either judicial or parliamentary supremacy when it comes to answering what law-making role judges ought to play in regulating employment contracts. To return to a point made earlier, the arguments presented are wide-ranging and often in direct conflict. This juxtaposition makes it difficult to reach a clear consensus as to how far the courts' law-making role ought to extend with respect to employment contracts.

This work has shown that terms implied by law are primarily a judicial technique, but parliament too can play a role in enacting terms implied by law by operation of statute. Throughout this chapter, and in those preceding it, judges have been admonished for failing (whether deliberate or not) to arrive at a clear position of when a term will or will not be implied by law into contracts generally, as well as into employment contracts specifically. Judges, who are as much law-makers as politicians, can remedy this uncertainty and generate clarity in the law by deciding to imply terms by law where necessary to fill gaps in classes of contracts, including in employment contracts. At the same time, however, judges may be wary of interfering by imposing obligations that were not otherwise consented to by the parties at the time of contracting. They may also fear straying too far into the realm of legislative action. The difficulty is that, absent judicial action, the legislature may be unwilling or unable to remedy a gap in a class or category of contracts, such as employment contracts.

Inaction by both the judiciary and legislature may ultimately mean that a gap in a class of contract, including in an employment contract, remains wide open and needs to be filled by way of a term implied by law. To avoid this impasse, the solution proposed is one that ensures coherence between the role of statute and the common law in implying terms by law as necessary incidents that shape those

---

[40] Gava (n 15) 759.

agreements. Therefore, attention now turns, first, to what amounts to coherence, and secondly, to how the courts and parliament are to be collectively responsible for ensuring that coherence.

Coherence is understood as the constant and uninhibited interplay between statute and judge-made law. Legislation will always require judges to decide matters involving its application. Statutes are increasingly becoming a source of judge-made law. It makes sense to refer to a 'kind of legal partnership between statute and common law'[41] as Professor Atiyah did in 1985. Similarly, Gleeson CJ once held that '[l]egislation and the common law are not separate and independent sources of law; the one the concern of parliaments, and the other the concern of courts. They exist in a symbiotic relationship.'[42] A symbiotic relationship involves the courts interpreting laws made by parliament, as well as parliament making laws phrased in general terms, knowing that the courts will apply that law to specific situations. The relationship allows for the courts to fill in any gaps they perceive as being left by parliament and to potentially alert parliament to any gaps in the law, thereby enabling parliament to legislate in response to a problem identified by the courts. Further, in a symbiotic relationship, 'legislative change may operate as a catalyst to prompt changes in judge-made law'.[43]

Each of these claims implies that the common law and statute are 'to a significant degree, products of the same inherently dynamic legal process'.[44] In support of this logic, Robert Williams contends that 'the common law [should be understood] not as a body of law whose change is impeded or blocked by a static body of rules, but as a process best served by the rational integration of judge-made and legislative law'.[45] Indeed, much has been written about the need for the common law and statute to work together as part of a 'coherent' system of law, instead of what Jack Beatson termed the 'oil and water' approach, which favours keeping the common law apart from its neighbouring but inferior relation, the statute.[46] In the context of Australian private law, Elise Bant has argued in favour of a more integrated approach to the application of statute and common law. Her view is that the interplay between statute and common law should be taken 'more seriously', so as to give rise to a more 'coherent private law as a whole'.[47] In the specific context of the relationship between the common law and statute law of employment, Mark Freedland has suggested that there is an 'intricate symbiosis' between the two sources of law.[48]

---

[41] P Atiyah, 'Common Law and Statute Law' (1985) 48 MLR 1, 6.
[42] *Brodie v Singleton Shire Council* (2001) 206 CLR 512 (HCA) [31].
[43] Leeming (n 30) 1021.
[44] S Gageler, 'Common Law Statute and Judicial Legislation: Statutory Interpretation as a Common Law Process' (2011) 37 Mon L Rev 1, 1–2.
[45] R Williams, 'Statutes as Sources of Law Beyond their Terms in Common-Law Cases' (1982) 50 Geo Wash L Rev 554, 599.
[46] J Beatson, 'Has the Common Law a Future?' (1997) 56 CLJ 291, 308, cited in S McLeish, 'Challenges to the Survival of the Common Law' (2014) 38 MULR 818, 826–7.
[47] E Bant, 'Statute and the Common Law' (2015) 38 UNSWLJ 367, 368.
[48] M Freedland, 'The Legal Structure of the Contract of Employment' in M Freedland and others (eds), *The Contract of Employment* (OUP 2016) 28, 34.

Davies has likewise suggested that in respect of labour law, '[i]t is not accurate in descriptive terms to regard the common law as foundational and statute law as an occasional intruder: the two are much more deeply intertwined'.[49] She goes on to say that because statute and the common law are so closely intertwined in this way, 'the courts should develop the common law alongside statutes to create a coherent system in line with the fundamental tenets of the Rule of Law'.[50]

Crucially, this chapter does not aim to determine conclusively whether judges or politicians ought to be ultimately responsible for shaping employment contracts through the implication of terms implied by law, either through the development of the common law or operation of statute. To do so would effectively deny the law-making function of the other. It may even obstruct the development of new legal rules with respect to employment contracts altogether. Any suggestion that either law-making function is preferable to the other with respect to employment contracts oversimplifies what is a complex and multilayered relationship. This chapter has endeavoured to uncover those layers by questioning the extent to which the courts or parliament ought to be responsible for shaping and constructing the norms of employment. Rather than advocating for either the courts or parliament to have greater influence than the other, this chapter makes a case for a closer symbiosis between the two branches of law-making with respect to employment contracts. Judicial law-making should not supersede legislative lawmaking with respect to employment contracts, and *vice versa*. One must inform the development and continuation of the other. The overarching benefit will be that employment contracts are continually shaped and will become reflective of contemporary norms.

With these understandings in mind, the following discussion offers two solutions that would reinvigorate both the courts and parliament working together in symbiosis in the future. Both proposals are made with the aim of avoiding uncertainty over the extent of the judicial law-making role in shaping employment contract law. The first proposal relates to the development of the common law, with the second relating to statutory change, both of which ought not to inhibit or impede the other.

First, in relation to the development of the common law, it might be said that judge-made law should, in general, uphold the notion of the parties' freedom to contract on their own terms and avoid interference by way of implying new terms by law. After all, parliament can step in and rectify any gaps by way of statutorily implied terms. However, the preferred (and arguably more coherent) approach is that when terms are implied by law through the operation of the common law, what ought to be reflected in those terms are the principles and values typically expressed in modern legislation concerning the employment relationship, including

---

[49] Davies (n 1) 74–75.
[50] ibid 95.

(but not limited to) legislation regulating discrimination in employment, unfair dismissal, unfair wages, and work health and safety. In essence, the existence of employment norms under statute serves to inform the development of the common law, and while this approach may appear controversial, it is well-placed to enhance coherence.

Putting this understanding into a practical scenario, what the High Court should have done in *Commonwealth Bank v Barker* was to fully analyse how and why Australia's statutory regime precluded the implication of the mutual trust and confidence term.[51] Instead, the court briefly mentioned Australia's extensive statutory employment regime:[52]

> Large categories of employment relationships are governed, at least in part, by statutory obligations expressed in industrial awards and agreements. There are laws dealing with unfair dismissal and the conditions of employment in relation to occupational health and safety. Anti-discrimination statutes of general application affect the conduct of the employment relationship ...

It then drew the blanket conclusion that because of Australia's extensive statutory protections in employment, this meant that, unlike in the United Kingdom, the mutual trust and confidence term was not necessary in Australia:[53]

> The regulatory history of the employment relationship and of industrial relations generally in Australia differs from that of the United Kingdom ... Judicial decisions about employment contracts in other common law jurisdictions, including the United Kingdom, attract the cautionary observation that Australian judges must 'subject [foreign rules] to inspection at the border to determine their adaptability to native soil'. That is not an injunction to legal protectionism. It is simply a statement about the sensible use of comparative law.

This reasoning is overly simplistic and lacks coherence. Ideally, the court should have critically analysed the statutory regimes mentioned and highlighted precisely how and why they covered the same field as the mutual trust and confidence term, making the term's implication unnecessary.

By contrast, the Full Court of the Supreme Court of South Australia in *State of South Australia v McDonald*[54] engaged in a more thorough analysis of the

---

[51] See further, V Sundra-Karean, 'The Erosion of the Implied Term of Mutual Trust and Confidence in Australian Employment Law: Are Common Law and Statute Necessarily Uncomfortable Bedfellows?' (2016) 45 CLWR 275, 287–90, which addresses the question of whether Australia's employment regime is so different from its English counterpart.
[52] *Commonwealth Bank v Barker* (n 4) 182–33.
[53] ibid 185.
[54] (2009) 104 SASR 344 (Full Court of the South Australian Supreme Court (SASCFC)).

particular statutory provisions in question and explained in detail the ways in which that regime prevented the implication of the mutual trust and confidence term. It considered that Mr McDonald's employment as a teacher and the statutory and regulatory framework that otherwise applied to that employment made the implication of the term unnecessary in his circumstances,[55] despite its apparent operation (noting that this decision occurred some years prior to the High Court of Australia's decision in *Commonwealth Bank v Barker*).

Secondly, the focus now shifts to the role of parliament in ensuring coherence. As this work's Conclusion reiterates, having parliament develop a set of model statutory-based default rules, which reflect existing common law terms implied by law into employment contracts, will go some way to alleviating confusion as to the underpinning norms of what it means to be employed under an employment contract. Such statutory-based default rules will serve to generate clarity, consistency, and a wider level of understanding between the contracting parties, their lawyers, and judges alike. It will serve to solidify, even codify, what have been routinely recognised as norms of employment at common law, removing doubt as to their necessity in the employment relationship in the future.

In developing these default rules, it is open to parliament to have them function as statutorily implied contractual terms, or as statutory rules that operate alongside the employment contract. It is debatable which regime would be beneficial to the parties to an employment contract. In her comments on the Consumer Guarantees shifting from statutorily implied contractual terms under the former *Trade Practices Act 1974* (Cth) to mandatory statutory rules under the *Australian Consumer Law*, Jeannie Paterson has mentioned that consumers can no longer 'rely on the law of contract to provide a remedy in the event of a failure to comply with [the Consumer Guarantees]'.[56] Parties to an employment contract may have the same experience, should the rules operate as mandatory statutory rules, rather than implied contractual terms. Paterson also highlighted that the measure of compensation and damages available to consumers for a breach of the Consumer Guarantees 'may not match the damages that would have been recovered under the law of contract'.[57] Whether the same could be said with respect to a breach of any statutory regime concerning employment contracts would largely depend on whether the remedies offered as part of the statutory regime are broader or narrower than those available under the common law of contract. In terms of generating greater certainty and less complexity in the law, there are undoubtedly arguments for and against either regime.

---

[55] ibid 398.
[56] J Paterson, 'The New Consumer Guarantee Law and the Reasons for Replacing the Regime of Statutory Implied Terms in Consumer Transactions' (2011) 35 MULR 252, 261.
[57] ibid 275.

In terms of who should be responsible for drafting proposed model terms in either England or Australia, it would be preferable for an independent panel of experts to draft the initial default rules in consultation with the legislature (and potentially the general public), which the legislature could then codify. Of course, the legislature would most likely amend the proposed terms, but at least the starting point for the default minimum terms would be theoretically objective. The courts would then be tasked with interpreting and applying those terms, should they come into question.

It is envisaged that the default rules would encompass those terms that already operate as terms implied by law through the common law. As is elaborated on in this work's Conclusion, there may be, for example, a case for including a good faith term. Less contentious examples might include a duty to obey lawful and reasonable orders, of fidelity, and to give reasonable notice on termination (albeit for far more limited circumstances in the English context). It could also include any further terms deemed necessary by parliament. These default rules would be useful because even when employment contracts are in writing, they are not always complete. Indeed, as reflected in Chapter 1, some employment contracts are not in writing at all[58]—even for employees at the highest executive level. Therefore, the potential for gaps in employment contracts is ever-present. There is clearly a benefit in having these rules operate as a default position to provide clarity.

The starting point for most of these default rules is that they would apply to all employment contracts, unless expressly excluded or altered by the parties. It is well understood that parties can contract out of such statutory default rules, yet by contrast, the aforementioned Consumer Guarantees under the *Australian Consumer Law* are mandatory standards, unable to be contracted out of. An equivalent English example exists under ss 6 and 20 of the *Unfair Contract Terms Act 1977* (UK), which prohibit any contracting out of the statutorily implied term in a sale of goods and hire purchase contract[59] that the seller or hirer has good title to (sell or hire) the goods. It is true that employers may exercise their superior bargaining power by using boilerplate clauses to specifically exclude non-mandatory default rules. As Bob Hepple once pointed out: 'The ... concept of contract which is utilised by the courts and tribunals is inherently biased in favour of the so-called rule making power of the employer.'[60] However, the effect of an employer drafting such an exclusion would be no different to that currently experienced in the employment relationship. As it stands, parties are already free to exclude terms implied by law, should they wish to do so.[61] On its face, the present suggestion would attract the same ability for parties to expressly exclude or alter the various default rules.

---

[58] See, eg, A Stewart, *Stewart's Guide to Employment Law* (5th edn, Federation Press 2015) 92.
[59] Found in the *Sale of Goods Act 1979* (UK) s 12.
[60] B Hepple, 'Restructuring Employment Rights' (1986) 15 ILJ 69, 81.
[61] See, eg, *Castlemaine Tooheys Ltd v Carlton & United Breweries Ltd* (1987) 10 NSWLR 468 (New South Wales Court of Appeal (NSWCA)), 492; *Johnson v Unisys Ltd* [2003] 1 AC 518 (HL) [18] and [24].

That said, while the ability to exclude such terms may be acceptable in some circumstances, this may not be the case for all default minimum rules. For example, as Chapter 5 made apparent, in English law, it is unlikely that this excludability would be permissible in respect of the mutual trust and confidence term. It would therefore be open to parliament to make some terms essential—and, consequently, non-excludable; essentially, akin in their operation and application to the non-excludable mandatory standards under the Consumer Guarantees. As argued more extensively in Chapter 6, there are several terms that ought to be viewed as essential—and consequently, mandatory, and non-excludable—in the employment relationship.

The creation of default minimum rules is not a new idea; Collins proposed it in 2001[62] and reaffirmed it in 2007.[63] But the *Commonwealth Bank v Barker* decision has since provided an important opportunity to reconsider its viability. When Collins initially put forward the idea, he asserted that a default set of implied terms would help to overcome obstacles and 'provide a legal sanction against opportunism'.[64] In his mind, 'further implied terms will be required to capture the implicit expectations of the parties [to the employment contract] on other matters'.[65] In addition, he suggested that any such rules would need to be 'clear and well-defined and their meaning confirmed by consistent interpretations'.[66] Ideally, they would be consistent with existing common law and statutory implied terms in employment contracts, but also include new terms as appropriate. In his later work, Collins emphasised that even though statutory and common law regulation of the employment relationship are 'on their own each ineffective for the task, a combination of the two [through combining implied terms and statutory controls] appears much more promising'.[67]

Importantly, any development of model statutory default rules must not limit the potential for the courts to develop new common law terms implied by law into employment contracts in the coherent manner envisaged above. To deny courts this law-making function would have the effect of leaving employment contracts with wide-open gaps needing to be filled, and potentially never addressed by parliament. The continuation of the courts' law-making function will enable judges to step in and fill the void in a situation where parliament is either unable or unwilling to respond. In that sense, both judicial and legislative law-making can work cohesively and alongside one another, with each informing the other, and crafting the normative understanding of being employed. This suggestion is made with a view

---

[62] See, eg, H Collins, 'Regulating the Employment Regulation for Competitiveness' (2001) 30 ILJ 17, 37.
[63] See, eg, H Collins, 'Legal Responses to the Standard Form Contract of Employment' (2007) 36 ILJ 2, 17–18.
[64] ibid 37.
[65] ibid 38.
[66] P Ingram, 'Justiciability' (1994) 39 Am J Juris 353, 368.
[67] Collins (n 63) 17.

to reinvigorating the collaboration between the judiciary and the legislature, and, ultimately, generating greater clarity as to the norms of employment.

Conclusion

At the very essence of any common law system, including those in England and Australia, there is an uncertain boundary between the role of the courts and parliament. This ambiguity has been especially prominent in the wake of the *Commonwealth Bank v Barker* decision, which cast even further doubt over the extent to which courts ought to determine the principles for the content and interpretation of employment contracts.

The main arguments as to how far the judicial law-making role ought to extend have been analysed and the importance of reinvigorating the symbiotic relationship between statute and the common law recognised. That discussion demonstrates that there is a wide range of different views on whether courts ought to determine the content of employment obligations, particularly where a contract is not clearly drafted, or not in writing at all. Moreover, the decision in *Commonwealth Bank v Barker* has exposed the potential for the courts to refuse to imply any new terms by law into employment contracts ever again, consequently diminishing the courts' future role in regulating employment contracts. *Commonwealth Bank v Barker* also cast doubt over the way in which courts will treat existing terms implied by law in the future. Essentially, if the decision in *Commonwealth Bank v Barker* is to be taken at face value, it suggests that there ought to be no judicial law-making role where there are defensible policy positions on both sides of an argument. Again, while the Australian decision is not binding on English courts, it exposes a potential approach that the judiciary in either jurisdiction may take if asked to shape employment contracts by implying a new term by law.

Despite these difficulties, this chapter ultimately presented a case for the preservation of a residual role for English and Australian courts in the regulation of employment contracts through terms implied by law, including existing and future terms. The notion of coherence between judicial and statutory law-making with respect to the development of terms implied by law was examined, followed by consideration of how the courts and parliament ought to be collectively responsible for ensuring that coherence. A recommendation was made for the creation of statutory default minimum rules for the employment relationship, while still emphasising that the courts must remain willing to imply terms by law into employment contracts as it is impossible for parliament to predict all future gaps that may need to be filled. These ideas are revisited as part of the reform options outlined in this work's Conclusion.

Conclusion

Reshaping Contracts for Work

This work has endeavoured to explore the common law's role in shaping contracts for work through the mechanism of terms implied by law. There has been a particular emphasis on constructing a theory of the nature of the employment contract, as distinct from other types of contracts for work, through the lens of terms implied by law. The present conclusion draws together the central arguments developed over the course of Chapters 1 to 4, returning to the more nuanced arguments encountered in Chapters 5 to 7: the extent to which employment can be regarded as a distinctive class of contract; the circumstances in which it is necessary to imply a term by law into the class of employment contracts; the question of whether the courts or parliament should be tasked with making laws with respect to employment contracts through the mechanism of terms implied by law; and finally, the interrelationship between a duty of mutual trust and confidence and good faith in the context of employment. This conclusion now applies a final overarching theory of the nature of the employment contract in relation to other types of work contracts through the lens of terms implied by law. In doing so, it makes a series of conclusions and recommendations as to the ways in which courts might shape the nature of the employment contract in the future. It suggests a rethinking of the courts' rationale for implying terms by law into employment contracts, compared in particular with the broader category of contracts for the performance of work.

Summary of the Argument

Chapters 1 and 2 of this work set out to assess the overarching influence of terms implied by law on the common law of contracts. The purpose of that discussion was to provide a standpoint from which to view the later analysis. The first chapter in particular set the scene by providing a survey of the law across both England and Australia that governs express and implied terms in contracts generally. In doing so, it considered the interplay between general contractual principles and their regulation of contracts for work. It also examined the relationship between implication and construction of contractual terms in both jurisdictions, including an examination of the policy considerations for the distinction between implication and construction. Consideration also turned to the relationship between implication and interpretation of terms. The general analysis from this chapter served as a precursor for the remaining content of this work.

Chapter 2 then illustrated the judicial effects of implying a term by law into a contract and how that action, irrespective of the contractual context, has the potential to fundamentally guide, shape, and alter the nature of the relationship between the contracting parties. As with Chapter 1, the analysis in this chapter was brief in recognition of the introductory nature of the debates raised, and their function as a backdrop to the work's remaining content.

With the content of Chapters 1 and 2 in mind, the next part provided a comparative, historical, and legal overview of terms implied by law into employment contracts primarily, but with added reference to other contracts for the performance of work.

Chapter 3 traversed the historical development of a selection of key terms already implied routinely into employment contracts. That historical analysis showed that most terms implied by law in both England and Australia previously functioned as norms in the former master and servant regime. In most instances, they originated as something other than terms implied by law, avoiding consideration of whether they are truly necessary in shaping what we now understand as instances of employment. Eventually, the terms came to be implied into all employment contracts as terms implied by law but lacked proper and careful justification for why that was the case.

Focussing on the more controversial duties of mutual trust and confidence and good faith Chapter 4 highlighted, through comparative explanation that, contrary to the position in English law, there is no implied term of mutual trust and confidence in Australian employment contracts. The status of a duty of good faith in Australian employment contracts also remains uncertain and open to future consideration. By contrast, the terminology of good faith in English law has proved a useful tool by which to stress the special obligations arising in the employment contract. However, there is room for debate, spanning both jurisdictions, as to whether there is indeed a marked difference between a duty of mutual trust and confidence and one of good faith.

The following part of this work shifted from the previous analytical-descriptive approach in Parts I and II to an openly normative attempt fundamentally to expose how courts might in the future shape employment contracts, as distinct from contracts for the performance of work, through the mechanism of terms implied by law. Keeping in mind the previous chapters' conclusions, its steps were carefully structured around the elements of terms implied by law into employment contracts specifically: employment contracts as a class of contract, instances in which it is necessary to imply a term by law into employment contracts, and, finally, an exploration of the judicial role of implying a term by law into the class of employment contracts.

Chapter 5 conducted an examination of the more nuanced issues associated with the distinctiveness of employment contracts as a class into which terms are implied by law. In that context, it reconciled that there is no consistent or universal understanding of employment contracts as a class.

Chapter 6 highlighted the issues surrounding the courts' assessment of when it is truly necessary to imply an existing or new term into employment contracts by law. Given that the question of whether a term implied by law can be excluded by a contrary express term is inextricably linked to the concept of necessity, this chapter considered the concepts of necessity and excludability of terms implied by law into employment contracts in conjunction with one another. Attention was also paid to obligations arising under statute, equity, and tort, and their potential to stymie the development of implied terms in contract. In essence, where a corresponding obligation exists in those other areas of law, it is arguably no longer necessary as a term implied by law in the contractual sense. Yet, as matters presently stand, it is not uncommon for a term implied by law imposing a contractual obligation on the employer under the contract of employment to sit alongside a concurrent obligation of the same kind. Chapter 6 ultimately arrived at the view that a broader policy-based necessity test for implying a term by law is preferred, and that when applied, it ought to be better articulated by the courts—a suggestion that is revived later in this Conclusion.

Discussion finally moved, in Chapter 7, to exploring the potential for judges to continue to make new law governing employment contracts in the face of ever-expanding statutory schemes. Analysed thus, the need for greater coherence between common law and statute was emphasised, building a case for the creation of statutory default minimum rules, which could operate without limiting the court's ability to imply new terms by law where appropriate—a recommendation that is revisited in this final chapter.

Overall, the breadth of this work, spanning the fields of both employment and contract law, and their crossover, and the comparison between England and Australia, has provided a rich tapestry of the current issues associated with implying terms by law into contracts for the performance of work. That backdrop now presents ample opportunity and rigour with which to approach the following discussion, which details four key ways in which the law regulating terms implied by law into employment contracts in particular can be reshaped. These options include, first, that there is a need for the courts to better articulate their understanding of what constitutes the 'employment contract' as a distinctive class of contract into which terms are implied by law, separate from the broader notion of 'contracts for the performance of work'. Secondly, courts must clarify the circumstances in which it is 'necessary' to imply a term by law into the class of employment contracts. Thirdly, the judicial role must be clarified in relation to the regulation of employment. Lastly, there ought to be greater judicial clarity about the interrelationship, if any, between a duty of good faith and mutual trust and confidence. Each of these claims is expanded upon in turn, with a view to utilising the mechanism of terms implied by law to arrive at a theory of what constitutes the employment contract, separate from other types of personal work contract.

Translating the Proposed Reshaping into Practice

A. Reclassifying Employment Contracts as a Class into Which Terms are Implied by Law

Chapter 5 identified that no consistent or universal understanding of employment contracts as a class into which terms are implied by law exists. Looking to broader academic, judicial, and legislative understandings of what constitutes the 'employment contract' does little to assist. If anything, such analysis emphasises that understandings as to what constitutes an employment contract are wide-ranging, only sometimes applicable, and therefore, inconsistent. There are actually many similarities between employment contracts and other types of contracts for the performance of work—particularly contracts for services—which make the judicial understanding of how to define and understand these contracts even more ambiguous.

Because of this ambiguity, there is an intelligible case for clarifying the categories of contract into which terms are implied by law in the employment context. Such clarity ought to be pursued to mandate increased rigour in determining the categories of employment contracts into which terms are currently, and may in the future, be implied by law. To generate such clarity, it is suggested that terms implied by law in employment be grouped into one of three main categories. This proposed classificatory technique would function in a manner similar to Mark Freedland's evocation of the three structural principles of 'exchange', 'integration', and 'reciprocity' described in Chapter 5, and their 'attributive function', which enables the assignment of normative incidents of effects to contracts of employment.[1]

The first proposed category is 'selective employment contracts', which encompasses terms implied by law that operate exclusively in respect of select types of contracts, as opposed to all instances of employment. Such a category would include terms presently implied by law into employment contracts, namely: the duty of employers to inform employees of their rights,[2] the duty of employees to hold inventions created in the course of their employment on trust for their employer,[3]

---

[1] Again, see, eg, M Freedland, 'The Legal Structure of the Contract of Employment' in M Freedland and others (eds), *The Contract of Employment* (OUP 2016) 28, 28–51.
[2] See, eg, *Scally v Southern Health and Social Services Board* [1992] 1 AC 294 (House of Lords (HL)), 307.
[3] *University of Western Australia v Gray* (2009) 179 FCR 346 (Full Court of the Federal Court of Australia (FCAFC)), 381 (and the authorities cited therein).

and, in the Australian context, the duty of both employers and employees to provide reasonable notice of termination[4] (recalling from Chapter 3 that this duty has been partially statutorily enshrined in English law; though, as discussed, there are some limited exceptions where the implied duty may still operate by virtue of the common law).

The second proposed category is that of 'non-exclusive employment contracts', which includes implied terms that have the potential to apply equally to other types of contractual relationships than employment alone. Typically, these default rules could be applied to 'contracts for the performance of work' in the general sense, noting that the label applies to more nuanced atypical and non-standard work relationships. As detailed in Chapter 3, apart from an implied duty to provide reasonable notice on termination, other implied duties in employment that may also apply to principal, host or hirer, and independent contractor or worker relationships include:

- a duty on an independent contractor or worker not to disclose confidential information and to remain loyal to their principal,
- a duty on a principal, host, or hirer to provide an independent contractor or worker with a safe place of work,
- a duty owed by a principal, host, or hirer to indemnify an independent contractor or worker for expenses innocently incurred during the performance of duties; and
- a duty owed by an independent contractor or worker to exercise reasonable care and skill in the tasks performed for their principal, host, or hirer.

On the face of it, there is nothing unique about any of these terms in the employment context to prohibit them from being applied to contracts for the performance of work, and beyond the realm of employment. Adrian Brooks even goes so far as to say that there really is 'no difference as to ... [implied] duties as to the contracts labelled as "employment contracts" from those which will arise under contracts labelled as "independent"',[5] and the same logic arguably applies with respect to worker contracts.

The mutual duty of cooperation also applies more broadly than in the context of employment. The High Court of Australia made this clear in *Secured Income Real*

---

[4] See, eg, *Byrne v Australian Airlines Ltd* (1995) 185 CLR 410 (High Court of Australia (HCA)), 429, noting the controversy that now exists concerning this duty, following the South Australian District Court's decision in *Kuczmarski v Ascot Administration Pty Ltd* [2016] SADC 65 (South Australian District Court (SADC), which has been discussed in Chapter 6 and is returned to below in Part D.

[5] A Brooks, 'Myth and Muddle—An Examination of Contracts for the Performance of Work' (1988) 11 UNSWLJ 48, 49.

Estate (Australia) Ltd v St Martins Investments Pty Ltd[6] when it affirmed the original principle stated by Griffith CJ in *Butt v M'Donald* that:[7]

> [I]t is a general rule *applicable to every contract* that each party agrees by implication, to do all such things as are necessary on his part to enable the other party to have the benefit of the contract.

The same sentiment was reflected in early English law, whereby the reciprocal duty of cooperation was said to exist not just in the context of employment, but to all contracts in a general sense.[8] Though, as Hugh Collins and others have explained, there remains scepticism as to the breadth of this duty in employment. While it undoubtedly applies to a whole workforce, the expectation of cooperation is probably even more heightened for staff in senior roles, such as managers and professionals, than it is for employees in the general sense.[9]

The final proposed category is that of 'exclusive employment contracts'. This category encompasses very rare instances of terms implied by law that fall exclusively into the realm of employment, with the primary example being an employee's duty to obey the lawful and reasonable instructions of their employer.[10] The reason for this is that the element of subordination on which the duty is premised is regarded as being at the very heart of the employment contract. It 'predates the contractual backcloth of the employment relationship and can be traced back to the 19th century master and servant laws'.[11] The present obligation of an employee to obey the lawful and reasonable orders of their employer has since been recognised as one of the 'identifying features' of employment.[12] In a leading English decision concerning the duty, *Laws v London Chronicle (Indicator Newspapers) Ltd*,[13] Lord Evershed labelled it as 'a condition essential to the contract of service'.[14] It has also been noted as the key characteristic 'which distinguishes ... [the employment contract] from other types of contract'.[15] In support of this contention, Sir Otto Kahn-Freund wrote that 'there can be no employment relationship without a power to

---

[6] (1979) 144 CLR 596 (HCA), 607, cited with approval in *Commonwealth Bank of Australia v Barker* (2014) 253 CLR 169 (HCA), 201.
[7] (1896) 7 QLJ 68 (Full Court of the Supreme Court of Queensland (QSCFC)), 70–71 (emphasis added).
[8] See, eg, *Mackay v Dick* (1881) 6 App Cas 251 (HL).
[9] See, eg, H Collins, K D Ewing, and A McColgan, *Labour Law* (2nd edn, CUP 2019) 152.
[10] As to an employee's duty to obey, see Chapter 3.
[11] D Cabrelli, *Employment Law in Context: Text and Materials* (OUP 2014) 193. See also S Deakin and F Wilkinson, *The Law and the Labour Market: Industrialisation, Employment and Legal Evolution* (OUP 2005) 61–62, 103; M Freedland and N Kountouris, *The Legal Construction of Personal Work Relations* (OUP 2011) 188.
[12] See, eg, *A-G (NSW) v The Perpetual Trustee Company (Ltd)* (1952) 85 CLR 237 (HCA), 299–300.
[13] [1959] 1 WLR 698 (Court of Appeal (CA)).
[14] ibid 700.
[15] C Sappideen and others, *Macken's Law of Employment* (8th edn, Lawbook Co 2016) 199–200.

command and a duty to obey, that is without this element of subordination in which lawyers rightly see the hallmark of the contract of employment'.[16]

At least in the English context, as detailed in Chapter 4, the duty of mutual trust and confidence is said to be one of the most remarkable and significant developments of the common law of the contract of employment in recent decades. So much so that Collins and others have reflected that it 'brings the common law closer into line with modern views about fairness in employment relations by controlling the abuse of managerial power ...'.[17] This view begs the question as to how defining and 'necessary' this particular term is, and, in turn, whether it is possible for an employer to be able to exclude a mutual trust and confidence term through the means of an express term. Recognising that there are limits to be placed on suitable express terms, whereby an employer can only validly give lawful orders to employees, there remains no strict prohibition on an employer prohibiting employees from expressly excluding the implied obligation not to act in a way that is likely to destroy mutual trust and confidence. Nevertheless, Douglas Brodie and Mark Freedland have separately reflected that the implied term of mutual trust and confidence ought to be considered so essential to the modern contract of employment that it should not be possible to exclude it through the mechanism of an express term.[18] It seems logical to accept those suggestions. In any event, it is unlikely that an employer would seek to deliberately exclude a term enabling it to behave in a contrary manner. Collins and others also warn that courts should be wary of interpreting contracts in standard form imposed on a take-it-or-leave-it basis to permit express exclusions of all implied terms, for example, avoiding any exclusion of the implied term all together.[19]

Moreover, in English common law, the implied term of mutual trust and confidence is one of only a few terms implied by law that continues to impose obligations on parties after the employment contract has been terminated (ie when the contract is in its post-employment mode). The same point applies in respect of the period prior to the formation of the contract of employment (ie when the contract is in the pre-employment stage). David Cabrelli highlights that the fact that the mutual trust and confidence term functions in this manner suggests that it forms part of the irreducible core of the contract of employment.[20] Taking these collective academic views, at least in the English context, the implied term of mutual trust and confidence perhaps also ought to be considered one of those terms that is applicable in the context of 'exclusive employment contracts', noting, of course, the

---

[16] O Kahn-Freund, *Labour and the Law* (Stevens for the Hamlyn Trust 1972) 9.
[17] Collins, Ewing, and McCoglan (n 9) 150.
[18] See, eg, M Freedland, *The Personal Employment Contract* (OUP 2003) 164–66; D Brodie, 'Beyond Exchange: The New Contract of Employment (1998) 27 ILJ 79.
[19] Collins, Ewing, and McCoglan (n 9) 152.
[20] See, eg, D Cabrelli, 'The Effect of Termination upon Post-Employment Obligations' in M Freedland and others (eds), *The Contract of Employment* (OUP 2016) 561, 575–76.

polarity this creates with the contrasting Australian position where the term has been found entirely unnecessary.

Beyond mutual trust and confidence, another duty that may find itself necessary in 'exclusive employment contracts', at least in England, is the newfound duty owed by an employer to conduct a disciplinary process fairly,[21] noting that this duty has been found separate and distinct from a duty of mutual trust and confidence.[22] As discussed in Chapter 4, it has not yet been the subject of judicial consideration in Australia. Thus, it remains unclear whether the same could be said of this duty in the Australian context.

Therefore, apart from the judiciary needing to fully articulate how it understands the employment contract at the general level, the author argues that in respect of terms implied by law in the employment context, clarity could also be achieved if the courts were to acknowledge that they were implying those terms into one of the three categories articulated above. This clarity ought to be achieved in respect of the categories of employment contracts into which terms are currently, and may continue to be, implied by law. Ideally, English and Australian courts ought to set clearer and more accurate boundaries as to the category of employment contract for which the term is considered necessary, in respect of both new terms and existing terms as they continue to be implied by law into such contracts in the future. The present approach of implying a term by law into the blanket class of 'all employment contracts' is over-generalised and, in many cases, inaccurate in respect of the term's necessity to all instances of employment. It is anticipated that by utilising these three classifications courts will be in a better position to conduct informed analyses of the new terms necessary to be implied as a matter of law in a situation of employment and, in turn, how existing terms implied by law in those contracts may be affected. Arguably, the more often courts rationalise the implication of a new or existing term by law into one of these three categories, the less they will feel as though they are creating law and more that they are ensuring the continuity of the common law.[23] Particularly in the Australian context, where the question of whether to imply a new term by law into the class of employment contracts arises, this approach will go some way to avoid *Commonwealth Bank v Barker*-like reasoning in the future, giving the courts greater confidence in exercising their judicial law-making functions without trespassing 'into the province of legislative action'.[24]

---

[21] See, eg, *Burn v Alder Hey Children's NHS Foundation Trust* [2022] ICR 492 (CA).
[22] ibid [37].
[23] See, eg, E Peden, 'Policy Concerns Behind Implication of Terms in Law' (2001) 117 LQR 459, 476.
[24] *Commonwealth Bank v Barker* (n 6) 185.

B. Defining When Terms Implied by Law are Necessary in Employment Contracts

Chapter 6 identified that the necessity test for implying a new term by law is uncertain in the way it is uniquely applied in England, and that the separate test operating in Australia must be clarified. Not only is this the case for employment contracts specifically, but also for other types of contracts more generally; the same test for implication applies when a term is sought to be implied into any contract by law. In relation to existing terms, the sense gathered from Chapter 6 is that, in general, the main reason accepted by judges for implying an existing term in law is because it has been implied in earlier cases, such that there is no need to reconsider its necessity in the present context. This approach is presumptuous and effectively sidesteps the gap-filling function of terms implied by law.

In English law, the current test for implying a term by law has seen the House of Lords emphasise that an 'incident' of the relationship must be 'necessary' to give effect to the transaction, and not simply 'reasonable' in the eyes of the court.[25] However, there is no explanation of whether necessity in this sense is a narrow and functional form of necessity (ie necessary to make the contract work in the strict sense), or whether it is founded on a broader policy-based notion of necessity (ie necessary for wider reasons of justice and policy). It seems logical to suggest that it is the latter, as the former seems more consistent with the test for establishing a term implied in fact.[26] There is, however, nothing conclusive to suggest either way. With that ambiguity in mind, it is worth contemplating that in *Crossley v Faithful & Gould Holdings*,[27] Dyson LJ described the necessity test for implying a term by law as 'protean' and 'elusive', and proposed what he viewed as an alternative test based on 'reasonableness, fairness and the balancing of competing policy considerations'.[28] In essence, his Lordship was a clear proponent for a wider policy-based version of the necessity test as it ought to apply in English law. Therefore, ambiguity exists as to whether the necessity test for implying a term by law as it currently applies in English law is one to be interpreted narrowly or broadly.

From Chapter 6 it became clear that, in Australia, there similarly appears to exist two iterations of the necessity test. The narrow interpretation espoused in *Byrne v Australian Airlines*[29] requires that the term to be implied by law must be necessary to ensure that the class of contract is not 'rendered nugatory, worthless, or ... seriously undermined'.[30] This test is in contrast to the wider interpretation

---

[25] See, eg, *Liverpool City Council v Irwin* [1977] AC 239 (HL).
[26] See, eg, *Marks & Spencer plc v BNP Paribas Securities Services Trust Company (Jersey) Ltd* [2016] AC 742 (UKSC) (Lord Neuberger).
[27] [2004] IRLR 377 (CA).
[28] ibid [34]–[36].
[29] *Byrne v Australian Airlines* (n 4) 452–53.
[30] ibid 450, 453.

from *University of Western Australia v Gray*, which allows for courts to take into account matters of justice and policy in determining what is necessary.[31]

While the formulation of the *Byrne v Australian Airlines* necessity test appears narrow in the way it is worded, it has the potential to be applied more widely. Indeed, the Full Court of the Federal Court in *University of Western Australia v Gray* recognised that possibility and suggested that notwithstanding the narrow wording of the *Byrne v Australian Airlines* test, it could be applied more broadly.[32] To be clear, this chapter operates on the premise that the narrow wording used in *Byrne v Australian Airlines* also means that the test is to be applied in a strict and functional sense.

The High Court in *Commonwealth Bank v Barker* did little to clarify which version of the test ought to be adopted when a new term is sought to be implied by law, or, indeed, how this would affect existing terms implied by law. While the High Court appeared to apply the narrow formulation of the necessity test from *Byrne v Australian Airlines* as a means of refusing the implication of the mutual trust and confidence term, its actual application of the test (ie its reasons for refusing the implication of the term) was wider, in that it was largely policy-based.

To achieve clarity, both English and Australian courts ought to fully engage with the necessity test for implying a term by law. They must openly decide which criterion ought to operate in respect of rationalising when it is necessary to imply a new term by law. Without that articulation, courts may avoid implying any new terms by law altogether, leaving gaps in contracts that need to be filled.[33] This possibility is not just relevant to employment contracts, but also to all types of contracts. To reiterate, all contracts attract the same necessity test when a new term is sought to be implied by law. Even so, a court could still decide that the particular matter would be better dealt with by parliament, thereby avoiding the implication on that broader basis. That potential for avoiding implication of a term by law was addressed in Chapter 7 and is revisited in Part C of this chapter.

It has become apparent that, notwithstanding having been previously presumed as necessary incidents applicable to all employment contracts, in reality most existing terms already implied by law are not actually necessary in *all* instances of employment. To be clear: not all existing terms implied by law into the class of employment contracts are vital to the maintenance and function of every employment relationship. Unfortunately, both English and Australian courts have neglected to consider the potential application of the formulation of the necessity test to existing terms implied by law into employment contracts, meaning that judicial

---

[31] *University of Western Australia v Gray* (n 3) 377–79.
[32] ibid 377.
[33] For a working example of how confusion surrounding the necessity test may stymie the development of a potentially newly available implied term (specifically, one which allows employees the right to disconnect), see, eg, G Golding, 'The Right to Disconnect in Australia: Creating Space for a New Term Implied by Law' (2023) 46(1) UNSWLJ 677, 699–704.

reasoning has become anomalous in respect of the status of those existing terms. Given the jurisprudential basis of the common law method, it is conceivable that courts in both jurisdictions may never undertake this exercise at all.

Nevertheless, given the potential for existing terms to be excluded if the narrow necessity test were to be applied retrospectively, this work argues that the broader view of necessity should be preferred, and it must be better articulated and understood. Despite the existence of the narrower necessity test, it is the wider test that ought to be applied, and better articulated, in order not to limit the instances in which gaps might need to be filled in respect of new terms in the future, even if for reasons of justice and policy. As suggested in Chapter 6, aiding the courts in better articulating that wider approach seems to be contingent on how the implied term will sit with existing law (whether that be statute or the common law); how any decision to imply it into a class or category of contracts will affect the parties to those agreements; and more expansive notions of what is deemed a fair and acceptable societal norm.

A key example of why this better articulated, broader view of necessity ought to be preferred, with the aim of preserving existing terms implied by law, involves the implied term requiring that an employer provide an employee with a safe place of work. Clearly, for broader policy-based reasons, where a statute covers the field, an equivalent common law term implied by law will not be necessary. Doing so would have no meaningful effect on the parties to the relationship because statute has already covered the same field. For the same reason, it would not be deemed a fair and acceptable societal norm in that context. Quite simply, there is no gap to be filled in circumstances in which statute has already performed the same role.

A consistent and better articulated application of a broader necessity test will also assist in delineating between terms implied in fact and those implied by law because the implication of a term in fact encompasses a business efficacy test, which is substantially similar to the narrow and functional version of the necessity test. To alleviate the risk of courts avoiding the implication of any new terms by law because they have applied broader policy-based reasoning, the discussion directly below considers how the judicial role ought to be clarified.

C. Clarifying the Judicial Role and the Potential for a Set of Statutory Default Rules Implied into All Employment Contracts

There are wide-ranging views as to whether the courts ought to determine the content of employment obligations. The High Court of Australia's reasoning in *Commonwealth Bank v Barker* opened the potential for common law courts to avoid implying any new terms by law into employment contracts, consequently diminishing their future role in regulating employment contracts. If English law adopted that same rationale, the potential for avoidance of any new implication would be similar. To evade such a situation, Chapter 7 established that greater coherence is needed between judicial and parliamentary made law insofar as the regulation of employment contracts through terms implied by law is concerned. That coherence could be best achieved by ensuring that when terms are implied by law into employment contracts through operation of the common law, what ought to be reflected in those terms are the principles and values typically expressed in modern employment legislation. Essentially, the two branches of the law will coincide, with one informing the development of the other.

Beyond the need for common law courts to fully analyse why a statute may or may not be inconsistent with a proposed term to be implied by law, Chapter 7 presented a statutory-based solution for avoiding future difficulties associated with how far the judicial law-making role ought to extend with respect to employment contracts. It involved combining statutory and common law implied terms to create a 'set of [default] rules ... [that] are presumed to apply [to regulate the employment contractual relationship]'.[34] It is anticipated that such an approach would require the legislature to initially take the lead in developing a default set of terms to be implied into all employment contracts.[35]

Even though a strong case for such legislative intervention exists, Chapter 7 reiterated that asking parliament to legislate to create the initial default minimum rules ought not to diminish the courts' ability to imply new terms by law into employment contracts, should they identify a gap. The default statutory rules should instead provide broad, principled guidance for cases in which gaps have already been identified. Both English and Australian employment relations are already governed by statutory and statutory-based regulation, perhaps to a heightened degree in Australia. This fact strengthens the argument for leaving regulation of terms of employment to parliament, or its agents (including industrial tribunals). However, gaps will always remain in the future, as will particular issues in which the common law plays an important role.

---

[34] H Collins, 'Regulating the Employment Regulation for Competitiveness' (2001) 30 ILJ 17, 37.

[35] This option for statutory reform through the creation of default rules could also extend to other types of contracts. However, a consideration of that broader possibility is beyond the scope of the present conclusion, which focuses on the shaping of employment contracts as distinct from broader contracts for the performance of work. In fact, the creation of statutory default rules may well solve problems for employment contracts, but not for other types of contracts. As such, it warrants separate and dedicated consideration.

D. Detailing the Precise Approach for Implying a Good Faith Term by Law into Employment Contracts

Chapter 4 highlighted that English courts have traditionally been highly averse to developing a general contractual duty of good faith.[36] A leading commentary on the issue notes that:[37]

> [I]n keeping with the principles of freedom of contract and the binding force of contract, in English contract law there is no legal principle of good faith of general application, although some authors have argued that there should be.

Gunther Teubner has also described good faith as an 'irritant' in English law. He sees it as an infection from European law, which does not accord with the inherent culture of the common law.[38]

Despite this defiance, the English position on a general duty of good faith appears to be evolving as a consequence of the English High Court decision concerning a distribution agreement, *Yam Seng Pte Ltd v International Trade Corporation Ltd*.[39] Justice Leggatt made the bold assertion in that case that: 'I respectfully suggest that the traditional English hostility towards a doctrine of good faith in the performance of contracts, to the extent it still persists, is misplaced'.[40] His Honour ultimately held that there was a term implied in fact into the contract in question that the parties would deal with each other in good faith.[41] Specifically, he held that good faith ought to be 'sensitive to context', but that it included the 'core value of honesty'.[42] His Honour described the test of good faith as an objective one: whether, in the particular context, reasonable people would regard the conduct as 'commercially unacceptable'.[43]

Irrespective of this recognition of the duty, the extent to which Leggatt J's decision will continue to be followed in England remains unclear.[44] As Brodie

---

[36] This tendency in England has been described in J Beatson and D Friedmann, 'From "Classical" to Modern Contract Law' in J Beatson and D Friedmann (eds), *Good Faith and Fault in Contract Law* (Clarendon Paperbacks 1995) 3, 14–15. Cf the early English rejection of that traditional position in R Powell, 'Good Faith in Contracts' (1956) 9 Curr Leg Probl 16, cited in A Bogg, 'Good Faith in the Contract of Employment: A Case of the English Reserve?' (2011) 32 Comp LL & PJ 729, 729.
[37] H Beale, *Chitty on Contracts* (31st edn, Sweet & Maxwell 2012) ¶1-039.
[38] See generally, G Teubner, 'Legal Irritants: Good Faith in British Law or How Unifying Law Ends Up in New Divergences' (1998) 61 MLR 11.
[39] [2013] 1 All ER (Comm) 1321 (High Court of Justice Queen's Bench Division (QB)). See the further discussion of this decision in J Paterson, 'Good Faith Duties in Contract Performance' (2014) 14 OUCLJ 283, 286–87.
[40] *Yam Seng v International Trade Corporation* (n 39) [153].
[41] ibid [131] and [146]. For further discussion on this decision, see, eg, D Campbell, 'Good Faith and the Ubiquity of the *"Relational"* Contract' (2014) 77 MLR 475; S Whittaker, 'Good Faith, Implied Terms and Commercial Contracts' (2013) 129 LQR 463.
[42] *Yam Seng v International Trade Corporation* (n 39) [141].
[43] ibid [144].
[44] See, eg, the later decision in *Mid Essex Hospital Services NHS Trust v Compass Group UK and Ireland Ltd (t/a Medirest)* [2013] EWCA Civ 200 (CA) [105], in which the English Court of Appeal cited

emphasised just after the relevant judgment was delivered, the law regarding a general duty of good faith across contracts generally 'is still in a decidedly embryonic stage',[45] and arguably that remains true today. That said, Brodie predicted that this situation would be 'likely to change sooner rather than later where the relationship can be viewed as analogous to employment'.[46] Indeed, that impetus seems to be gathering now, with Brodie having recently identified the impact of the rise of good faith as a key driver of the future of the employment contract.[47] There is even more that can be gleaned from the Canadian experience, where good faith is viewed as a core 'organising principle' in contract law generally.[48] Since 2019, there have also been several rulings relating to the implied duty of good faith under English law, and the courts seem to be sending a consistent message in their findings.[49] While it is accepted law that there is no general duty of good faith in English commercial contracts, a duty can be implied where it is in accordance with the presumed intention of the parties and their contractual relationship, functioning as a term implied in fact. Collectively, these more recent authorities commonly show that if the courts are able to find that a relational contract exists, they are more likely to be able to imply a duty of good faith between the parties, subject to the facts.

As to the application of the good faith duty in employment, Alan Bogg explains that 'some caution is warranted before we fix upon a characterisation of [good faith in] English contract law in general, and the English contract of employment in particular'.[50] In making this claim, Bogg draws on the work of Simon Whittaker and Reinhardt Zimmerman, who assert that any statements about the English common law's rejection of good faith often 'must be qualified to such an extent as to make these bold general statements appear little more than caricatures'.[51] Whittaker and Zimmerman go on to mention that 'the law of special contracts is far less hostile to

---

Yam Seng v International Trade Corporation (n 39), but did not base its decision on the principles stated by Leggatt J.

[45] D Brodie, 'Fair Dealing and the World of Work' (2014) 43 ILJ 29, 43.
[46] ibid.
[47] D Brodie, *The Future of the Employment Contract* (Edward Elgar 2021)Part V.
[48] See, eg, *Bhasin v Hrynew* [2014] 3 SCR 494 (Supreme Court of Canada (SCC)). See also, the related commentary arising from this decision, J McCamus, 'The New General "Principle" of Good Faith Performance and the New "Rule" of Honesty in Performance in Canadian Contract Law' (2015) 32 JCL 103; J Robertson, 'Good Faith as an Organising Principle' (2015) 93 Can Bar Rev 809; S O'Byrne and R Cohen, 'The Contractual Principle of Good Faith and the Duty of Honesty in *Bhasin v Hrynew*' (2015) Alta L Rev 1; H MacQueen and S O'Byrne, 'The Principle of Good Faith in Contractual Performance' (2019) 23 Edin L R 301.
[49] See, eg, *Bates v Post Office Ltd (No 3)* [2019] EWHC 606 (QB); *Teesside Gas Transportation Ltd v CATS North Sea Ltd* [2019] EWHC 1220 (Commercial Court (Comm)); *Zedra Trust Co (Jersey) Ltd v Hut Group Ltd* [2019] EWHC 2191 (Comm); *UTB LLC v Sheffield United Ltd* [2019] EWHC 2322 (High Court of Justice Chancery Division (Ch Div)); *Russell v Cartwright* [2020] EWHC 41 (Ch Div); *Morley v Royal Bank of Scotland plc* [2020] EWHC 88 (Ch Div).
[50] Bogg (n 36) 730.
[51] ibid.

the idea of a good faith doctrine that its general counterpart'.[52] They cite the employment contract as a 'leading example of such a phenomenon'.[53]

Bogg then explains that '[w]hat history discloses is how recently the contract of employment [has] displayed elements of good faith in its basic constitution'.[54] He identifies that a duty of good faith in English employment contracts came to fruition in the late 1970s following, first, the development of the concept of terms implied by law, and second, the emergence of the mutual trust and confidence term.[55] He specifically cites 1977 as the year in which the development of the duty of good faith as a term implied by law in employment 'coincided with the judicial articulation of the mutual trust and confidence term'.[56] Recently, English authorities have tended to support the notion that there is actually a single obligation encompassing both a duty of mutual trust and confidence in employment and a duty of good faith. In that sense, both duties have come to be treated as one and the same.[57]

There are four key reasons for this apparent 'transformation of the contract of employment into a contract of good faith'.[58] First, it was largely because of judicial thinking reconfiguring the concept of the English employment contract. Specifically, the regulatory gap left by the disappearance of collective bargaining during that time (and the good faith functions fulfilled by that system of collective bargaining) 'necessitated a creative regulatory response by the common law and the crafting of a contractual good faith duty'.[59] Secondly, the courts had developed a 'distinctive employee-protective philosophy compared with the dominant "judicial philosophy of market individualism"'.[60] Thirdly, some judicial speeches given at that time pointed to the influence of relational contract theory as underpinning the shift toward contractual good faith in employment.[61] Fourthly, there was a deep normative reconfiguration of the employment contract in the English common law, such that employment was no longer considered a mere exchange of wages for work and, due to the inherent subordination of the employee to employer, the employee was seen as especially vulnerable to abuses of power by the

---

[52] S Whitaker and R Zimmerman, 'Good Faith in European Contract Law: Surveying the Legal Landscape' in S Whitaker and R Zimmerman (eds) *Good Faith in European Contract Law* (CUP 2000) 7, 41.
[53] ibid.
[54] Bogg (n 36) 741.
[55] See, eg, ibid 742.
[56] ibid, 746–47, citing B Hepple, *Rights at Work: Global, European and British Perspectives* (Sweet & Maxwell 2005) 51–52.
[57] See, eg, *Johnson v Unisys Ltd* [2003] 1 AC 518 (HL) [24]; *Eastwood v Magnox Electric plc* [2005] 1 AC 503 (HL) [11]; *Russell v Trustees of the Roman Catholic Church* (2007) 69 NSWLR 198 (New South Wales Court of Appeal (NSWCA)) [32]; *Rogan-Gardiner v Woolworths Ltd* [2010] WASC 290 (Western Australia Supreme Court (WASC) [125]–[126]. See also D Cabrelli, 'Discretion, Power and the Rationalisation of Implied Terms' (2007) 36 ILJ 194, 201–02.
[58] Bogg (n 36) 746–47.
[59] ibid 749.
[60] ibid.
[61] See, eg, ibid. The concept of employment contracts as 'relational' is examined further in Chapter 5.

employer.[62] As Brodie elucidates, this focus on 'human dignity' has generated a distinctive version of good faith in English employment contracts.[63] Brodie also commented that nowadays in English law, '[g]ood faith ... has assumed a central role in the life of the employment contract and has acted, and continues to act, as a catalyst for further evolution at common law'.[64]

Despite its recognition and being apparently synonymous with mutual trust and confidence, that does not mean that there is not more that the English courts could do to further articulate and more clearly delineate the necessity for the duty of good faith in the context of employment. There remains scope and potential for further understanding and articulation of the duty as it exists in its own right.

By contrast, the Australian position as to the existence of a good faith duty in employment contracts is far less resolved. Notwithstanding the High Court of Australia's refusal to imply a term of mutual trust and confidence in *Commonwealth Bank v Barker*, the potential for a duty of good faith was deliberately left open. A range of conflicting authorities exist in respect of the duty's status in contracts generally and employment contracts specifically. In either context, the duty has the potential to function as a term implied by law or in fact, as a rule of construction, or not at all. Assuming it exists, there is also widespread confusion as to the duty's likely content.

If it were to operate in employment, any good faith obligation will need to be distinguished from the mutual trust and confidence obligation already rejected by the High Court in *Commonwealth Bank v Barker*. It has been argued that there may be no practical distinction between a duty of good faith and one of mutual trust and confidence. Assuming that argument is correct, the High Court's refusal to imply a mutual trust and confidence term by law in *Commonwealth Bank v Barker* could well mean that there is similarly no need to imply a good faith duty by law into employment contracts. That said there is still the possibility that the two duties could be understood separately. To repeat a point made in Chapter 4, prior to *Commonwealth Bank v Barker*, Joellen Riley Munton argued that the two duties were related, but remained separate.[65] Following *Commonwealth Bank v Barker*, it remains to be seen how the courts will handle this apparent distinction, if at all.

Returning briefly to the decision in *Commonwealth Bank v Barker*, the High Court's reasons for refusing to imply a term of mutual trust and confidence were

---

[62] This reconfiguration was expressed by Lord Hoffman in *Johnson v Unisys* (n 57) who held that: 'Freedom of contract meant that the stronger party, usually the employer, was free to impose his terms on the weaker. But over the last 30 years or so, the nature of the contract of employment has been transformed. It has been recognised that a person's employment is usually one of the most important things in his or her life. It gives not only a livelihood but an occupation, an identity and a sense of self-esteem. The law has changed to recognise this social reality', cited in Bogg (n 36) 750.

[63] D Brodie, 'Mutual Trust and Confidence: Catalysts, Constraints and Commonality' (2008) 37 ILJ 329, 339.

[64] ibid 32.

[65] J Riley, 'Siblings but Not Twins: Making Sense of "Mutual Trust" and "Good Faith" in Employment Contracts' (2012) 36 MULR 521.

flawed in several ways. The court purported to apply the narrow necessity test for refusing the term's implication, yet its broader policy-based reasoning suggested otherwise. Part of its reasoning also suggested that Australia's statutory regime would cover the field that would otherwise be taken up by a mutual trust and confidence term, and consequently, the term was unnecessary. However, as already discussed in Part C, the court failed to conduct any detailed analysis of the statutory regimes mentioned to fully analyse whether they really did cover the field that would otherwise be taken up by the implied term. The court also suggested that a matter such as whether there ought to be a mutual trust and confidence term constituted a matter better dealt with by parliament. Hence, it was not appropriate for the court to make a ruling as to its existence in any event. However, this reasoning appeared to unduly limit the courts' law-making function, making it seem that courts ought not to imply any new terms by law into employment contracts in the future. Taking stock of this combination of erroneous logic, had the High Court reasoned differently to avoid these flaws, it may have achieved a different result in respect of the implication of the mutual trust and confidence term. If that been the case, it may have meant that a good faith term does have a place as a term implied by law into Australian employment contracts.

With the High Court's erroneous reasoning in mind, and assuming that a duty of good faith is deemed distinct from one of mutual trust and confidence, recent authorities, both in England and Australia, indicate that if a good faith duty were to operate in employment, it would likely apply to regulate employers' discretionary powers conferred by the contract (rather than all acts of the employer under the contract).[66] If that were the case, then the duty would likely apply when the exercise of that discretionary power affects the employees' enjoyment of the contract's essential benefits.

While this appears to be the most logical operation of a good faith duty in employment at common law, there may also be a statutory solution that would be equally applicable in English and Australian law. A duty of good faith could operate as a model statutory term, similar to those discussed above at Part C. In fact, the inclusion of a good faith term was alluded to in Collins' proposal of model terms in the employment contract.

In concluding these practical illustrations, it is important to keep in mind the caveat set out in Part C of this chapter that while there is the potential for each of the recommendations in Parts A to D to be adopted in both English and Australian law, such approaches have not yet been embraced coherently by either English or Australian courts, or at the parliamentary level. As Chapter 7, in particular, sought to show, however, there is clear impetus for the courts and parliament to achieve

---

[66] See, eg, the further discussion as to how the duty might operate in respect of the exercise of discretionary powers in Chapter 4. As to future predictions regarding the role of good faith in an employer's exercise of discretionary powers, see further, Brodie (n 63) 160–62.

greater coherency and for both to give way to context-specific approaches in respect of how contracts for the performance of work continue to be shaped. It is the goal of this work to suggest ways in which that shaping can usefully occur.

Rethinking the Rationale

Despite several challenges, terms implied by law continue to play an important gap-filling role in English and Australian employment contracts. As argued over the course of Chapters 4 to 7 in particular, and solidified earlier in this conclusion, there are ways in which clarity can be achieved to ensure that implying terms by law remains a viable judicial technique through which courts can shape employment contracts as distinct from contracts for the broader performance of work.

A firm judicial determination as to the nature of the employment relationship, utilising the three main categories for implication by law in employment described in Part A of this chapter, as well as making a definitive decision on the proper application of the necessity test as suggested in Part B, would assist courts in making decisions about whether to imply both existing and new terms by law into employment contracts. It is envisaged that utilisation of these categories would set boundaries within which the courts can develop any new terms implied by law in employment. It would also inform the continuing operation of existing terms implied by law in employment. Instead, employment lawyers have been left guessing: What is the true nature of the employment relationship as distinct from other types of agreement for the performance of work, and, in turn, how should employment contracts be defined as a category into which terms are implied by law? How does the necessity test now apply to existing terms implied by law? Which necessity test is the correct one to apply when seeking to imply a new term by law—the narrow or wide test?

Furthermore, as proposed in Part C of this chapter, parliament ought to play the primary role by creating a statutory default minimum set of terms to govern the employment relationship in both jurisdictions. Arguably, it is a step too far to suggest that parliament ought to take over the field completely. This claim diminishes the judicial role too greatly and presumes that there are presently no gaps and that, in future, there will be no gaps to be filled, other than by parliament through legislation.

This apparent limit on the court's future role suggests that parliament ought to step in and create a default set of minimum rules to regulate the employment relationship, some of which ought to be considered mandatory and not capable of exclusion by the parties. However, in creating a default set of terms, it would be exceedingly difficult (if not impossible) for parliament to foresee all situations in which a term might need to be implied at some point in the future. Essentially, it is not possible for parliament to predict all future gaps that may require filling. The courts should therefore remain willing to imply new terms by law in order to accommodate these situations. These situations will necessarily be far more limited should parliament implement a default minimum set of implied terms. If the set of default minimum rules existed, coherence and arguably fairness in the law would be enhanced, and the roles of the courts and parliament clarified. It has been proposed that any statutory rules reflect what is already contained in the common law through terms implied by law into employment contracts, with the potential addition of a good faith term. However, it would always be open to the court and the parties themselves to go further as needed. The courts would then be tasked with interpreting, applying, and potentially adding to those terms, should they come into question.

The conclusions drawn here collectively present a powerful case for future reform in respect of the legal test for implying terms by law in employment, a test that has been largely haphazardly applied by English and Australian courts to date. This work's overarching proposal is that parliament should intervene, and that a suitable appellate court ought to reform and clarify the common law in respect of terms implied by law into employment contracts, as well as contracts more broadly. These legislative and judicial changes need not stand alone. In recognising the need for greater coherence between statute and the common law, the changes ought to coincide. In making these suggestions, this work has provided original insights into the operation of an important feature which shapes both English and Australian employment contracts as distinct from other contracts for the performance of work. Most importantly, it is hoped that the findings and conclusions will provide the reader with an informed understanding of the law associated with terms implied by law into employment contracts. As a whole, this work has sought to offer insight into the ways in which the legal test for their implication can be refined to confront the continuing challenges associated with the shaping of employment contracts, as distinct from other contracts for the performance of work. It is hoped that the rethinking of the rationale for implying terms by law in order to shape employment contracts as distinct from broader contracts for work will provide employment law with just such a model for suitable development in a clear yet nuanced way, and that the preceding chapters have presented some initial pointers towards the path that might be followed in its adoption.

Rethinking the rationale at the heart of terms implied by law into employment contracts enables conceptual clarity in the face of factual complexity. What, though, are the normative implications of the resolutions proposed in this concluding chapter? The purpose of this work was not only to provide a technical analysis and to develop theoretical proposals. Once slotted into the broader edifice of the contract of employment as the core instrument shaping the employment relationship, the four proposals set out in this conclusion have the potential to restore coherence to the scope of employment law. These proposals bring the complexities of different types of work arrangements back to a state of clarity and better understanding of the scope of the contract of employment as distinct from other types of contracts for the performance of work. This conceptual restoration of scope will on occasion go hand in hand with an extension of the application of existing employment norms beyond their current reach. This is the main practical outcome of the proposed rethinking. By specifically identifying areas for reshaping, the four proposals set out in this conclusion therefore enable the contract of employment to regain its functionality in complex employment settings. As discussion of the existing law concerning terms implied by law into contracts generally showed in Chapter 1, terms implied by law are intimately linked to shaping the contract of employment in both English and Australian law. In this final analysis, the four proposals put forward can ultimately be justified as no more than a restoration of coherence in the personal scope of employment law.

Bibliography

Acreman T J, 'The Long Road to a Wide Ambiguity Gateway' (2016) 42 Aust Bar Rev 12
Adams-Prassl A, 'Inequality in the Impact of the Coronavirus Shock: Evidence from Real Time Surveys' (IZA Institute of Labour Economics Discussion Paper No 13183, April 2020)
Adams-Prassl J, '*Autoclenz v Belcher* (2011): Divining "The True Agreement Between the Parties"' in ACL Davies, J Adams-Prassl, and A Bogg, *Landmark Cases in Labour Law* (Hart Publishing 2022) 299
Adams Z and others, *Deakin and Morris' Labour Law* (7th edn, Hart Publishing 2021)
Anderman S, 'The Interpretation of Protective Employment Statutes and Contracts of Employment' (2000) 29 ILJ 223
Anderson G, Brodie D, and Riley J, *The Common Law Employment Relationship: A Comparative Study* (Edward Elgar 2017)
Arnow-Richman R, 'Mainstreaming Employment Contract Law: The Common Law Case for Reasonable Notice of Termination' (2015) 66 Fla LR 1513, 1529
Atiyah P, *The Rise and Fall of Freedom of Contract* (Clarendon Press 1979)
Atiyah P, 'Common Law and Statute Law' (1985) 48 MLR 1
Atkinson J, 'Implied Terms and Human Rights in the Contract of Employment' (2019) 48 ILJ 515
Atkinson J, '*Johnson v Unisys Ltd* (2001): A Compelling Constitutional Vision of Common Law and Statute?' in ACL Davies, J Adams-Prassl, and A Bogg, *Landmark Cases in Labour Law* (Hart Publishing 2022) 267
Austen-Baker R, *Implied Terms in English Contract Law* (2nd edn, Edward Elgar 2017)
Bant E, 'Statute and the Common Law' (2015) 38 UNSWLJ 367
Barmes L, 'Common Law Implied Terms and Behavioural Standards at Work' (2007) 36 ILJ 35
Beale H, *Chitty on Contracts* (31st edn, Sweet & Maxwell 2012)
Beatson J, 'Has the Common Law a Future?' (1997) 56 CLJ 291
Beatson J and Friedmann D, 'From "Classical" to Modern Contract Law' in J Beatson and D Friedman (eds), *Good Faith and Fault in Contract Law* (Clarendon Paperbacks 1995) 3
Bingham T, 'Singapore Academy of Law Annual Lecture 2001: From Servant to Employee: A Study of the Common Law in Action' (2001) 13 S Ac LJ 253
Blackstone W, *Commentaries on the Laws of England* (13th edn, Dublin 1796)
Bogg A, 'Good Faith in the Contract of Employment: A Case of the English Reserve' (2011) 32 Comp LL & PJ 729
Bogg A, 'Common Law and Statute in the Law of Employment' (2016) 69 Curr Leg Probl 67
Bomball P, 'Statutory Norms and Common Law Concepts in the Characterisation of Contracts for the Performance of Work' (2019) 42 MULR 370
Boyle M, 'The Relational Principle of Trust and Confidence' (2007) 27 OJLS 633
Brodie D, 'The Heart of the Matter: Mutual Trust and Confidence' (1996) 25 ILJ 121
Brodie D, 'Beyond Exchange: The New Contract of Employment (1998) 27 ILJ 79
Brodie D, 'A Fair Deal at Work' (1999) 19 OJLS 83
Brodie D, 'Mutual Trust and the Values of the Employment Contract' (2001) 30 ILJ 84

Brodie D, *The Employment Contract: Legal Principles, Drafting and Interpretation* (OUP 2005)
Brodie D, 'The Employment Contract and Unfair Contracts Legislation' (2007) 27 Leg S 95
Brodie D, 'Mutual Trust and Confidence: Catalysts, Constraints and Commonality' (2008) 37 ILJ 329
Brodie D, 'How Relational is the Employment Contract?' (2011) 40 ILJ 232
Brodie D, 'The Employment Relationship and Fiduciary Obligations' (2012) 16 Edin L R 198
Brodie D, 'Fair Dealing and the World of Work' (2014) 43 ILJ 29
Brodie D, 'Relational Contracts' in M Freedland and others (eds), *The Contract of Employment* (OUP 2016) 145
Brodie D, 'The Autonomy of the Common Law of the Contract of Employment from the General Law of Contract' in M Freedland and others (eds), *The Contract of Employment* (OUP 2016) 124
Brodie D, 'The Dynamics of Common Law Evolution' (2016) 32 IJCLL&IR 45
Brodie D, *The Future of the Employment Contract* (Edward Elgar 2021)
Brodie D, 'Constructive Dismissal: The Contractual Maze' (2022) 33 KLJ 151
Brodie D, '*Malik v BCCI*: The Impact of Good Faith' in ACL Davies, J Adams-Prassl, and A Bogg, *Landmark Cases in Labour Law* (Hart Publishing 2022) 245
Brodie D, 'The Demise of the Relational Contract of Employment' (Paper presented at the Phillipa Weeks Lecture in Labour Law, ANU College of Law, Australian National University, Canberra, 16 November 2022)
Brooks A, 'Myth and Muddle—An Examination of Contracts for the Performance of Work' (1988) 11 UNSWLJ 48
Brooks A, 'The Good and Considerate Employer: Developments in the Implied Duty of Mutual Trust and Confidence' (2001) 20 UTas LR 29
Brown W and others, *The Individualisation of Employment Contracts in Britain* (DTI, Employment Relations Research Series, URN 98/934, 1998)
Burrows A, 'The Relationship Between Common Law and Statute in the Law of Obligations' (2012) 128 LQR 232
Cabrelli D, 'The Implied Duty of Mutual Trust and Confidence: An Emerging Overarching Principle?' (2005) 34 ILJ 284
Cabrelli D, 'Discretion, Power and the Rationalisation of Implied Terms' (2007) 36 ILJ 194
Cabrelli D, *Employment Law in Context: Text and Materials* (OUP 2014)
Cabrelli D, 'The Effect of Termination upon Post-Employment Obligations' in M Freedland and others (eds), *The Contract of Employment* (OUP 2016) 561
Cabrelli D, *Employment Law in Context: Text and Materials* (4th edn, OUP 2020)
Cabrelli D and D'Alton J, *Furlough and Common Law Rights and Remedies* (*UK Labour Law Blog*, 8 June 2020) <https://uklabourlawblog.com/2020/06/08/furlough-and-common-law-rights-and-remedies-by-david-cabrelli-and-jessica-dalton/> accessed 20 December 2022
Cairns J, 'Blackstone, Kahn-Freund and the Contract of Employment' (1989) 105 LQR 300
Calabresi G, *A Common Law for the Age of Statutes* (Harvard University Press 1982)
Campbell D (ed), *The Relational Theory of Contract: Selected Works of Ian Macneil* (Sweet & Maxwell 2001)
Campbell D, 'Good Faith and the Ubiquity of the *"Relational"* Contract' (2014) 77 MLR 475
Carter J, *Contract Law in Australia* (6th edn, LexisNexis Butterworths 2013)
Carter J, *The Construction of Commercial Contracts* (Hart Publishing 2013)
Carter J and Courtney W, 'Implied Terms in Contracts: Australian Law' (2015) 43 ABLR 246
Carter J and Peden E, 'Good Faith in Australian Contract Law' (2003) 19 JCL 155

Carter J and others, 'Terms Implied in Law: "Trust and Confidence" in the High Court of Australia' (2015) 32 JCL 203

Chighine L, *Commonwealth Bank of Australia v Barker*—No Implied Term of Mutual Trust and Confidence in Employment Contracts, But Door Still Open for Good Faith' (2015) 28 AJLL 77

Chin D, 'Implied Terms and the Stifling of Innovation in the Employment Contract' (Paper presented at the Eight Biennial National Conference of the Australian Labour Law Association, St Kilda, 4 and 5 November 2016)

Churches S, 'The Presumption of Yearly Term in a General Contract of Employment and the Plight of the Modern Manager, or the Black Death and the Malady Lingers On' (1979) 10 UQLJ 195

Clarke L, 'Mutual Trust and Confidence, Fiduciary Relationships and Duty of Disclosure' (1999) 30 ILJ 348

Clayton A and Mitchell R, *Study on Employment Situations and Worker Protection in Australia: A Report to the International Labour Office* (Centre for Employment and Labour Relations Law, University of Melbourne, 1999)

Collins H, 'Market Power, Bureaucratic Power and the Contract of Employment' (1986) 15 ILJ 1

Collins H, 'Independent Contractors and the Challenge of Vertical Disintegration' (1990) 10 OJLS 353

Collins H, *Regulating Contracts* (OUP 1999)

Collins H, 'Regulating the Employment Regulation for Competitiveness' (2001) 30 ILJ 17

Collins H, *The Law of Contract* (4th edn, CUP 2003)

Collins H, 'Legal Responses to the Standard Form Contract of Employment' (2007) 36 ILJ 2

Collins H, *Employment Law* (2nd edn, OUP 2010)

Collins H, 'The Contract of Employment in 3D' in D Campbell, L Mulcahy, and S Wheeler (eds), *Changing Concepts of Contract* (Palgrave Macmillan 2013) 65

Collins H, 'Implied Terms: The Foundation in Good Faith and Fair Dealing' (2014) Curr Leg Probl 1

Collins H, 'Contractual Autonomy' in A Bogg and others (eds), *The Autonomy of Labour Law* (Hart Publishing 2015) 45

Collins H, 'Implied Terms in the Contract of Employment' in M Freedland and others (eds), *The Contract of Employment* (OUP 2016) 471

Collins H, 'Is a Relational Contract a Legal Concept?' in S Degeling, J Edelman, and J Goudkamp (eds), *Contract in Commercial Law* (Thomson Reuters 2016)

Collins H, 'Dependent Contractors in Tax and Employment Law' in G Loutzenhiser and R de la Feria (eds), *The Dynamics of Taxation: Essays in Honour of Judith Freedman* (Bloomsbury Publishing 2020) 117

Collins H, 'Employment as a Relational Contract' (2021) 137 LQR 426

Collins H, 'Relational and Associational Justice in Work' (2023) 24 Theor Inq Law 26

Collins H, Ewing K D, and McCoglan A, *Labour Law* (2nd edn, CUP 2019)

Collins P, *Putting Human Rights to Work: Labour Law, the ECHR, and the Employment Relation* (OUP 2022)

Connolly A and Stewart D (eds), *Public Law in the Age of Statutes: Essays in Honour of Dennis Pearce* (Federation Press 2015)

Cornish W, 'Law and Organised Labour' in W Cornish and others (eds), *The Oxford History of the Laws of England: Volume XIII* (OUP 2010) part III, 667

Cornish W, *The Oxford History of the Laws of England: Volume XIII* (OUP 2010)

Courtney W and Carter J, 'Implied Terms: What is the Role of Construction?' (2014) 31 JCL 151
Countouris N and De Stefano V, 'The Future Concept of Work' in K Arabadjieva and others (eds), *Transformative Ideas—Ensuring a Just Share of Progress for All* (European Trade Union Institute 2023) 93
Creighton B and Stewart A, *Labour Law* (5th edn, Federation Press 2010)
Davies ACL, 'Judicial Self-Restraint in Labour Law' (2009) 38 ILJ 278
Davies ACL, 'The Relationship Between the Contract of Employment and Statute' in M Freedland and others (eds), *The Contract of Employment* (OUP 2016) 73
Davies ACL, 'Terms Implied into the Contract of Employment by Legislation' in M Freedland and others (eds), *The Contract of Employment* (OUP 2016) 427
Deakin S, 'The Evolution of the Contract of Employment, 1900–50' in N Whiteside and R Salais (eds), *Governance, Industry and Labour Markets in Britain and France* (Routledge 1998) 212
Deakin S, 'Does the 'Personal Employment Contract' Provide a Basis for the Reunification of Employment Law?' (2007) 26 ILJ 68
Deakin S and Wilkinson F, 'Labour Law and Economic Theory: A Reappraisal' in H Collins, P Davies, and R Rideout (eds), *Legal Regulation of the Employment Relation* (Kluwer Law International 2000) 42
Deakin S and Wilkinson F, *The Law and the Labour Market: Industrialisation, Employment and Legal Evolution* (OUP 2005)
Dicey A V, *Introduction to the Study of the Law of the Constitution* (Macmillan 1885)
Dickens L, 'Exploring the Atypical: Zero Hours Contracts' (1997) 26 ILJ 262
Dietrich J, 'What is Lawyering?' (2006) 65 CLJ 549
Dixon B, 'Common Law Obligations of Good Faith in Australian Commercial Contracts—A Relational Recipe' (2005) 33 ABLR 87
Dixon W M, 'Good Faith in Contractual Performance and Enforcement—Australian Doctrinal Hurdles' (2011) 39 ABLR 227
Dworkin R, 'Law as Interpretation' (1982) 9 Crit Inq 179
Elias P, 'Changes and Challenges to the Contract of Employment' (2018) 38(4) OJLS 869
Elias P, Napier B, and Wallington P, *Labour Law: Cases and Materials* (Butterworths 1980)
Feinman J M, 'Contract After the Fall' (1987) 39 Stan LR 1537
Finn P, 'Statutes and the Common Law' (1992) 22(1) UWALR 7
Flannigan R, 'Employee: Fiduciary' (2016) 19 CLELJ 509
Flannigan R, 'The (Fiduciary) Duty of Fidelity' (2008) 124 LQR 274
Fraser A, 'The Employee's Contractual Duty of Fidelity' (2015) 131 LQR 53
Frauenfelder S, 'Implied Terms—Are the *BP Refinery* Criteria Broken?: A Theoretical and Empirical Analysis' (2022) 38(2/3) JCL 103
Freedland M, *The Contract of Employment* (Clarendon Press 1976)
Freedland M, *The Personal Employment Contract* (OUP 2003)
Freedland M, 'Contract of Employment to Personal Work Nexus' (2006) 35 ILJ 1
Freedland M, 'Constructing Fairness in Employment Contracts' (2007) 36 ILJ 136
Freedland M, 'Otto Kahn-Freund, the Contract of Employment and the Autonomy of Labour Law' in A Bogg and others (eds), *The Autonomy of Labour Law* (Hart Publishing 2015) 29
Freedland M, 'The Legal Structure of the Contract of Employment' in M Freedland and others (eds), *The Contract of Employment* (OUP 2016) 28
Freedland M and Kountouris N, *The Legal Construction of Personal Work Relations* (OUP 2011)

Gageler S, 'Common Law Statute and Judicial Legislation: Statutory Interpretation as a Common Law Process' (2011) 37 Mon L Rev 1

Gallagher D, 'Independent Contracting: Finding a Balance Between Flexibility and Individual Well-being' in K Näswall, J Hellgren, and M Sverke (eds), *The Individual in the Changing Working Life* (CUP 2008) 108

Gava J, 'The Rise of the Hero Judge' (2001) 24 UNSWLJ 747

Godfrey K, 'Contracts of Employment: Renaissance of the Implied Term of Trust and Confidence' (2003) 77 ALJ 764

Godfrey K, 'The Renaissance of the Implied Term of Trust & Confidence' [2003] 88 ACLN 29

Golding G, 'Terms Implied by Law into Employment Contracts: Are They Necessary?' (2015) 28 AJLL 113

Golding G, 'The Role of Judges in the Regulation of Australian Employment Contracts' (2016) 32 IJCLL&IR 69

Golding G, 'The Distinctiveness of the Employment Contract' (2019) 32 AJLL 170

Golding G, 'The Origins of Terms Implied by Law into English and Australian Employment Contracts' (2020) 20 OUCLJ 163

Golding G, 'Employment as a Relational Contract and the Impact on Remedies for Breach' (2021) 30 Griffith L Rev 270

Goldsworthy J, 'Implications in Language, Law and the Constitution' in G Lindell (ed), *Future Directions in Constitutional Law* (Federation Press 1994) 158

Good Work: A Response to the Taylor Review of Modern Working Practices (HM Government, February 2018) <https://assets.publishing.service.gov.uk/government/uploads/system/uploads/attachment_data/file/679767/180206_BEIS_Good_Work_Report__Accessible_A4_.pdf> accessed 20 December 2022

Gordley J, *The Philosophical Origins of the Modern Contract Doctrine* (Clarendon Press 1991)

Gray A, 'Good Faith in Australian Contract Law After *Barker*' (2015) 43 ABLR 358

Hale Baroness, 'Legislation or Judicial Law Reform: Where Should Judges Fear to Tread?' (Annual Society of Legal Scholars Conference, Oxford, 7 September 2016)

Harlow C, 'Changing the Mindset: The Place of Theory in English Administrative Law' (1994) 14 OJLS 419

Hay D, 'Master and Servant in England: Using the Law in the Eighteenth and Nineteenth Centuries' in W Steinmetz (ed), *Private Law and Social Inequality in the Industrial Age* (OUP 2000) 227

Hepple B, 'Restructuring Employment Rights' (1986) 15 ILJ 69

Hepple B, *Rights at Work: Global, European and British Perspectives* (Sweet & Maxwell 2005)

Hillbrick L, 'Why the High Court Went Too Far in Rejecting the Implied Term of Mutual Trust and Confidence in Its Entirety, in the Context of Constructive Dismissal Claims' (2018) 31 AJLL 45

Hodder J, 'Employment Contracts, Implied Terms and Judicial Law-Making' (2002) 33 VUWLR 475

Hogg M, *Promises and Contract Law: Comparative Perspectives* (CUP 2012)

Honeyball S, 'Employment Law and the Primacy of Contract' (1989) 18 ILJ 97

Honeyball S and Pearce D, 'Contract, Employment and the Contract of Employment' (2006) 35 ILJ 30

Howe J and Mitchell R, 'The Evolution of the Contract of Employment in Australia: A Discussion' (1999) 12 AJLL 113

Huscroft G, 'Romance, Realism, and the Legitimacy of Implied Rights' (2011) 30 UQLJ 35

Hutchinson T and Duncan N, 'Defining and Describing What We Do: Doctrinal Legal Research' (2012) 17 Deakin L R 83

Ingram P, 'Justiciability' (1994) 39 Am J Juris 353
Irving M, *The Contract of Employment* (LexisNexis Butterworths 2012)
Irving M, 'What Is Special about the Employment Contract?' (Paper presented at the Industrial Relations Society of South Australia Conference, Adelaide, 19 October 2012)
Irving M, 'Australian and Canadian Approaches to the Assessment of the Length of Reasonable Notice' (2015) 28 AJLL 159
Irving M, *The Contract of Employment* (2nd edn, LexisNexis Butterworths 2019)
Jacoby S, 'The Duration of Indefinite Employment Contracts in the United States and England: An Historical Analysis' (1982) 5 Comp Labour Law 85
Jensen D, *Theories, Principles, Policies and Common Law Adjudication* (2011) 36 Aust J Leg Philos 34
Kahn-Freund O, *Labour and the Law* (Stevens for the Hamlyn Trust 1972)
Kahn-Freund O, 'On Uses and Misuses of Comparative Law' (1974) 37 MLR 1
Kuehne G, 'Implied Obligations of Good Faith and Reasonableness in Performance of Contracts: Old Wine in New Bottles?' (2006) 33 UWALR 63
Langstaff B, 'Overconfidence in the Implied Term? Court Out ... ' (Paper presented at the Industrial Law Society Conference, Oxford, 19 September 2014)
Langstaff B, 'Changing Times, Changing Relationships at Work ... Changing Law?' (2016) 45 ILJ 131
Leeming M, 'Theories and Principles Underlying the Development of the Common Law—The Statutory Elephant in the Room' (2013) 36 UNSWLJ 1002
Lindsay The Honourable Mr Justice, 'The Implied Term of Trust and Confidence' (2001) 30 ILJ 1
Macaulay S, 'Non-Contractual Relations in Business: A Preliminary Study' (1963) 28 Am Soc Rev 55
MacCormick N, *Institutions of Law* (OUP 2007)
Macneil I, 'The Many Futures of Contract' (1974) 47 S Cal L Rev 691
Macneil I, 'Contracts: Adjustment of Long-Term Economic Relations Under Classical, Neoclassical, and Relational Contract Law' (1978) 72 N W L Rev 854
Macneil I, *The New Social Contract: An Inquiry into Modern Contractual Relations* (Yale University Press 1980)
Macneil I, 'Values in Contract: Internal and External' (1983) 78 N W L Rev 340
Macneil I, 'Exchange Revisited: Individual Utility and Social Solidarity' (1986) 96 Ethics 567
Macneil I, 'Barriers to the Idea of Relational Contracts (The Complex Long-Term Contract, Structures and International Arbitration)' in F Nicklisch (ed), *Der Komplexe Langzeitvertrag. Strukturen und Internationale Schiedsgerichtsbarkeit* (Müller Juristischer Verlag 1987) 277
Macneil I, 'Relational Contract Theory as Sociology: A Reply to Professors Lindenberg and de Vos' (1987) 143 JITE 272
Macneil I, 'A Brief Comment on Farnsworth's "Suggestions for the Future"' (1988) 38 JPLE 301
Macneil I, 'Contract Remedies: A Need for a Better Efficiency Analysis' (1988) 144 JITE 6
MacQueen, H and S O'Byrne, 'The Principle of Good Faith in Contractual Performance' (2019) 23 Edin LR 301
Mason A, 'The Judge as Law-Maker' (1996) 3 JCULR
Mason A and Gageler S, 'The Contract' in P Finn (ed), *Essays in Contract* (The Law Book Company 1987) 1
McCamus J, 'The New General "Principle" of Good Faith Performance and the New "Rule" of Honesty in Performance in Canadian Contract Law' (2015) 32 JCL 103

McCarry G, 'Damages for Breach of the Employer's Implied Duty of Trust and Confidence' (1998) 26 ABLR 141
McLeish S, 'Challenges to the Survival of the Common Law' (2014) 38 MULR 818
Merrit A, 'The Historical Role of Law in the Regulation of Employment: Abstentionist or Interventionist?' (1982) 1 Aust J L & Soc 56
Mitchell C, 'Behavioural Standards in Contracts and English Contract Law' (2016) 33 JCL 234
Moir M, 'Discretion, Good Faith and Employer Control Over Executive Remuneration' (2011) 24 AJLL 121
Mummé C, '*Bhasin v. Hrynew*: A New Era for Good Faith in Canadian Employment Law, or Just Tinkering at the Margins?' (2016) 32 IJCLL&IR 117
Murray J, 'Conceptualising the Employer as Fiduciary: Mission Impossible' in A Bogg and others, *The Autonomy of Labour Law: Essays in Honour of Mark Freedland* (Hart Publishing 2015) 337
Neil I and Chin D, *The Modern Contract of Employment* (Lawbook Co 2012)
O'Byrne S and Cohen R, 'The Contractual Principle of Good Faith and the Duty of Honesty in *Bhasin v Hrynew*' (2015) Alta L Rev 1
O'Grady P, 'Nothing Implied: Construction as a Means of Curbing the Excessive Use of Power in Employment Contracts' (Paper presented at the Eight Biennial National Conference of the Australian Labour Law Association, 4 and 5 November 2016)
O'Grady QC P, 'Nothing Implied: Construction as a Means of Curbing the Excessive Use of Power in Employment Contracts' (2017) 30 AJLL 137
Owens R, Riley J, and Murray J, *The Law of Work* (2nd edn, OUP 2011)
Paterson J, 'Terms Implied in Fact: The Basis for Implication' (1998) 13 JCL 103
Paterson J, 'The New Consumer Guarantee Law and the Reasons for Replacing the Regime of Statutory Implied Terms in Consumer Transactions' (2011) 35 MULR 252
Paterson J, 'Good Faith Duties in Contract Performance' (2014) 14 OUCLJ 283
Paterson J, Robertson A, and Duke A, *Principles of Contract Law* (5th edn, Lawbook Co 2016)
Pearce D, Campbell E, and Harding D ('Pearce Committee'), *Australian Law Schools: A Discipline Assessment for the Commonwealth Tertiary Education Commission* (Australian Government Publishing Service 1987)
Peden E, '"Cooperation" in English Contract Law—To Construe or Imply?' (2000) 16 JCL 56
Peden E, 'Incorporating Terms of Good Faith in Contract Law in Australia' (2001) 23 SLR 223
Peden E, 'Policy Concerns Behind Implication of Terms in Law' (2001) 117 LQR 459
Peden E, *Good Faith in the Performance of Contracts* (LexisNexis Butterworths 2003)
Peden E, 'When Common Law Trumps Equity: The Rise of Good Faith and Reasonableness and the Demise of Unconscionability' (2005) 21 JCL 226
Peden E, 'Contract Development Through the Looking-Glass of Implied Terms' in J T Gleeson, J A Watson, and E Peden (eds), *Historical Foundations of Australian Law* (Federation Press 2013) 201
Peel E, *Treitel: The Law of Contract* (13th edn, Sweet & Maxwell 2011)
Phang A, 'Implied Terms Revisited' [1990] JBL 394
Phang A, 'Implied Terms, Business Efficacy and the Officious Bystander—a Modern History' [1998] JBL 1
Powell R, 'Good Faith in Contracts' (1956) 9 Curr Leg Probl 16
Prassl J, *The Concept of the Employer* (OUP 2015)
Prassl J, *Humans as a Service: The Promise and Perils of Work in the Gig Economy* (OUP 2018)

Quinlan M, 'Pre-Arbitral Labour Legislation in Australia' in S Macintyre and R Mitchell (eds), *Foundations of Arbitration* (OUP 1989) 29

Reid Lord, 'The Judge as Lawmaker' (1972) 12 JSPTL 22

Reiter B, 'The Control of Contract Power' (1981) 1 OJLS 347

Reynold QC F, 'Bad Behaviour and the Implied Term of Mutual Trust and Confidence: Is There a Problem?' (2015) 44 ILJ 262

Riley J, 'Mutual Trust and Good Faith: Can Private Contract Law Guarantee Fair Dealing in the Workplace?' (2003) 16 AJLL 1

Riley J, *Employee Protection at Common Law* (Federation Press 2005)

Riley J, 'The Boundaries of Mutual Trust and Good Faith' (2009) 22 AJLL 73

Riley J, 'Siblings but Not Twins: Making Sense of "Mutual Trust" and "Good Faith" in Employment Contracts' (2012) 36 MULR 521

Riley J, 'Uneasy or Accommodating Bedfellows? Common Law and Statute in Employment Regulation' (Paper presented at the Phillipa Weeks Lecture in Labour Law, ANU College of Law, Australian National University, Canberra, 25 September 2013)

Riley J, 'Before the High Court—"Mutual Trust and Confidence" on Trial: At Last' (2014) 36 SLR 151

Riley J, 'The Definition of the Contract of Employment and its Differentiation from Other Contracts and Other Work Relations' in M Freedland and others (eds), *The Contract of Employment* (OUP 2016) 321

Riley J, 'The Future of the Common Law in Employment Regulation' (2016) 32 IJCLL&IR 33

Riley Munton J, *Labour Law: An Introduction to the Law of Work* (OUP 2021)

Robertson J, 'Good Faith as an Organising Principle' (2015) 93 Can Bar Rev 809

Sanders A, 'Fairness in the Contract of Employment' (2017) 46 ILJ 508

Sappideen C and others, *Macken's Law of Employment* (7th ed, Lawbook Co 2011)

Sappideen C and others, *Macken's Law of Employment* (9th edn, Lawbook Co 2022)

Seddon N C, Bigwood R A, and Ellinghaus M P, *Cheshire and Fifoot's Law of Contract* (10th edn, LexisNexis Butterworths 2012)

Silink S and Ryan D, 'Vicarious Liability for Independent Contractors' (2018) 77 CLJ 458

Simms V, 'Is Employment a Fiduciary Relationship' (2001) 30 ILJ 101

Smith I, Barker A, and Warnock O, *Smith & Wood's Employment Law* (14th edn, OUP 2019)

Stewart A, 'Good Faith and Fair Dealing at Work' in C Arup and others (eds), *Labour Law and Labour Market Regulation: Essays on the Construction, Constitution and Regulation of Labour Markets and Work Relationships* (Federation Press 2006) 579

Stewart A, *Stewart's Guide to Employment Law* (5th edn, Federation Press 2015)

Stewart A, *Stewart's Guide to Employment Law* (7th edn, Federation Press 2021)

Stewart A and McCrystal S, 'Labour Regulation and the Great Divide: Does the Gig Economy Require a New Category of Worker?' (2019) 32 AJLL 4

Stewart A and Nosworthy B, 'Employees and Indemnity' (2011) 27 JCL 18

Stewart A and others, *Intellectual Property in Australia* (6th edn, LexisNexis Butterworths 2014)

Stewart A and others, *Creighton and Stewart's Labour Law* (6th edn, Federation Press 2016)

Summers S, 'Similarities and Differences between Employment Contracts and Civil or Commercial Contracts' (2001) 17 IJCLL&IR 5

Sundra-Karean V, 'The Erosion of the Implied Term of Mutual Trust and Confidence in Australian Employment Law: Are Common Law and Statute Necessarily Uncomfortable Bedfellows?' (2016) 45 CLWR 275

Swanton J, 'Incorporation of Contractual Terms by a Course of Dealing' (1988) 1 JCL 223

Swanton J P, 'Implied Contractual Terms: Further Implications of *Hawkins v Clayton*' (1992) 5 JCL 127

Tan Z X, 'Disrupting Doctrine? Revisiting the Doctrinal Impact of Relational Contract Theory' (2019) 39 Leg S 98

Taylor M and others, *Good Work: The Taylor Review of Modern Working Practices* (July 2017) <https://www.gov.uk/government/uploads/system/uploads/attachment_data/file/627671/good-work-taylor-review-modern-working-practices-rg.pdf> accessed 20 December 2022

Teubner G, 'Legal Irritants: Good Faith in British Law or How Unifying Law Ends Up in New Divergences' (1998) 61 MLR 11

Tolhurst G and Carter J, 'The New Law on Implied Terms' (1996) 11 JCL 76

Traynor R, 'Statutes Revolving in Common Law Orbits' (1968) 17 Cath U L Rev 401

Tsuruda S, 'Good Faith in Employment' (2023) 24 Theor Inq Law 206

Veneziani B, 'The Evolution of the Contract of Employment' in B Hepple (ed), *The Making of Labour Law in Europe* (Mansell Publishing 1986) 31

Warren M, 'Good Faith: Where Are We At?' (2010) 34 MULR 344

Wedderburn Lord, *The Worker and the Law* (3rd edn, Penguin 1986)

Whitaker S and Zimmerman R, 'Good Faith in European Contract Law: Surveying the Legal Landscape' in S Whitaker and R Zimmerman (eds), *Good Faith in European Contract Law* (CUP 2000) 7

Whittaker S, 'Good Faith, Implied Terms and Commercial Contracts' (2013) 129 LQR 463

Williams R, 'Statutes as Sources of Law Beyond their Terms in Common-Law Cases' (1982) 50 Geo Wash L Rev 554

Wilmot-Smith F, 'Express and Implied Terms' (2023) 43(1) OJLS 54

Wynn-Evans C, 'Of Portmanteaux and Bridgeheads' (2004) 33 ILJ 355

Yihan G, 'New Distinctions within Terms Implied in Fact' (2016) 33 JCL 183

Zweigert K and Kötz H, *An Introduction to Comparative Law* (3rd edn, Clarendon Press 1998)

Index

For the benefit of digital users, indexed terms that span two pages (e.g., 52–53) may, on occasion, appear on only one of those pages.

Note: Tables and figures are indicated by *t* and *f* following the page number

anti-discrimination laws 137–38, 170–71, 191–92
   see also disability; discrimination
awards 72–75, 141, 164, 192
   see also Modern Awards

Bogg, Alan 103–4, 210–11
breach
   contract, of 29–30, 61, 67–68, 84, 87, 92, 165, *see also* contract
   implied term, of an 60–61, 85, 87, 89, 92–94, 142, 161–62
   statutory duty, of a 29–30, 193, *see also* statutory
Brodie, Douglas vii–viii, 86–87, 103–5, 109, 122–24, 136, 139–40, 143, 146–47, 151, 155–56, 186, 203, 209–12

Cabrelli, David vii–viii, 40–41, 101–2, 203–4
care
   duty of 52–54, 73–74, 76, 78, 174–76, 179–80, 201, 207, *see also* implied terms
Carter, John 24–25, 30–32, 95, 97–98
Casual Employment Information Statement 18–19
class 117–58
   contract, of 3–4, 8, 10, 28, 43, 110, 117–60, 197–204, *see also* contract
Collins, Hugh vii–viii, 2, 19
common law
   coherence with statute, and 10–11, 14, 110, 183–84, 187, 189–96, 199, 207–8, 214–16, *see also* statute
compensation *see* damages
   see also remedies
confidentiality
   duty of 57, 60–61, 66–68, 77, 79, 174–75, 178–80, 201, *see also* implied terms
construction
   distinct from implication, as 5–6, 17, 31–35, 40–41, 70, 82–83, 96, 108, 110, 113, 154, 197–98, 212, *see also* implied terms

contract
   breach of *see* breach
   class of *see* class
   interpretation of *see interpretation*
   oral, with terms that are *see* express terms
   repudiation of *see* repudiation
   terms 18–20
   in writing, with terms that are *see* express terms
contract of employment
   application of general principles of contract law, and the 122–26, 144, 156–57
   courts' imposition of particular duties, and the 139–43
   courts' inability to exclude particular duties, and the *see* excludability
   distinctive class of contract, as a *see* class
   operation of particular statutory rules, and the 29–30, 117, 136–39, 157, 193, 208, 214–15, *see also* statutory
   relational contract, as a 104–5, 108, 111–12, 117, 120, 135, 141, 147–57, 209–12
   statutory default rules, and *see* statutory
   termination of *see* termination of employment
   see also contract of service; employment; service
contract of service *see* contract of employment
   distinct from a contract for services, as 135–36, 157
   see also employment; service
contract for services *see* independent contractors
   distinct from a contract of service, as 135–36, 157
   see also contractors; non-standard performance of work
contractors *see* independent contractors
   see also contract for services; non-standard performance of work; self-employed, services
cooperation
   duty of 31–32, 61, 68–70, 93, 95–96, 118–19, 146, 174, 201–2, *see also* implied terms

custom and usage
    implied term based on 17–22, 26–28, 34–35, 37–38, 164, *see also* implied terms

damages 29–30, 53, 60, 83–85, 87–88, 91–93, 175–76, 193
    see also compensation; remedies
Davies, ACL 182, 190–91
Deakin, Simon 2, 135, 143
deemed employees 136–39, 157
discrimination *see* anti-discrimination laws
    see also disability
disability
    discrimination on the basis of 170–71
    see also anti-discrimination laws; discrimination

employment *see* contract of employment
    see also contract of service; service
excludability 9, 117, 143–48, 174–75, 194–95, 203
    see also contract of employment
express terms 18–22
    oral 19–20
    in writing 19
    see also contract

Fair Work Commission 18–19
Fair Work Information Statement 18–19
fidelity
    duty of 57, 60–63, 77–78, 174–75, 177, 179–80, 194, *see also* implied terms
fiduciary duties 51, 54–55, 61, 64–78, 86, 121, 141, 166
fixed-term employment 63, 75–76, 173–74
Freedland, Mark 40–42, 62–63, 118–19, 134, 139, 146–47, 190–91, 203

gig work(ers) 4–5
    see also contract for services; independent contractors; intermediate categories; limb (b) workers; self-employed; services; non-standard performance of work; workers
good faith 3–5, 7–8, 10, 50, 67–68, 80–83, 85–86, 102–13, 145–47, 154–56, 175, 194–200, 209–14

health and safety *see* work health and safety
hirer *see* principal
    see also host
host *see* principal
    see also hirer

human rights
    implied terms in contracts of employment, and 183–84
    see also implied terms
implied terms
    application in contracts for the non-standard performance of work, and *see* non-standard performance of work
    breach of *see* breach
    custom and usage, based on *see* custom and usage
    distinct from construction, as *see* construction
    distinct from express terms, as *see* express terms
    employees, owed by 57–68
        confidentiality, of *see* confidentiality
        fidelity, of *see* fidelity
        hold inventions on trust, to *see* inventions
        obey, to *see* obedience
        reasonable care and skill, to exercise 57, 63–64, 77–79, 177–80
    employers, owed by 52–57
    fact, in 23–25
        indemnify, to *see* indemnification
        inform employees of their rights, to 52, 55–57, 76–77, 177, 200–1
    fact/law distinction, and the 30–31
    gap fillers, as 1, 22
    human rights, and *see* human rights
    mutually, owed 68–76
        cooperate, to *see* cooperation
        mutual trust and confidence, not to destroy *see* trust and confidence
        reasonable notice, to provide *see* notice
    normative function of *see* normative
    parties' intentions, and 23–24, 31, 38–39, 209–10
indemnification
    employees, of 52, 54–55, 76, 78, 174–77, 179–80, 201, *see also* implied terms
independent contractors 4–5, 13, 49, 52–55, 57, 59, 62–64, 78–80, 101, 111–13, 117, 125–38, 157, 201
    see also contractors; self-employed; services; non-standard performance of work
intermediate categories
    worker, of 2–3, 126–27
    see also gig work(ers); limb (b) workers; non-standard performance of work; workers
interpretation
    contracts, of 5–6, 21–22, *see also* contract
    extrinsic evidence, and 21–22

INDEX   229

inventions
  ownership of 57, 64–66, 77, 79, 167, 174–75, 178–80, 200–1, *see also* implied terms
Irving, Mark 88, 120–21

Johnson exclusion zone 87
  see also unfair dismissal
judicial law-making 187–89
  coherence and predictability, and 187
  democratic legitimacy, and 187–88
  efficiency, and 188
  faith in an impartial judiciary, and 189
  flexibility, and 185–86
  see also legislative; parliamentary; statutory

Kahn-Freund, Sir Otto 12, 202–3

legislative *see* statutory
  see also judicial law-making; parliamentary
limb (b) workers 57, 59–60, 78, 173
  see also gig work(ers); intermediate categories; limb (b) workers; non-standard performance of work; workers
loyalty *see* fidelity
  see also implied terms

Macneil, Ian 149–50, 155–56
managerial prerogative
  exercise of 90–91
master and servant
  legislative regime 7, 51, 59, 62–64, 66, 70–71, 75–77, 112, 198, 202–3
  relationship 57–60, 77, 140
methodology 11–12
  comparative research 12
  doctrinal research 11–12
  historical research 11–12
minimum standards
  statutory 29–30, 71–72, 74–76, 79, 136–37, 173–74, 194–96
Modern Awards *see* awards
mutual trust and confidence *see* trust and confidence
  see also implied terms

necessity 159–80
  broad/wide test of 8–9, 12, 97, 101–2, 159–80, 199, 205–7, 212–14
  excludability and absolute 172–78
  historical background to the test of 160–62
  narrow/functional test of 8–9, 159–60, 164–71, 176–80, 205–7, 212–14
  test in Australia, application of the 164–72
  test in England, application of the 160–64

non-standard performance of work 1–11, 13–14, 17, 19, 22, 29, 36–40, 44–45, 49–55, 57, 59–60, 62–66, 68–80, 100–2, 111–12, 150, 173–78, 198–202
  see also gig work(ers); implied terms; intermediate categories; limb (b) workers; non-standard performance of work; workers
normative
  terms implied by law, function of 1–2, 4–5, 8, 11–14, 17, 34–37, 39–42, 44, 50–52, 104–5, 110, 118–19, 139, 159, 172, 195–96, 198, 200, 211–12, 215–16
  see also implied terms
notice
  display or delivery, through 20
  pay in lieu of 72–73
  prior course of dealing, through
  reasonable *see* reasonable notice
  termination of employment contracts, of 71

obedience
  duty of 42–43, 57–60, 77–78, 120, 145, 172–73, 175–76, 178–80, 194, 202–3, *see also* implied terms

parliamentary *see* statutory
  see also judicial law-making; legislative
parol evidence rule 19–20
patents
  ownership of 65–66, 79
Paterson, Jeannie 27, 110, 193
Peden, Elisabeth 37–38, 95, 107–8
policy
  considerations 4–6, 8–10, 12, 14, 40–42, 44, 82, 94–95, 98–99, 101–2, 111–13, 124–25, 145, 159, 163–73, 176, 179–80, 182, 187–88, 196–207, 212–13
principal
  independent contractor, and 2–3, 13, 52, 57, 59, 62, 64, 78–80, 107, 125, 150, 201
  see also hirer; host

reasonable notice
  termination on 68–77, 79, 165, 172–74, 179–80, 194, 200–1
  see also implied terms
remedies 85, 88, 110, 183, 193
  see also compensation; damages; statutory
remuneration
  bonuses 90–91, 154–55
representation
  mere 19–20
  see also warranty
repudiation 58–59, 75–76, 84

Riley Munton, Joellen vii–viii, 5, 87, 95–96, 108, 136–37, 171, 212

self-employed *see* independent contractors
   see also contractors; non-standard performance of work; services
service
   contract of *see* contract of employment
   see also employment
services
   contract of *see* independent contractors
   see also contractors; services; non-standard performance of work
sham contracting arrangements 146–47
slavery
   contract of 70–71, 165, 173–74
statement *see* representation
   see also express terms
statute
   coherence with common law, and *see* common law
statutory
   default rules 11, 31–32, 39, 139–40, 144, 146, 156–57, 163–64, 193–96, 199, 201, 207–8
   duty, breach of *see* breach
   implied terms 18, 29–30, 191–95, *see also* implied terms
   law-making *see* judicial law-making
   remedies 193, *see also* remedies
   rules in the contract of employment, operation of particular see *contract of employment*
   see also legislative; parliamentary
Stewart, Andrew 21–24, 127, 171

termination of employment 68, 70–77, 79, 83–85, 87–88, 91–93, 95–96, 99, 136–37, 153–54, 165, 172–74, 179–80, 194, 200–1, 203–4
torts 7–9, 36, 51–54, 76–78, 112, 129, 131–32, 159–61, 172, 175–76, 179–80, 199
trade unions 147
trust and confidence
   Australian law, in 87–99
   beyond employment, and application 100–2
   English law, in 83–87
   mutual duty of 83–102
   see also implied terms

unfair dismissal 83–85, 87, 89, 136–37, 191–92
   see also Johnson exclusion zone

vulnerable workers 79–80, 104–5, 109, 142, 211–12

warranty
   representation, as compared to a 19–20
   see also representation
work health and safety 64, 73–74, 137, 145, 175–78, 191–92, *see also* health and safety
workers 2–3, 18–19, 49–55, 57, 59–60, 62–64, 68, 75–76, 78–80, 101, 111–13, 117–19, 125–38, 157, 173, 201
   see also contract for services; gig work(ers); independent contractors; intermediate categories; limb (b) workers; self-employed; services; non-standard performance of work
wrongful dismissal 57–58, 84

zero-hour(s) contract 2–3, 119